THE NEW TESTAMENT EPISTLES

THE CLASSIC BIBLE BOOKS SERIES

The Book of Job: Why Do the Innocent Suffer?
Introduced and Edited by Lawrence Boadt; Foreword by Alice Thomas Ellis

Genesis: The Book of Beginnings
Introduced and Edited by Lawrence Boadt; Foreword by Sara Maitland

The Gospel of St John: The Story of the Son of God
Introduced and Edited by John Drane; Foreword by Piers Paul Read

The Great Sayings of Jesus: Proverbs, Parables and Prayers
Introduced and Edited by John Drane; Foreword by Richard Holloway

The Hebrew Prophets: Visionaries of the Ancient World
Introduced and Edited by Lawrence Boadt; Foreword by Desmond Tutu

The New Testament Epistles: Early Christian Wisdom
Introduced and Edited by John Drane; Foreword by Roger McGough

The Psalms: Ancient Poetry of the Spirit
Introduced by Lawrence Boadt and F. F. Bruce; Edited by Lawrence Boadt;
Foreword by R. S. Thomas

Revelation: The Apocalypse of St John
Introduced and Edited by John Drane; Foreword by Richard Harries

Sayings of the Wise: The Legacy of King Solomon
Introduced and Edited by Lawrence Boadt; Foreword by Libby Purves

The Song of Solomon: Love Poetry of the Spirit
Introduced and Edited by Lawrence Boadt; Foreword by John Updike

Stories from the Old Testament: Volume I
Introduced and Edited by Lawrence Boadt; Foreword by Monica Furlong

Stories from the Old Testament: Volume II
Introduced and Edited by Lawrence Boadt; Foreword by Morris West

+++

THE NEW TESTAMENT EPISTLES
Early Christian Wisdom

+++

Partially abridged from the text of the Revised English Bible

INTRODUCED AND EDITED BY JOHN DRANE
FOREWORD BY ROGER McGOUGH

St. Martin's Griffin
New York

ISBN 0-312-22103-7 paperback

Library of Congress Cataloging-in-Publication Data

Bible. N.T. Acts. English. Revised English. 1999. New Testament Epistles :
    early Christian Wisdom, partially abridged from the text of
    the Revised English Bible / foreword by Roger McGough ;
    introduction by John Drane.
        p.   cm. -- (The Classic Bible Series)
    ISBN 0-312-22103-7
    I. Bible. N.T. Epistles. English. Revised English. 1999.
    II. Title. III. Series.
    BS2617.5.A3 1999
    227'.052064--dc21
                                                            99-15307
                                                            CIP

First published in Great Britain by Lion Publishing plc, 1997.
First St. Martin's Griffin edition: January 2000.
        10 9 8 7 6 5 4 3 2 1

Contents

Foreword   7

Acknowledgments   8

Introduction   9

The Acts of the Apostles   9

The General Epistles   13

The Epistles of Paul   25

The Epistles of John   54

The New Testament Epistles in Literature   61

Themes and Images   62

The Acts of the Apostles   177

The General Epistles   227

The Epistle of James   228

The Epistle to the Hebrews   235

The First Epistle of Peter   248

The Epistle of Jude   256

The Second Epistle of Peter   258

The Epistles of Paul

The Epistle to the Galatians   *265*

The First Epistle to the Thessalonians   *274*

The Second Epistle to the Thessalonians   *279*

The First Epistle to the Corinthians (abridged)   *282*

The Second Epistle to the Corinthians (abridged)   *300*

The Epistle to the Romans (abridged)   *312*

The Epistle to the Colossians   *331*

The Epistle to Philemon   *337*

The Epistle to the Ephesians   *339*

The Epistle to the Philippians   *347*

The First Epistle to Timothy   *353*

The Epistle to Titus   *360*

The Second Epistle to Timothy   *363*

The Epistles of John   *369*

The First Epistle of John   *370*

The Second Epistle of John   *376*

The Third Epistle of John   *377*

Index of Primary Sources   *379*

Foreword

As part of a series of New Testament readings, the BBC invited me to record a selection from St Paul's letter to the Romans, a hair-raising experience that brought me face to face with the sheer power of language.

I remember that beginning a sentence was like taking off in a small plane. I would try to enunciate clearly and give meaning to the text, but I could see that the full stop was six or seven lines away. Would I run out of breath? Would I make it without losing control?

It was a bumpy journey but thankfully I arrived safely. What struck me, though, was the clarity, intellect and energy that shone through a language many times removed from the original.

'The world is charged with the grandeur of God', wrote Gerard Manley Hopkins. 'It will flame out, like shining from shook foil'. To be able to see God in everything and everybody around us is his great gift, and once we acknowledge that gift, then, as Erasmus says,

> These writings bring you back
> to the living image of that
> most holy mind,
> the very Christ himself,
> speaking, healing, dying, rising...

Roger McGough

ACKNOWLEDGMENTS

The text of 'The New Testament Epistles in Literature' has been selected from *A Dictionary of Biblical Tradition in English Literature*, edited by David Lyle Jeffrey, copyright © 1992 by permission of Wm B. Eerdmans Publishing Co.

The text of the epistles of John has been taken from the *New Jerusalem Bible* copyright © 1985 by Doubleday, a division of Bantam Doubleday Dell Publishing Group, Inc. and Darton, Longman and Todd Ltd. Used by permission of Doubleday, a division of Random House, Inc. and Darton, Longman and Todd Ltd and Doubleday and Company Inc.

The text of Acts and the epistles of Paul has been taken from the Revised English Bible, copyright © 1989 by permission of Oxford and Cambridge University Presses.

The text of the General epistles has been taken from the New Revised Standard Version of the Bible, copyright © 1989 by the Division of Christian Education of the National Council of the Churches of Christ in the USA.

Excerpt from *The Dumb Founding* by Margaret Avison, reprinted by permission of WW Norton and Company Inc. and by permission of McClelland & Stewart, Inc. *The Canadian Publishers*: page 149.

Excerpt from 'Choruses from "The Rock"' in *Collected Poems 1909-1962*, copyright 1936 by Harcourt Brace & Company, copyright © 1964, 1963 by T.S. Eliot, reprinted by permission of the publisher: page 115.

Excerpt from 'Little Gidding' in *Four Quartets*, copyright 1942 by T.S. Eliot and renewed 1970 by Esme Valerie Eliot, reprinted by permission of Harcourt Brace & Company: page 80.

Excerpt from 'Seven Stanzas at Easter' from *Telephone Poles and Other Poems* by John Updike. Copyright © 1961 by John Updike. Reprinted by permission of Alfred A Knopf Inc.: page 116.

W.B. Yeats, extract from 'The Second Coming', reprinted with the permission of Simon & Schuster from *The Poems of W.B. Yeats: A New Edition*, edited by Richard J. Finneran. Copyright © 1924 by Macmillan Publishing Company, renewed 1952 by Bertha Georgie Yeats: page 176.

INTRODUCTION

The Acts of the Apostles

Every book of the New Testament tells us something about the life of the earliest Christians. The letters written by Paul and other church leaders are the kind of information modern social historians would use and value, while even the gospels tell us a great deal about their first readers. But it is the book of Acts that tries to give some kind of historical account of the early years of Christianity. This book is a companion volume to the gospel of Luke. They were both written to the same person, 'Theophilus': the gospel to tell the story of the life and teaching of Jesus, and the book of Acts to tell how the work that Jesus began was developed by his followers into a worldwide Christian movement.

Acts does not tell the story of all the apostles, and the book has most to say about Peter and Paul, together with a few incidents from the lives of other early Christian leaders such as Philip, John, James the brother of Jesus, and Stephen. The story is told in two parts. The first deals mainly with events in Jerusalem and elsewhere in Palestine, and here Peter is the leading character (chapters 1–12). The second section tells the remarkable story of Paul (chapters 13–28).

Who wrote the book of Acts? Or, to put the question more accurately, who wrote the two volumes, Luke and Acts? They were certainly both written by the same person. Both were written for Theophilus, in identical style and language. All the evidence points to Luke, the Gentile doctor who accompanied Paul on some of his travels.

The date of Acts is more complex, with eminent scholars arguing for both the sixties and the eighties of the first century – though the balance of probability seems to favour a date in the eighties, perhaps around AD85.

The value of Acts

The Acts of the Apostles is occasionally referred to as a history of the early church. So it is, but it is not a comprehensive history. It is a deliberately selective story, drawing attention to those people and movements which Luke believed to be especially significant. When he wrote his gospel, Luke adopted exactly the same procedure – selecting those aspects of the life and teaching of Jesus which meant most to him. In similar fashion, Acts highlights those incidents which for Luke typified the trend of events among the first Christians. He wanted to show how Christianity spread from Jerusalem to Rome, and everything that records, and the way he records it, is intended to illuminate that transition. In the process, he omits many things modern readers might like to know. What happened to Peter? How did James get on in the church of Jerusalem? And what about those other apostles of whom we know little more than their names? These questions were not relevant to Luke's purpose, and so he never mentions them.

This means that his story is also an interpretation of the progress of the early church. All history, of course, is an interpretation of past events. When you read the newspaper, you are not getting a 'factual' account of what it describes: you are getting facts plus comment, as the reporter tries to indicate what they mean. So by saying that Luke gives an interpretation of early church history we are not implying that he simply invented it all. If nothing had happened, there would have been nothing to interpret! But what we have in Acts is the way that Luke, from his own presuppositions and background, saw what took place, and what it meant.

There are in fact a number of reasons for thinking that the picture we have in Acts is an essentially authentic reproduction of life in the period it describes.

In the prologue to his gospel (Luke 1:1–4) Luke tells us how he worked: he read all that he could find, sifted through it and then wrote his own considered account of what had happened. In the case of the gospel, we can see how he went about it, for we possess at least one of his source documents (Mark). The way he uses Mark shows that he was a very careful writer, aware of the need to reproduce his sources accurately and without distortion. We have no direct knowledge of his sources for Acts, though it is widely supposed that he relied on written information for his story of early events in Jerusalem and Samaria (chapters 1–9). If so, he would probably take the same care in compiling the story in Acts as he had previously taken with the gospel. In addition to that, he was himself personally present for at least some of the events in Acts (the 'we passages').

Luke's picture of life in the earliest Palestinian churches is consistent with what we would expect. The theology he attributes to those earliest Christian believers is much less sophisticated than the theology either of Paul or of the church later in the first century. For example, Jesus is still referred to as 'the Messiah' (Christ) in Acts 2:36, 3:20, 4:27, and he can be called 'the Servant of God' (Acts 3:13, 26; 4:25–30), or even in one instance, 'the Son of man' (a title much used by Jesus himself but found nowhere in the rest of the New Testament except Acts 7:56). The Christians are called simply 'disciples' (for example, in Acts 6:1–7; 9:1, 25–26), and the church itself is 'the Way' (Acts 9:2; 19:9, 23; 24:14, 22), Professor Norman Perrin has described all this as 'extraordinarily realistic… the narratives of Acts are full of elements taken directly from the life and experience of the church'.

This same realism features in Luke's description of the Roman world and its officials. He always uses the right word to describe Roman administrators, sometimes words that would only be familiar to people living in particular cities. Sergius Paulus and Gallio are correctly designated 'proconsuls' (Acts 13:7–8; 18:12). Philippi is accurately described as a Roman colony, ruled by the *Strategoi* (Praetors). This is an unusual word to find in a literary source, but it has been discovered on inscriptions, showing that it was the colloquial term used in Philippi itself (Acts 16:12, 20–22). Thessalonica also has its own name for its rulers, who are called 'politarchs' (Acts 17:8). This title was once thought to be a mistake, because it is not found in Latin or Greek literature. But subsequent archaeological discoveries have shown that Luke was right to describe the authorities at Thessalonica in this way. There are also many other points at which Luke's stories can be shown to depend on direct and reliable knowledge of the Roman world as it actually was at the time it is describing.

11

The same concern for authenticity can also be seen in Luke's presentation of the problems of the early church. The only real controversy that appears in Acts is concerned with the relationship of Jewish and Gentile Christians. But this argument soon became less important, and after AD70 it was of no importance at all, except on a theoretical level. At the time when Luke was writing, other issues were far more prominent: heresy and orthodoxy, and false teaching of various kinds. But he never tries to import the problems of a later day into the story of Acts, though he does show how the earlier experience of conflict resolution was relevant to the controversies of his own time.

There is just one point which may at first sight appear to contradict this generally positive evaluation of Luke's trustworthiness as a historian. This is his treatment of Paul. It is certainly true that things Paul is concerned with in Acts are often quite different from the issues that typically arise in his letters. In fact, Acts never even hints that he wrote any letters! But this is not as strange as it might seem. When Paul wrote letters, he was writing to Christians. But when he speaks in Acts he is usually addressing non-Christians. There has been plenty of speculation about the content of Paul's initial preaching to the Galatians, Corinthians, Thessalonians and others, but we cannot know for certain what he told them. We can be sure that he would present his message in a different way to engage the attention of those who were not Christians than he did when trying to correct the errors of church members. It is noteworthy that in the only instance when Acts gives us an address to Christians by Paul (Acts 20:17–38), the substance of his message is not materially different from the typical content of his letters. Even the sermon at Athens (Acts 17:22–31) has close similarities with what he wrote on the same subject in Romans 1:18 – 2:16.

The purpose of Acts

Though he does not address their problems directly, Luke must have hoped that his first readers would learn something from his story to help their own Christian thinking. He may therefore have had at least three primary aims in view.

Perhaps the main thing that comes out clearly from Acts is the conviction that Christianity is a faith with the potential to change the world. Indeed, through Paul and others it *did* change the world, and the secret of its success was the way in which these early Christians had the power of the Holy Spirit working within them. Luke encourages his readers to follow the example of those who had gone before them, and to do for their generation what Paul had achieved in his.

But then Luke also seems to go out of his way to emphasize that Christianity can have good relationships with the Roman empire. On the one hand, he commends the Christians to Rome itself, as he stresses that their faith is the true successor of Judaism – and Judaism, of course, was a recognized religion within the empire. But he also encourages his readers themselves to take a positive attitude towards the empire, depicting its officials as good and upright, and by implication suggesting that a maniac like Nero was the exception rather than the rule.

In view of what he says at the beginning of his gospel, we must also take seriously the fact that Luke claimed to be the first historian of Christianity. His two books are addressed to Theophilus in order to inform him about the facts relating to Christian faith. Moreover, the procedure that Luke adopted for compiling his story suggests that he had a historian's interest in finding out about the past for its own sake. As the church became established as a significant institution in the Roman world, it was important for its members to know their origins and history, and Luke was perhaps the first person to set some of it down in a systematic form.

The General Epistles

We shall never fully understand the story of the early church without appreciating that the Christian movement was deeply rooted in the Jewish faith. Jesus was a Jew, as were all his original disciples, and so were most if not all the converts on the Day of Pentecost. But even in the earliest days, people like Stephen were asking whether Christianity was just another sect within Judaism, or whether it was meant to become something distinctive and new. These questions became more pressing once Paul and others had moved out into the wider world to take the good news about Jesus to people with no previous Jewish connections. Paul clearly regarded himself as the 'apostle to the Gentiles', yet wherever he travelled he always took his message first to the local Jewish synagogue. As a result, many of the issues dealt with in his letters have a distinctively Jewish flavour – questions about the Old Testament Law, and the nature of Christian belief and behaviour over against Jewish traditions.

These issues were to become increasingly important for every aspect of life in the early church, as Christians took over the Jewish scriptures (the Hebrew Bible) as part of their own authoritative writings (the Old Testament). They naturally needed to know what relationships there might be between the inherited faith of Israel and their own new experience of Jesus and the Holy Spirit. Paul's epistles deal repeatedly with this question. But there are other writings in the New Testament which show how other Christians were tackling these issues. These 'general epistles' are mostly shorter than Paul's letters, and they are also for the most part considerably less complex. But they are no less valuable for that, for they give us direct access to areas of the church's life and thinking that are mentioned nowhere else in the New Testament.

James

Judaism had always been deeply concerned with behaviour. In the Roman world, Jewish people were often distinguished not so much by what they thought as by what they did. They circumcised their male children, kept the Sabbath day apart and observed complicated laws about food. These were the things that announced to the Romans that the Jews were different. But they were not the only things. For the Jewish people also had a comprehensive code of moral behaviour. Many of the things that were taken for granted in a pagan lifestyle were avoided by Jews – not just because they were un-Jewish, but because they seemed to be against the Law of God.

The foundation of Jewish morality had been laid many centuries before in the Old Testament. Besides its concern with matters of religious ritual, the Torah has a strong moral core, in the Ten

Commandments and elsewhere (especially Deuteronomy). It was concerned to ensure that worshippers in ancient Israel should carry their religious beliefs over into the affairs of everyday life. As Amos and other Old Testament prophets never tired of pointing out, it was a waste of time to make high-sounding religious affirmations in the temple if they meant nothing in the market-place.

Jesus' own message had been largely concerned with this theme, and the letter of James is very similar: it emphasizes that religious belief is worthless if it does not affect the way people live. Devotion to God does not end at the door of the church. It only begins there: 'What God the Father considers to be pure and genuine religion is this: to take care of orphans and windows in their suffering and to keep oneself from being corrupted by the world.' The heart of real devotion to God is to love one's neighbour as oneself – and without deeds that will put such sentiments into action, religious faith is worthless.

Like Jesus, James uses many illustrations to deliver his message. He draws a vivid verbal picture of the apparent splendour of a rich person. Like the flowers whose beauty he tries to copy, his day will soon be over: 'The sun rises with its blazing heat and burns the plant; its flowers fall off, and its beauty is destroyed. In the same way the rich man will be destroyed…' James also turns his attention to the dangers of thoughtless talk. The tongue is just like a rudder, which can steer a ship many times larger than itself; its influence is out of all proportion to its size – and if we are not careful it can make trouble for ourselves and other people. Once a person loses control of their tongue, it can create conditions like a forest fire, which is started by just one small spark but is very difficult to put out.

The book of James has no coherent 'argument' as such, but its message would not be lost on its readers. These people were suffering the kind of discrimination that James mentions, and they are urged to be patient and to trust in God for deliverance. What God has promised will come true, and God's people will be vindicated in the end.

There are several unsolved questions about the letter of James. But two things are quite clear: it is an intensely Jewish writing, and it is concerned above everything else with correct behaviour. Some have thought it so Jewish that they have doubted whether it is really Christian. Martin Luther had no time for it, and dismissed it as 'a right strawy epistle – for it has no evangelical manner about it'. Others have pointed out that James mentions the name of Jesus in only two places, and that when he gives examples for his readers to follow, he chooses Old Testament figures like Abraham, Job, Elijah and even the prostitute Rahab rather than Jesus. No significant facts about Jesus are mentioned anywhere in the book – not even his death and resurrection. Indeed, if we were to look for other books of a similar kind, we would most easily find them in books like Proverbs in the Old Testament and other so-called 'Wisdom' books that were popular with Jewish readers in the time of Jesus.

Some have therefore suggested that James was not written by a Christian at all, and that the two references to Jesus were inserted at some later date when Christians became embarrassed by the existence of this apparently Jewish book in their scriptures. But there is no evidence to support this idea. A later Christian editor who set out to change a Jewish book in to a Christian one would surely have inserted far more references to specifically Christian ideas than just two mentions of the name of Jesus.

The message of James is in general very much in harmony with the teaching of Jesus. But there is more than just a superficial similarity between them. For there are many detailed points at which James' advice corresponds closely to specific aspects of Jesus' teaching.

The words of James and the words of Jesus are not *identical* in any of these passages. But the language used and the sentiments expressed are so similar that it seems obvious there must be some connection. The most likely explanation is that the writer of James knew these sayings of Jesus in a slightly different form from how we know them from the New Testament gospels. The gospel materials circulated by word of mouth for some time before they were written down, and the fact that some of this teaching has a more primitive form in James than it does in Matthew suggests that James had access to it at an earlier stage than the writers of the gospels.

The epistle of James may well have originated among those followers of Jesus who remained in Galilee after the main centre of the church moved to Jerusalem. It is impossible to prove this, of course, for we know next to nothing about such Galilean believers. But the message of James would be especially appropriate to those who were worshipping in the Jewish synagogues of rural Palestine, and at the same time trying to put into practice what Jesus had taught them. Such people may easily have been tempted to substitute religious formality for the spiritual realities of which Jesus had spoken – and, as a relative minority, they would also be open to the kind of persecution that James mentions.

If this was the book's background, it may also explain why it went unrecognized in the wider church for so long. Its eventual association with an important person like James of Jerusalem would then have been a means of justifying its inclusion in the canon of the New Testament. It could also reflect the possibility that the church in Jerusalem was included in 'God's people in the Dispersion', to whom James was originally despatched at an early stage in the history of the church.

Hebrews

The temple in Jerusalem occupied a special place in the life and thinking of Jewish people. The first temple was built in the time of Solomon, at the height of ancient Israel's political expansion. That structure was destroyed by Babylonian invaders in the 6th century BC, though it was subsequently replaced by a far less impressive building. In 20BC, Herod the Great decided to build a new temple that would be as grand as any monument in the Roman world. But he did not live to see it finished. The work was so ambitious and costly that it went on for something like eighty years. By the time it was completed, the Jews were in revolt against the Romans, and soon afterwards it was destroyed by the Roman general Titus in AD70, and was never rebuilt. This was the temple that Jesus and the first Christians knew, and it was a centre of devotion for Jewish believers from all over the Roman empire. There were also Jewish synagogues in every town or city where there was a Jewish population of any size. Worship in the synagogue was not the same as worship in the temple. Most of the rites prescribed in the Old Testament could only be carried out in the temple. This was where priests offered sacrifices – and all the great religious festivals had special significance when celebrated in the Jerusalem temple. Jews from all over the empire went there to worship in its holy places.

How did all this relate to Christian faith? For Gentile believers, with no previous connection with the Jewish faith, this question seemed trivial. But for those with a Jewish heritage, it was of fundamental importance. The early church took Jewish moral standards for granted. But in reality, the Torah was far more than a collection of ethical teachings. It also contained detailed regulations for the proper conduct of worship. What was to be done with the ritual practices of the Jewish religion?

This question inspired the New Testament book of Hebrews. Its author encourages and advises his readers in a way that suggests they were being persecuted – perhaps because of their resistance to accepting Jewish practices. The early chapters of Acts show how difficult religious fanatics could could make life for Christian believers, and some scholars believe a similar situation is envisaged here. On the other hand, Christians throughout the Roman empire must always have been tempted to try and link themselves to Judaism, especially in times of persecution – for Judaism was a permitted religion under Roman Law, whereas at this stage Christianity was not.

The writer of Hebrews argued that it was both pointless and unnecessary for Christians to keep the ritual requirements of the Old Testament Law. For him, the message of Jesus was God's final word. Previous prophets in ancient Israel had spoken in God's name to the people of their own time, but they were now all superseded by Jesus. Jesus is compared in turn to the angels who Jewish tradition identified with the giving of the Torah, and also with Aaron, the archetype of every Jewish priest. But as 'Son of God', Jesus was greater than all of them. Yet because of his human experience, he understood how people felt when faced with the power of evil. He was the fulfilment of all Judaism's aspirations, 'a great high priest' who both summed up and fulfilled all that had gone before.

When was Hebrews written?

Various dates have been suggested, ranging from the early sixties to the end of the first century. It cannot have been written later than about AD90, for it is referred to in 1 Clement which was written in Rome no later than AD96.

The writer of Hebrews has a lot to say about the kind of worship described in the Old Testament. Some statements seem to imply that it was all still happening: 'The same sacrifices are offered for ever, year after year... the sacrifices serve year after year to remind people of their sins...' (10:1–3). If this was actually happening in the temple at Jerusalem, then the book can be dated before AD70. On the other hand, Hebrews never refers to the temple, but always to the tent of worship in the desert. The regulations for worship were the same in each case, of course, and probably of the same origin. But if Hebrews is, in effect, an exposition of Old Testament passages, then it would be irrelevant whether or not the temple still stood. At the same time, if the temple had already been destroyed it is hard to believe that the author would not have mentioned it, for the literal destruction of the Old Testament ritual in AD70 was the final confirmation of the whole argument of his book.

If Hebrews was directed to readers in Rome, then the statement that they had not yet given their lives for the gospel would seem to point to a time before Nero's persecution came to a climax in AD64. The earlier persecution they had suffered could then have been connected with the disturbances that led Claudius to expel the Jewish people from Rome for a time in AD48.

We may tentatively conclude that Hebrews was written by an unknown author in the period leading up to Nero's persecution. Its first readers were a group of Hellenist Jewish Christians in Rome who were trying to escape the political consequences of being known as Christians by adopting the ritual of Judaism. They wanted the protection that the empire gave to Jews. But they also wished to enjoy the privileges of being Christians. The author of Hebrews deplored such a selfish attitude. In his opinion, not only were they betraying their fellow-Christians, their acquiescence in Jewish rituals was also in effect a denial of what Jesus had done for them. If they truly wished to serve him, they must be prepared to stand up and be counted as his followers, whatever the cost might be.

1 Peter

The debates in the early church about Jewish morality and ritual were the symptoms of a much more fundamental concern. In Old

Testament times, to be a member of the people of God was not simply a matter of behaving in the same way as other like-minded people. It also involved inclusion in the special covenant relationship that God had established with Israel's ancestor Abraham, and renewed with Moses at Mt Sinai.

This theme is central to the first epistle of Peter, which argues that Gentile Christians are now the true successors to the people of God in Old Testament times. It also asserts that they have achieved this position as a result of their response in faith to what God has done for them through Jesus. Like the family of Abraham before them, Christians can know God not because of their own piety or understanding, but solely through God's free expressions of love for them. In the case of Israel, this had been largely through the events of history, particularly the exodus. Now, God's love had been shown afresh in 'the costly sacrifice of Christ, who was like a lamb without defect or flaw'.

After an initial greeting and thanksgiving to God, the letter turns to exhortation. Peter's readers are encouraged to celebrate God's goodness to them, 'even though for a little while you may have to suffer various trials'. The writer tells them that such trials are insignificant when set against God's power. Christians already know something of this power in the new life that they enjoy through Jesus. They can also look forward to 'the Day when Jesus Christ is revealed', when they will meet him face to face. Simple Gentile believers may find this difficult to understand – even the angels cannot fully do so – but what is happening to them now, and the destiny that is waiting for them in the future, is all part of God's plan that was first revealed in the Old Testament.

The writer then goes on to remind his readers that acceptance of the good news about Jesus imposes responsibilities as well as bestowing privileges. Faith in Christ is not merely a private experience, but something to be shared with others, in deed as well as word. Christ's death and resurrection has 'set you free from the worthless manner of life handed down by your ancestors', and the recollection of that should lead Christians to obey God, and share God's love with other people.

They should also grow and develop in their Christian experience, being as eager for spiritual nourishment as babies are for their mothers' milk. As they grow as Christians, so they can 'come as living stones, and let yourselves be used in building the spiritual temple, where you will serve as holy priests to offer spiritual and acceptable sacrifices to God through Jesus Christ'. As Christians mature in this way, they will demonstrate how they are 'the chosen race, the King's priests, the holy nation, God's own people'.

There is not another passage of comparable length in the whole New Testament where more Old Testament imagery that was originally applied to Abraham and his descendants is taken over and applied to the Christian church, the 'new Israel'.

Peter goes on to remind his readers that as God's people, they have different standards from non-Christians. They are as much at home in pagan society as 'strangers and refugees'. Their only true allegiance is to God and so everything they do should be intended to glorify God alone. Even when they have to 'endure the pain of undeserved suffering', they can look to the example of Jesus. For 'when he was insulted, he did not answer back with an insult; when he suffered, he did not threaten, but placed his hopes in God, the righteous Judge'.

Exactly the same principles should determine how Christians behave at home. Christian wives should be ready to share the love of Christ with their husbands – and they for their part must treat their wives with respect and understanding. In a word, every believer should follow the advice of Jesus: 'Love one another... and be kind and humble with one another. Do not pay back evil with evil or cursing with cursing; instead, pay back with a blessing.'

Finally, Peter gives advice to those who are, like himself, 'elders' or 'shepherds' in the church. Instead of being domineering, they should be 'examples to the flock', recognizing that the church will flourish only when all its members have 'put on the apron of humility' to serve one another. In doing so, they are following the example of Jesus, who himself had worn the apron of a slave to wash his disciples' feet. But above all, they must not lose their trust in God in the midst of persecution.

Who wrote 1 Peter?

1 Peter was well-known and widely read in the church from quite early times. 1 Clement refers to it (AD96), as also does Polycarp (AD70–155), while Irenaeus stated towards the end of the second

century that it was written by the apostle Peter himself. There are good reasons to accept this view of its authorship:

Much of its teaching is exactly what we would expect from a disciple of Jesus. Many aspects echo the teaching of Jesus himself, sometimes following it quite closely. The author contrasts the readers' knowledge of Jesus, which was second-hand, with his own first-hand knowledge, and he seems to have witnessed both the trials (2:21–24) and the crucifixion of Jesus (5:1). Some scholars also believe that certain passages contain allusions to gospel stories in which Peter was particularly involved. Others, however, have claimed that if this letter was the work of Peter, then we would expect to read much more about Jesus. But this argument depends on the mistaken assumption that authors will write everything they know in everything they write. We should also remember that Peter's reminiscences of the life and teaching of Jesus may well have been recorded in a comprehensive way already, in the gospel of Mark.

If Peter did indeed write this letter, then obviously we must date it before his death in the persecution of Christians begun by Nero in AD64 or 65. But dating it more precisely than that depends on our interpretation of the various references to persecution that occur throughout the letter. These indicate that 1 Peter was written as Nero's persecution was in its early stages. We have no certain evidence that it eventually spread to Asia Minor. But even if it did not, the official persecution in Rome would certainly have encouraged people elsewhere to despise the Christians in their own cities. We do know that Peter was in Rome at the time. The term 'Babylon', used by this letter, was a favourite code word for Rome among the early Christians. As Peter saw what was happening there, he felt it would only be a matter of time before such a great evil spread to other parts of the empire. He wanted Christians to know that when their time of trial came, they were not alone in their suffering. Others were suffering too. But most important of all, God would not fail to care for them, for they were the covenant people.

Jude and 2 Peter

The influence of false teachers is the subject of two of the most obscure books of the New Testament: Jude and 2 Peter. These books clearly belong together, for almost the whole of Jude (in a slightly modified form) is contained in 2 Peter. But otherwise, neither book contains any information to help us identify their original readers.

The way in which Jude and 2 Peter oppose false teachers suggests that they originated in a situation quite similar to that dealt with in the opening chapters of the book of Revelation. The term 'gnosis' (knowledge) is not actually mentioned, but these teachers are described as 'psychics' ('controlled by their natural desires'), and we know that this was a technical term used by later Gnostics. These people certainly laid a great emphasis on their own spiritual experiences and they argued that because they themselves had been 'raised' to a new level of spiritual life, they had also been released from the normal constraints of Christian morality. But all this was unacceptable to those in the mainstream of the church. Jude reminds them that even in Old Testament times God had punished people for the same kind of wrongdoing – and unless his readers were prepared to repent, they could expect to share the same fate.

2 Peter also suggests that these people were denying the reality of the future coming of Jesus. No doubt they argued that since they themselves had already been spiritually 'raised' to heaven, there would be no further need for the kind of literal resurrection hope held by the majority of the early Christians. In any case, they said, nothing had happened, even though the church had fervently expected Jesus to return in glory. This argument had first been put forward by Paul's opponents in Corinth. But 2 Peter introduces a new answer to it, by asserting that God operates with a different time-scale from people: 'There is no difference in the Lord's sight between one day and a thousand years...' The fact that the end has not yet arrived does not mean that God's promises have failed. Quite the opposite is true, for the delay in the coming of Jesus is itself an expression of God's patience in allowing men and women more time to repent.

Authors and dates

Neither Jude nor 2 Peter contains any information linking them to specific events or people in the early church. The only way we can understand their background is by trying to fit them into what we know about the development of the early churches in general. A number of indications seem to suggest that both these books belong to the end of the New Testament period, rather than the time of the apostles:

A minority of scholars have tried to explain the origin of these books by recourse to their opening sentences. For both of them appear to be claiming to be the work of people who flourished in the age of the apostles themselves. 'Jude, servant of Jesus Christ, and brother of James' (Jude 1) is almost certainly meant to be that Jude who is named in the gospels as a brother of Jesus and of James in Mark 6:3; while 'Simon Peter' is clearly intended to identify the author of 2 Peter as the apostle himself (2 Peter 1:1). But there are other problems involved here:

The early church had a number of doubts about both these books. Jude is mentioned occasionally by the early Church Fathers, but 2 Peter is mentioned nowhere before the works of Origen (AD185–254), and as late as the fourth century both of them were regarded either as spurious or of doubtful value. This at the very least must suggest that they were not generally recognized as writings of leaders of the first generation of Christians.

Coupled with this, there is general agreement among scholars that if 1 Peter is the work of Peter, the disciple of Jesus, then 2 Peter is not. Many writers in the early church were perplexed by the differences between the two, for in style of writing, theological emphasis and general outlook they are so different that it is impossible to think the same person wrote them both. So if we are correct to connect 1 Peter with Peter himself, then we must look elsewhere for an explanation of 2 Peter.

An ingenious solution to this problem was proposed by Dr John Robinson. He points out that the writer of Jude says he was in the process of writing a letter when he became aware of a more urgent need to communicate with his readers immediately – and in response to that, he wrote the letter of Jude (Jude 3). But what was the original letter he was writing? In view of the many similarities between them, could it have been 2 Peter? And could it be that the earlier letter referred to in 2 Peter 3:1 was not 1 Peter, but Jude? Dr Robinson goes on to suggest that Jude may have been writing as Peter's representative, and he points out that according to Acts 15:14, the leaders of the Jewish church commonly referred to Peter as 'Simon', which could explain the unusual use of that name in the opening sentence of 2 Peter.

If Jude and 2 Peter both originate from a group of Peter's disciples, this would explain the similarities and the differences between 1 and 2 Peter. It could also explain why certain sections of 2 Peter (like the description of the transfiguration of Jesus in chapter one) have struck many readers as authentic reminiscences of Peter himself. Perhaps what we have in both these short letters is a fresh application of the teaching of Peter to the concerns and interests of a Hellenistic Jewish Christian congregation somewhere in Asia Minor towards the end of the first century.

As the years passed, the church had to change and adapt itself to deal with new threats and take advantage of new opportunities. But it never forgot that its thinking and behaviour must always be firmly anchored in the experiences and outlook of those first followers who had actually known Jesus. Had it not been for the continuing commitment of a small group of Palestinian peasants, the wider world would never have heard this life-changing message. It was not easy for them. Their courage and boldness was rewarded with persecution, and even death. But their own experience of Jesus was such that they had no thought of turning back.

The Epistles of Paul

Paul the letter-writer

When Paul wrote letters to the Christians who were under his care, he naturally followed the common style of the day. We have an example in Claudias Lysias' letter to Felix. An ancient letter usually followed a more or less set pattern:

It always began with the name of the writer, and then named the person it was sent to. Paul follows this quite closely.

Then follows the greeting, usually a single word. Paul often expanded this to include the traditional Hebrew greeting (*shalom*, 'peace') together with a new, Christian greeting ('grace' – in Greek very similar to the normal everyday greeting).

The third part of a Greek letter was a polite expression of thanks for the good health of the person addressed – usually expanded by Paul into a general thanksgiving to God for all that was praiseworthy in his readers. Next followed the main body of the letter. In Paul's letters this is often in two parts: doctrinal teaching (usually in response to questions raised by his readers) and then advice on Christian living. Personal news and greetings came next. Paul generally included news of the churches and prominent individuals in them.

Paul's letters often contain a note of exhortation or blessing in his own handwriting, as a kind of guarantee of the genuine and personal nature of the letter.

Finally, ancient letters ended with a single word of farewell, which Paul almost always expands into a full blessing and prayer for his readers.

Galatians

Though Galatians is not an especially long and involved letter, it is not always very easy to understand Paul's meaning. This is partly because the letter was written hastily in the middle of a raging controversy. In such circumstances people do not express themselves in the ordered way they would in calmer moments. The complexity of his expression also stems from the subject-matter. For Paul was very much at home in the Hebrew scriptures, and quotes them with great freedom as he expounds the twin principles of liberty and equality within the Christian fellowship.

Paul's letter falls into three main sections, dealing in turn with three false ideas that had been propounded by the Jewish Christians ('Judaizers') who had visited the Galatian churches.

Did Paul have any authority?

The Judaizers had claimed Paul was not a proper apostle, because he had not been accredited by the original apostles in Jerusalem.

Therefore he had no right to give any directions to new Christians, nor ought they to pay attention to what he said. Paul's reply to all this is in Galatians 1:10 – 2:21. He makes it quite clear that he needed no authorization from Jerusalem or anywhere else, since he had himself met with the risen Christ.

Christians and the Old Testament

After dealing with this attack on his own credentials, Paul appeals briefly to the Galatians' own experience before going on to consider the second false claim put forward by these Judaizers. What the Galatian Christians knew of Christ ought to have shown them that they had received the Holy Spirit (the mark of the true Christian, Romans 8:9) not because they obeyed the Old Testament Law, but because they had exercised faith in Jesus (Galatians 3:1–5).

This leads straight into an attack on another part of the Judaizing teachings. In the Old Testament the promise of the Messianic kingdom was given to Abraham and his descendants (Genesis 17:7–8). The Judaizers therefore argued that anyone wishing to be in the Messianic kingdom must become members of Abraham's family by circumcision and continued obedience to the Old Testament Law (Genesis 17:9–14). Paul addressed this in three ways, by appealing to the Old Testament itself.

In Galatians 3:6–14, he points out that the blessings promised to Abraham belong to 'all who believe' (verse 9). Abraham had faith in God, and this faith was the basis of his acceptance by God (Genesis 12:1–4; see also Hebrews 11:8–12, 17–18). At the same time, 'all who rely on works of the law are under a curse' (verse 10). Everyday experience and the Old Testament both proved that in practice it was impossible to be justified in God's sight by keeping the Law.

But was not the Law God's highest revelation in the Old Testament, surpassing all that had gone before it? No, says Paul. Since the Law (or Torah) came into effect long after Abraham's time, it could not possibly alter a direct promise made to him by God. The 'inheritance' promised to Abraham could not be obtainable by both Law and promise (verse 18).

Paul now takes the argument to its logical conclusion (Galatians

3:25 – 4:7). The Old Testament Law was only a temporary thing, effective from the time of Moses 'till the offspring should come to whom the promise had been made' (verse 19). Now, the 'offspring' *had* come in Jesus Christ. So the era of the Law must be finished, and to those who had faith in him, Christ would give freedom from the Law.

Freedom and legalism

By trying to put themselves under the jurisdiction of the Law, the Galatians were in effect undermining what God had already done for them in Christ. Paul was fearful that if they did this, he had laboured over them in vain (4:8–11). So he goes on to deal with another argument put forward by the Judaizing teachers. They had given 'scriptural' reasons to suggest that Christians ought to keep the Torah and to be circumcised. Paul answers in three ways.

Paul looks again at the status of the Law (4:21 – 5:1). Again he appeals to the story of Abraham, this time using the incident of Sarah (a free woman) driving out Hagar the slave. This, he says, is an allegory of the superior position of the good news in Christ over against the legalism of the Jewish Law.

Paul answers the queries about circumcision (5:2–12). He makes it clear that circumcision is of no value either way to Christians. It makes no difference whether Christians are circumcised or not. Their standing before God depends on no external signs but on 'faith working through love' (5:6). In the case of people like the Galatians, to submit to circumcision would actually be a denial of what Christ had done for them (5:2). In any case to be circumcised also obliged people to observe the whole of the Jewish Law (5:3) – the very thing that Paul had just rejected, and which experience showed to be impossible anyway. The freedom that Christ brings is clearly incompatible with the 'yoke of slavery' (5:1) brought by circumcision and the Law.

Paul deals with the problem of Christian behaviour (Galatians 5:13 – 6:10). The Jews were distinguished from other groups in the ancient world by their moral standards, which they got from the Old Testament Law. The false teachers who visited Galatia had argued that if Christians did not follow the Jewish Law, they would have no guide for their conduct, and would be indistinguishable from the pagans around them.

Paul deals with the accusations of the Judaizers on this score by making four important statements:

First (5:13–15), 'freedom' in Christ does not mean Christians are free to do what they like. Since the Holy Spirit aims to produce in Christians a Christ-like character, their freedom should obviously be demonstrated in ways that are consistent with his behaviour.

Secondly (5:16–26), though the Christian gospel does not lay down a list of dos and don'ts, 'those who belong to Christ Jesus have crucified the flesh with its passions and desires' (5:24). So the Christian's life will be marked out by the fruit of the Spirit. Christian faith demands something much more radical than the imposition of rules and regulations from the outside: the Christian's whole personality should be revolutionized as attitudes and behaviour are changed from within.

Thirdly (6:1–6), Christians should beware of judging others. They ought to recognize that they themselves could have no moral strength to do what was right, apart from the power of the Holy Spirit. They are to 'fulfil the law of Christ' by bearing 'one another's burdens' (6:2). This is very different from keeping externally imposed rules and regulations by their own efforts.

Fourthly (6:7–10), Paul sums up his advice. In order to reap the harvest of eternal life, they must sow not to the flesh – their own self-indulgence – but to the Spirit – their new life given by Jesus Christ.

Then, finally, in Galatians 6:11–18, Paul makes a last appeal to his readers, with two further points against his opponents followed by two balancing statements about his own belief and practice.

His opponents, in spite of their high pretensions, were in fact spiritually bankrupt (6:12). They 'want to make a good showing in the flesh', the very thing that Paul had denounced in the previous section of his argument (Galatians 6:8: 'he who sows to his own flesh will from the flesh reap corruption'). They are also inconsistent, even on their own understanding: though they emphasize the outward sign of circumcision they are not willing to accept the spiritual discipline involved in keeping the Old Testament Law.

For Paul, the truth revealed to him by the risen Christ was greater than anything else. So he says finally that the only real cause of boasting before God is that the Christian has been crucified to the world, through the cross of Christ.

1 Thessalonians

After the usual introduction, Paul begins by commending his readers for their faithfulness to the Christian message. Paul had told them how the risen and living Christ had revolutionized his own life, and he had challenged them to allow Christ to do the same for them by the power of the Holy Spirit. The Thessalonians had fully accepted this message, and the result had been that a strong church had been established. In addition, by the example of their changed lives, the Christian message had been commended to the pagan world around them.

Nevertheless, there was something lacking in their faith (3:10). So Paul set out to advise on the difficulties Timothy had reported to him.

How should Christians behave?

One thing that often posed a problem for converted pagans was the question of personal morality. In the wider society of the day immorality of all kinds was normal. From what Paul says in chapter 1 of this letter, it is clear that the majority of the Thessalonian Christians had been enabled by the power of the Holy Spirit to overcome the pressure to be like their fellow citizens in this respect. But it was still necessary to reinforce what he had no doubt told them when he founded their church (4:1–8).

In a world in which the established order was rapidly changing, and in which men and women were frantically grasping at whatever religion came their way, one of the most important things the church could do was to display the love of Christ (4:9–12). Was not this what Jesus himself had taught? 'By this everyone will know that you are my disciples. If you have love for one another' (John 13:35). The advice is here repeated and reinforced by Paul.

What about the future?

One thing above all was troubling the church at Thessalonica. They understood well the relationship that ought to exist among the members of their church. But what about those Christians who had died shortly after Paul's departure from the city? Paul found the answer to that in his conviction that the Lord he knew was present in the church by the operation of the Holy Spirit would one day come back openly and triumphantly (4:13–18), Meanwhile, the Thessalonian Christians should not worry unduly about loved ones who had died: 'since we believe that Jesus died and rose again, even so, through Jesus, God will bring with him those who have fallen asleep' (4:14).

Paul realized there was danger in emphasizing only what God would do in the future. So he reminded the Thessalonian Christians that their belief in the future return (or *parousia*) of Jesus was no excuse for inactivity in the present. Some people may not be prepared for 'the day of the Lord', but Christians ought to be. Their business was not to try and calculate 'the times and the seasons' (5:1), but to 'encourage one another and build one another up' (5:11).

Living the Christian life

Finally, Paul gave some advice on various topics, summarizing all that he had said before (5:12–21).

In the church, the Christians should: respect those who laboured among them – the elders whom Paul had presumably appointed in their church; be at peace among themselves (a repetition and reinforcement of what he had said in 4:9–12); encourage one another in their faith in Christ (5:14). In their everyday life, the Christians should: return good for evil (5:15) – one of the most characteristic marks of the Christian (see also Matthew 5:44); 'rejoice always' (5:16). In their individual relationship to God, the Christians must: live in an attitude of prayer (5:17); allow the Holy Spirit to direct their lives (5:19–20).

Paul signs off with his usual blessing and greeting, making a last appeal and promise to his readers. He knew that the secret of the

Christian faith was the work of the living Christ operating in the lives of his followers. This was what he wanted them to keep in the forefront of their minds: 'He who calls you is faithful, and he will do it' (5:24).

2 Thessalonians

Despite Paul's advice in his first letter, the Thessalonians were soon diverted from the importance of God's faithfulness. They began instead to speculate on what Paul had said about the state of Christians who died, and the expected return (*parousia*) of Jesus. It was not long before Paul had to write another letter to help sort out the difficulties which, to some extent, the Thessalonian Christians seem to have created for themselves out of certain parts of his first letter. Paul's second letter, known as 2 Thessalonians, is found alongside his first in our New Testament.

In this second, shorter letter to the Thessalonians Paul clarifies three main points:

1. The church and its enemies: From what he says in 2 Thessalonians 1:5–12 it appears that the church had come under increasingly fierce persecution. This was to be expected; for the more widely known their love and Christian character became, the more could their enemies be expected to increase. The Jews and Romans never bothered about a religious faith that meant nothing to those holding it; but the revolutionary character of the life of the Thessalonian church naturally drew their attention to what was going on. It would be impossible to turn the world upside down without provoking some reaction! Paul reminds these Christians that though for the moment things may be difficult, God is on their side, and will ultimately vindicate them.

2. The church and the future: A more subtle form of 'persecution' had also come into the church, with the appearance of letters claiming to be written by Paul and his associates (2 Thessalonians 2:1–12). Fanatics of some kind had taken advantage of Paul's mention of the *parousia* of Jesus in his earlier letter, and used the occasion to put their own point of view on the subject.

Paul had to warn the Thessalonian Christians 'not to be quickly shaken in mind or excited, either by spirit or by word, or by letter purporting to be from us, to the effect that the day of the Lord has come' (2:2). The precise meaning of the suggestion that 'the day of the Lord has come' is unclear. In 1 Corinthians we find mention of people who thought that the resurrection (which was associated with the end of things), and the *parousia* of Christ had already taken place. On the basis of this belief they indulged in all kinds of immoral practices (1 Corinthians 15:12–58). But it is difficult to connect the two groups of people in any direct way. In any event, Paul goes on to emphasize here that in his view the *parousia* of Jesus was not an event that could take place invisibly or mystically (which would need to be the case if it had already happened). On the contrary, he fixes his own hope firmly in history by making it clear that certain historical events connected with 'the man of lawlessness' (2:3–12), would herald the return of Christ.

3. The church and society: The outcome of the interest in future events that had arisen in Thessalonica was that some of the Christians had stopped living a normal life. They had opted out of work and were idly waiting for Christ to return, an attitude Paul criticized severely. He regarded the Christian not as someone who shirked duties by becoming a religious hermit, but as someone who played a full part in the life of the community. People who did not do this, however 'spiritual' their motive, should be disciplined by the church. It was not very often that Paul instructed a church to take disciplinary action against one of its members, but this was one such case. Of course, the other Christians were to do this in a way that brought glory to the Lord whom they were serving: 'Do not look on him as an enemy, but warn him as a brother' (3:15).

Even with all their problems, however, the Thessalonian Christians had learned the true secret of the Christian way of life Paul had shown them. They were rapidly becoming the kind of congregation of which Paul could be proud: 'your faith is growing abundantly, and the love of every one of you for one another is increasing' (1:3).

1 Corinthians

Corinth was an important sea port on one of the busiest routes in the Mediterranean, and one of the most cosmopolitan cities anywhere in the empire. In the streets of Corinth military men from Rome, mystics from the East and Jews from Palestine continually rubbed shoulders with the philosophers of Greece. When Paul had preached the good news about Jesus in this city, people from all sections of society responded, and came to form the new church there.

Men and women from very diverse spiritual and intellectual backgrounds brought with them into the church many assorted concepts and ideas. While Paul was with them, the various sections of the young congregation were held together. But on his departure they began to work out for themselves the implications of their Christian faith, and naturally produced many different answers.

A divided church

As a result the church at Corinth had for all practical purposes been divided into four different groups, of which Paul speaks in 1 Corinthians 1:10–17. Some traced their spiritual allegiance to Paul, others to Apollos, others to Cephas, while yet others claimed only to belong to Christ (1:12–13). These four parties clearly reflect the diverse backgrounds of the Corinthian Christians:

The 'Paul Party' would consist of libertines – people who heard Paul's original preaching on the freedom of the Christian and concluded from it that, once they had responded to the gospel, they could live as they liked.

The 'Cephas Party' were undoubtedly legalists – people like the Judaizers, who believed that the Christian life meant the strict observance of the Jewish Law, both ritual and moral.

The 'Apollos Party' were probably devotees of the classical Greek outlook. According to Acts 18:24–28, Apollos was a Jew from Alexandria, 'an eloquent man, well versed in the scriptures'. As an educated Alexandrian Jew, Apollos would naturally be an acceptable teacher to those Christians at Corinth with a Greek philosophical background.

The 'Christ Party' probably consisted of a group who considered themselves superior to the groups that had developed around the personalities of ordinary mortals. They wanted a direct contact with the cosmic Christ, much as they had experienced direct mystical contacts with the deities of the eastern Mystery religions.

In 1 Corinthians we can see how each of these groups was at work, spreading its own ideas and emphases. *The libertines*, who claimed to follow Paul, encouraged the whole church not to worry about open immorality (5:1–13). *The legalists*, claiming to follow Cephas' example, raised the old question of what kind of food Christians should eat – but this time the argument was over food that had been offered in pagan temples before being sold to the public (chapters 8–9). *The philosophers*, followers of Apollos, were insisting they had a form of wisdom superior to anything Paul had proclaimed (1:18–25). *The mystics*, claiming they were following Christ, were inclined to argue that the sacraments of the church acted in a supernatural way, giving automatic protection against the natural results of their immoral activities (10:1–13). The resurrection had already come, they claimed, they had been raised in a mystical way with Christ (15:12–19), and were now living on a super-spiritual level of existence, far beyond the grasp of the followers of people like Paul, Cephas or Apollos (see also 4:8).

The combination of these different types of extremism led in the second century to the formation of a heterodox movement known as 'Gnosticism', and we can see here in Corinth the first stirrings in this direction. But at the time, Paul was not concerned with giving a name to it. All he saw was one of his largest churches thrown into utter confusion by fanatics operating from four different directions.

This was totally against all that he understood the Christian message to be. When he first visited Corinth Paul had declared the cross of Christ and his resurrection to be 'of first importance' for Christian faith (1 Corinthians 15:3–7; 1:18–25). This was the only basis on which men and women of diverse cultures could be reunited. Whatever Paul, Apollos or Cephas had done in their own name was of no consequence. So Paul repeated his basic message as the answer to the problems of the Corinthian church: 'No other foundation can anyone lay than that which is laid, which is Jesus Christ' (3:11).

Having established this starting-point, Paul went on to look at some of the specific problems of the Corinthian church: problems concerned with their attitudes to non-Christian standards and institutions, and with their attitudes to one another in the gatherings of the church.

The church's belief

Finally, Paul deals with what he regarded as the core of essential Christian belief. It was also one of the main elements in the problems of the Corinthian church: the resurrection of Christ.

Some members of the church were claiming that in their mystical experiences they had already been raised to a new spiritual level above that achieved by ordinary Christians. This belief was linked with a misunderstanding about the resurrection of Jesus, and Paul deals with it in two ways.

First he reminds the Corinthians of the firm historical foundation on which belief in Jesus' resurrection is based (15:3–11). In doing so, he provides the earliest account in the New Testament of the resurrection of Jesus. Secondly he goes on to show how, if the resurrection happened historically (as he and the other apostles believed), this would guarantee that Christians also will be raised at the last day in the same way as Jesus had been raised from death. Because of the centrality of Jesus' resurrection for the whole of Christian belief, anyone who denied this by spiritualizing it into mystical experiences was really denying the basis of the Christian faith: 'if the dead are not raised, then Christ has not been raised. If Christ has not been raised, your faith is futile and you are still in your sins... we are of all people most to be pitied' (15:16–18).

More arguments in Corinth

This was not the end of Paul's correspondence with the Christians at Corinth. He must have been at least partly successful in persuading them to change their minds, for we hear nothing more of questions about the resurrection, or marriage, or things like food bought in the pagan temples. But there were still problems, this time especially connected with the arrival of messengers – 'apostles' as they called themselves – probably from Judea. Paul had already dealt with such people in the churches of Galatia. But those who came to Corinth were not 'Judaizers' in the strict sense. They were not trying to persuade the Corinthians to become Jews by accepting circumcision and the Law. They were aiming to persuade them to transfer their allegiance away from Paul to the Jewish leaders of the original church in Jerusalem. Paul had apparently chosen to visit the church at Corinth while these people were in residence there – and this is the 'painful visit' to which he refers. It was certainly painful for Paul, for he was insulted by these 'false apostles' and their claims that his authority was questionable. He left in a hurry – something he was later to regret, for it seemed to confirm what his opponents were saying about him.

As a result the Corinthian Christians were left in a turmoil. Who were the real apostles, and how could they tell the difference between true and false? Their loyalty swung from one to the other, and in order to clarify the issues Paul wrote to them yet again. The letter he wrote this time was our 2 Corinthians.

2 Corinthians

1 Corinthians has a clear line of argument from beginning to end. But 2 Corinthians often reads more like an anthology of Paul's advice on different subjects. Some think this is just what it is: a collection of two or three letters that were originally written quite independently, and later joined together by an editor. This would be a standard procedure in the ancient world, and in principle anyone collecting Paul's letters together would be quite likely to fit in more than one of them into the same standard length book.

What, then, does 2 Corinthians have to say about the fresh problems faced by Paul and the Corinthian Christians? The letter falls naturally into four main sections:

1. Facing up to problems: Paul knew that he needed to explain the turbulent nature of his relationship with the Corinthian church. But what about the question of true and false apostleship? Paul clarifies his thinking on both topics in his opening thanksgiving section (1:3–11), affirming not only his affection for the church in Corinth, but also his conviction that suffering and weakness are in some way an inevitable part of following Christ. To cope with persecution, Paul needs to trust wholeheartedly in God. But he also needs the prayerful support of his readers. His relationship with them is not all one-sided: he needs their prayers just as much as they need his guidance.

Paul also needed to reassure the Corinthians of his trustworthiness. His unexpected visits and letters, and last minute changes of plan had given them the impression he was unstable (1:12 – 2:4). They had concluded he was afraid to visit them because he knew that at bottom the claims of the 'false apostles' were true. Paul obviously felt these criticisms deeply, and defends himself against the charge that he was acting selfishly.

2. What is an apostle? The major point at issue was Paul's authority as an apostle. Paul introduces this subject by expressing gratitude for what God had done in his life. Because of his experience of the living Christ, he is a part of 'Christ's victory procession' (2:14). As such, he is in a close personal relationship to Christ himself. But that does not allow him to boast in a triumphalist way about his own abilities. Quite the opposite, for endowment with God's Holy Spirit brings great responsibilities, and it is the recognition of this that makes Paul different from the other so-called 'apostles' who had arrived in Corinth.

Unlike those who had come from Jerusalem, Paul did not depend on official letters to establish his credentials. He was content for the validity of his work to be judged by its results – the changed lives of his converts, and his own lifestyle (3:1–18).

But did this mean that Christian apostles would be living a super-spiritual sort of existence, unaffected by the regular problems of everyday life? Not at all, asserts Paul (4:1–15). Though the gospel is a powerful, life-giving message, God had chosen to entrust it to 'common claypots'. No one takes special care of everyday crockery, which inevitably becomes chipped and cracked in the course of ordinary use. This is exactly what true servants of Christ can expect: 'we are often troubled... sometimes in doubt... badly hurt... always in danger of death for Jesus' sake...' (4:7–11). Furthermore, this had been Jesus' own experience, culminating in the agonizing despair of the cross. But after the cross had come the resurrection – and for Paul, this is the key to understanding the Christian life.

Reflecting on the physical dangers he had faced led Paul onto the subject of life after death. This had already been a major subject of 1 Corinthians. But now in 2 Corinthians, Paul's perspective has changed. He asks different questions – no doubt as a result of his recent narrow escapes from death (presumably in Ephesus, 2 Corinthians 1:9). What he says is one of the most complex passages in all his letters (5:1–10). But two things are quite clear: (i) he is still opposed to the views of those Corinthians (and later Gnostics) who claimed that 'resurrection' was a matter of a person's inner spiritual experience; and (ii) he still clings to the Jewish belief in a bodily existence after death, rather than resorting to the Greek view of an immortal soul that would survive the disposable body.

Even this however was only the final outworking of what was already happening in the lives of Christian people. Like Jesus, Paul saw a tension between what God would do in the future when the kingdom comes in all its perfection, and what God is doing now in the lives of those who follow God's way. Christians' thinking, behaviour, standards and values, should all reflect here and now the reality of God's living presence: 'No longer, then, do we judge anyone by human standards... Those who are joined to Christ are a new being, the old is gone, the new has come' (5:16–17). This reached to the very heart of Paul's understanding of the death and resurrection of Jesus, and was the basis of all his work as an evangelist: 'God was in Christ, reconciling the world' (5:19).

Paul then turns to warn the Corinthians that the Christian lifestyle should be wholly different from a secular lifestyle. Christians must reflect God's own values and standards (6:14 – 7:1). Modern readers of this passage often imagine that Paul writes about personal morality, especially marriage relationships. That would be covered by what he says, but his advice is far more wide ranging. There is something fundamentally incompatible between the accepted standards of the pagan world and the standards of the Christian gospel – and believers must be prepared to put God first in every area of life, not just where they find it convenient.

3. Looking to the future: Paul now moves on to the effects of his 'painful letter', which had apparently led to a change of heart on the part of the Corinthians – a change which Titus had reported (7:5–16). It was presumably on that basis that Paul felt it was now appropriate to invite them to make a contribution to the collection he was organizing for the financial relief of the church in Jerusalem (8:1 – 9:15). This was not the first time the Corinthians had heard of this

(1 Corinthians 16:1–4). But their stormy relationship with Paul had prevented anything being done about it until now. Paul urges them to be generous not simply out of a sense of duty, but as a loving response to what God had done for them. He also believed that such an act of generosity would improve relations between the Gentile churches he had established around the empire and the exclusively Jewish congregations back in Palestine (9:1–15).

4. Authority and charisma: In this section Paul again takes the offensive. Perhaps he had heard of yet further challenges to his authority even while he was in the process of writing. This time it seems he was being criticized because of his personality. 'Paul's letters are severe and strong,' his Corinthians opponents were saying, 'but when he is with us in person, he is weak, and his words are nothing' (10:10). Clearly, he lacked the charismatic appeal of the 'false apostles' who had come to Corinth. They did not suffer from self-doubt as he did, but were always boasting about their mystical experiences and spiritual maturity. Paul does not answer these charges comprehensively now. He has already done so in his previous discussion of the relationship between weakness and power in the lives of God's servants. He tackles the subject less systematically here, suggesting that these others only seem so impressive because 'They make up their own standards to measure themselves by, and they judge themselves by their own standards' (10:12). Indeed, worse than that. For he accuses the Corinthians of accepting 'anyone who comes to you and preaches a different Jesus, not the one we preached; and you accept a spirit and a gospel completely different from the Spirit and the gospel you received from us' (11:4).

Paul then launches into a wide-ranging attack on those who were questioning his own credentials on this spurious basis – dealing in turn with his relationship to the Corinthian church (11:1–6), his style of life (11:7–11), and the ultimate source of his authority (11:12–15). Far from showing him to be second rate, his suffering and persecution actually demonstrate the reality of his calling (11:16–33).

The 'false apostles' also seem to have been claiming more spectacular manifestations of the Holy Spirit's gifts than Paul. We certainly know that was a perennial focus for argument in Corinthian church life (1 Corinthians 12–14). Paul recognized that boasting about such things does no good – but he needed to set the record straight and point out that he too had 'visions and revelations given me by the Lord' (12:1). But he still returns to the theme of suffering and weakness as the cornerstone of his apostolic status: it is only as people recognize their own weakness and trust entirely in God that they can speak of being truly Christian (12:7–10).

Finally, Paul reminds them that he will be visiting Corinth again, and they would do well to put their lives in order before he arrives. Despite what his opponents have claimed, he is prepared to denounce them face to face. But it would be much happier for everyone if they would get back to the basis of the gospel first, and recognize that it is only when they each acknowledge their human weakness that God's power can work effectively in their lives (13:1–10).

So Paul came to the end of what was probably the most complicated letter he ever wrote. Like Galatians, the Corinthian letters were written in the white heat of controversy, which only adds to our difficulties in understanding them. Paul was under attack by his friends as well as his enemies. This must have given him considerable reason to pause and think out his gospel again. He wanted to avoid the pitfalls of the past without in any sense compromising his basic position that in Christ all barriers of race, sex and social standing are removed, and all men and women stand equal in the freedom given to them by the Holy Spirit. It was probably thoughts of this kind that dictated the form of Paul's next major letter, which is quite different from any of those we have looked at so far.

Romans

Rome was naturally Paul's ultimate goal in spreading the good news about Jesus throughout the empire. But Rome had already been evangelized, and had a flourishing church. Many of the Christians in Rome were probably of Jewish origin, and Paul realized that some of them may have been influenced against him. Judaizing Christians may well have been there saying it was necessary for all Gentile converts to observe the Law of the Old Testament, and if Roman Christians had heard of what was happening in Corinth they could have been confirmed in their false impression of Paul and his message.

Rome was crucial to the evangelization of the empire – and Paul also recognized a need to re-state his own gospel in a form that was not open to misinterpretation, either by sympathizers or by opponents. So he decided to prepare for his visit to the capital by writing a letter to the church there, containing a reasoned statement of his own beliefs. This was the letter to the Romans.

Paul was clearly in a more reflective mood when he wrote Romans than when he penned Galatians or any of the Corinthian letters, but it is not a comprehensive statement of the whole of his theology. Several important aspects of his thinking do not feature here at all – not least his belief in the future return of Jesus (*parousia*) and about life after death. What he says on the nature of the church in Romans is also very limited when compared with his fuller exposition of this theme in 1 Corinthians.

Romans is best understood as a more carefully articulated account of some of the major themes of Galatians and 1–2 Corinthians (1 Corinthians in particular). The nineteenth century scholar J.B. Lightfoot claimed that 'the epistle to the Galatians stands in relation to the Roman letter, as the rough model to the finished statue'. This strikes the right note, except that the Corinthian situation also cannot have been far from Paul's mind at the time. What we have in Romans is a restatement of the argument of Galatians, as seen through the spectacles of what had taken place in Corinth.

Because Romans is so closely based on Paul's previous letters to the Galatians and to the Corinthians we do not need to summarize it in such great detail here.

The letter falls into three major sections:

1. How Christians know God: The first part of Romans, chapters 1–8, is one long theological argument starting from a text in the prophet Habakkuk: 'the just shall live by faith' (Habakkuk 2:4). Here Paul argues in a way very familiar from Galatians; indeed many of the points he makes are the same. Everyone, whether Jew or Gentile, is under the power of sin. Apart from Christ there is no way of escape from God's condemnation of sin (1:18 – 3:20). Yet it is possible to receive 'the righteousness of God', that is, release from

God's sentence of condemnation and the power to share in God's own goodness. This is something that can be obtained only through faith in Christ, and not by doing good works (3:21 – 4:25).

As in Galatians, Paul illustrates his theme from the life of Abraham (4:1–25). He then goes on (5:1 – 8:39) to describe the results of this new relationship with God: freedom from the wrath of God; freedom from slavery to sin; freedom from the Law; and freedom from death through the working of the Spirit of God in Christ. 'In all these things we are more than conquerors through the one who loved us' (8:37).

These are all themes that Paul had dealt with before in either Galatians or Corinthians. But in Romans we find several new elements, all of which are clearly the outcome of Paul's experience in seeing his message misunderstood and misapplied in the churches. Paul deals directly with the problem of antinomianism in 6:1 – 8:39. He makes it clear that though Christians are set free from the rule of all external law as a way of gaining acceptance from God, they have in fact entered into a new kind of service – no longer 'slaves of sin' (6:17), but now 'slaves of God' (6:22). Christians have been set free not to do as they please, but so that the Holy Spirit within them might help them to be 'conformed to the image of God's Son' (8:29). This is the teaching of Galatians as seen by Paul after his experiences in Corinth.

2. Israel and salvation: In chapters 9–11 Paul moves on. He is concerned with the fact of Israel's apparent rejection of this salvation he has been describing. He points out that God's present neglect of the Jews does not contradict either the promises in the Old Testament or God's justice. It is Israel's own fault, for choosing the way of 'works' rather than the way of faith. But Paul was still convinced that God's rejection of Israel was not final. Even in the midst of unfaithfulness, there was a faithful remnant (11:1–10). The present repudiation of the Jews was an integral part of God's plan for the ultimate salvation of people from all races (11:11–36).

3. How Christians should behave: Paul then moves away from strictly theological statements to write about the practical application of God's righteousness in Christian living (12:1 – 15:13). Here he deals with the Christian's relationship to the church (12:1–8), to other people (12:9–21) and to the state (13:1–10). He sums up

Christian duty as a whole in the words 'love is the fulfilling of the Law' (13:10). He emphasizes again that standards of Christian morality are to be produced not by an artificial set of rules and regulations imposed from outside, but by the power of the Holy Spirit working within the believer. But the end result of the Spirit's work will be that the Law of God is in fact observed, and the key idea of this law is love. Paul illustrates this by reference to two live issues: the eating of vegetables in preference to meat (14:1 – 15:6; a similar case to the question of meat bought from pagan temples), and the general attitude of Jews and Gentiles towards one another within the church (15:7–13).

In this letter we have a mature statement of the gospel as Paul understood it. It was a gospel that did not depend on keeping rules and regulations. It was rather a radical message of a living Christ who wanted to enrich the lives of his followers. Under his direction they would discover a way of living that would be pleasing to God, beneficial to other people, and personally enriching. Accepting that help needed to come from outside was a notion no one liked, whether Jew or Gentile. But all the same Paul was convinced that it was 'the power of God for salvation', appropriated through faith in Christ, and put into practical effect by the power of the Holy Spirit working in the believer's life.

Colossians

Though Colossae was not far from Ephesus, where Paul had worked for three years, he never visited it. A major element of his mission strategy was that he would establish his own work in a central location, from which his converts could then take the gospel into surrounding areas. This is what happened in Colossae, where the church was founded by Epaphras, who may have been one of Paul's converts in Ephesus.

Epaphras visited Paul during his later imprisonment in Rome, and gave him a generally encouraging report of the Colossian church. But one thing was causing real concern, namely the spread of a false teaching which modern readers often call 'the Colossian heresy'. It was a combination of practices like those Paul opposed in Galatia, with the sort of beliefs held by the 'Christ party' in Corinth. The racial exclusivism of people like the Judaizers had been combined with the intellectual exclusivism common in many pagan religious cults of the day. As a result a group of people in the Colossian church considered themselves better Christians than the others. These people held that a complete and lasting salvation could not be achieved simply by faith in Christ, as Paul had taught. In addition to simple faith, it was also necessary to obtain an insight into divine things through secret knowledge given in a mystical way.

Such knowledge could be acquired by taking part in various ritual practices (circumcision, for example), not eating certain foods, and observing Jewish festivals and Sabbaths. The Colossian heretics must have seemed very similar to the Judaizers whom Paul encountered in Galatia, who also wanted to impose circumcision and other Jewish rituals on Gentile converts. But the rationale for doing these things was quite different in Colossae than it had been in Galatia.

The Galatians had been tempted to observe the Old Testament Law as an integral part of keeping the religious covenants of the Old Testament. The Judaizers had told them they could not be a part of God's people unless they first became Jews, by accepting the claims of the Old Testament Law. But in Colossae, these observances were part of a radical ascetic agenda, searching for something that would help check 'the indulgence of the flesh', and thereby heighten 'spiritual' awareness. These people were not 'legalists' like the Judaizers, and the fact that they chose to achieve their aims by using certain parts of the Old Testament Law was only coincidence. This is very clear from Paul's reply to them, as he deals not with the issues of law and grace (as in Galatians), but with the basic moral issues raised by any kind of ascetic practice.

In his letter to the Colossian church, Paul deals with this matter by emphasizing again that believers can find all they need in Christ. Like the later Gnostics, some of the Colossians had been suggesting that other supernatural agencies were needed, and that Jesus was just one of several possible manifestations of God. Against this, Paul firmly asserts that 'In Christ all the fullness of God was pleased to dwell' (Colossians 1:19). Indeed, he went further than this by emphasizing that in Jesus 'the whole fullness of deity dwells *bodily*' (2:9).

45

The Colossians claimed they needed to experience something deep and mysterious if they were to find full salvation, and Paul agreed with them. He could even describe his own work as the presentation of 'the mystery'. But far from being something deep and hidden, this 'mystery' was the very thing that lay at the heart of all Paul's preaching: the simple fact of Christ's own life within them (1:27). Whatever the Christian may need, it can all be found in Christ, 'in whom are hid all the treasures of wisdom and knowledge' (2:3).

Paul then went on to remind his readers of all the benefits they had as Christians, some of which they were now trying to achieve by other, mystical means. Whoever they are, and whatever experiences they claim to have, all Christians stand equal before God. All have the same temptations to face (3:5–11), and there is only one way for all of them to overcome such temptations. 'Set your minds on things that are above, not on things that are on earth. For you have died, and your life is hid with Christ in God... Hence there cannot be Greek and Jew, circumcised and uncircumcised, barbarian, Scythian, slave, free person, but Christ is all, and in all' (3:2, 11).

Instead of following a false set of values based on their own worthless speculations, the Colossians ought again to remind themselves that the true ambition of the Christian must be to become like Christ (3:12–17): 'Whatever you do, in word or deed, do everything in the name of the Lord Jesus, giving thanks to God the Father through him' (3:17).

By their emphasis on asceticism and speculation the Colossian teachers had removed Christian faith from the arena of real life. But Paul was convinced, as always, that following Christ should make a difference to everyday living. So he ends his letter by showing how the power of Christ that lives in the Christian (1:27) works itself out in the family (3:18–21), at work (3:22 – 4:1), in the church (4:2–4), and in life in general (4:5–6).

Philemon

Along with the letter to the church in Colossae, Paul also sent a personal note to one of its leading members: Philemon. He must have been quite affluent, for the Christians met for their regular meetings in his house (verse 2). Like everyone else in his position in the Roman empire, Philemon had a number of slaves. One of them, Onesimus, had run away from Colossae, perhaps taking some of Philemon's possessions with him (verses 18–19). But he had met Paul, and as a result he became a Christian himself.

Paul knew it was his duty – both as a citizen and as a Christian – to return Onesimus to his master. There were legal penalties in the Roman empire for anyone harbouring runaway slaves – and in addition, Paul could see that any other course of action would threaten the bonds of Christian friendship that existed between himself and Onesimus. It was for these practical reasons that Paul therefore sent Onesimus back to Colossae, along with this short personal letter. Of course Paul's action in doing this raises other questions about his attitudes to slavery as an institution. In particular, modern readers will wish to ask how this episode fits in with Paul's categorical statements elsewhere that freedom is at the very heart of the Christian gospel (e.g. Galatians 3:28).

Here we should notice that Paul does explicitly express the hope that he is not returning Onesimus to exactly the same position as he was in before. He sends him back as 'not just a slave, but much more than a slave: he is a dear brother in Christ' (verse 16). And he instructs Philemon: 'welcome him back just as you would welcome me' (verse 17). Indeed, more than that. For many scholars think that Paul was actually asking for Onesimus to be released from his service so that he could return to work full-time with Paul as a Christian missionary (verses 11–14).

We do not know what happened when Onesimus got back to Colossae. He may have been set free and returned to Paul, to become a leading figure in the Christian churches of the area. At the beginning of the second century, Ignatius mentions an Onesimus who was leader of the church at Ephesus, describing him as 'a man of inexpressible love' and 'an excellent bishop' (Ignatius, *To the Ephesians* 1). If this was the same person, that would explain why a short personal letter to Philemon should be preserved and included in the official collection of Paul's letters to churches. In any case, presumably Philemon must have complied with Paul's request – otherwise no-one would have wished to preserve this little note.

Ephesians

Colossians refers to another letter: 'When this letter has been read among you, have it read also in the church of the Laodiceans; and see that you read also the letter from Laodicea.' Laodicea was quite near to Colossae, and Paul wanted the churches to exchange letters.

There is no 'letter to the Laodiceans' in the New Testament. Noting this omission, the church of the early centuries lost no time in producing a letter of that name, which survives in Latin, and may also have been available in Greek. But this letter is certainly not authentic, and merely consists of bits and pieces from Paul's other letters strung together in an aimless way.

Could it be, though, that we do in fact possess a copy of the real 'letter from Laodicea' to which Paul referred – except we know it as Ephesians? This letter contains in a fuller and more carefully argued form the same kind of teaching about the person of Christ as in Colossians, but without the pointed references to the local Colossian heresy.

Three other things also suggest that Ephesians was probably intended for other churches in the area as well as for the Christians at Ephesus. The words 'at Ephesus' in Ephesians 1:1 (the only indication that this letter was destined for that city) are not found in the best and oldest manuscripts of this letter. Some modern versions of the New Testament put the words 'at Ephesus' in the margin, to indicate this.

There are no personal greetings in this letter, though Paul probably had more friends in Ephesus than anywhere else.

The second-century Gnostic leader Marcion called Ephesians 'the letter to the Laodiceans'.

Ephesians was probably a circular letter addressed to a number of different congregations. The words 'at Ephesus' in Ephesians 1:1 would be found in the copy that went to that city, while the copy referred to in Colossians 4:16 would have the words 'at Laodicea' instead.

In Ephesians, Paul again emphasizes the central place of Christ in the plan of God and in the life of Christian believers. He begins by reminding his readers of the great privileges they possess in Christ.

Though the people to whom he was writing had previously 'lived in the passions of their flesh' (Ephesians 2:3), God had put them in a new position. They had been 'made... alive together with Christ... and raised... up with him, and made to sit with him in the heavenly place' (2:5–6). Every individual Christian had become a part of the new creation in which God planned 'to unite all things in Christ, things in heaven and things on earth' (1:10).

Some of the people who read Paul's letter had been told these things before by Paul himself. For this was his special ministry: 'to preach to the Gentiles the unsearchable riches of Christ' (3:8); and to demonstrate how those 'riches' could be received and enjoyed in real life. Some of his readers may have been influenced by false teaching like the Colossian heresy. They would find the true satisfaction they desired only if they were willing to be 'filled with all the fulness of God' (3:19), which is found nowhere else but in Christ.

After setting out this profound description of Christ as Saviour of the world and as the source of all physical, mental and spiritual knowledge and activity, Paul went on to draw out the practical implications of it all. If his readers were indeed members of Christ's body, new people and children of God, they must show by their actions who they really are.

Did Paul write Ephesians?

In most of Paul's letters we are always close to the heartbeat of the apostle, and usually not far from controversy. It takes little imagination to envisage the furious arguments that led to the writing of Galatians or 1–2 Corinthians, for example. But in Ephesians things are different. The discussion is much more serene and settled, and seems to progress independently of any direct involvement with opponents, or indeed any specific identifiable readers.

A number of other arguments can also be presented, which together support the suggestion that perhaps Paul never actually wrote this letter.

Ephesians is certainly different. But there is nothing in it that cannot legitimately be seen as the product of further reflection on some of the significant themes of Paul's other prison letters. It could be that just as his earlier handling of the controversy in Galatia led him to articulate his thinking more carefully in his later letter to Rome, so his argument with the Colossian heretics prompted a similar process which culminated in the writing of Ephesians. In any event, if it was not penned by Paul himself, it must certainly have been compiled within his circle of close acquaintances, and with first-hand knowledge of his thinking.

Philippians

With the exception of Philemon, this is the most personal of Paul's letters. It was written to acknowledge a gift that the Philippian church had sent to Paul to help him financially while in prison. A messenger called Epaphroditus had brought the gift from Philippi, and was a great help to Paul during his short stay in Rome. Most of Paul's letter, sent back to Philippi with Epaphroditus, is concerned with personal matters affecting Paul's possible release, and expressing his warm affection for the Philippian Christians.

Paul always felt especially close to the Christians in Philippi. Theirs was the first church he established on European soil – and it was also apparently one of the few that had not been torn apart by damaging arguments about Christian faith and behaviour.

Paul begins with an appreciative expression of thanks to God for all that these Christians had meant to him (1:3–11). Unlike some others, they had consistently 'helped me in the work of the gospel from the very first day until now' (1:5). This is why he was able to accept their financial generosity (1:7) – something that he felt unwise in the case of more volatile congregations such as that in Corinth (1 Corinthians 9:8–18). Because of their open and friendly attitude, he can be confident that their Christian living will be marked by 'the truly good qualities which only Jesus Christ can produce, for the glory and praise of God' (1:11).

He continues to sound this note as he brings them up to date with his own situation in prison (1:12–30).

But there was one thing that bothered Paul about the church at Philippi. Some of the Christians were quarrelling with each other. Paul later names two argumentative women, Euodia and Syntyche (4:2–3)

– but they were not the only ones. In urging them to 'look out for one another's interests, not just for your own' (2:4), Paul quotes from an early hymn that was no doubt familiar to his readers, and probably to Christians in other churches as well (2:6–11).

This is the only place in Paul's letters where he gives the example of Jesus as a pattern for Christian behaviour (2 Corinthians 8:9–10 is very similar). Modern Christian preachers who tell their listeners to follow Jesus' example usually have in mind the kind of things that Jesus did during his ministry. The gospels give us many examples of his compassion, care and good works. But it is quite striking that Paul never urges Christians to follow this example. In those places where he does give Jesus as a model for Christian living, he refers to Jesus' abandonment of all that was his when he became a human person. This idea was very important for Paul, and lay at the heart of much of his thinking. In order to be a Christian at all, people must be prepared to give up themselves and all that they are completely to Christ. This was the lesson he had learned on the road to Damascus, when he himself responded in faith to the demands of the risen Jesus. It runs like a golden thread through the fabric of all his letters.

Paul now moves on to explain in greater practical detail what it means for a Christian's life to be infused with the life of the risen Jesus himself.

Finally, he closes this most joyful of all his letters with advice on a number of topics. He reminds his readers that, like him, they can have 'the strength to face all conditions by the power that Christ gives' (4:13), for 'my God will supply all your needs' (4:19).

1 and 2 Timothy and Titus

The 'pastoral epistles' (1 and 2 Timothy and Titus) are quite different in both style and content from Paul's other letters. They were written to advise other leaders of the early church. Both Timothy and Titus are mentioned elsewhere as Paul's companions, though they also worked independently of Paul: Titus in Crete, and Timothy in Ephesus. These three letters are very similar to each other, and were probably written at about the same time. They deal with four main subjects.

1. False teachers: Many of Paul's letters were written in response to threats from various opponents: Judaizers in Galatia, ascetics in Colossae, and Jewish Gnostics of some sort in Corinth. Timothy and Titus were facing similar problems, and were under pressure to abandon the gospel message as Paul had delivered it to them.

This teaching consisted of several elements that we have met before. The Old Testament Law was certainly involved, for some of the troublemakers are identified as 'converts from Judaism, who rebel and deceive others with their nonsense'. It seems that these people were using the Old Testament for their own ends, for Timothy is reminded that 'the Law is good if it is used as it should be'. The specific argument seems to have been about sex and food, with some claiming that true spiritual enlightenment could only come through a life of asceticism in which material bodily existence was denied as far as possible. But Timothy is urged to remember that 'Everything God has created is good; nothing is to be rejected...'

These people probably had leanings towards a Jewish form of Gnosticism. There is indeed a specific mention of 'the profane talk and foolish arguments of what some people wrongly call 'knowledge' (Greek *gnosis*)'. Like later Gnostics, they wanted to deny that this world is really God's world – and so the sooner they could escape from it, the better. The fact that Timothy's opponents were arguing about 'myths and endless genealogies which promote speculation...' and had 'lost their faith in foolish discussions' supports this identification. But of course there was more than one way to belittle bodily existence. Asceticism was not the only option: extreme permissiveness was another. And at least one group mentioned here seems to have chosen this alternative: 'they will hold to the outward form of our religion, but reject its real power'. For Paul, the Christian gospel had always been about changing lifestyles, not about provoking arguments.

2. True belief: In response to all this, Timothy and Titus are encouraged to reaffirm the basic elements of true Christian faith. They must continue to deny the idea that God does not care about the world we live in. The fact that Jesus himself was both truly human and truly divine clearly contradicted such a notion.

Not only did Jesus come into this world to share God's love: he became personally involved with sinful people. The essence of salvation therefore is not to be found in philosophical speculation, but in humble acceptance of God's love and mercy as demonstrated in the life, death and resurrection of Jesus. Those who have their theological priorities right will show it in the way they live – not motivated by money, but by 'the true words of our Lord Jesus Christ'.

3. Christian behaviour: This theme keeps coming up throughout these three letters. Several passages spell out in more detail how Christians ought to behave. Family relationships, relationships in the church, and attitudes to secular governments should all reflect the best aspirations of the ancient world, 'so that no one will speak evil of the message that comes from God'.

4. Christian leadership: As we might expect, there is much advice here to Titus and Timothy about their own conduct. They are to be examples of good behaviour to all whom they serve. But they must also have courage to stand firm for the truth, recognizing that the gospel depends not on personal opinions but on God. They must ensure that those whom they appoint to serve in leadership capacities in their churches also have the same qualities, and are the sort of people whom others can admire.

Did Paul write the pastoral epistles?

The three letters we refer to under the combined title 'the pastoral epistles' (1 and 2 Timothy and Titus) are very different from Paul's other letters. They were written not to churches, but to two individuals who were working among groups of young Christians: Timothy at Ephesus and Titus in Crete. In form, subject-matter and style these three letters are very similar to each other. But in all these respects they are quite distinct from Paul's other letters. The differences are so striking that many scholars today say that these three letters could not have been written by Paul himself.

The real strength of the suggestion that the pastoral epistles were not written by Paul lies in the style and vocabulary of the letters. These differences could perhaps be explained by reference to the different subject matter, to the fact that Paul was now an older man, or even to the fact that he was using a different secretary. It is also possible that the style of a letter written by Paul himself may have been revised later to make it into better Greek.

All the evidence of the early Church Fathers supports the view that Paul had some connection with these letters – and certainly, they do not reflect life in the church at a period far removed from his lifetime. Some have drawn attention to similarities between the pastoral epistles and Luke–Acts, and have suggested that Paul's friend and companion Luke could have written them in their present form after the apostle's death, using Paul's rough drafts as his starting point.

The Epistles of John

Like the gospel of John, 1 John tells us why it was written. In chapter five, the writer says, 'I am writing this to you so that you may know that you have eternal life – you that believe in the Son of God'. The gospel of John was written to demonstrate that Jesus was Messiah and Son of God – and to win people to faith in him. By contrast, 1 John was written to people who were already Christian believers, but who needed to be reassured of the truth of what they believed.

The heretics

It is not difficult to see why they needed such reassurance. Like the churches mentioned in Revelation, the church to which they belonged was suffering from the activities of 'false prophets'. These false prophets had originally been church members themselves. But they had left, and were now trying to subvert it from the outside. Of course, that was not how the false teachers saw things. They believed they had received special revelations that were not given to ordinary church members. They spoke of 'knowing' God in an intimate way, through the special operation of the Holy Spirit in their lives. They also believed that this enabled them to live on a different plane from ordinary Christians. They were already spiritually 'perfect', living in full appreciation of the 'light' which was God's personal essence – and so the normal earth-bound rules of Christian morality no longer applied to them.

All this sounds remarkably similar to the claims of Paul's opponents in Corinth. They too were claiming that because of their special mystical experiences, they were no longer bound by the normal constraints of human existence. They believed that through these mystical experiences they had already been raised to a new spiritual level far above that enjoyed by ordinary Christians. It was, they said, just as if the resurrection had already come. They might seem to be living in this world, but really they had been totally liberated from it, and so they no longer shared its concerns.

Docetism

But there is a new element in 1 John. For the 'false prophets' mentioned here had a distinctive understanding of the person and significance of Jesus himself. It is clear from what he says that John's opponents were denying that Jesus was the Messiah and the Son of God. It was not that they denied that Jesus had revealed the power of God. But they found it difficult to see how an ordinary human person could reveal the character of the eternal God. So they asserted that Jesus was not truly human at all.

Greek thinking always upheld a strong separation between this world in which we live, and the heavenly, spiritual world where God is. The Old Testament prophets had always believed that God's activity could be seen in the affairs of human experience. But Greek thinkers regarded life in this world as a miserable existence. The true destiny of men and women, they claimed, was not here, but in the spiritual world inhabited by God. True salvation, therefore, could only consist in the escape of a person from the 'prison' of this world into the life of the spirit world. There were many theories to explain precisely how this could be accomplished, and it is obvious that the desire for such liberation was what motivated both Paul's opponents in Corinth, and the false teachers of the church to which 1 John was addressed.

At the beginning, Christians were interested in such ideas mainly because they were attracted by the promise of exciting mystical experiences. But as these mystics began to think out the theological implications of their experience, they inevitably found it hard to cope with the church's belief that Jesus had somehow come direct from God. For if God was a part of that other mystical, supernatural world, then there was no way in which God could also be a real human person. For the all-powerful God of Greek philosophy to be imprisoned in the life of a human being would be a contradiction in terms.

One way out of the dilemma was to suggest that Jesus had only *seemed* to be the Messiah or Son of God. This view was 'Docetism' (from the Greek word *dokeo*, 'to seem'), and it was the opinion that is opposed in 1 John. Many of the early Church Fathers mention people with such beliefs. Irenaeus, 2nd century bishop of Lyons, tells how the apostle John once went to a public bath-house in Ephesus. But when he got there, John refused to take a bath because Cerinthus, a prominent Docetist, was also there.

Some have suggested that 1 John was a direct reply to Cerinthus himself, for he argued that the 'divine essence', or 'Christ', came into the human Jesus at his baptism, and left him before the crucifixion – and 1 John includes a statement that looks like a reply to this: 'Jesus Christ is the one who came with the water of his baptism and the blood of his death. He came not only with the water, but with both the water and the blood.' But Cerinthus had many other ideas not mentioned at all in 1 John, and the problems dealt with in this letter are undoubtedly less complex than the theology of Cerinthus and his followers. Indeed, with the exception of their speculation about the person of Christ, the heretics of 1 John have much more in common with Paul's opponents in Corinth, and it is probably more accurate to regard them as an intermediate stage between the Corinthian heretics and the fully-developed Gnostic systems of the second century.

1 John

The author of 1 John clearly had no time for these people. He denounced their beliefs and opposed their practices in every section of his letter. He realized all too well the strong pressure that they were placing on the members of the church, and he went out of his way to assure them that they, and not the heretics, were the ones who had the truth.

But it is not easy to find any logical argument here. Some scholars have tried to rearrange John's letter to make it fit together more logically. Others have explained what they regard as inconsistencies by supposing that the letter went through more than one edition and is therefore the work of more than one writer. But none of these suggestions is particularly convincing. The book contains not just the author's response to the heretics. It is also a part of his own theological reflection on the situation which he faced, and for that reason it is more a work of art than a book of theology. It can usefully be compared to a musical composition, in which the main theme is first expounded, and then is taken up and developed and elaborated as the composer moves on to other themes and ideas yet always returning to the original concept.

Whatever the form of the argument, the message of 1 John is crystal clear. Like every other New Testament writer, John is convinced that mystical experiences, however elevated, are totally irrelevant to Christian faith unless they affect the way people behave. It is no use talking about being liberated into the world of light, unless God's light truly informs and inspires human behaviour. To say that mystical experiences actually release people from the power of evil is unrealistic and untrue. Anyone who claims to be perfect and free from the influence of sin is fooling himself.

True Christians must 'live just as Jesus Christ did' – but they must also accept the reality of their moral poverty, and accept the forgiveness that only Jesus can give. Living like Jesus is a practical affair; it is a matter of loving other people, and this means that anyone who despises others (as the Docetists did) can hardly claim to be doing God's will. In reality, they are just indulging their own selfishness.

The fact that such people could ever have been a part of the church should serve to emphasize that the day of judgment is not far off. The others must not be intimidated by them. Whatever the heretics may claim, those in the church are the true recipients of the Holy Spirit, and they are the ones who have been accepted by God. Not that they have done anything to deserve that love. But having been adopted as God's children, they should ensure that they continue to do as God wants. Just as Christ loved them, so they must love one another – then they can be sure that they are truly living in harmony with the Holy Spirit, and in personal union with God.

But telling the true from the false is not just a matter of human judgment. There is a test of belief that can distinguish the heretics from the true believers: 'Anyone who acknowledges that Jesus Christ came as a human being has the Spirit who comes from God. But anyone who denies this about Jesus does not have the Spirit from God.' Having God's spirit naturally leads to love, just as God's own essence is love. It also leads to obedience to God's commands, and to final victory over all that is opposed to God's will. With this assurance, true Christians can be certain that they will know and understand God in a way that the Docetists never could.

2 and 3 John

2 and 3 John are related very closely to 1 John, though they are quite different types of literature. Unlike 1 John, they are short, personal letters, one addressed to a church and the other to an individual called Gaius. Their author calls himself 'the Elder'. In 2 John he warns his readers about wandering teachers 'who do not acknowledge that Jesus Christ came as a human being' (2 John 7–11). He was concerned that these people should not be welcomed into the church, and because of this many scholars think 2 John must have been written before 1 John, for in 1 John the heretics had already been excluded from the church (1 John 2:19).

3 John advises Gaius about a man by the name of Diotrephes. He was aspiring to be the leader of the church, and 'the elder' says that he intends to pay a short visit to correct 'the terrible things he says about us and the lies he tells' (3 John 9–10). There does not seem to have been any major theological disagreement between 'the elder' and Diotrephes. What 3 John reflects is the nature of power struggles at a stage when new patterns of the church leadership were beginning to emerge. As the apostles and their representatives died, the corporate leadership of the earliest churches began to disappear, and new leaders tried to assert themselves. Eventually there would be the formal appointment of just one authoritative leader in each local church, instead of the plurality of elders there had originally been.

Perhaps 'the elder' represented the older form of church organization, and was concerned at the emergence of just one person claiming to be the church's leader. In the second century, anyone with the title of 'elder' would themselves have been part of the organized hierarchy of the church. But the writer of these letters clearly does not belong in that context. He was obviously highly respected by his readers, but does not seem to have had absolute authority over them. He can only appeal to them to do what he believes to be right.

John Drane

THE NEW TESTAMENT EPISTLES IN LITERATURE

Themes and Images

Charity, Cupidity   *62*

Conscience   *80*

Conversion   *89*

Despair   *96*

Faith   *101*

Freedom, Bondage   *116*

Grace, Works   *124*

Heaven   *131*

Hell   *135*

Holy Spirit   *140*

Incarnation   *150*

Predestination   *154*

Resurrection   *162*

Second Coming   *167*

Themes and Images

Charity, Cupidity

The opposition *caritas / cupiditas,* while reflecting a basic moral distinction in the Bible, owes its particular formulation in Western tradition to difficulties encountered by St Jerome in rendering several biblical words for love accurately in available Latin equivalents. The Old Testament Hebrew word *'ahab,* while generally referring to spontaneous desire, applies to a range of human and divine expressions of affection. Another word, *hesed,* is used to connote deliberately chosen affection, loyalty, and kindness, typically translated by the King James Version as 'mercy' (cf. *raham,* 'to have compassion', Deuteronomy 30:3). Any of these terms may be involved in connection with sexual love, fraternal love, or God's love for his people. In Greek literature before the New Testament *eros* is the most common word for love; it suggests spontaneity (like *'ahab*) and yet is almost always sexual in connotation, even when, as in the erotic narratives of classical mythology (e.g., Leda and the swan), it refers to the love of the gods for human persons. In Platonic discourse, 'noble *eros'* can refer to the human quest for 'God' (cf. Plato, *Symposium*). When the Septuagint translators tried to find Greek equivalents for the familiar Hebrew words for love they rejected *eros* because of its overwhelming cultural associations with libidinous activity, choosing instead the obscure *agape* to translate *'ahab; eros* appears only once in the Septuagint, in a prostitute's invitation to sexual promiscuity (Proverbs 7:18). The New Testament eschews *eros* altogether. It makes limited use of *philia* ('love', 'affection, as for a spouse') to describe parental love (Matthew 10:37), the disciples' love for Jesus (John 21:15–17; 1 Corinthians 16:22), and Jesus' love for Lazarus (John 11:3, 36), as well as God's love for Jesus (John 5:50) and for his people (John 16:27; Revelation 3:19). It is never used, however, to describe human love for God. The principal New Testament word is *agape, agapao* (in English Bibles usually translated 'love', though twenty-nine times in the King James Version as 'charity'). In St Paul's first epistle to the Corinthians (13:4–8), *agape* (Vulgate *caritas;* King

James Version 'charity') is succinctly described in negative as well as positive terms. Charity is not jealousy, conceit, ostentation, arrogance, self-centredness, and resentment (various expressions of self-love); it is rather expressed in patience, kindness, truth, righteousness, hope, benevolence, and endurance (self-transcending love).

The King James Version 'charity' derives from Latin *caritas* (and its 13th-century French equivalent *charité*). St Jerome chose *caritas* ('love', 'esteem', 'affection') and *dilectio* ('delight', 'love', 'high esteem') to translate Greek *agape*, knowing that they were imprecise Latin equivalents, themselves overlapping in Roman usage. He then chose *cupiditas* ('lust', 'desire', 'passion', 'ambition') to translate *agapao* in cases where the object of the affection or desire was of a carnal order – e.g., 'Demas, in love with this present world' (2 Timothy 4:10). In 1 Timothy 6:10 (King James Version 'the love of money is the root of all evil') Jerome renders Greek *philargyria* in the same way: '*radix malorum cupiditas est*'. *Caritas* and *cupiditas* thus become, in the Vulgate New Testament and early commentary upon it, divergent, even polar, words for love, the neutral Latin word for which was usually *amor* (cf. *eros*, 'desire'). What determines whether the *amor* is *caritas* or *cupiditas* is its object, or, in St Augustine's more precise formulation, the intention the 'lover' bears towards the object. The Vulgate translator's attempt to characterize the 'sense', as Jerome was wont to say, rather than the semantic 'letter' in translating the Bible, is basic to subsequent Western usage. Developing the distinction in a passage of enormous influence, Augustine writes:

> I call 'charity' the motion of the soul toward the enjoyment of God for His own sake, and the enjoyment of one's self and of one's neighbour for the sake of God; but 'cupidity' is a motion of the soul toward the enjoyment of one's self, one's neighbour, or any corporal thing for the sake of something other than God. (*De doctrina Christiana*, 3.10.16)

In other words, desire (*amor*) never remains neutral, but is sharply defined by intention and object. Moreover, the intentions and objects of *caritas* and *cupiditas* are not compatible, so that 'the more the reign of cupidity is destroyed, the more charity is increased' (3.10.16). For

Augustine this is the fundamental spiritual conflict figured in every ethical choice, internally or externally. Vice and virtue, depredation and beneficence, wounding and healing – all manner of opposites are a relative function of choice between cupiditous and charitable promptings of the will. Augustine is thus able to reduce the pedagogical strategy of the Bible to a single governing precept: 'Scripture teaches nothing but charity, nor condemns anything except cupidity, and in this way shapes the minds of men.'

Numerous positive studies of the 'virtues' of *caritas* in the 12th century, notably including two by the Cistercians St Bernard of Clairvaux *(De Diligendo Deo)* and Aelred of Rievaulx *(Speculum Caritatis)*, are effectively what we should today style 'psychological' treatments of their subject. Bernard related both to inward promptings, saying: 'Only Charity can convert the soul, freeing it from unworthy motives' *(De Diligendo,* 12). Aelred's *Speculum Caritatis* theologically anticipates St Thomas Aquinas; psychologically it recapitulates Augustine. One of its major themes is the inner peace which derives from charity, and the role charitable affection can play in overcoming the disordering psychic effects of cupidity. The condition of charity is 'Sabbath rest', enjoyed in this life as a prefiguration of the life to come. He argues further that practical charity is illuminated by the order of priorities established in the Great Commandment (Deuteronomy 6:5; Matthew 22:37–40): love of God ought to be uppermost, followed by love of one's neighbour, with self occupying the humblest rung in one's ladder of affection. If this hierarchy of the 'law of love' is inverted, cupidity reigns, and with it inevitably idolatry (3.2–6). 'Choice', Aelred says, 'is the beginning of love, whether it be *caritas* or *cupiditas*.' In practice, then,

> Charity means that in the first place we have chosen something we are permitted to have; that we have gone about attaining it in the right way, and that having attained it we enjoy it in the way that God meant it to be enjoyed. Charity implies a wise choice and an enjoyment that will benefit us. It begins as a choice, it develops as the pursuit of something good, and comes to its term in enjoyment. But if we choose unwisely, and seek what we have chosen in a

wrongful manner, and end by abusing what we have acquired, this is greed, and the root of all evil. But charity is the root of all that is good (3.8).

For Aquinas, 'Charity is driven out, not because sin is strong, but because the human will subjects itself to sin.' Conversely, 'Charity brings to life again those who are spiritually dead' (*De Caritate*, 1.24). It is capable of overcoming cupidity's sorry effects, if chosen in repentance by the errant soul (*Summa Theologica*, 2a–2ae.23.2). In its requirement of responsibility, charity is ennobling (cf. Richard of St Victor, *De Trinitate*, 3.2), it has the character of human friendship with God (Aquinas, *De Potentia*, 9; *De Caritate*, 1.3), and it is the basis of perfection in all the other virtues (*Summa Theologica*, 1a–2ae.114.4; *De Virtutibus Cardinalibus*, 2). Accordingly, Aquinas concludes, 'we must look for the perfection of the Christian life in charity' (*Summa Theologica*, 2a–2ae.184.1–2; *De Perfectione Vitae Spiritualis*, 5). For mystical writers like pseudo-Dionysius, Richard of St Victor, or the author of *The Cloud of Unknowing*, the ultimate perfection of *caritas* is achieved in the mystical union of the soul with God.

Just as *cupiditas* was frequently associated with carnal lust, so *caritas* was often identified by Aquinas and others with *castitas*, chaste affection. Aquinas observes that 'chastity' has both and literal and metaphorical sense:

> By a figure of speech, accordingly, spiritual chastity is engaged when our spirit enjoys God, with whom it should be joined, and refrains from enjoying things God does not mean us to mingle with: *I have espoused you one husband, that I may present you a chaste virgin to Christ*. So also may we speak of spiritual fornication, when our spirit delights in embracing things against God's fair order: *thou hast played the harlot with many lovers*. Chastity in this sense is a characteristic of every virtue, each of which holds us back from contracting illicit unions. Yet charity is at the centre of every virtue, and so also are the other theological virtues, which unite us immediately with God. (*Summa Theologica*, 2a–2ae.151.2)

The persistence of this association means that in medieval and Renaissance literature especially, a cupiditous abuse of chastity can serve as an exemplum prompting to charity. This appears to be the case in Chaucer's *Merchant's Tale*, where the distinctly selfish and uncharitable motivation of old Januarie in acquiring his young bride May in the marketplace is debated in terms of its consequences for 'peace' or 'discord' by Justinus and Placebo.

Chaucer typically stresses a hierarchical aspect to the relation of *cupiditas* and *caritas*. The lower love, either through bitter experience of its imperfections in fact or through the virtues of vicariously apprehended sorrow, can be instrumental in a lover's progress to higher love (cf. Gower's *Confessio Amantis*). In Dante's *Vita Nuova*, for example, the narrator pictures himself as loving Beatrice first in an erotic, carnal way (Sonnets 1–7), then gradually for the character in her which the 'God of love himself' admires (7), and finally (16.1) for the sake of Love himself to whom her virtues, he sees at last, are to be referred. Chaucer's *Knight's Tale* juxtaposes the concord of a chaste married love (Theseus and Hippolyta) with unchaste, discordant passions (Palamon's and Arcite's feelings for Emilye), yet only so as to show how charitable judgment and chaste marriage can in the end restore what Theseus calls 'the fair cheyne of love', that order of Divine Providence by which God established the creation (1.2987–3074; cf. Dunbar's 'Of Luve Erdly and Divine', a similar 'progress' poem).

Connection of charity with the Law of Love is the subject of a treatise by 14th-century spiritual writer Richard Rolle, in which sin, especially mortal sin, is made the 'enemy of love' at each level – self, neighbour, and God (Jeffrey, 155–61). A similar theme runs through Langland's *Piers Plowman*, where the Tree of Charity has roots of Mercy and Pity for its trunk (B.16.3–5). By the same token, *Caritas* in *The Castle of Perseverance* tells Humanum Genus that she informs other virtues and is the enemy of vice, particularly *invidia*:

> To Charite, Man, have an eye,
> In al thinge, Man, I rede.
> Al thy doinge as dros is drye,
> But in charite thou dyth thy dede.
> I distroye alwey Envye... (1602–06)

The communion into which Humanum Genus is invited is the Eucharistic 'Love Feast', in which sacrament, as 15th-century preacher John Mirk puts it, the Christian should understand charity to be 'enfleshed' each time it is offered at the altar (*De Solemnitate Corporis Christi*, ed. Erbe, 168-69). A Wycliffite treatise of the same period, *Of Servants and Lords*, advises its hearers that 'whoever is most in charity will be most readily heard by God, whether he be a shepherd or a common labourer, whether he be in the church or out in the field.' To summarize: medieval texts typically emphasize the crucial nature of choice (intention or *animus* of heart); the ordinate hierarchy of affections (the Law of Love, or Great Commandment); and the foundational relationship of *caritas* and *cupiditas* to all the other vices and virtues respectively.

Renaissance texts of the 16th century innovate materially upon the medieval paradigm. Calvin, for example, discusses charity as pertaining to the Ten Commandments in detail (rather than the summarizing Law of Love). The two tables of the Decalogue, he assumes, are divided into injunctions concerning the 'cultivation of piety' and 'how we are to conduct ourselves towards our fellow men.' Worship is what we owe to God, 'charity... he enjoins us to have towards our fellow men' (*Institutes*, 2.8.11–12). The parable of the Good Samaritan (Luke 10:36) illustrates the principle in its widest sense for Calvin (*Institutes*, 2.8.55), which is to say that charity for him is less to be understood as a matter of intentions of the heart, or their object, than in terms of external social 'works' – a point which characterizes his later argument against Sadoleto that faith rather than charity is the first cause of salvation (since charity is a matter of works, *Institutes*, 3.18.8). Though St Paul actually contrasts benevolence, or 'bestowing one's goods to feed the poor' (1 Corinthians 13:3), with *agape* (King James Version 'charity'), Calvin's emphasis is basic to a shift in English usage after the Reformation, in which 'charity' becomes an outward action in relief of one's neighbour, or even political toleration, while 'love' denotes the inward feeling or prompting of the heart. 'Cupidity' largely retains its established meaning – self-love in its cruder forms – though it ceases to be prominent. 'Hate' begins to emerge as the usual opposite to 'love', while when 'charity' is used in its new social sense, its opposites include 'greed' and 'selfishness'.

Already in the 17th century this semantic shift can be observed in even a moderate Calvinist like George Herbert, in whose poetry 'charitie' appears but three times – twice with but a residue of the medieval sense ('Love-joy'; 'Trinitie Sunday'). In the third instance ('The Church-floore') it is paired with 'love' in such a way as to suggest that he uses one word for the inward, the other for a complementary outward action: 'But the sweet cement, which in one sure band / Ties the whole frame, is *Love* / And *Charitie*' (10–12). Confirmation comes in his prose, where Herbert uses 'charity' thirty times to signify the parson's duty: 'a debt of Charity to the poor' (*A Priest to the Temple,* 11.6); 'any present good deed of charity' (10.6) is proper to the faithful parson, 'exposing the obligation of Charity, and Neighbour-hood' (19.34), 'so is his charity in effect a Sermon' (12.17). The entire second book of Sir Thomas Browne's *Religio Medici* (1642) is devoted to charity in Herbert's sense of the word – sensitivity and response to the need and miseries of others, and, above all, toleration of their various differences of religious and political opinion. Indeed, after this period, 'charity' becomes synonymous with toleration for many writers (e.g., Norris, Locke, Tillotson).

For Puritan writers this was not so, yet the emphasis upon love as a duty was, if anything, stronger. In John Winthrop's famous mid-Atlantic lay sermon aboard the *Arabella* ('A Model of Christian Charity') he tied charity to the 'double law', the 'law of nature and the law of grace, or the moral law and the law of the gospel.' Charity is above all an exemplary witness of Christian obedience to these laws:

> Whatsoever we did or ought to have done when we lived in England, the same must we do, and more also where we go. That which the most in their churches maintain as a truth in profession only, we must bring into familiar and constant practice: as in this duty of love we must love brotherly without dissimulation, we must love one another with a pure heart fervently, we must bear one another's burdens, we must not look only on our own things but also on the things of our brethren.

Charity is here a covenant obligation; the Lord has 'ratified this covenant and sealed our Commission, [and] will expect a strict performance of the articles contained in it' (ed. Miller, 82).

The old usage of *caritas* did, however, continue side by side with the new usage for a time – even selfconsciously so. One element which continued to attract Renaissance poets was the old connection of *caritas* and *castitas*, charity and chastity, though in Protestant poets especially it is likely that this owes as much to the Neoplatonic notion that to move towards God was to renounce the flesh, as to the formulations of Aquinas or Aelred. In Spenser's *Faerie Queene*, for example, Charity (Charissa) is a daughter of Dame Coelia of the House of Holiness. Her characterization as a paragon of chastity may seem at first glance at odds with her description:

> She was a woman in her freshest age,
> Of wondrous beauty, and of bounty rare,
> With goodly grace and comely personage,
> That was on earth not easie to compare;
> Full of great love; but Cupids wanton snare
> As hell she hated; chaste in worke and will;
> Her necke and brests were ever open bare,
> That ay thereof her babes might sucke their fill;
> The rest was all in yellow robes arayed still.

Charity here is allied to 'married Chastity', rather than virginity. Later in the poem Britomart is the representative heroine of the Book of Chastity. Her 'charity' is an active virtue: she subdues the forces of lust, then marries Artegall in an alliance of Justice and Mercy to reproduce Spenser's model for married chastity. Britomart's opposite in this connection is Malecasta ('corrupted chastity'), the wanton and lustful lady of the night who entertains in Castle Joyous, and who corresponds exactly to medieval figurations of *cupiditas* as *luxuria* (e.g., *Roman de la Rose*; cf. *Sir Gawain and the Green Knight*).

Shakespeare reflects these associations in *The Tempest*, where Miranda, who represents the 'wonder' of *caritas*, is strongly identified with chastity. In *King Lear* Cordelia, whose love is 'nothing', or no-thing, and which knows 'no cause', functions also as a representation of charity and married chastity to counter the *cupiditas* and *luxuria* of her sisters. Milton's *Comus* cannot be well understood apart from the tradition which would read the Lady's chastity as a prima facie manifestation of Christian charity. Chastity in this light still figures in the valiant struggle of the *miles Christi* to overcome sin in the world – a figuration particularly transparent in Bunyan's *Pilgrim's Progress*, where Charity is one of the virgins who (with Discretion, Prudence, and Piety) arm Christian with the sword and shield of faith.

Other lineaments of biblical and medieval tradition are apparent throughout Renaissance literature. In Henry More's 'Charity and Humility', the linkage clearly pertains to self-effacing love for God and then others, a love which for More may never be self-generated because of pride's inevitable complicity. Catholic convert Richard Crashaw's '*Caritas Nimia,* Or the Dear Bargain' is a poem about *agape*, God's unparalleled and almost incomprehensible love expressed at Calvary. The poet can scarcely reckon with 'the bargain':

> If my base lust
> Bargain'd with death and well-beseeming dust,
>> Why should the white
>> Lamb's bosom write
>> The purple name
>> Of my sin's shame?

Crashaw's 'On a Treatise of Charity' provides an interesting counter-Reformation reprise of the Reformers' derogation of charity (construed as 'works' or 'merit') in contrast with 'justifying faith'. What can happen in such a scorning, says Crashaw, is that all sense of *caritas* love for God as a 'sacrifice of the heart' in worship gets lost and love grows cold. He yearns for a spiritual renewal in which the hypocrite will no longer be regarded as 'upright... / Because he's stiff, and will confess no knee', but rather the altar and its representative sacrifice will once more, even as in biblical times, be central. Then,

> ... for two turtle-doves, it shall suffice
> To bring a pair of meek and humble eyes;
> This shall from henceforth be the masculine theme
> Pulpits and pens shall sweat in; to redeem
> Virtue to action; that life-feeding flame

That keeps religion warm; not swell a name
Of faith, a mountain-word, made up of air,
With those dear spoils that want to dress the fair
And fruitful charity's full breasts, of old,
Turning her out to tremble in the cold.
What can the poor hope from us? when we be
Uncharitable even to Charity.

Restoration and 18th-century literature tends either to codify the Calvinist and Puritan emphasis, or to define charity against such codifications by appeal to classical and rationalist authors. Matthew Prior's poem 'Charity' is a verse paraphrase of 1 Corinthians 13, a dialogue in Hudibrastic couplets written, he says, with ideal rational readers like Socrates or Montaigne in mind (*Poems*, 252). On his view, Paul's 'charity' is the practice of a temperate balance and mean enjoined by the knowledge that in this world all things are equivocal. Swift's 'Letter to a Young Gentleman', advising him on his desire to enter the ministry, adduces Socrates as authoritative on the greatest of the theological virtues, 'charity' (his own definition proves indeed to be a blending of Socratic and Pauline wisdom). In his *Sermon on the Trinity* charity is a 'duty', as, he says, Socrates teaches (*Sermons*, ed. Landa, 159). In his sermon on 'Brotherly Love' charity is prudential temperance, standing firm in the Anglican middle of the road between two enemies, 'the Papists and Fanaticks' (*Sermons*, 172). Even John Wesley, whose Methodist 'Love Feasts', system-disturbing works of mercy and emotional spirituality, identify him with Swift's 'fanaticks', could stress the priority of love as Christian duty. Advising a correspondent to steer clear of mystics like Boehme, he counsels him to 'keep in the plain, open Bible way. Aim at nothing higher, nothing deeper, than the religion described in our Lord's Sermon upon the Mount, and briefly summed up by St Paul in the 13th chapter to the Corinthians' (*Letters*, 5.342).

For all this apparently unarguable similarity, and the Methodists' intensive involvement in ministries of relief to prisons, mental hospitals, orphanages, and the like, they were keenly disliked by latitudinarian churchmen and their sympathizers both for an apparent Spartan severity and their insistence that faith, not accrued 'charity', was the redemptive agent in human salvation. For example, in his sermon 'The Nature and Necessity of Self-Denial' (1737), the 'Calvinist-Methodist' George Whitefield opposes what a medieval preacher would have called *cupiditas, luxuria,* and *superbia* to 'denying our self-will', denying 'the pleasurable indulgence and self-enjoyment of riches', and denying 'pride of the understanding.' What he calls 'the medicine of self-denial' is based upon imitation of the self-sacrificing love of Christ, the apostles, and martyrs – their *agape* or *caritas.* In his homiletic description of 'The Almost Christian' (1738) he says of such a person that even his apparently charitable actions proceed 'not from any love to God or regard to man, but only out of a principle of self-love – because he knows dishonesty will spoil his reputation and consequently hinder his prosperity in the world.' In a style reminiscent of William Law (a major influence upon Whitefield) he adds that the nominal Christian 'is no enemy to charitable contributions, if not too frequently requested. But then he is quite unacquainted with the kind offices of "visiting the sick and inprison'd, clothing the naked, and relieving the hungry"' (ed. Jeffrey, 302).

Latitudinarian preachers such as Isaac Barrow, Archbishop John Tillotson, Bishop Benjamin Hoadley, and Samuel Clark countered such preaching with their own more relaxed doctrines. On their modified Pelagian view, human nature is essentially, not accidentally, benevolent. Salvation is dependent upon active charity, which is 'natural to mankind' (although, in a world corrupted and confused by bad custom and miseducation, an inducement of future rewards and punishments seems to be required). Comprehensive and energetic charity is a specific manifestation of 'good nature'; such charity is not mere almsgiving but rather 'universal love of all mankind, embracing friend and enemy, and limited only by the opportunity, position, or political power of the individual' (i.e., the latitudinarians set off their view also from the proto-positivistic 'politic charity' of Hobbes and Mandeville). Like Whitefield they censured self-love (especially avarice, ambition, vanity, and hypocrisy), but unlike him they stressed the priority of the epistle of James ('Faith, if it hath not works, is dead', James 2:17) over Paul's epistle to the Ephesians ('For by grace are ye saved through faith; and that not of yourselves: it is the gift of

God: Not of works, lest any man should boast', Ephesians 2:8–9).
The 'hero of faith' is here a 'hero of works', so to speak. The truly
heroic individual is not the powerful, wealthy, or prestigious person
but the 'good man', whose moral superiority is typically described in
terms of benevolence (e.g., R. Steele's *The Christian Hero,* 2701,
Spectator, no. 248; Henry Fielding's 'Of True Greatness'). Isaac
Barrow's sermon 'On Being Imitators of Christ' provides a pattern in
terms of which one may understand Fielding's preface and opening
chapters in *Joseph Andrews* (1742). The historian's task, says Barrow, is
to provide examples of the 'good man' which emphasize his *chastity*
with respect to himself (control of reason over the passions), the
biblical model for which is Joseph resisting the advances of Potiphar's
wife, and his *charity* with respect to society, the biblical model for
which is Abraham, the epitome of faith revealed in works and hence
of active charity. But the good historians will depict, says Barrow,
human imperfections as well as virtues because a flawless model of
righteousness would induce only despair. In *Joseph Andrews* (1.11–13)
treatment of the theme of charity is characterized by Parson Abraham
Adams, whose recasting of the parable of the Good Samaritan stresses
good works rather than faith. Fielding's *Tom Jones* (1749), a 'man of
good feeling', is less plausibly a representative of chastity. Rather, 'no
better than he should be', in Fielding's phrase, he progresses from
wanton amours towards wisdom ('Sophie' Western), union with
whom entails a presumably chaste marriage and a return to Paradise
Hall. But for Fielding, as for the latitudinarian divines, a little cupidity
is infinitely to be preferred to the slightest whiff of 'hypocrisy' or
'affectation', which Fielding (in *Shamela* and *Tom Jones*) calls the
source of the 'truly ridiculous', the laughable but pitiable morality of
self-love.

William Cowper's long poem *Charity* (1782) is on the side of
Whitefield (whom he admired). Like Hannah More's 'Ode to Charity'
of the same period, it associates charity less with outward actions of
benevolence – though these are discussed in detail – than in terms of
an inward peace of relationship with God which overflows into loving
actions toward humanity. But if More's pragmatic view of charity is
barely tacit in her poem (she was in fact energetic in founding and
funding charity schools for children), in the palpably Calvinist

Cowper (a virtual recluse) it gets top billing. Like More, Cowper invokes Charity as a muse by whose guidance he will write her praise, lest a writer's vanities should obscure the subject, 'whether we name thee Charity or Love'. Cowper takes up the theme of the *socius* first: 'God, working ever on a social plan, / By various ties attaches man to man' (15–16). His 'hero' of charity is the explorer Cook, who

> ... lamented, and with tears as just
> As ever mingled with heroic dust –
> Steer'd Britain's oak into a world unknown,
> And in his country's glory sought his own,
> Wherever he found man, to nature true,
> The rights of man were sacred in his view.
> He sooth'd with gifts, and greeted with a smile,
> The simple native of the new-found isle...

Cook's antithesis, for Cowper an icon for *cupiditas,* is Cortez, 'odious for a world enslav'd'. 'Mammon makes the world his legatee', he continues: the ugly slave trade is 'most degrading of all ills, that wait / On man' (155–56) and 'an epitome of all that defiles charity and a Christian name' (179–217). For Calvinist Cowper this is the effect of innate depravity, which revelation (if not reason) shows to be the true opponent of charity (337–44); Socrates therefore must be corrected by Scripture:

> Philosophy, without his heave'nly guide,
> May blow up self-conceit, and nourish pride;
> But, while his province is the reas'ning part,
> Has still a veil of midnight on his heart;
> 'Tis truth divine, exhibited on earth,
> Gives Charity her being and her birth. (373–78)

Here he means *agape,* charity in the older sense, which is then celebrated in an extended paraphrase of 1 Corinthians 13 (412–34). True charity must thus be distinguished from alms (447–68); indeed, the motivation for 'subscription' from wealthy donors is suspect (469–84), and even what sum is collected 'the office clips as it goes'. For what is commonly called 'charity' to be meritorious, and not merely affectation, vanity, and hypocrisy, it must be an overflowing of *caritas:*

No works shall find acceptance, in that day
When all disguises shall be rent away,
That square not truly with the scripture plan,
Nor spring from love to God, or love to man...
True charity, a plant divinely nurs'd,
Fed by the love from which it rose at first,
Thrives against hope; and, in the rudest scene,
Storms but enliven its unfading green;
Exub'rant is the shadow it supplies;
Its fruit on earth, its growth above the skies.
(557–60; 573–78)

What Cowper wishes to do, in effect, is to affirm Whitefield's 'charity' against that of the Latitudinarians, rooting the meaning of charity in the primary relationship between the individual and God rather than between the individual and his neighbour. In this he was consistent with the raison d'être of 'charitable' social reforms among the 18th-century Methodists and even with the usage of closet-Catholic Christopher Smart, in whose (most charitable) poetry charity is an axiom of gratitude, the root of all virtues (cf. Aquinas):

Thus in high heaven charity is great,
    Faith, hope, devotion hold a lower place;
On her the cherubs and the seraphs wait,
    Her, every virtue courts, and every grace;
See! on the right, close by th' Almighty's throne,
In him she shines confest, who came to make her known.

Deep-rooted in my heart then let her grow,
    That for the past the future may atone;
That I may act what thou hast giv'n to know,
    That I may live for THEE and THEE alone,
And justify those sweetest words from heav'n,
'THAT HE SHALL LOVE THEE MOST TO WHOM
THOU'ST MOST FORGIVEN.'

Smart said elsewhere, in more medieval fashion than perhaps he knew: 'For I have translated in the charity, which makes things / better & I shall be translated myself at the last' (Jubilate Agno). But desire to achieve the goals of charity as benevolence without the encumbrance of religious characterizations of social responsibility were growing stronger. Jeremy Bentham, with his plan to reform the British Poor Law (1795) and plans to create a modern welfare state, finds 'charity' *ab initio* a distasteful and even demeaning term. For Bentham, the function of a 'national charity company' is not to dispense kindness or generosity, but to accord basic human rights.

For the most part, Romantic poetry lacks interest in charity defined as benevolence or alms. On the other hand, love is a primary subject, both in its divine and human modes of expression. Wordsworth's very conception of the poet, in his preface to *Lyrical Ballads* (1802), is 'the rock of defence of human nature; an upholder and preserver, carrying everywhere with him relationship and love' (ed. Zall, 52). But the 'love' of Romantic poetry is hard to identify with the *agape* or *caritas* of Christian tradition; even when it draws upon mystical Christian writers like Jacob Boehme, Romantic 'love' is rather the integrative force binding the disparities of individual and community experience together in a comprehension, however vaguely formulated, of the divine purpose in Creation. To this ideal of love, narrow *Selbheit* (Boehme) or *Ichheit* (Schelling) is still, like self-centredness, the technical opposite to unitive love. But the means by which the Romantic poet transcends his ego is not worship; it is what Shelley calls 'the expression of the imagination'. In his *Defence of Poetry* (1821),

> The great secret of morals is love, or a going out of our own nature and an identification of ourselves with the beautiful which exists in thought, action, or person, not our own. A man, to be greatly good, must imagine intensely and comprehensively; he must put himself in the place of another and of many others; the pains and pleasures of his species must become his own. The great instrument of moral good is the imagination... Poetry enlarges the circumference of the imagination. (Ed. Clark, 277, 282–83)

In other words, the 'good' and hence heroic person manifests love not in active works of benevolence or alms, but rather – in a curious but perhaps predictable sentimentalizing of the Latitudinarians and Methodists both – by vicarious imagination of the plight of the less fortunate. But in the usage of Romantic poets, Shelley and Byron in particular, 'love' covers 'a multitude of sins', often by becoming a name for many of them. If Coleridge takes *philia*, friendship, to be the paradigm for 'love', Shelley is more visceral. As he puts it,

> That profound and complicated sentiment which we call love… is rather the universal thirst for a communion not merely of the senses but of our whole nature, intellectual, imaginative, and sensitive… This want grows more powerful in proportion to the development which our nature receives from civilization, for man never ceases to be a social being. The sexual impulse, which is only one and often a small part of these claims, serves from its obvious and external nature as a kind of type or expression of the rest, as common basis, an acknowledged and visible link. ('On the Manners of the Ancient Greeks')

Thus, according to M.H. Abrams,

> In the broad Romantic application of the term love… all modes of human attraction are conceived as one in kind, different only in object and degree, in a range which includes the relations of lover to beloved, children to parents, brother to sister, friend to friend, and individual to humanity. The orbit of love was often enlarged to include the relationship of man to nature as well. (*Natural Supernaturalism*, 297)

Here one returns to Greek *eros*. Augustine's basic distinction *caritas / cupiditas* is accordingly by this point not only blurred but in some instances reversed. Further, the laissez-faire morality of Shelley or Byron comes to have its counterpart in broader social terms, leading writers such as Carlyle (in *Past and Present*) to lament 'our present system of individual Mammonism' in which 'cash payment is… the sole nexus of man with man.' None of this has to do with love, Carlyle insists, only with the lust of meaner desires (*Works*, 10.257, 272–74). Each of these developments complicates thought about 'charity' for

Victorian Christians, without doing much to clarify cupidity or another contrastive vice. Charity thus becomes what Matthew Arnold would call a 'problem'; preoccupation with the virtues of vicarious identification often produces ethically evasive exegesis. An example is provided by Ruskin, who writes:

> You know how often it is difficult to be wisely charitable, to do good without multiplying the sources of evil. You know that to give alms is nothing unless you give thought also; and that therefore it is written, not 'blessed is he that *feedeth* the poor', but 'blessed is he that *considereth* the poor.' And you know that a little thought and a little kindness are often worth more than a great deal of money. Now this charity of thought is not to be exercised towards all men. There is assuredly no action of our social life, however unimportant, which, by kindly thought, may not be made to have a beneficial influence upon others; and it is impossible to spend the smallest sum of money, for any not absolutely necessary purpose, without a grave responsibility attaching to the manner of spending it.

Ruskin goes on to talk about consumer 'ethics', about whether 'the sum we are going to spend will do as much good spent in this way as it would if spent in any other way' (*Lectures on Architecture and Painting*, 44). But Ruskin is also able to indicate succinctly the self-serving rationalizations (quite well) anticipated by Bentham:

> We have heard only too much lately of 'indiscriminate charity', with implied reproval, not of the Indiscrimination merely, but of the Charity also. We have partly succeeded in enforcing on the minds of the poor the idea that it is disgraceful to receive; and are likely, without too much difficulty, to succeed in persuading not a few of the rich that it is disgraceful to give. (*Munera Pulveris*, Appendix 6)

Charles Dickens, in his *A Christmas Carol* (1843), set out to contrast cupidity and charity in terms practical enough that the dangerous ephemerality of this debate should become clear, but had only limited success. In such an environment, 'charity' soon gave *caritas* a bad name. George Bernard Shaw, a Fabian Socialist, was among those who later rejected the concept as misnomer, exploring as alternative values the grand idealism of a Christian socialist clergyman in *Candida* (1898), and a naive but well-motivated Salvation Army charity in *Major Barbara* (1907) – a play which not only satirizes the disguising of self-interest as 'duty', but teaches that 'poverty is the worst of crimes' and that the *lack* of money is the root of all evil. Shaw's impatience with traditional Christian notions of charity surfaces again in *The Intelligent Woman's Guide to Capitalism and Socialism* (1928). (G.K. Chesterton's book-length study of his friend continues a debate over the subject which had been at the core of their testy friendship for many years.)

The Romantics' strong desire to find in idealized love (*amor/eros*) the unifying and integrating of all experience had been notoriously sidetracked into erotic confusions of that purpose. Yet their idealism persists in a significant strain of religious as well as secular poetry. The erotic mysticism of Christina Rossetti, with its theme of the spectre bride or bridegroom (*The Hour and the Ghost; The Ghost's Petition*), and her sublimation of sexual desire as the pilgrim's longing for 'a better country' (cf. Hebrews 11:13–16) in *Marvel of Marvels* and *Passing away, saith the World* lend to the traditional medieval language of *caritas* eerily erotic overtones precisely inverse in their function to the de-eroticizing allegories of the Song of Solomon by St Bernard of Clairvaux. Patmore's postconversion poetry (he became a Catholic in 1864) similarly blurs *agape* and *eros* (e.g., *The Unknown Eros*, 1877), to the point where his spiritual advisers asked him to destroy a long manuscript, his *Sponsa Dei*, in which the confusion had apparently become identification.

The orthodox English poet of the modern period has thus had two misprisions to answer. These are the Enlightenment tendency to split charity as benevolence to the neighbour off from its roots in *caritas* as love directed toward God above all things, and the Romantic and post-Romantic tendency to dissolve the distinction in a cosmic love so ambiguous that *eros* or *cupiditas* can be its most apparent vital expression (cf. D.H. Lawrence's *Apocalypse*). In strikingly diverse poets the strategy has been similar: to try to re-establish the vertical or hierarchical relation of the precepts of the Great Commandment so that, in typical Augustinian fashion, *caritas* in the community of men and women is comprehensible only in terms of its referential governance by each person's prior love for God. Thus John Keble's 'Charity the Life of Faith' (*The Christian Year*, 1827) takes as its epigraph 1 John 3:13–14: 'We know that we have passed from death unto life, because we love the brethren.' The test of regeneration, the presence of supreme love for God and not self, is love for those who love him also. To do this is, in effect, to love Christ both in his divine and human nature:

> Wouldst thou the life of souls discern?
> Nor human wisdom nor divine
> Helps thee by aught beside to learn:
> Love is life's only sign.
> The spring of the regenerate heart,
> The pulse, the glow of every part,
> Is the true love of Christ our Lord,
> As man embrac'd, as God ador'd.

But this is what T.S. Eliot also says in *Little Gidding*. The 'liberation' from cupiditous 'attachment to self and to things and to persons', he writes, lies in a type of love which is 'not less of love but expanding / Of love beyond desire, and so liberation / From the future as well as the past.' When this love is shared abroad, then, all people, even Englishmen like those who fought bloody (religious) civil wars, will be 'folded in a single party', and 'All manner of thing shall be well / By the purification of the motive / In the ground of our beseeching' ('Little Gidding', 3). In other words, desire itself shall be redeemed.

David L. Jeffrey
University of Ottawa

Conscience

The noun *conscience* appears thirty times in the King James Version of the New Testament (in the Revised Standard Version it occurs twenty-eight times in the New Testament, and once to translate the much broader Hebrews *leb* [King James Version 'heart'] in 1 Samuel 25:31).

In all cases but one (John 8:9) the King James Version is translating Greek *syneidesis* (e.g., Romans 2:15; 9:1; 13:5; 2 Corinthians 1:12; 4:2; 1 Timothy 4:2; Hebrews 10:2; 1 Peter 3:16, 21).

Most New Testament terms acquire their content from Old Testament precedent (equivalent or near equivalent), but not so this word; not only the term but the concept appears to owe to a particularly Greek ethos. Moreover, the noun is to some degree an intellectual or 'literate' term; including two instances (Acts 23:1; 24:16) where St Paul's dialogue is being reported, twenty-one of its biblical occurrences are attributable to Pauline theological discourse. The related verb, *synoida*, is found earlier (from the 6th century BC) and is colloquial, meaning 'to know in common with', or perhaps 'to be conscious of' or 'aware'; the reflexive form *synoida emauto*, 'I know with myself', begins to approximate, in classical writings, the sense of the later New Testament noun derived from it – *syneidesis* – a neologism first appearing in Greek only in the century before Christ.

Philologists regard such a development as instanced here with utmost interest. Following the shift from a verb (*synoida [emauto]*) to a noun, *syneidesis* signifies not merely another action performed by the self; it is now an agent within the self, literally 'the self that knows with itself'. The development of the noun form of the word thus signals 'the recognition of an alter ego, another self within the self that observes the self and then testifies as to what it sees'.

The new noun *syneidesis* does not occur in any of the four gospels (King James Version 'conscience' in John 8:9 translates the reflexive verb), where Hebraic orientation is strong. In the writings of Paul, however, educated in Greek literature and culture, the noun occurs repeatedly. Since 'conscience' is nowhere defined by Paul, we must assume that he expected his readers to be able to gather the sense he intends, partly by contrasting hellenic and Judaic thinking. Writing to the Romans, he indicates certain differences between the perspective of Jews, who possess the external constraint of the law, and Gentiles, who do not: 'For when the Gentiles, who have not the law, do by nature the things contained in the law, these, having not the law, are a law unto themselves: Which shew the work of the law written in their hearts, their conscience also bearing witness, and their thoughts the mean while accusing or else excusing one another'

(Romans 2:14–15). Paul then uses this distinction to sharpen another, that between the Jew who 'rests in the law' (v. 17) and his circumcision (v. 25) merely in the sense of outward observance, and one who has internalized the law, having written it in the heart, where it can best bear its witness (cf. Acts 23:1; Romans 9:1; 2 Corinthians 1:12). This person will be a better Jew, the one of 'conscience', so to speak: 'he is a Jew, which is one inwardly; and circumcision is that of the heart, in the spirit, and not in the letter; whose praise is not of men, but of God' (Romans 2:29). 'Circumcision of the heart' (cf. Leviticus 26:41; Deuteronomy 10:16; 30:6; Jeremiah 6:10) here is tropic, congruent with Old Testament language; it adds specific biblical content to a novel Greek tropic noun, derivative rather of hellenic philosophical language.

The Latin translation of New Testament *syneidesis* is *conscientia*, a compound of *con*, 'together', and *scire*, 'to know' (paralleling the original Greek compound). If in classical Latin *conscientia* typically means something like 'consciousness' or 'knowledge', not typically of an ethically charged nature, in Christianized usage already in the 4th century and widely by the 13th century it has acquired the fuller, spiritualized sense found in the New Testament. St Thomas Aquinas (*De Veritate*, 17.5) illuminates a general medieval application of Paul when he says:

> Spiritual and inward ties are stronger than bodily and outward ones. Our duty to a human superior is material and external, for legal authority works by managing temporalities. All that will be changed at the last trump, when Christ shall have put down all rule and all authority and power. Therefore conscience is more to be obeyed than authority imposed from outside. For conscience obliges in virtue of divine command, whether written down in a code or instilled by Natural Law. To weigh conscience in the scales against obedience to legal authority is to compare the weight of divine and of human decrees. The first obliges more than the second, and sometimes against the second.

The notion of self-consciousness as we know it is a further development. It arises later, after the Renaissance and Reformation, when writers like Descartes and Montaigne could begin to distinguish between a 'true' self, the inner and self-conscious identity (e.g. Descartes' *cogito ergo sum*) and an artificial or outer self (Montaigne's 'artifice'). When Locke (in 1632) adopts the new word *consciousness*, he distinguishes it from *conscience*, defining it as 'perception of what passes in a man's own mind'; as in classical Latin *conscientia* perception is separated from evaluation.

One difficulty which presents itself to study of the concept of conscience in English literature, even where it is an apparent function of biblical tradition, is that *conscience* and *consciousness* (Latin *conscius*, 'knowing something with others', 'being privy to') could be used almost interchangeably up to the 19th century The possible doubleness of some usages becomes apparent in *Sir Gawain and the Green Knight*, for example, where the hero is said to search his 'conscience' to try to understand the meaning of his hostess' entry into his bedroom (1197).

In Langland's personification of Conscience (*Piers Plowman* B.19), as in the debates of Good and Bad Angels contesting for the soul of Everyman, Mary Magdalene, or Doctor Faustus, or in Bunyan's characterization of Mr Conscience in *The Holy War*, conscience acts as an external witness; the internal sense, as when Paul uses 'conscience' (1 Corinthians 4:4) to say that he knows nothing against himself, is by the Renaissance capable of ironic and more complex assignation. Milton has Eve withdraw at first from Adam's courting, so impelled by 'her virtue and the conscience of her worth' (*Paradise Lost*, 8.102).

Conscience in these examples clearly bears witness to personal history – one's own past actions – as measured against divine standards. Some passages in the New Testament have contributed greatly to this sense. In 1 Corinthians 8:7–12 and 10:25–29 Paul speaks of the duty of Christians to respect the conscience of a 'weak brother' whose faith might be destroyed by careless actions of those with less tender conscience. As C.S. Lewis suggests, *syneidesis* here means not simply shared knowledge but 'judgment as to what is right or wrong'. In Romans 13:5 Paul joins this meaning of conscience with the Jewish notion of the wrath of God, the internal pain of conscience gnawing at a person for his sins becoming parallel to the punishment of the wicked which God administers in the world. But what is at stake is the potential of the conscience to be educated – sensitized or desensitized – not merely by knowledge of the law but also by the accretion of experience. 1 Timothy 4:2 and Titus 1:15 teach that the scar of sin weakens the conscience and upsets the mind or the power of choice in matters of future conduct. A 'defiled conscience', or what St Thomas Aquinas (in *De Veritate*, 17.5) calls an 'erring conscience', is a result of bad moral education, so to speak. In Shakespeare's *Henry 8* the possibility that a conscience may become corrupted through persistent error is suggested in Lord Chamberlain's remark concerning Henry's despondency and aggravation: 'It seems the marriage with his brother's wife has crept too near his conscience.' Suffolk then replies, 'No, his conscience has crept too near another lady' (2.2.17–18). Excusing morally or politically dubious actions on the grounds of 'reasons of conscience' (especially by public officials) came to be regarded as a scandalous abuse of the New Testament term. Bishop Jeremy Taylor takes up Aquinas in his *Ductor Dubitantium* (1660) when he writes:

> Nothing is more usual, than to pretend *Conscience* to all the actions of men which are publick, and whose nature cannot be concealed. If arms be taken up in a violent warre; inquire of both sides, why they ingage on that part respectively? they answer, because of their Conscience. Ask a Schismatick why he refuses to joyn in the Communion of the Church? he tels you, it is against his Conscience: and the disobedient refuse to submit to Laws; and they also in many cases pretend Conscience. Nay, some men suspect their brother of a crime, and are perswaded (as they say) in Conscience that he did it: and their Conscience tels them that *Titius* did steal their goods, or that *Caia* is an adulteress. And so Suspicion; and Jealousie, and Disobedience, and Rebellion are become *Conscience*; in which there is neither knowledge, nor revelation, nor truth, nor charity, nor reason, nor religion. (1.26)

Taylor's admonition is directed against abuse of 'good conscience' (Hebrews 9:9; 10:2, 22; 13:18), which inculcates abstinence from reproach or reproachability; the result of such corruption is 'bad conscience' (cf. Milton, *Areopagitica*).

In the general Christian frame of reference 'the conscience' becomes in popular discourse a kind of storehouse of moral principles or knowledge of good and evil. This omnibus sense of the term with its Pauline overtones reverberates throughout literature. Chaucer's use of the word to describe the tears the Prioress sheds because of her 'conscience and tendre herte' at the sight of a mouse in a trap (*General Prologue*, 150) appears to be ironically loaded, but the irony is dependent upon a normative expectation that *conscience* means the ability to judge between right and wrong in one's actions (rather than mere 'sensibility' or tenderness). Thus Shakespeare talks of deeds 'done in the testimony of a good conscience' (*Love's Labour's Lost*, 4.2.2). In Middle English *conscience* took the place of the earlier term *inwit*. We also have Spenser's 'grieved conscience' (*Faerie Queene*, 1.10.23), and Shelley's 'accuser conscience' (*Cenci*, 2.2.120) and 'hounds of Conscience' (5.1.9). George Herbert calls conscience in his poem of that title an insidious 'pratler', a carping adversary he can only silence by purging himself in the Eucharist.

In the Septuagint Wisdom 17:11 reads: 'Wickedness condemned by an internal witness is a cowardly thing and expects the worst, being hardpressed by conscience [*syneidesis*]' (cf. Wisdom 2:15). Subtle and ironic variations on this theme are common in English literature. Thus, the murderer in Shakespeare's *Richard 3* says that this knowledge or conscience 'makes a man a coward' (1.4.132), and Richard himself apostrophizes 'Coward Conscience' (5.3.180). Lord Henry in Wilde's *The Picture of Dorian Gray* argues that: 'Conscience and cowardice are really the same things. Conscience is the trade-name of the firm' (chapter 1).

A 'bad conscience' is in the Christian context usually associated with fear of God's ultimate judgment. The writer in tune with biblical language sees conscience bearing witness against him on Judgment Day in terms of external standards to which all persons are held accountable by God. Robert Herrick, a 17th-century Cavalier poet whose amatory verse suggests that he may have had as much reason to feel the 'prick of conscience' as anyone, makes the relation explicit ('To his Conscience'):

> Can I not sin, but thou wilt be
> My private *Protonotarie?*

> Can I not wooe thee to passe by
> A short and sweet iniquity?
> I'le cast a mist and cloud, upon
> My delicate transgression,
> So utter dark, as that no eye
> Shall see the hug'd impietie:
> *Gifts blind the wise,* and bribes do please,
> And winde all other witnesses:
> And wilt not thou, with gold, be ti'd
> To lay thy pen and ink aside?
> That in the mirk and tonguelesse night,
> Wanton I may, and thou not write?
> It will not be: And, therefore, now,
> For times to come, I'le make this Vow,
> From aberrations to live free;
> So I'le not feare the Judge, or thee.

The 'norm' from which he has been aberrant, he owns, is not subjective or relativistic, despite his natural inclination to wish it so. This is the apprehension Coleridge describes in 'Lines suggested by the last words of Berengarius':

> No more 'twixt conscience staggering and the Pope
> Soon shall I now before my God appear,
> By him to be acquitted, as I hope;
> By him to be condemned, as I fear. (1–4)

Belief that the normative standard in terms of which conscience speaks is indeed objective, eternal, and expressed in the law as rooted in the holiness of God is basic to dramatic conflict in Marlowe's *The Tragicall Historie of Doctor Faustus*. It helps to explain why Faustus, stung by his conscience and fretting over the fact that he has denied God, succumbs to despair. (Marlowe's play has been linked to another, *The Conflict of Conscience,* by his contemporary Nathaniel Wood.) Goethe's Faust has less difficulty with conscience, partly because, like the Übermensch of Nietzsche's *Also Sprach Zarathustra* or the manly hero of his *Genealogy of Morals* (part 2), he is true to the instinct to mastery, especially self-mastery, an 'autonomous and supra-moral man' who may with impunity shun the 'bad conscience' which arises from 'the will to mistreat oneself' (*Antichrist*, 55).

Some of the Church Fathers understood conscience to be a divine faculty in humans (e.g., St Augustine, *De utilitate credendi*, 34). Similarly, Oscar Wilde's Dorian Gray claims that conscience is the image of God in mankind: 'It is the divinest thing in us' (chapter 8). Antonio in *The Tempest* scoffs at the idea – 'I feel not this deity in my bosom' (2.1.278) – but Milton's God says, 'I will place within them as a guide My umpire conscience' (*Paradise Lost*, 2.194–95). Marvell describes conscience as 'that Heaven-nursed plant', the reward of whose tilling in the earthly garden is sanctity in heaven ('Upon Appleton House', 353–60). Yet Milton's famous cry in his *Areopagitica* could be readily adapted to libertarian as well as evangelical purposes: 'Give me the liberty to know, to utter, and to argue freely according to conscience, above all liberties.' Browning later defines conscience as 'the great beacon-light God sets in all' (*Stafford*, 4.2.178).

The claim that conscience was itself a divine lawgiver led to the troublesome conclusion that different persons acknowledge different inner laws. Consequently, we have the notion of 'Liberty of Consciences' which appears in Butler's *Hudibras* (1.1.765) or Robinson Crusoe's self-congratulatory boast just before departing from the island that he had 'allowed liberty of conscience throughout my dominions' to a Protestant, a Catholic, and a pagan. Shakespeare's *Henry 8* focuses on the battle between the primacy of 'private conscience' (5.2.178–80) and the authority of the Church, and Launcelot Gobbo's humorous dialogue with his conscience in *The Merchant of Venice* (2.1.1–32) echoes the explicit discussion of Aquinas on this question (*De Veritate*, 17.5; cf. *2 Sententiae*, 44.2.2). Robert Bolt's *A Man for All Seasons* presents the other side of the coin, yet Sir Thomas More is made to argue from the same premise: 'I believe when statesmen forsake their own private conscience for the sake of their public duties... they lead their countries by a short route to chaos' (Act 1). These plays seem to pit a Catholic or 'foundational' point of view, which tends to find the ultimate guide to personal conscience in an external authority and tradition, against a post-Reformation disposition to find guidance by letting conscience itself interpret and apply the gospel. The *Sermons* and *Analogy of Religion*

(1736) of the Anglican Bishop Butler, for example, anticipate a more general post-Enlightenment or Latitudinarian view (cf. Tillotson's sermons): individual conscience is made the pivot of ethics – perhaps not precisely what the apostle Paul had in mind. A generation earlier Dryden's *The Hind and the Panther* had joined the debate against such views by investigating the consequence of letting 'private conscience' be the guide against 'her claim to church auctority' (1.478–80). A harbinger of 19th- and 20th-century developments is Wordsworth's *Excursion,* where the author insists that the aesthetic awareness of nature leads inevitably to the ethical imperatives of conscience and that victory in life is 'entire submission to the law / Of conscience – conscience reverenced and obeyed' (4.224–25).

The older idea of conscience as witness to God's law came under direct attack in the Victorian period. Matthew Arnold, in a celebrated chapter in *Culture and Anarchy,* decried as repressive the 'Hebraic impulse' which had inculcated 'strictness of conscience' or a sense of sin in mankind throughout history, advocating in its place a new Hellenism which would sponsor a 'spontaneity of consciousness' free yet not anarchic. What Arnold really argues for, in effect, is the relativity of conscience, its independence from biblical law or revelation. (Arnold's aversion to a 'guilty' conscience may seem to parallel that of Freud, though for Freud the negative element in self-consciousness is associated also with Pauline and hence 'hellenistic' internalization.) It is here that the seeds of the radical separation of conscience as a term for ethics and 'consciousness' as one for psychology were first planted. James Joyce widened this split even further. In *A Portrait of the Artist as a Young Man* Stephen Dedalus leaves behind both the priesthood and Ireland 'to forge in the smithy of his soul the uncreated conscience of his race.' Stephen dismisses the traditional 'ache of conscience' he feels as a result of his sins earlier in the book in order to become both internal and external lawgiver, the standard himself by which to judge the acts of his countrymen. Ultimately, he substitutes a personal aesthetic conscience for an ethical one. Wilde's *The Picture of Dorian Gray,* on the other hand, where the portrait of the hero acts as 'a visible emblem of conscience', apprehends a profound psychic disturbance in the unresolved modern split between psychology / aesthetics and theology / ethics. *A Case of Conscience*, by James Blish (1958), is a space-age fantasy whose protagonist, a Jesuit priest and scientist Father Ruiz-Sanchez, attempts to resolve a crisis among a race of reptilian aliens so totally reliant upon reason that they have become incapable of faith or belief, and hence socially paralyzed.

Dominic Manganiello
University of Ottawa

Conversion

Despite the nominal Christianization of Europe by the 12th century, conversion has remained an important feature of religious experience in the West, and figures importantly as a centre of interest in English poetry, fiction, and drama.

The term appears in the Old Testament (*shub; also panah; hapak; sabab*), in later prophetic writings to refer to the return from captivity (Isaiah 1:27; Jeremiah 29:14; Ezekiel 16:53), and in other places figuratively meaning to turn back to God (1 Samuel 7:3; 1 Kings 8:33; Isaiah 19:22; Hosea 6:1; 7:10). Gentile conversion to Judaism, a relatively rare phenomenon in the Old Testament, involved circumcision; this is how Josephus reads the 'turning' in Esther 8:17 (*Antiquities*, 11.6.13); in later times such converts were not considered 'perfect' Jews because their conversion was 'not above suspicion' (Yebamot 24b).

The term as it appears in the Septuagint and New Testament is typically *strepho, epistrepho,* or a cognate, used figuratively to signify a turning from wrongdoing to right (Matthew 13:15; Mark 4:12; Luke 22:32; Acts 9:35; 11:21; 14:15; 15:19; 26:18; 2 Corinthians 3:16; 1 Thessalonians 1:9; James 5:19ff.). The word *hypostrepho*, meaning to turn away from right to wrong, is used in 2 Peter 2:21.

In the Bible, conversion has both a divine and human aspect. In the Old Testament, it is God who 'turns back' Israel, or 'turns his people to himself', and while this is less explicit in the New Testament, the action of the Holy Spirit seems always to be implied in conversion. The human side of conversion involves repentance and faith. When the 'call' to repentance is heard in a New Testament context, the individual first turns from idolatry, Satan, or worship of the 'dead letter' in an authentic repentance which involves renunciation of past sins. But 'the call is not simply a command to fulfil particular moral obligations to "amend one's life"' (K. Rahner, *Concise 'Sacramentum Mundi'*, 292); the individual completes his or her 'revolution' by turning to God in true faith and heartfelt commitment. In most New Testament instances this is the process whereby unbelievers become followers of Christ (e.g., Acts 3:19; 1 Thessalonians 1:9), but a renewal of believers can also be signified (Luke 22:32). Such acts of conversion may be sudden, as in the cases of Paul (Acts 9) and the Philippian jailer (Acts 16), or gradual, with a period of preparation, as in the cases of the Ethiopian eunuch (Acts 8) and the centurion Cornelius (Acts 10).

By the 3rd century baptism of new converts from paganism, often involving exorcism, took place on the eve of Easter or Pentecost. In a dramatic ceremony, candidates renounced evil, professed faith in Christ, and promised obedience to him, then were given new garments and sometimes gifts of milk and honey, symbolizing their beginning of the 'new life' (*International Standard Bible Encyclopedia*, 1.769).

St Augustine writes in the *Confessiones* of the effect upon himself and others of the dramatic conversion of Victorinus, the great Roman orator, who, like St Ambrose, was led to the church to make his profession by St Simplicianus (8.2.3–5). He then recounts his own struggles with carnal appetite, spiritual pride, and professional vanity (8.8–11), before yielding at last to the tears of contrition. In reflection on an account of the conversion of St Anthony (whose 'call' was the text in Matthew 19:21), and having heard the prompting of the Spirit in the form of children's singing over the wall *tolle lege*, 'pick it up and read it', he grasped his copy of St Paul's epistle and his eyes fell on Romans 13:13–14: 'Not in rioting and drunkenness, not in chambering and wantonness, not in strife and envying. But put ye on the Lord Jesus Christ, and make not provision for the flesh, to fulfil the lusts thereof' (8.12.29). The apropos of Augustine's 'call' to conversion is abundantly evident from the account (*confessio*) of his life to this point; the denouement is a swift release into tranquillity: 'for instantly, as the sentence ended – by a light, as it were, of security infused into my heart – all the gloom of doubt vanished away.'

Augustine's account of his own conversion proved seminal for subsequent Christian literature and has influenced, in a variety of ways, the conversion accounts of Luther, St Ignatius Loyola, Pascal, Kierkegaard, and others.

Although the rapid nominal Christianization of Europe made adult conversion gradually less frequent, so that the term came at last to be applied to the taking of holy orders by St Gregory the Great and others, referring especially to monastic profession (e.g., *Epistle* 48; 50), it was used also of notable incidents which combine the two senses – as in the conversions of St Francis and St Dominic. That of St Francis in particular, with his dramatic casting away of his father's clothes to step naked into the protective enfolding of the bishop's surplice in front of the whole village, recalls in extravagant form early Christian baptismal liturgy described by Augustine and St John Chrysostom (Thomas of Celano, *Vita*, 1.3; 1.6.14–15).

The best known of early English conversion stories is that of King Edwin of Northumbria, recorded by the Venerable Bede. In it two pagan counsellors give their opinion in favour of such a conversion, the one on materialist grounds, for greater benefits, the other out of a yearning for greater certainty about what lies beyond mortal life, which he likens to the flight of a sparrow out of the stormy winter night for a fleeting moment through the warm, lighted hall, then again into the darkness (*Hist. Ecclesiastes* 2.13). The *Emendatio Vitae* of Richard Rolle (circa 1340) begins with a chapter '*De Conversio*', which he describes as a 'turning away from the world and sin, the devil and flesh' and a 'turning to God... from changeable to unchangeable good'; Rolle is here reflecting Gregory's sense of 'conversion' to the contemplative life, although the text admits of a more general application. In Chaucer's *Canterbury Tales*, *The Second Nun's Tale* of St Cecelia, coming near the end of the pilgrimage, is about the sanctity of an early Christian who proved an instrument of grace in the conversion of Romans all around her, including even her tormentors. This classic hagiographical theme, reflected also in *The Clerk's Tale*, is moved from 'historical' setting (in the 2nd century) to contemporary 'autobiography' in the next tale. Here the Canon's Yeoman confesses his erstwhile allegiance to the 'false chanoun', a predatory alchemical magus; in the process of confessing he also 'turns' away from his old master, joining the pilgrimage to Canterbury and a new profession. *The Parson's Tale* sums up the meaning of turning away from sins (in repentance) and turning towards God (in acceptance of Christ's grace through faith informed by love).

Medieval lyrics often put the appeal to conversion in still more urgent terms, sometimes reflecting a Franciscan spiritual emphasis on the need for an affectual, not merely intellectual response to God's offer of grace in Christ. The language, however, from the lyric 'Lord, thou clepedest me' (C. Brown, *Religious Lyrics of the XIVth Century*, no. 5) to Friar James Ryman's 'Revert, revert' (Jeffrey, *Law of Love*, 121) is often Augustinian; the former poem is based on a passage in *The Confessiones* (8.5), the latter on Augustine's *vertere, revertere, convertere* wordplay (8.7.16). Ryman's verses conclude with Jesus speaking to the sinner: 'I axe namore, man, but thyne herte. Revert, revert, revert, revert.' The Augustinian model also lies behind Dante's *Vita Nuova*, an allegorical essay with love poems to Beatrice in which he describes his conversion from carnal to spiritual love.

In the drama, it might be argued, morality plays like *Everyman* are essentially conversion plays; some saints' plays certainly are – including the Digby *Mary Magdalen* and *The Conversion of St Paul*. In the Paul play biblical language and incident directly inform the play; in *Mary Magdalen* the biblical narrative is extensively augmented by use of the *legenda*. In Shakespeare's *Henry IV (2)*, there is a vestige of this pattern when Prince Hal recognizes that he must rise from folly to pursue his regal duty; he puts off his former counsellor , his 'old man', characterized by Falstaff, saying:

> Presume not that I am the thing I was,
> For God doth know, so shall the world perceive,
> That I have turned away my former self,
> So will I those that kept me company. (5.5.60–63)

The Reformation introduced new views of the nature and necessity of conversion. The most significant of these is the terse view of Calvin, in which the penitent's response to the Word in contrition is downplayed and conversion seen as the work of God alone: 'If it is like turning a stone into flesh when God turns us to the study of rectitude, everything proper to our own will is abolished, and that which succeeds in its place is wholly of God' (*Institutes*, 2.3.6). Otherwise, he argues, 'if any, even the minutest, ability were in ourselves, then would also be some merit.' Accordingly, Calvin has little else to say on the subject except notably that conversion involves not only justification but also sanctification. Luther links conversion to repentance and faith. Pietist writers, including especially those influenced by Arminian theology like some of the dissenters and later Wesley in England, gave the element of 'personal decision' a greater prominence. The Anglican *Homilies Appointed to Be Read in Churches* subsumes these matters under sermons on 'Salvation', 'The True and Lively Faith', and 'Repentance', tending to follow a middle way between Luther and Catholic thought on the one hand and Calvin on the other.

John Donne offers a classic Augustinian example of conversion as repentance of a nominal believer in 'Good Friday, 1613, Riding Westward', which moves from 'forraigne motions' to a paradox in which, in response to Calvary, the speaker says, 'I turne my backe to thee, but to receive, / Corrections', and then pleads that the divine image will be restored in him by grace: 'That thou may'st know mee, and I'll turne my face.' Bunyan's *Grace Abounding to the Chief of Sinners* (1666) describes his own conversion as a gradual awakening following the reading of two devotional books belonging to his wife, Dent's *Plain Man's Pathway to Heaven* and Bayly's *Practice of Piety*. Defoe's *Robinson Crusoe* presents the marooned hero who discovers a Bible in the ship's wreckage, begins to read it, and 'not long after' is moved to repentance and conversion, something he later enjoins also upon his servant Friday. As is characteristic of Puritan treatments of conversion, the focus falls upon the individual encounter with Scripture, followed by a prompting by the Holy Spirit to repentance and resolution to declare faith in Christ and 'confess him before men' – the latter 'confession' providing much of the substance of Defoe's conversion narrative.

John Dryden, whose conversion to Roman Catholicism is reflected in the sceptical fideism of his *Religio Laici* and *The Hind and the Panther*, represents the conversion of a heathen philosopher Apollonius to the essentially rationalist arguments of St Catherine in his play *Tyrannic Love* (1670). Swift suspects Presbyterians,

Anabaptists, Independents, and Quakers of being 'emissaries' of the Jesuits, presumably because they each preached a species of radical adult conversion (*The Abolishing of Christianity in England*). The growth of pietism in the 18th century, often derided under the name 'enthusiasm', has much to do with the development of which Swift was apprehensive. John Wesley's High Church revivalism was substantially altered by his contact with the Moravians, who aspired to the life of the primitive Church and stressed the all-importance of conversion. The Arminian bias in subsequent Wesleyan thought split the Methodist movement; George Whitefield remained Calvinist, and, with other evangelicals of moderate Calvinist persuasion, emphasized 'predestination unto salvation' although retaining more of a conversionist theology than is found in Calvin. Augustus Toplady, author of 'Rock of Ages' ('Nothing in my hand I bring....') wrote that "Tis true that none can come except as they are *drawn* by God's Spirit. But 'tis also no less true that those are drawn who come, and that all who come shall be graciously received' (quoted in Wright, *Toplady and Contemporary Hymn-Writers*, page 242). Conversion is thus proof of election. 'Rock of Ages' was explicitly anti-Wesleyan, addressed to 'The Holiest Sinner in the World', and pleading 'Save me from its [sin's] guilt and power' – where Wesley taught that conversion saves from the guilt of sin but not its power. Toplady thus accords with Calvinist contemporaries in believing conversion to include sanctification as well as justification.

Dickens' *A Christmas Carol* is perhaps his clearest secularized version of the evangelical conversion experience. As with Calvin himself, or Bunyan, conviction of sin (accompanied by terror over the prospect of damnation) is the first stage in the conversion process. The 'time-spirits' of past, present, and future take the place of the Holy Spirit in producing conviction in Scrooge, following whose repentance 'Christ' is reborn in him as charity, or kindliness. With Wesley's followers as well as those of Whitefield, Doddridge, and others preaching in public places about repentance and conversion, anonymous satiric pamphlets soon sprang up with titles such as *Fanatical Conversion* (1779) and *The Temple of Imposture* (1778), in which Mahomet the arch-imposter declares:

In servile Imitation of my Plan,
Priests now in Tabernacles fish for Man.
There, to thy Honour, Goddess, thou canst see
M[ada]n, R[omai]ne, and W[esle]y, mimic *me*.

Other 18th-century treatments of conversion vary from *Tom Jones'* gentle transformation in the fashion of Augustine and Dante in Fielding's great novel (1749) to John Newton's extremely popular *Authentic Narrative* (1764), a spiritual autobiography which may in part have influenced that of his friend and protégé, William Cowper. Cowper's *Memoir*, containing the account of his conversion, is influenced also by Augustine's *Confessiones*. His *Conversation* is a poetic plea against vain and idle talk (including religious talk of those who vainly rely on baptismal regeneration) and for the transformed 'conversation in the Spirit' of those who have experienced the 'new birth'.

The 19th century offers a variety of literary treatments of conversion. Wordsworth, whose naturalism excluded much of Christian supernaturalism, writes in *Peter Bell* (1798; revised 1819, 1827, 1832) of a moral rather than religious conversion, effected through a chain of natural events. The Oxford Movement, which saw figures of evangelical persuasion such as J.H. Newman move towards Rome while sons of High Churchmen, like Pusey and Keble, stayed, is indicative of a growing emphasis on Augustinian or Pauline conversion in 19th-century English Catholicism. A reaction to Romanticism and to various forms of romanticized faith, it helps in part to account for the appeal of the Catholic Church to the sons of notable evangelical statesman William Wilberforce, three of whom, with both his daughters and their husbands, became Catholics. While Keble's *Christian Year* upholds paedobaptism instead of conversion, Newman writes of the transforming 'voice, speaking so clearly in my conscience and in my heart' (*Apologia pro Vita Sua*, 219). Francis Thompson's 'The Hound of Heaven', rich with echoes of the Psalms, records how 'I fled Him, down the nights and down the days', but moves to a point of recollection where 'ever and anon a trumpet sounds', and Christ the trumpeter, 'him who summoneth', turns him to himself at last.

In Protestant circles the emphasis on conversion was being expressed in strikingly similar terms, as in C.H. Spurgeon's sermon 'Regeneration' (Sermon 14 on John 3:3). A novel like Dickens' *Little Dorrit*, with its metaphors of birth and rebirth, is closer in many respects to Spurgeon than to the apocalyptic romanticism of Carlyle. Carlyle's Teufelsdröckh experiences a conversion of *Weltanschauung* momentous enough that he wakes to visions of 'a new Heaven and a new Earth', the product of a 'Spiritual Newbirth' occasioned by his assertion of his personal freedom. Most religious conversions in the 19th-century novel, however, are after the pattern of Dostoevski's *Crime and Punishment*, conducted offstage.

In the 20th century, G.B. Shaw's *Major Barbara* is a Fabian socialist's sceptical look at the Christian 'socialism' and conversion theology of the Salvation Army of William Booth. Shaw's stated opinion was that conversion is impossible, so that a savage converted to Christianity means Christianity converted to savagery (cf. *Androcles and the Lion*; *The Shewing-Up of Blanco Posnet*).

A conversion to Anglo-Catholicism was to redirect and subsequently recharacterize the major poetry of T.S. Eliot, who reflects on the new birth in his 'Journey of the Magi'. Eliot's conversion was not well received by critics at the time; subsequently it has become a major source of interest in defining his poetics. Margaret Avison's *The Dumbfounding* (1966) is a more recent poetic diary of conversion in which are found echoes of Eliot and Donne, as well as of Augustine and Paul. In it the familiar tension between personal freedom and death to self for the sake of 'new life' in Christ marks a strong continuity with ancient as well as modern explorations of the 'psychology' of conversion.

David L. Jeffrey
University of Ottawa

Despair

The term *despair* appears only four times in the King James Version (1 Samuel 27:1; Ecclesiastes 2:20; 2 Corinthians 1:8; 4:8), but the concept of religious despair as it formed through patristic literature and into the Renaissance was understood to have its roots in a wide range of biblical texts, including texts other than those in which the word itself appears.

Central to the concept of despair in Christian tradition is the Pauline distinction between 'godly' sorrow, prompted by a recognition of one's sinfulness, which leads to repentance, and 'worldly' sorrow, which is self-preoccupied and does not seek a remedy of grace: 'For godly sorrow worketh repentance to salvation... but the sorrow of the world worketh death' (2 Corinthians 7:10). The distinction is crucial to the early Fathers, who see worldly sorrow as a sin rather than merely a pitiable malady, and as the instrument of Satan. They define despair in terms of its spiritual opposite, presumption – despair evidencing a lack of confidence in Christ's mercy, and presumption an overconfidence in such mercy (e.g., St Augustine, *Patrologia Latina,* 38.778; St John Chrysostom, *Patrologia Graeca*, 61.75; 62.447–48).

Chaucer, in *The Parson's Tale*, examines despair in the context of his discussion of Sloth, a vice dominated by loss of hope and inability to do good works. 'This horrible synne is so perilous that he that is despeired, ther nys no felonye ne no synne that he douteth for to do, as sheweth wel by Judas' (*Canterbury Tales*, 10.695). In Sackville's 'Induction' in *Mirrour for Magistrates* (1563), Sorrow guides the persona / narrator to the depths of Hell where, passing by personifications of Revenge, Maladie, and Warre, he meditates despairingly on the defects of the world. The stories of tyrannical princes which follow reveal the errors of arrogance and presumption.

In early English drama, especially in the morality tradition, despair is portrayed in the protagonist's sinful absorption with his depravity. In *Mankind* (circa 1465) the central character expresses suicidal desperation: 'A rope, a rope! I am not worthy.' Despair first appears as a personified figure in John Skelton's allegorical examination of princely morality, *Magnificence* (1515; ed. Scattergood, 1983):

> In tyme of dystresse I am redy at hande;
> I make hevy hertys, with eyen full holowe.
> Of farvent charyte I quenche out the bronde;
> Faythe and good hope I make asyde to stonde.

In Goddys Mercy, I tell them, is but foly to truste...
(2285–89)

Mischief offers a choice of a knife or a rope, but rescue comes in the form of Good Hope. The rope and dagger subsequently appear frequently in the iconography of Despair.

Dispayre appears among the temptations to Wastefulness, the protagonist of George Wapull's morality play *The Tyde Tarryeth No Man* (1576) – using rhetoric and logic to bring Wastefulness to believe that his sins are outrageous and his soul beyond repair. Wastefulness bids the world and his wife farewell and announces that he will end his 'life with cord or knyfe'. He is rescued by Faithful-Few and through prayer 'that wicked Monster of Dispayre' is banished. Wastefulness learns that God's Justice (the Old Dispensation) has been overridden by God's Mercy (the New Dispensation).

Edmund Spenser's allegorical portrait of Despair (*Faerie Queene*, 1.9.33–54) is probably the best known in English literature. A gaunt, hollow-eyed, and ragged cave-dweller, he assails Redcrosse Knight with accusations of his sinfulness, arguing that the longer he lives the greater will be his guilt, and counsels that suicide is the most reasonable remedy. Redcrosse, moved by Despair's rhetoric, lifts a dagger and prepares to take his life; but Una, snatching the weapon away, reprimands him and bids him to 'arise, and leave this cursed place'. She immediately leads him to the house of Holiness where he is instructed in repentance. Despair is left behind, condemned to an eternity of unsuccessful suicide attempts.

Giles Fletcher, in his *Christs Victorie and Triumph* (1610), patterns his personification of Despair on Spenser's reclusive deceiver Archimago, including the clerical disguise which satirizes the false comforts offered by the Roman Church. Despair, the agent of Satan, is the first of the three tempters introduced to Christ. Fletcher's association of Despair with the initial temptation faced by Christ in the wilderness (Matthew 4:3–4) borrows from expositors such as Lancelot Andrewes, who called the first temptation the temptation to 'murmur against God' (*The Wonderfull Combate betweene Christ and Satan*, 1592). The second tempter in Fletcher's scheme is the traditional opposite of Despair, the tyrant Presumption.

Phineas Fletcher, Giles' brother, uses a female allegorical figure for Despair, 'a sad ghastly Spright' who wishes for death but cannot die (*Apollyonists*, 1627, 1.15). Another Spenserian imitator, William Browne, brings his protagonist to a fork in a road where he must choose between Repentance and Despair. He is given direction by a heavenly choir just as he is about to make the wrong choice (*Britannia's Pastorals*, 1613–16, 1.5). In Anthony Copley's *A Fig for Fortune* (1596) the protagonist is advised to kill himself by Cato's ghost, 'a spirit of Despair and self-Misdoom', which combines the classical image of suicide with Christian allegory. This protagonist is able, through his own powers of recognition, to reject Despair.

John Donne, in his 'Biathanatos' (circa 1607), engages in a lengthy and erudite consideration of suicide – distinguishing between suicide and martyrdom on the basis of intention. His two *Anniversary* poems, marking the untimely death of the daughter of his patron, portray a decayed world on the brink of despair which regains its sense of worth from the memory of Elizabeth Drury. George Herbert, in 'The Bag', casts off despair by recounting the extraordinary grace of Christ – especially his unstinting forgiveness of grievous sin and injury to himself in the Passion. The poet, having recited the 'strange story' of Jesus' love, is able to defy his adversary, 'Harke, Despair away'.

In his 'Definition of Love', Andrew Marvell adapts the theological understanding of despair to amorous verse, suggesting that his love was 'begotten by Despair / Upon Impossibility'. Borrowing from the tradition that sees despair leading to godly sorrow and thus inaugurating the spiritual journey, Marvell asserts that 'magnanimous Despaire alone / Could show me so divine a thing' as Love.

Burton's *Anatomy of Melancholy* bases its learned paramedical discussion of despair on traditional sources, defining it as the malady of those who cannot believe in divine mercy and the prospect of their salvation, and naming Satan as the principal agent and procurer of this mischief. The symptoms of despair, says Burton, are sleeplessness, a trembling heart, and a sorrowful mind. And many (including such biblical characters as Cain, Saul, and Judas) 'make away themselves.' Those afflicted with despair, he argues, should consider the sins of such as Job, David, Peter, and Paul, and learn that no crime is so great that it cannot be pardoned.

A memorable dramatic treatment of despair is afforded by Marlowe's *Doctor Faustus* in which the protagonist, at the end of his twenty-four-year pact with Mephistopheles, rejects the Old Man's counsel to repent and the Scholar's reminder of the infinity of God's mercy and chooses his own damnation, dying with cries of despair on his lips: 'See, see, where Christ's blood streams in the firmament! One drop would save my soul, half a drop. Ah, my Christ!' Many of Shakespeare's characters are beset by despair. Richard III, the presumptive tyrant, hears the ghosts of his victims taunt him with the refrain, 'Despair and die' (*Richard III,* 5.3). Hamlet contemplates whether suicide is to be preferred to bearing the ills of life. King Lear confronts despair in Gloucester's view of the universe bereft of purpose and his own experience of the absence of justice.

In *Paradise Lost* Milton associates despair directly with Satan, whose unresolved despair informs his daring attack on Adam and Eve. Eve, after the Fall, loses hope and proposes that she and Adam 'seek Death' (*Paradise Lost,* 10.989–1007), but Adam counsels repentance, the first step in their regeneration and their emergence from crippling sorrow. In Bunyan's *Pilgrim's Progress* the giant Despair imprisons Hopeful and Christian in Doubting Castle, urging them to commit suicide. Christian, like Spenser's Redcrosse Knight, is susceptible to the arguments of Despair, but Hopeful urges patience; discovering a key called Promise, the pair eventually escape. (In part 2, the giant Despair is slain and Doubting Castle is levelled.)

Since the 17th century the allegory of Despair has all but disappeared from English literary tradition. Prominent biblical figures who fell into despair have, however, continued to attract literary interest (e.g., Swift's 'Judas'; Byron's *Cain*). Lady Gregory, in 'The Story Brought by Brigit' (1924), combines an Irish folk story with the material of a Passion play. Her characterization of Judas shows him overtaken by despair: 'Dogs tearing, hounds hunting, a rock frozen in the waves. A wave of ice and a wave of fire – that is the wages of the betrayal of the King!'

Religious despair is a prominent theme in the writings of William Cowper, whose preoccupation with his own sinfulness prompted several suicide attempts and much mental distress. Despite having collaborated with John Newton on a considerable body of hymns celebrating confidence in God's grace and his own salvation, his last original poem, 'The Castaway', expressed again the despair he once referred to as 'a sentence of irrevocable doom in my heart':

> No voice divine the storm allayed,
> No light propitious shone,
> When, snatched from all effectual aid,
> We perished, each alone;
> But I beneath a rougher sea,
> And whelmed in deeper gulfs than he.

In Emily Dickinson's poem 'It was not Death, for I Stood Up' (no. 510) a form of desperate meaninglessness is mistaken for death:

> But, most, like Chaos – Stopless – cool
> Without a Chance, or Spar –
> Or even a Report of Land –
> To justify – Despair. (20–23)

Twentieth-century literature is replete with characters caught in purposeless and despairing lives. Theodore Roethke, in 'In a Dark Time', portrays agony and isolation: 'I know the purity of pure despair, / My shadow pinned against the sweating wall.' John Barth's *The Floating Opera* (1956) traces the suicidal steps of its protagonist, and in Arthur Miller's *Death of a Salesman* (1949) Willie Loman responds with suicide to the futility of his life. The traditional resolution of despair through a Christian acceptance of the power of grace is seldom portrayed: even in a work with an implied biblical subject matter such as Archibald MacLeish's *J.B.* (1956) Jobian despair is resolved by the power of human love to overcome the crippling inaction engendered by unresolved guilt.

Faye Pauli Whitaker
Iowa State University

Faith

The most concise biblical definition of faith is found in the epistle to the Hebrews: 'Faith is the substance of things hoped for, the evidence of things not seen' (11:1). In this chapter faith is exemplified by memorable figures from salvation history who, having heard the call of God, obeyed at once. By faith they became heirs of the covenant and pilgrims on earth searching for a better heavenly country (11:13, 16).

The writer explains that 'through faith we understand that the worlds were framed by the word of God' (11:3); that is, faith grants the possibility of understanding things one can never know with evidential certitude. Faith also prompted the parents of Moses to hide him in the bullrushes despite Pharaoh's edict: faith gives courage to choose the good, or life itself, without fear of the consequences (11:23). Faith also sees one through persecution because of loyalty to the word of God (vv. 24–28, 35–39), even though receipt of God's promises is not complete in mortal life (cf. St Augustine, *Enchiridion*, 6–8).

The cornerstone of New Testament faith is the resurrection: 'If Christ be not raised, your faith is vain' (1 Corinthians 15:17). Because miracles (especially the resurrection) are central to the meaning of faith, the commitment of faith is intrinsically resistant to purely rational analysis. Nor does it depend upon a consensus of human judgment (Romans 3:3; cf. 14:22–23). For the writer to the Hebrews, faith is at bottom simply an acknowledgment of Jesus as 'author and finisher of our faith' (Hebrews 12:2); hence, 'without faith it is impossible to please him' (Hebrews 11:6).

The term *faith* is used in a variety of ways in English literature, most derived, through centuries of tradition, from the Bible itself. First, in the Old Testament, the Hebrew noun has the basic sense of trustworthiness and corresponds to the verb 'to believe' (e.g., Deuteronomy 7:9; Psalm 89:1–33). It normally refers to the 'faithfulness' of God rather than the 'faith' of persons (cf. Romans 3:3; Galatians 5:22). The substantial development of this term, however, is in the New Testament (cf. John 3:1–5). Jesus refers to faith strong enough to work miracles (Matthew 17:20; 9:28); the sense here is of absolute trust (cf. Latin *fiducia*) or reliance upon the preexisting faithfulness of God; to believe God is to rely on his word (e.g., Genesis 15:1–6; Exodus 4:15, 28–30). The degree to which individuals trust God, as the story of St Peter's attempt to walk out to meet Christ on the water suggests, is the degree to which they can overcome the typical limitations of their human nature (Matthew 14:23–33). Here the word of God which must be trusted is Jesus himself.

Second, St Paul says that faith is a product of the word written and the word preached: 'Faith cometh by hearing, and hearing by the word of God' (Romans 10:17). While faith thus defined must have an intellectual content, mere assent to facts or truths does not count as 'saving' faith: as the characterization of Mephistopheles in Marlowe's *Doctor Faustus* makes clear (e.g., 1.3.320–27), 'the devils also believe, and tremble' (James 2:19). Faith does not merely 'accept the gospel'; it accepts it as God's irrefragable word (2 Thessalonians 2:13).

Third, 'faith without works is dead' (James 2:17–26), not proscriptively but evidentially. For the 'faith which comes by hearing' is also acceptance of the truth about one's self; hence repentance and faith which 'justifies' are intimately connected (Acts 2:38–44; 17:30, 34; 26:20). St Thomas Aquinas insists that the person must be primary in the act of faith; just as an individual's word is believed, so also the formal aspect of faith consists in the fact that God is believed (*Summa Theologica* 2.2.q.11,a.1; q.2,a.2). In the 'act of faith', says Aquinas, a person enters into a personal relationship with the God who speaks to him.

Finally, the term 'the Faith' signifies the whole body of Christian doctrine and precept; this use of the term has its origin in the letters of Paul, where Greek *pistis* is used as such a metonym (Galatians 1:23; 1 Timothy 4:1, 6; cf. Romans 1:5). It is in this latter sense that the epistle of Jude exhorts its readers 'that ye should earnestly contend for the faith which was once delivered unto the saints' (v. 3). *Fides* so defined is unitive (the word is cognate with Sanskrit *bhidh*, 'unite' or 'bind together'); and in the New Testament the goal of faith is said to be unity (Ephesians 4:5, 13).

The burden of early patristic commentary falls on the second and fourth aspects of faith, what Tertullian called the 'rule of faith' – the core of credal and catechetical doctrine necessary to salvation (or membership in the church). St Augustine illustrates the chief reason for this focus in his *Enchiridion* – protection of the fledgling church from rampant syncretism and heresy. He is also at pains to say that persons are not saved 'through the merit of their own works' or by the determination of their own free will, but are dependent upon grace. He quotes Paul, 'By grace are ye saved through faith; and that not of yourselves: it is the gift of God: Not of works, lest any man should boast' (Ephesians 2:8–9). But that his readers may understand good works are not wanting 'in those who believe' Augustine is careful to quote also the following verse, 'For we are his workmanship, created in Christ Jesus unto good works, which God hath before ordained that we should walk in them' (v. 10; *Enchiridion*, 30–31).

Despite concern for the 'rule of faith', matters of faith soon grew too theologically complex for simple and untutored laypeople. The *praeambula fidei* or *antecedens fidem*, as 13th-century scholastics called them, were 'antecedent' philosophical questions concerning the nature of humanity, the character of God, the demonstrability of moral law, the problem of knowledge, and the relationship of nature and grace (to name a few). This corpus was elaborated with such dense and laboured prolixity that matters of reason and faith could seem almost at odds. One of Aquinas' major efforts was to resolve this problem: reason, he said, enables us to perceive the 'divine signs'; however, it is grace which makes us to see *in* them a call to personal faith (*Summa Theologica* 2.2.q.1,a.5 ad 1). But an unfortunate effect of the sheer industry as well as method of the scholastics was that the rational element proved more amenable to philosophical analysis. The questions of grace operating at a personal level to create faith or of God's faithfulness being the foundation of faith's possibility, clear in both Augustine and Aquinas, tended to slip into the background. *Fides quaerens intellectum*, faith seeking understanding, was the privilege of a few: for the majority all that was held necessary (or possible) was *fides in ecclesiam* or 'implicit faith'.

Partly for this reason, faith is often opposed to heresy or apostasy in medieval poetry. In *St Erkenwald* the first Roman missionary to Britain, St Augustine of Canterbury, is praised for having 'preched he here the pure fayth and plantyd the trouthe' (13). The term 'god fayth' (good faith) is found dozens of times in works of the *Pearl* Poet, Langland, and Chaucer with much the same value as in modern usage, except that on occasions it bears a residue of its origins in the notion of 'God's faithfulness' as the model for trustable intent, usually reinforcing the natural pun: 'In god fayth quoth the godman with a goud wille' (*Sir Gawain and the Green Knight*, 1969).

The Augustinian monk Martin Luther found implicit faith unsatisfactory. Studying Paul's letter to the Romans, he discovered anew the Pauline doctrine of justification by faith, in the initial sense above, and also as declared in Ephesians 2:8–9. His resulting opposition to any evidence of justification by works or merit (the sale of indulgences, quantified penances, etc.) put him on his collision course with the authority of Rome, and at the same time, inadvertently perhaps, established the modern notion of faith as essentially a personal and hence subjective matter: *Hier steht ich.* 'Every man is responsible for his own faith, and he must see to it for himself that he believes rightly. As little as another can go to hell or heaven for me, so little can he believe or disbelieve for me; and as little as he can open or shut heaven or hell for me, so little can he drive me to faith or unbelief' (*Secular Authority*, 211). That is, no sacrament of the church, be it baptism or penance, can, for Luther, give 'justifying faith'. Accordingly, the scholastic's 'faith informed by love' was not sufficiently articulate for Luther: sacrifice did not for him 'grant' faith; sacrifice only became meaningful where faith was already established in the heart. 'What justified Abel was by no means his sacrifice, but his faith; for by this he gave himself up to God, and of this his sacrifice was only the outward figure.' Luther was not fond of the epistle of James and felt it should possibly be dropped from the canon because of its emphasis on works. His rejection of natural theology in favour of the Reformation formula *sola fide*, *sola scriptura*, *solus Christus* set him sharply at odds with the orthodox Catholic definition of 'faith' in its sense of *fides in ecclesiam*.

Calvin, who disputes Augustine and Erasmus that Hebrews 11:1 provides a definition of faith, nevertheless offers an Erasmian modification of Luther's emphasis: 'It is faith alone which justifies, but the faith which justifies is not alone' (*Commentary on James*, 2:14–25; cf. *Commentary on Hebrews*, 11:1; for his own definition of faith see *Institutes* 3.2.7, 14). On the dispute concerning faith and works, or, as it was styled, between Paul and James, Calvin observes: 'When Paul says we are justified by faith, he means precisely that we have won a verdict of righteousness in the sight of God. James has quite another intention, that the man who professes himself to be faithful should demonstrate the truth of his fidelity by works' (*Commentary on James*, 2:21). Thus Calvin sees the arguments of Paul and James as distinct but complementary.

The 16th century in England was characterized by a collapsing of all previous *distinctiones* of discussion concerning faith into matters of catechism and conformity. The 1562 *Articles of Religion* of the Church of England and the *Official Homilies Appointed to Be Read in Churches* of the same year, although largely drafted by Cranmer, were an imposition of 'consensus' in the form of an itemized 'test of faith'. St Thomas More had suggested in his *Utopia* that this was not a proper definition of the Christian state, and he is famous for reminding his accusers (in the spirit of Romans 3:3; 14:22–23) that faith does not depend upon a consensus to be valid. Protestant poetics, as developed in Sidney's *Defence of Poetry* (1579–80), argues that poetry is to be preferred to philosophy as a means of teaching virtue because, in effect, it naturally engages the mystery of faith – meaning here something not unlike 'the suspension of disbelief'. In Spenser's *Faerie Queene* the personification of faith is not in the minor character Fidessa but in the Redcrosse Knight himself and in Una, who comprise faith in its institutional and unitive senses.

Seventeenth-century treatments tend to deal with a broader spectrum of the theological and psychological aspects of faith. Donne, whose language about faith in his poems is often applied to courteous or amorous analogy, reflects in his '1613 Ecologue' that 'As, for divine things, faith comes from above, / So, for best civil use, all tinctures move / From higher powers' (65–67); in his verse letter to the Lady Carey he wishes 'to speake things which by faith alone I see' (12), not the hidden things of God, of course, but such as he imagines of the lady in question. Similarly, in 'To the Countesse of Bedford', he parodies a theological commonplace: 'Reason is our Soules left hand, Faith her right, / By these we reach divinity, that's you.' Faith is here again a synonym for innocence of experience which nonetheless imagines it. In another theological allusion,

> Then back again to implicit faith I fall,
> And rest on what the Catholique voice doth teach.
> That you are good: and not one Heretique
> Denies it. (15–18)

On a higher plane, when he wishes to compliment George Herbert's mother in 'To the Lady Magdalene Herbert', he compares her to her namesake, saying that in Mrs Herbert 'An active faith so highly did advance, / That she once knew, more than the Church did know, / The resurrection.' As a priest and student of theology, however, Donne was keenly aware of the tendency of rationalism to kill personal faith and prays in his 'Litanie', 'Let not my mind be blinded by more light / Nor Faith, by Reason added, lose her sight.'

Herbert's poem on faith celebrates its power to transform vision and understanding:

> Faith makes me any thing, or all
> That I beleeve is in the sacred storie:
> And where sinne placeth me in Adam's fall,
> Faith sets me higher in his glorie. ('Faith', 16–20)

In a passage later much admired by John Wesley, Jeremy Taylor warns against equating faith with mere belief. He writes that

> though a great part of mankind pretend to be sav'd by Faith, yet they know not what it is, or else wilfully mistake it, and place their hopes upon sand or the more Unstable water [i.e., their baptism as an infant]. Believing is the least thing in a justifying Faith. For Faith is a conjunction of many Ingredients; and Faith is a Covenant, and Faith is a law, and Faith is Obedience, and Faith is a work, and indeed is a sincere cleaving to and a closing with the termes of the gospel in every instance, in every particular. (*Righteousness Evangelical*, 1663, 205)

While neither Henry Vaughan nor Herbert would in the end disagree with Taylor, Vaughan's conversion poems in *Silex Scintillans* (1650) include one on 'Faith' which stresses the centrality of belief. Observing how 'when the Sun of righteousness / Did once appear' the limitations of natural revelation as well as the Law and its liturgy ceased to have spiritual power in themselves, he describes how in their stead:

> So are now *Faith, Hope, Charity*
>   Through him Compleat;
> Faith spans up blisse; what sin, and death
>   Put us quite from,

> Lest we should run for't out of breath,
>   Faith brings us home;
> So that I reed no more, but say
>   *I do believe,*
> And my most loving Lord straitway
>   Doth answer, *Live.* (35–44)

Vaughan, converted in part through the poetry of Herbert, in this respect joins with him in anticipating the mainstream of evangelical piety in the 18th century.

At the same time a sceptical fideism influenced by developments among French Catholic writers was gaining ground in England. Its roots trace to earlier writers such as Pico della Mirandola, who published (1520) a six-book argument, itself indebted to Sextus Empiricus, dedicated to showing the insufficiency of human reason for certitude. Dividing all philosophers into three groups – the dogmatists who claim certitude, the academics who deny, and the sceptics (or Pyrrhoists) who do neither but rather doubt, Mirandola placed himself in the last category.

This line of thinking influenced Montaigne's *Apology for Raymond Sebond* (1580), which argues that human learning may be dangerous and quite often useless, whereas 'only humilitie and submission is able to make a perfect honest man. Every one must not have the knowledge of his dutie referred to his own judgment, but ought rather to have it prescribed unto him, and not be allowed to chuse it at his pleasure and free will' (*Essays,* trans. Florio, 2.189). Montaigne applies this argument for the necessity of 'higher authority' to 'the lawes of religion and Politik decrees'.

Montaigne's disciple Pascal, of Jansenist (French Augustinian) sympathies, and a near contemporary of Jeremy Taylor, applied Montaigne's argument more directly to matters of faith: 'If we submit everything to reason, our religion will have no mysterious and supernatural element. If we offend the principles of reason, our religion will be absurd and ridiculous' (*Pensées,* trans. Trottier, 78). In effect, it is more rational to submit to authority in religion, says Pascal, than not: 'There is nothing so conformable to reason as the disavowal of reason.'

In the Church of England, whose officially 'rationalist' position was still closely reflected in Richard Hooker's *The Laws of Ecclesiastical Polity* (1593–97), Montaigne and Pascal were nearly anathema, and in the 18th century the influence of 'Port-Royal' mystical fideism was roundly repudiated in pulpit and treatise alike. The appeal of Catholic fideism of this stripe to figures as diverse as John Wesley, John Fletcher, Elizabeth Rowe, and William Cowper made the evangelical and Methodist adherents susceptible to hysterical charges of Jesuitical subterfuge, a 'secret Catholicism'.

Ironically, this association was made possible by Catholic apologetic strategies for undermining Calvinist and Anglican 'rational religion', including such famous and controversial works as Father Simon's *Critical History of the Old Testament* (trans. 1682) – which called into question the reliability of the text of the Bible itself. Sceptical fideism had not since Aquinas been welcomed by Catholic theologians as a means of 'defending the faith' *inside* the Church. (Montaigne and Thomas Browne were alike put on the Index.) Hence the Jesuits opposed Jansenism in France with passionate intensity, even as they and others used parallel arguments in England to achieve apologetic objectives. *Fiat Lux* (1661) by the Franciscan John Canes begins by establishing a case for scepticism concerning the powers of reason and ends by leading the reader to fideist submission to the authority of the Church. Although this was 'answered' by John Owen's *Animadversions* (1662), in which the Independent pastor and spiritual writer analyzed Canes' strategy, pointing out that it steers 'poor unstable souls... to the Borders of Atheism, under a pretense of leading them to the Church' (156), in fact the tactic was quite effective in a number of cases.

Despite the efforts of Chillingworth (*Religion of Protestants*, 1638), Stillingfleet (*Rational Account of the Protestant Religion*, 1665), and Tillotson (*The Rule of Faith*, 1666), Anglican theology during this period may have, in fact, proved weakest in the point it most wished to defend – a rationally grounded faith, with the more rational buttressing for faith arguably coming from Dissenters such as Richard Baxter, John Owen, and literary apologists such as John Milton, whose prose works as well as poetry show he was not shy of attempting a rational justification of faith.

The popular mind in this period was, however, quite evidently open to such a sceptical fideism, as is well evidenced by the remarkable popularity of Sir Thomas Browne's *Religio Medici* (1642) through the 17th and early 18th centuries. Browne suggests, in ways which also recall Donne's 'Litany 7', that it is better to remain in ignorance and believe than to strive for that knowledge which seems to make belief unnecessary. Browne comments that it is the devil's stratagem to persuade us to 'raise the structures of... Reason', while using the resulting overbalance 'to undermine the edifice of... Faith' (*Works*, 1.31–32). The task of an intelligent person of science and learning is also then to teach 'haggard and unclaimed reason to stoop to the lure of Faith.... And this I think is no vulgar part of Faith, to believe a thing not only above, but contrary to Reason, and against the arguments of our proper Senses' (17–18). (Here Browne almost precisely anticipates Kierkegaard, who also drew on Pascal.)

Browne's *Religio Medici* was one of the most important books in the life of John Dryden; Father Simons' *Critical History* was another. Together they led Dryden to reject the rationalist apologetic of the Church of England and to conclude with Burnet that 'there was no certain proof of the Christian religion, unless we took it from the authority of the church as infallible' (Burnet, *History*, 1.1.335). The choice for one convinced of the sceptical argument was thus between atheism and submission to the authority of Rome, and for Dryden, as Louis Bredvold has observed, 'scepticism became a high road leading from Anglicanism to Rome' (Bredvold, *The Intellectual Milieu of John Dryden*, 1934, page 86). His own *Religio Laici* (1682), its title drawn from Browne, and his *The Hind and the Panther* (1687) reflect this movement to a Catholic definition of faith. In the first poem, that reason which 'pale grows... at Religion's sight' leads him to cry out for dependable authority: 'Such an *Omniscient* Church we wish indeed; / 'Twere worth *Both Testaments,* and cast in the *Creed*...' (282–83). In the second poem Dryden urges: 'Let reason then Her own quarry fly... how can finite grasp Infinity?' (104–05; cf. *Religio Laici*, 39–40, 114).

The real issue defining faith grew out of what might have been seen in earlier times as a lack of faith; a profound need for certitude made the central question in this period one of authority. For most Protestants authority remained in the Bible itself and was mediated through individual reason and judgment; Catholics, seeing the apparent undependability of this process, found certitude in the infallible authority of Rome. For a Protestant, faith was to be grasped and integrated in personal terms; for a Catholic, faith was more pronouncedly implicit and an institutional matter.

Accordingly, literary discussions of faith in the 18th century tend to confuse faith as personal belief and subscription to ecclesiastical authority more readily even than their 16th- and 17th-century precedents. Subjectively asserted personal belief, a central feature in the spirituality of Quakers (the 'inner light'), Baptists, Congregationalists, and a variety of Dissenters, was dismissed by rationalist latitudinarians such as Archbishop John Tillotson and philosopher John Locke (*Discourse Concerning Human Understanding*, chapter 19) as lamentable 'enthusiasm'. Against the appeal to personal experience of 'enthusiasts' Tillotson typically argues for the rational ethical principles of 'Christian religion', effectively a reduction of the content of faith to 'observable duty' and moral principles (Sermon 1, 1695: 'Of the great Duties of Natural Religion, with the Ways and Means of Knowing them') which are to be derived by observation from general human practice.

The question of authority, of its origin and relation to institutional faith, is explored in Swift's ecclesiastical satire *A Tale of a Tub* (1704), in which Martin (i.e., Luther, but here identified with the Anglican Church), Jack (Calvin and the Dissenters), and Peter (Roman Catholicism) adulterate their inherited vestments of faith. (Although Martin comes off least scathed, he is not entirely spared.) An implicit purpose of Swift's work is to ask the question, 'What has happened to original faith?' For a Catholic like Alexander Pope, whose 'Messiah' (1712) parallels Isaiah and the *Pollio* of Virgil, answering the question could lead to a different conclusion altogether from Dryden's, one in which the Deist's universalism seems a way out of the impasse. In a poem which he later affixed to his *Essay on Man* (1734), Pope pledges his faith to the

> Father of All! In every Age,
> In every Clime ador'd,
> By Saint, by Savage, and by Sage,
> Jehovah, Jove, or Lord! ('The Universal Prayer')

In some respects the evangelical revival under Wesley accented the confusion, even in its own attempt to revitalize personal faith. Among the Dissenters, Isaac Watts – a rigorous Cartesian, author of a student textbook on *Logick* (1725), and a Calvinist – laid strong emphasis upon rational grounding for faith. However, one of his own parishioners, Elizabeth Rowe, wrote her popular poems and *Devout Exercises* (1737) almost completely under the influence of the Port Royal mystics. John Wesley, despite his strong rationalist tendencies, articulated a doctrine of salvation which, like Luther's, depended on personal faith alone ('The Scripture Way of Salvation', 1765), stressing the subjective element of personal experience as the measure of faith. For the evangelical Anglican writer Hannah More, the rational foundation of faith suggested in Calvinist theology toughened her early neo-Gothic Romanticism and made her later work outward, analytical, and apologetically directed; for the Calvinist evangelical Cowper, whose emotional instability eventually predominated in his work, the question of personal faith was increasingly entangled in subjective uncertainty. His poetry emphasizes hope ('Hope', 'Lively Hope, and Gracious Fear') rather than certitude, and when addressing faith he takes refuge in the Augustinian-Calvinist doctrine that faith cannot be self-generated and must be given by God ('Praise for Faith', in *Olney Hymns*, 65).

The subjective element in faith, even the self-generation of faith, is a bridge leading to the Romantics. The faith in 'divine Nature' and in himself which Wordsworth works out in 'The Prelude' is derived, like the self-generated 'system' of Blake's theology, from earlier Christian epistemologies, and faith as a means of knowing for Wordsworth is, as for Wesley, a matter of 'inner light.' In 'Resolution and Independence' 'Genial faith, still rich in genial good' (38) is a threatened tranquillity, one supported only by the resolve which gives 'human strength' (112). When he reflects, however, on institutional faith, Wordsworth finds it in decay ('Decay of Piety'), and in his 'Ecclesiastical Sonnets' he wonders about an earlier age in which 'faith thus sanctified the warrior's crest / While from the Papal Unity there came, / What feebler means had failed to give, one aim / Diffused thro' all the regions of the West' (no. 9). Now, in another age, that Unity is attested 'By works of Art, that shed, on the outward frame /

Or worship, glory, and grace, which who shall blame / That ever looked to heaven for final rest?'

It was not the ardent atheism of Shelley and Byron, nor Coleridge's laborious journey from Unitarianism to Trinitarian faith, nor Coleridge's influence through *Aids to Reflection* (1825) on Sterling, Kingsley, and the young Christian socialists which most accurately anticipated the balance of the 19th century. Rather, it was Wordsworth's idealization of art as a means of faith. Aestheticism, variously developed by the Morrises, Christina Rossetti, the Pre-Raphaelites, and even Oscar Wilde, is fundamentally a movement from identifying the shape of faith with its expression in art and architecture to a substitute faith in art itself, or 'faith in the sublime.' As such, like the Christian socialism of Kingsley, Fabian socialism of G.B. Shaw, or Marxism of William Morris, faith is no longer faith in the biblical sense, but rather an optimism and even reverence concerning human achievement.

Matthew Arnold, an ardent opponent of faith in the biblical sense in *Literature and Dogma* (1873), *God and the Bible* (1887), and *St Paul and Protestantism* (1870), could, while placing his faith in the same liberal sphere, nevertheless mourn a loss of religious faith of the sort that gives a kind of quiet certitude. His famous 'Dover Beach' is, among other things, a lament for an age which has used up all its mythologies.

From the perspective of the 17th century, at least, the romanticized fideism of Tennyson would have seemed ill-formed and substantially without biblical content; the poetry of Robert Browning seems as tantalized by the power of faith (*Saul*) as, in earlier times, its perversion (a theme in the dramatic monologues), but nonetheless it lacks any substantial positive address to personal faith. Despite some apparent similarities in the subject matter of religious poetry, the underlying *pietas* had been radically altered. The theme of the loss of faith, or rejection of faith, so vivid in the fiction of Hardy (see especially *Jude the Obscure*) and the poetry of Swinburne (e.g., 'Hymn of Man'), overshadowed the theme of 'faith given', as in Francis Thompson's 'Hound of Heaven', or 'faith experienced', as in the poems of Hopkins.

Much of the same was true in America. Earlier Calvinist and

Puritan poets wrote confidently of a faith they securely possessed because it had been granted by God and passed on in the covenant of grace, but they had relatively little to say about the personal struggle to find faith. Faith, too, could become a matter of 'manifest destiny'. James Russell Lowell celebrates the rewards of public faith in his famous Harvard 'Oration Ode' (1810) when he writes "Tis not the grapes of Canaan that repay, / But the high faith that failed not by the way.' The content of the faith Lowell has in mind is surely biblically derived, but tends to be literarily directed to a revelation of the divine in nature, in a manner distinct from Wordsworth only to the degree that it maintains more of the familiar language of institutional piety. William Cullen Bryant's 'Forest Hymn' represents a more widespread aspiration (cf. 'I Cannot Forget with what Fervid Devotion'):

> Be it ours to meditate
> In those calm shades thy milder majesty,
> And to the beautiful order of thy works,
> Learn to confirm the order of our lives.'

For the Calvinist rebel Melville such sentiments as Bryant (or Transcendentalists like Thoreau) expressed and the ideals of public faith of a 'covenant America' were two sides of the same coin, and alike repulsive. In *The Confidence-Man* (1857) he has Satan himself come on board the American ship of faith, *Fidele*, and by taking up the arguments of scepticism familiar from Father Simon's *Critical History* and Montaigne, demonstrate that there are in fact no biblical Christians on board.

In the 20th century public or institutional faith has largely ceased to be a vital issue. James Joyce's *Portrait of the Artist as a Young Man* is one of the last major treatments of the theme of loss of faith familiar from the 19th century. The modern era, perhaps more than any previous, emphasizes individual personal identity and has produced some literarily significant individual pursuits (and affirmations) of biblical faith. The classic case is T.S. Eliot, whose Dryden-like progress grows through a dark and weary scepticism ('Mr Eliot's Sunday Morning Service', *The Waste Land*, and 'The Hollow Men') to a revelation of personal faith ('Journey of the Magi') and finally an affirmation of public faith (e.g., *Four Quartets*). In *Choruses from the Rock,* heavily influenced by medieval and 17th-century spiritual writers, Eliot asks his readers to

> Remember the faith that took men from home
> At the call of a wandering preacher
> Our age is an age of moderate virtue
> And of moderate vice
> When men will not lay down the Cross
> Because they will never assume it.
> Yet nothing is impossible, nothing,
> To men of faith and conviction.
> Let us therefore make perfect our will.
> O God, help us. (8)

Novelist and Catholic convert Graham Greene views the age as one of frankly immoderate vice. *Brighton Rock* (1938) introduces his notion of the only plausible ground of faith, not a rational theology but a realization of the 'otherness', 'the appalling strangeness of the mercy of God'. *The End of the Affair* (1951) is designed to suggest, from a Catholic perspective, the modern need for personal faith; his earlier novel *The Power and the Glory* (1940) in its penultimate scene offers a back-porch analysis of the divergence between a subjective Lutheran and rigorously objective Catholic definition of faith.

Attempts at a traditionalist theology of faith have been made from the Catholic perspective by G.K. Chesterton (*Orthodoxy; The Everlasting Man*) and from the Anglican by C.S. Lewis (*Surprised by Joy; Mere Christianity*), both writers enjoying wide popularity as Christian apologists, lay theologians, and writers of fiction. In these authors, as in the poets David Jones (*Anathemata; The Sleeping Lord*) and R.S. Thomas (*Pieta; Laboratories of the Spirit*), there is evident nostalgia for the clearer definitions of an earlier age, but also a principled working out of a biblical tradition of faith in the secular modern context.

While American literature of the later 20th century offers fewer notable examples of such declarative addresses to faith, a similar recrudescence is discernible. Sometimes, as in the case of John Updike, it comes in the voice of American antinomianism, and hence, as in Updike's 'Seven Stanzas at Easter', surprises:

> Make no mistake: if He rose at all
> it was as His body;
> if the cell's dissolution did not reverse, the molecules
> reknit, the amino acids rekindle,
> the Church will fall.

The stark 'either/or', on reflection not so surprising in a Lutheran and American writer, leads Updike to impatient rebuke of 19th- and 20th-century poetry about faith:

> Let us not mock God with metaphor,
> analogy, sidestepping, transcendence;
> making of the event a parable, a sign painted in the
> faded credulity of earlier ages:
> let us walk through the door. (*Telephone Poles and Other Poems*, 72–73; cf. 1 Corinthians 15:17; Acts 14:27)

In another fashion, Flannery O'Connor makes much the same point in her short story 'The Enduring Chill'. In it a sceptical young student, embarrassed by what he imagines to be intellectually lowbrow origins, aspires to affect a Catholic prospect on faith partly because he imagines it to be much more 'rational' and partly because he hopes it will offend his Baptist mother. The humour of the story lies in the young man's outrage and defeat when the garrulous Irish Jesuit priest who comes to give him last rites insists that the 'faith which comes by hearing' can only be obtained by his first accepting the truth about himself: 'How can the Holy Ghost fill your soul when it's full of trash?' the priest roars. 'The Holy Ghost will not come until you see yourself as you are – a lazy, ignorant, conceited youth!' (*The Complete Stories*, 377; cf. 2 Timothy 1:6–14).

David L. Jeffrey
University of Ottawa

Freedom, Bondage

The interrelated motifs of freedom and bondage serve as major organizing principles in the Bible and biblical tradition. In the creation story (Genesis 1), God gives each creature freedom to live and multiply in a good world, and to humanity the added freedom of ruling over the lower creation. In Genesis 2, God decrees: 'Of every tree... thou mayest freely eat: But of the tree of the knowledge of good and evil, thou shalt not eat...' (Genesis 2:16–17), thereby establishing the boundary which when trangressed will determine humanity's subsequent loss of freedom, its bondage on earth to sin and death.

In the New Testament the earthly life of Jesus begins in a humble stable in the symbolic bondage of swaddling wraps for the Word made flesh (Luke 2:7; John 1:14); it ends in humiliating submission to the bondage of death on the cross and entombment in linen burial cloths. Though sought after as a political messiah, Jesus repeatedly declares his kingdom and the liberty of its citizens in spiritual terms. He proclaims his role as liberator from the letter of the old law (Mark 2:27) and imposes the more difficult demand of an inner righteousness which will fulfil the spirit of the old (Matthew 5:17–48). He promises, by bearing the burden of the new law with his followers, to make it light (Matthew 11:29–30). In his resurrection, he leads captivity captive (Ephesians 4:8) and robs death of its sting (1 Corinthians 15:55–56).

St Paul constantly and paradoxically emphasizes the continuing sense of bondage to sin in the flesh, and joy in freedom from that sin in Christ (Romans 6:14–23; Galatians 5:1; etc.); St Peter who, like Paul, was imprisoned more than once for the sake of the gospel, uses 'prison' as a metaphor for the bondage suffered by sinners in hell (1 Peter 3:19–20). St John, writing to churches helpless before the bondage of political and military occupation, devotes much of his Revelation to visions of God's wrathful justice against those who oppress the poor and faithful, and affords a vision of blissful freedom in the New Jerusalem after these oppressors have been overcome. The Bible thus begins, climaxes, and ends in acute consciousness of the tension between freedom and bondage.

In subsequent times the modes of freedom proclaimed or sought have been influenced by biblical precedent. Some early Christians sought deliverance from this world in a martyr's death. Like John, others awaited the realization of apocalyptic hopes. Midrashic literature shows that Jews, too, continued to hope for deliverance in the day of the Lord as prophesied in Isaiah 2, Zechariah 14, and elsewhere; in the meantime they could see each Sabbath as a limited respite figuring the future time of deliverance (*Midrash on Psalms*, trans. W.G. Braude, 786).

Origen came to believe, under the influence of pagan thought, that the doctrine of eternal bondage for sinners in hell was inconsistent with a belief in genuine human freedom and God's justice and goodness. His complex solution, involving a curative hell and a doctrine of rebirth, had lasting influence, although it was judged heretical. St Augustine follows Paul in stressing the bondage of fallen humanity to sin: he argues that the will is free in terms of its responsibility for choices made but is bound to make evil choices unless delivered through the goodness and mercy of God in Christ. He advances a doctrine of predestination rooted in Romans 8:29: some persons are apparently incapable of responding to God's liberating initiative. Boethius wrote his influential *De Consolatione Philosophiae* in response to his actual bondage in prison. Like Augustine, he takes up the thorny questions of fate and providence, foreknowledge, predestination, and free will, finally confessing that inferior human reason cannot of itself attain the mode of divine knowledge in which these issues resolve themselves. True freedom for Boethius is freedom of the will to choose intelligible or higher good, and it may not be diminished by physical bondage. To choose such freedom is indeed the only way to preserve rationality.

It is in this sense that medieval English writers understood the promise of Jesus concerning belief in his word, 'And ye shall know the truth, and the truth shall make you free' (John 8:32). The phrase concludes each line of Chaucer's 'Balade de Bon Conseil', which suggests that fortune's adversity, an inevitable condition of 'wrastling for this world', may be overcome by appeal to God's mercy and 'godeness' for spiritual deliverance: 'Unto the world leve now to be thral', he concludes, 'And trouthe the shal delivere, it is no drede.' Among his numerous treatments of this theme, Chaucer offers in his Knight of *The Canterbury Tales* a concise insight into medieval understanding of the relation between freedom and bondage. In response to Harry Bailey's terms for a story contest en route to Canterbury, the Knight forgoes his privilege of station and draws straws with the company to see who shall have the less desirable lot of initial narrator. As fortune would have it, the lot falls to him,

> And whan this goode man saugh that it was so,
> As he that wys was and obedient
> To kepe his foreward by his free assent,
> He seyde, 'Syn I shal bigynne the game
> What, welcome be the cut, a Goddes name!'
> (*General Prologue*, 1.850–54)

Having bound himself by his 'foreward' (promise), he now assents in freedom to that condition. He 'freely obeys'. His tale, unsurprisingly, contrasts the infelicity and unreason of those who make physical bondage their 'reality' with those who know the rational felicity of preserving inward, spiritual freedom.

Medieval lyrics and carols, as well as 'Harrowing of Hell' plays, make use of patristic typology in which Christ is the 'key of David'.

> O clauis David inclita,
> Dans viam in portis,
> Educ nos de carcere
> Et de umbra mortis

is the incipit to both a Latin hymn and the 16th-century English carol which 'translates' it:

> O David, thow nobell key,
> Cepter of the howse of Isreall,
> Thow opyn the gate and geff us way...
> And saue vs fro owre fendys felle.

> We be in prison; vn vs haue mynde,
> And lose vs fro the bonde of synne,
> For that thou losest no man may bynde.
> (R. Greene, *The Early English Carols*, no. 2)

Optimism concerning the potentiality of human freedom in this life re-emerged for a time in the Renaissance. Pico della Mirandola's 'Oration on the Dignity of Man' (circa 1486) rests its hopes under God in 'moral philosophy and dialectic' as a means to 'set us free' so that 'Gabriel, the "strength of God", shall abide in us, leading us through the miracles of nature and showing us on every side the merit and the might of God.' But English writers of the 16th century remained more aware of the tension. Spenser, working within the patterns of Christian redemption in the first book of his *Faerie Queene,* characterizes the strict limits to earthly freedom: Redcrosse can freely imitate Christ in liberating Una's parents and their lands from the Satanic dragon, but he is not free to enjoy full union with his heavenly bride until his earthly quest is done.

John Donne's sense of the paradoxical relationship between freedom and bondage is reflected amply in his poetry as well as his sermons, perhaps most memorably in the appeal of 'Holy Sonnet 14':

> Take me to you, imprison me, for I
> Except you enthral me, never shall be free
> Nor ever chaste, except you ravish me.

George Herbert's poetry is replete with analogous reflections on the paradoxical relationship between apparent bondage (which comes as a result of obedience to God) and true inner freedom (e.g., 'The Collar'; 'Obedience'). This theme is central to Bunyan's *Pilgrim's Progress* (another work written in prison), and it is prominent in Milton's relation of obedience and love in *Paradise Lost.*

Milton takes an affirmative view of the potential for good in human freedom of choice without minimizing the difficulties and pains involved: 'I cannot praise a fugitive and cloistered virtue', he writes, 'that never... sees her adversary, but slinks out of the race' (*Areopagitica,* ed. Hughes, 728). Milton's writings demonstrate repeatedly the power of the individual to exercise obedient freedom, standing firm in testing circumstances (*Comus*; *Paradise Lost,* especially book 12; *Samson Agonistes*). Such freedom is perhaps most notably dramatized in Christ's reasoned and scripturally obedient refusal of Satan's temptation in *Paradise Regained.*

The theme is amplified in numerous 18th-century poems (e.g., Christopher Smart's *Jubilate Agno*) and hymns, perhaps most memorably in Charles Wesley's 'And Can it Be', which relates Christ's free sacrifice to human liberty, in terms echoing (perhaps unconsciously) medieval Latin hymns on the harrowing of hell:

Long my imprisoned spirit lay,
Fast bound in sin and nature's night.
Thine eye diffused a quick'ning ray;
I woke; the dungeon flamed with light.
My chains fell off, my heart was free,
I rose, went forth, and followed thee.

Spiritual deliverance is also a major theme in the fifth book of William Cowper's *The Task*, where Cowper argues (cf. John 8:32) that 'Grace makes the slave a freeman':

He is the freeman whom the truth makes free
And all are slaves
beside. There's not a chain
That hellish foes, confed'rate for his harm,
Can wind around him, but he casts it off
With as much ease as Samson his green wyths...
His freedom is the same in ev'ry state;
And no condition of this changeful life,
So manifold in cares, whose ev'ry day
Brings its own evil with it, makes it less:
For he has wings that neither sickness, pain,
Nor penury, can cripple or confine.
No nook so narrow but he spreads them there
With ease, and is at large. Th'oppressor holds
His body bound; but knows not what a range
His spirit takes, unconscious of a chain;
And that to bind him is a vain attempt
Whom God delights in, and in whom he dwells.
(5.598, 733–34, 767–78)

With the Enlightenment, however, and the Romantic period, important changes in dominant use of the word *freedom* affect the way in which the biblical opposition is understood and applied. Use of the words *free* and *freedom* to mean simply independence or escape from restraint – in Herbert's 'The Collar' still a mere counterfeit of true freedom – begins to assert itself even in contexts where biblical allusion is involved, as the primary understanding. Partly this is a result of chiliastic attachments to national identity – in Britain and in America – of the biblical concepts of election and covenant: political liberty under present regimes becomes identified with exodus freedom, liberty from Egyptian bondage (or Babylonian captivity), so that biblical deliverances formally allegorized or spiritualized in prevalent exegesis, commentary, and allusion now become typologized as analogues, effectively, for modern state polity or privilege. Such a tendency is evident, for example, in Cowper's *Expostulation* (1782), where England is the object of praise:

> Freedom, in other lands scarce known to shine,
> Pours out a flood of splendour upon thine;
> Thou hast as bright an int'rest in her rays
> As ever Roman had in Rome's best days.
> True freedom is where no restraint is known
> That scripture, justice, and good sense, disown,
> Where only vice and injury are tied,
> And all from shore to shore is free beside. (588–95)

This is also the dominant usage of Thomas Paine, and of Rousseau and Voltaire. Hence it figures largely in the rhetoric of poetry admiring the French and American Revolutions. In American romanticism, with Whitman, or in English romanticism, with Blake, emphasis on the individual's personal liberty is opposed to the restraint of social conventions or the curb of kings and priests (cf. Wordsworth, Byron, Shelley). Thus, whereas the medieval emphasis in understanding the relationship between truth and freedom is inward and spiritually directed, the post-revolutionary understanding is chiefly libertarian or political. In Julia Ward Howe's 'Battle Hymn of the Republic' (1862) the last stanza effectively makes an analogy of what formerly would have been distinguished – spiritual and political freedom: 'As he [Christ] died to make men holy let us die to make men free / – His truth is marching on.' This understanding proves surprisingly amenable to Marxism and modern 'liberation theology'.

In American literature at the popular level, Emerson's luminous essay 'Self-Reliance', with its insistence that 'No law can be sacred to me but that of my nature', follows Rousseau and Montaigne in making the psychology of individual liberty – even to the point of anarchy – the essence of freedom's meaning. In historical perspective Emerson may appear somewhat confused: he commences with an apparent acknowledgment of biblical and Boethian wisdom which actually asserts the contrary of his own thesis. Wordsworth's similar concern in the *Prelude* with 'genuine freedom' is also largely divested of biblical associations. Freedom becomes more or less the prerogative of the absolute ego of Fichte's *Wissenschaftslehre,* despite Coleridge's criticism that such self-assertion is 'a crude egoismus, a boastful and hyperstoic hostility to NATURE as lifeless, godless, and altogether unholy' (*Biographia Literaria,* 1.101–02). Wordsworth's 'bondage' in *The Prelude* (1805) is still to be understood as spiritual bondage, though his 'liberation' is won by the advent of self-mastery, including especially mastery of consciousness, rather than by Milton's or Chaucer's obedience to biblical precept:

> A captive greets thee, coming from a house
> Of bondage, from yon City's walls set free,
> A prison where he hath been long immured.
> Now I am free, enfrancis'd and at large.
> ...With a heart
> Joyous, nor scar'd at its own liberty,
> I look about...
> Enough that I am free. (1.6–33)

As a result, though biblical allusion may lurk in the shadows, the tension in much Romantic and post-Romantic poetry between freedom and bondage is characterized by a strikingly post-biblical definition of the term *freedom*: whereas for Chaucer the word is largely other-directed and bespeaks a benefit of obedience (Middle English *fredom* is glossed in medieval French by *largesse*), for Wordsworth its meaning is largely self-directed and signifies a triumph of self-mastery. For Chaucer's Knight to love 'trouthe, honour, fredom and curtesye' is thus to cherish a different sort of character than is admired by Wordsworth, despite the latter's allusively Pauline phrasing:

> Oh! who is he that hath his whole life long
> Preserved, enlarged this freedom in himself?
> For this alone is genuine Liberty. (*Prelude,* 13.120–23)

Most subsequent literary use of the binary opposition has only vestigial connection to the biblical concepts.

Elizabeth Bieman
University of Western Ontario

Grace, Works

'For by grace are ye saved through faith; and that not of yourselves. It is the gift of God: not of works, lest any man should boast. For we are his workmanship, created in Christ Jesus unto good works, which God hath before ordained that we should walk in them' (Ephesians 2:8–10). These words of St Paul situate theological grace in its traditional relationship to salvation, faith, personal freedom, and merit.

In secular Greek, *charis* had been used with aesthetic and social connotations, and could suggest that which is 'gracious', 'artful', 'charming', or even, as in the case of a superb wine, 'exquisite'. The gracious acts of a host prompt gratitude: the word for 'thanks' is also *charis*. And it is a kind of noble generosity which grants favour to suppliants. It is the last context which most closely approximates the usage of Paul, who uses the word almost twice as often as all other biblical writers together. Paul's essential message is that 'saving' grace is uniquely God's to give (Romans 5:15; Ephesians 2:5); justification is clearly an act of God and cannot be claimed as a right by anyone; hence it must be received as a gift (Galatians 2:17–21). This excludes the possibility of the recipient taking credit for it, 'boasting' (1 Corinthians 1:29, 31), or 'glorying' (Galatians 6:14), except in the cross of Christ. In this sense, the term can imply the whole impact of Christ's incarnation and ministry (Titus 2:11). Grace is not an entity which God dispenses, but the quality of forgiveness and the thanksgiving in freedom which it invites; to experience that reciprocity is a matter of relationship rather than possession – a typically Pauline definition of what it means to live in a 'state of grace'. (The later definition of the Council of Trent uses this phrase in a narrower sense, to mean sanctification by grace [e.g., of absolution] for receipt of the Blessed Sacrament.)

In Paul's epistles justifying or saving grace is thus set against not only the Law but also human works or moral effort. There are at least two theological meanings of the term *works* in Scripture, both of which are taken up in later literature. First, there are what Paul calls 'the works of the law', obedience to covenant requirements (Torah) which focuses especially on the ceremonial commands, or Halakah. These had been adduced by some of Paul's contemporaries as the proper means of achieving a right relationship with God. Paul emphatically denies that for followers of Jesus these suppositions are appropriate (Romans 3–4; cf. 9:31–33; 11:6; Galatians 2:14 – 5:14). Attempting to earn one's own way to God does not produce or add to salvation, he argues. Rather, it detracts from Christ's work on the cross and is thus a type of apostasy. There are, however, 'good works' (as opposed to 'dead works', Hebrews 9:14; 'works of the flesh', Galatians 5:19, or 'works of darkness', Romans 13:12), and they are a necessary expression of a person committed to God, the fruit of every true conversion. So St James (2:14–26) argues that an intellectual conversion to orthodoxy without practical works is useless and unredemptive. Jesus points to his works as evidence of his relationship with the Father (John 14:10–11) and expects the same from his followers (Matthew 5:16). Repeatedly the New Testament calls Christians to such 'works', which are mainly charitable actions (2 Corinthians 9:8; Ephesians 2:10; Colossians 1:20; 2 Thessalonians 2:17; 1 Timothy 6:18; Hebrews 10:24). These will be the basis of future judgment (1 Corinthians 3:13–15; 1 Timothy 5:25; 1 Peter 1:17; Revelation 20:11–15; 22:12; cf. Matthew 25), and even now they are being examined and judged in this world by Christ, who knows all (Revelation 2–3).

A related issue in subsequent interpretation of the Pauline definition of grace concerns whether grace is given to an individual because of his or her faith, or whether personal faith is itself the effect of God's grace. Paul himself does not appear to notice a problem here, nor does he try to set grace and faith in any causal relationship (Ephesians 2:8–9; Romans 4:16) – faith is simply the manner of receiving the gift and acknowledging that it is free and unmerited (Romans 3:21–31). In his epistle to the Galatians, accordingly, Paul takes up the traditional contention of Judaism that persons may gain favour with God by moral and religious achievement, countering with an insistence that one has status with God only through faith – which is to say, in effect, only through accepting one's salvation as an unearned 'gracious' gift from God. Paul argues in Romans that Israel's own divine election should be understood in this way: Israel was chosen by grace (11:5) and not because 'of works, but of him that calleth' (9:11). What Scripture shows to be most remarkable about God's grace towards humankind is its sheer extravagance, a 'grace abounding' – always exceeding expectations as much as deserts (Romans 5:15, 18; 2 Corinthians 4:15; Ephesians 1:7, 23; 2:7).

Old English poetry with its emphasis on the Old Testament develops the notions of 'glory', 'power', and salvation from the experience of uncertain exile in places where later poetry will talk of the experience of an 'inward' grace. Old English *are,* as in the opening lines of 'The Wanderer' (*'Oft him anhaga are gebide…'*), can mean 'mercy' but also 'honour', 'glory', or, in the social sense, 'grace'. The strong Nordic idea of perseverance in hardship may seem to colour some Old English poetry with a slight Pelagian tint, but grace is more often simply displaced as a principal subject because of the stronger appeal of Old Testament heroism and the motifs of exile and pilgrimage.

Middle English poetry tends, by reason of later catechetical formulation and a parallel social concern for grace as 'courtesy', to see Christ's action on the cross less in terms of its raw heroism (cf. 'The Dream of the Rood') and more as a gracious and divine noblesse oblige. This pattern is still clear in the Anglo-Norman poem 'Christ's Chivalry' (D. Jeffrey and B. Levy, *The Anglo-Norman Lyric,* 1989, no. 29). Grace in this period is closely connected to mercy: 'Mercy and grace moste hem then stere', writes the *Pearl* poet (*Pearl,* 623), speaking of 'enabling' grace. The *Pearl* poet consciously opposes any idea of salvation by works, not only in *The Pearl* itself but in *Cleanness,* where all guilt is said to be forgiven only through grace (731). But grace is universal: 'alle called on that cortesye and claymed his grace' (1097). The great theme of *Pearl* is that 'the grace of God is gret inogh' (612, 624, 625, 636, 648, 660) for any who are brought into the kingdom by the water of baptism which flowed from the wound of Christ on the cross (649–53). The idea that the font of every grace is the Passion of Christ is Bonaventuran as well as Augustinian, but *Pearl* is particularly an ally of 14th-century English theologians such as Bradwardine,

Fitzralph, and Wyclif against resurgent neo-Pelagian and semi-Pelagian notions of 'merited grace'. For Chaucer's Parson, repentance is crucial to the operation of grace; without it no one may see God.

After the Reformation grace is treated in English literature from a diversity of theological perspectives. The contrast of grace and works is not so evident in Renaissance literature, in part because of the position taken in the *Official Homilies* (1562) of the Church of England. The three-part sermon 'Of Good Works annexed unto Faith' (1.5), construing the connection in terms of the apparent split between the apostle Paul and the epistle of James, concludes that good works are indeed necessary and profitable, though only if performed in faith (cf. also 'Of good Works; and first of fasting', 2.4). Shakespeare's *Measure for Measure* sets itself a 'straw man' (Angelo) who embodies a Calvinist Puritan notion of grace by election, then uses the Puritans' favourite texts from Romans to make the point that mercy is to be preferred to justice; indeed, that mercy is a function of grace. The gracious Duke ('your Grace') motivates reconciliation wherever he obtains the cooperation of human will in his kingdom. His arch rival, the strife-making Lucio, knows well enough the biblical doctrine of grace, and Shakespeare uses him comically to highlight his point that the role of God's grace in human affairs is simpler and more to be valued than the theological warfare with which it was burdened in the 16th century. Speaking to a bewildered pair of 'gentlemen', ostensibly about the subject of a 'grace' before meals, Lucio says mischievously, 'Grace is grace, despite of all controversy. As, for example, thou thyself art a wicked villain, despite of all grace' (1.2.25–27) – a statement concerning the sinner's absolute need of grace with which no theological party could disagree.

John Donne, raised a Catholic but later an Anglican priest, knew both principal traditions: in his poetry 'sinne insinuates twixt just men and grace' ('Elegie on Mrs Boulstred'); grace, however, keeps the soul from sin ('Death', 36). A person may fall into mortal sin, but contrary to the conclusion of Marlowe's Faustus, 'Yet grace, if thou repent, thou canst not lacke' ('Holy Sonnet 4'). It is God, nonetheless, who gives the grace necessary for repentance and conversion (cf. Aquinas, *De Veritate*, 28.2). In 'Goodfriday 1613', Donne concludes by praying, 'Restore thine Image, so much, by thy grace, / That thou may'st know mee, and I'll turne my face' – lines which recall the notion of Chrysostom and Aquinas that what God recognizes in persons, by the presence of grace, is his own handiwork or 'reflection', and that there is thus, in Aquinas' words, 'no conversion to God unless God turn us' (*Summa Theologica* 1a–2ae.109.6; cf. John 6:44). The principle, if not the phrasing, is here conformable to Calvin as well. George Herbert's 'Grace' is a poem about the powerlessness of the best-intended Christian endeavour without grace; Herbert's good preacher will, accordingly, follow the model of Jesus in his teaching, by bringing 'out of his treasure things new and old; the old things of Philosophy, and the new of Grace' (*A Priest to the Temple*, 23). Herbert implies by this contrast, here and elsewhere, that grace cannot be reduced to precept or analysis; the Parson like anyone else must in the face of his own sin and inadequacy 'creep to the throne of grace' ('Discipline') and 'throw' himself there in recognition of his own inability to understand and unworthiness to administer the mysteries of faith and the sacraments (*A Priest to the Temple*, 22). In his 'Prayer before Sermon' he comes there again:

> O brand it in our foreheads forever: for an apple once we lost our God, and still lose him for no more; for money, for meat, for diet: But thou Lord... hast exalted thy mercy above all things; and hast made our salvation, not our punishment, thy glory: so that then where sin abounded, not death, but grace superabounded...

Here the throne of mercy, clearly, is the font of grace.

Grace Abounding to the Chief of Sinners, or the brief Relation of the exceeding Mercy of God in Christ to his poor servant John Bunyan (1666), drawing its title from Paul (Romans 5:15–20; cf. 6:1), is a homiletic spiritual autobiography focusing on the unmerited as well as the 'abounding' character of grace. Bunyan's discussion of grace is more intense and 'enthusiast' than Jeremy Taylor's eloquent description of grace in 'daily experience' (*Via Intelligentia*, 31ff.), but the underlying understanding is Calvinist in both cases, to the degree that Taylor's comments (1662) may serve as an introduction to Bunyan's text.

The Enlightenment tended to highlight other objects of admiration. One effect of this was to deflect poets from religious subjects altogether. Alexander Pope began his prodigious career with paraphrases, one of which, 'done by the author at 12 years old', is of Thomas à Kempis: 'Speak, Gracious Lord, oh speak; thy Servant hears', and asks for 'grace to hear' and 'grace afford' to receive the word of God. Fifteen years later, attuned to a time in which Nature and Reason were seen by the Deists (as well as some Anglicans and Catholics) as prompting human virtue more often than grace, Pope understands grace as, in effect, a backstop to reason: 'If I am wrong, Thy Grace impart / To find that better Way' ('The Universal Prayer'). At the height of his career, in his *Essay on Man* (1730–32), he proclaims that 'The gen'ral ORDER, since the whole began, / Is kept in Nature, and is kept in Man' (1.5.171–72), and that 'Whatever is, is right' (1.10.294). Here Pope illustrates the degree to which a doctrine of grace is sustainable in its strong form only where there is a correspondingly strong sense of a fallen and disjointed world. Pope resists Catholic as well as Protestant theological efforts to split Grace and Nature, Grace and Works (or 'Virtue') (12.2.80–92).

Two poets of the next generation, one Catholic and one Anglican (and Calvinist), each in his own way distressed by Reason's evident fallibility and Nature's corruptibility by human sin, give grace a more central place. Christopher Smart sees himself as a beneficiary of particular saving grace, comparing himself to the healed King Hezekiah in 'Hymn to the Supreme Being', while in *Jubilate Agno* he reiterates the theme that human history and nature are alike redeemed by grace, and their beauty and health hence made known in grace or, to put it another way, recognized in the act of thanksgiving. Hence: 'the Sin against the HOLY GHOST is INGRATITUDE.' It is grace which helps one see redemption's work, grace which makes one grateful:

> 'Tis the story of the Graces,
> Mercies without end or sum;
> And the sketches and the traces
> Of ten thousand more to come.

> Lift, my children, lift within you,
> Dread not ye the tempter's rod;
> Christ our gratitude shall win you,
> Wean'd from earth, and led to God.
> (*Hymn* 22, 'Gratitude')

William Cowper views grace in a strict Calvinist light, 'grace undeserv'd – yet surely not for all!' ('Truth', 483) – i.e., grace is made available independently of human volition and effort, or even in spite of it. Human choices are not, however, entirely irrelevant for Cowper, since though the will may not choose grace, it can refuse it once offered:

> Grace leads the right way: if you choose the wrong,
> Take it, and perish; but restrain your tongue.
> Charge not, with light sufficient, and left free,
> Your wilful suicide on God's decree.
> ('Truth', 17–20)

Cowper's priest at Olney, John Newton, less rigidly Calvinist than his parishioner and always mindful of his own radical conversion from sordid profiteering in the slave trade (*Authentic Narrative*, 1764), composed the hymn 'Amazing Grace'. Its celebration of grace is written in the spirit of Smart's gratitude and ties its experience in Pauline and Augustinian fashion to the inception of faith, 'the hour I first believed'.

In the 19th and 20th centuries grace at least as a subject in poetry is either almost entirely diffused in Nature (as in the Romantics and Tennyson) or else subsumed in the matter of salvation (as in Francis Thompson's 'The Hound of Heaven', in which the persistent love and grace of Christ rescues the narrator despite his utter lack of desert: 'How hast thou merited – of all men's clotted clay the dingiest clot?'). If it is 'saving grace' which characterizes the poetry of Catholic converts such as Thompson and Belloc, 'habitual grace' is celebrated by Hopkins:

> the just man justices;
> Keeps grace: that keeps all his goings graces;
> Acts in God's eye what in God's eye he is –
> Christ. ('As Kingfishers')

but each in such a way as to reveal the imprint not only of post-Tridentine but the medieval theology of grace. For Hopkins, as for the Romantics, nature, too, reveals grace in its beauty, though it must yield at last to 'God's better beauty, grace' ('To What Serves Mortal Beauty').

T.S. Eliot conjures in *Ash Wednesday* with the face of Christ looking down from the cross and reflects that there is 'no place of grace for those who avoid the face' (5.18), ending his poem with the plea: 'And let my cry come unto Thee'. In the American poet Richard Wilbur's 'Grace', a poetic reflection on Hopkins, there is a consideration of the degree to which grace in nature, habitual grace, and human freedom expressed in choice come together; perfect grace is then perfect freedom, even where 'piety makes for awkwardness'.

David L. Jeffrey
University of Ottawa
Peter H. Davids
Langley, British Columbia

Heaven

The primary meaning of *heaven* in the Bible is 'that which is above the earth'. Although it can refer (in either singular or plural) to the sky or heavenly bodies, its important religious meaning is the transcendent 'other' world, the abode of God. Throughout the Old Testament God is called the Lord of heaven and is pictured as dwelling in a transcendent heaven (e.g., Genesis 14:19; Exodus 20:22; Deuteronomy 4:36; Psalm 103:19; Ecclesiastes 5:2). The epithet 'God of heaven' is recurrent in the Old Testament (e.g., 2 Chronicles 36:23; Nehemiah 2:4; Daniel 2:18, 19).

Throughout the Bible the term *heaven* appears as a synonym and metonym for God (Genesis 49:25; Luke 15:18, 21; John 3:27). Heaven is also the abode of angels, as in the Old Testament vision of Jacob – in which angels were seen ascending and descending a ladder which reached from earth to heaven (Genesis 28:12–13) – and numerous New Testament passages (Matthew 18:10; Mark 12:25; Luke 2:15).

Two aspects of heaven are distinctive to the New Testament.

Heaven is said to be the place from which Christ came and to which he returned (John 3:13; 6:33, 38, 50, 51, 58; Luke 24:51; Acts 1:11). In the epistles the ascended Christ is pictured as one 'who is gone into heaven, and is on the right hand of God' (1 Peter 3:22; cf. Ephesians 6:9; Colossians 4:1). The New Testament also pictures heaven as the place where believers are glorified and eternally present with God (Colossians 1:12; 1 Peter 1:4). The greatest repository of passages picturing heaven as the abode of God and glorified believers is the book of Revelation, where the word appears more than fifty times and where chapters 4, 7, 19, 21, and 22 contain the most extensive descriptions of heaven in the Bible. In Revelation 21 – 22, heaven and earth are pictured as joined in the New Jerusalem, the antitype of Eden. Like the paradisal garden, the heavenly city has a tree of life and fountain of pure water issuing from its centre (from under the throne of God, a detail also foreshadowed in Zechariah 14:8).

In rhetorical terms, heaven is generally described in one of five ways: (1) contrast, in which the qualities of heaven are set over against those of earth or hell; (2) negation, in which imperfections are denied to heaven; (3) analogy, in which heaven is likened to some feature of earthly reality; (4) distancing, in which the mystery of heaven is preserved by picturing it as remote from ordinary human experience; and (5) conceptual imagery, in which terms such as bliss, joy, and peace are used to suggest a realm which transcends physical reality.

The greatest medieval vision of heaven, Dante's *Paradiso*, is Italian, but it had a profound impact upon English and other literatures. The English work most similar to it is *Pearl*, a dream vision which pictures heaven as a city of jewels and light, inhabited by glorified saints and distanced from earth by a river. The Old English *Doomsday* poem concludes with a detailed picture of the glory of those who will dwell in heaven. For morality plays like *Everyman*, heaven is the acknowledged destination of every Christian soul after this life; *contemptus mundi* literature takes for granted the contrast between the eternal heavenly realm and the transience of earthly things.

In the Renaissance, Spenser pictures heaven at the end of the November eclogue of *The Shepheardes Calender,* in *An Hymne of*

Heavenly Love and *An Hymne of Heavenly Beauty,* and in *The Faerie Queene,* 1.10.55–58. Marlowe's *Doctor Faustus* repeatedly alludes to the Christian concept of heaven as a place of transcendent glory and reward. Giles Fletcher's *Christ's Victorie and Triumph* is an exalted poetic description of heaven, while Bunyan's *Pilgrim's Progress* makes the Celestial City the goal of his protagonist's quest. Heaven is, for Bunyan, the joyous end, God's place, which renders worthwhile all the perils and rigors of earthly wayfaring. Milton picks up an idiom familiar in Shakespeare (e.g., *A Midsummer Night's Dream,* 1.1.207; 2.1.243), to 'make a heaven of hell' or 'hell of heaven', to characterize the rejection of an objective paradise by the self which insists on its autonomy. Satan's thesis, that 'The mind is its own place, and in itself / Can make a Heav'n of Hell, a Hell of Heav'n' (*Paradise Lost,* 1.254–55), while a harbinger of modernist epistemologies, is here his attempt to rationalize away his eternal loss of heaven's joys.

Milton's elaborate treatment of heaven reflects the Reformers' (especially Calvin's) emphasis upon a carefully imaged heaven as the goal of Christian pilgrimage. Heaven appears as a major part of Milton's imaginative world even in his early poetry (e.g., 'On Time', 'At a Solemn Music', 'Lycidas', and Sonnets 9, 14, 19, 23). The heaven presented in *Paradise Lost,* especially books 3, 5, and 6, is a transcendent reality accommodated to human eyes and shaped to a surprising degree by free creaturely action. A revolt of the angels leads to war in heaven, a mining of heaven's floor, the invention of cannons, and a short-term transformation of the landscape. Such a heaven appears to be a realm of process and contingency, though Milton's God says emphatically that he is approached by neither necessity nor chance.

Heaven is also one of the most important subjects of 17th-century lyric poets such as Vaughan ('Peace', 'They Are All Gone into the World of Light'), Crashaw ('A Hymn to… Saint Teresa'), Traherne ('Shadows in the Water', 'Felicity'), Herbert ('Heaven'), and Herrick ('The White Islands: or Place of the Blest'). Descriptive pictures of heaven are most predictable in poetic elegies; examples include Donne's *Second Anniversarie* and Dryden's 'Ode on the Death of Mrs. Anne Killigrew.'

The Saints' Everlasting Rest (1650), the most popular treatise on heaven in the 17th century, presents at great length the felicity of the blessed, a felicity which includes all the activities appropriate to and delighted in by the rational soul. The fourth part of the work is a manual on heavenly meditation. This devotional method, preached also by the popular Puritan divine Richard Sibbes, represented within Reformed tradition the strategy of the affirmative way evidenced much earlier in Dante's *Paradiso:* earth is seen as the pilgrim way to heaven.

In the Enlightenment, English letters saw an abundance of casual references to heaven, but virtually all of these alluded either to the natural domains of sky and stars or, in a religious context, to a vague transcendent realm which admits of no detailing.

Bolder treatments are evident again with the 19th-century poets. In *The Excursion,* Wordsworth presents a heavenly afterlife as the only suitable context for human affections 'else betrayed and lost.' In book 14 of *The Prelude* he traces out the course of spiritual love, necessarily ending in 'Eternity, and God.' Tennyson, in his eclectic poem celebrating Arthur Hallam, *In Memoriam* (1850), presents his conviction that heaven must involve a continuation of personal and self-conscious life along with the recognition of and reunion with loved ones; moreover, it must allow for growth and service. These sentiments are echoed by Robert Browning, through a variety of dramatic spokesmen, in *The Ring and the Book.* In 'Paracelsus' Browning argues that heaven must also involve the opportunity to correct earthly error. Heaven makes notable appearances, also, in the poetry of Francis Thompson ('The Kingdom of God'), Gerard Manley Hopkins ('The Starlight Night'), and Emily Dickinson ('I Never Saw a Moor', 'Heaven has Different Signs to Me'), and in T.S. Eliot's play *Murder in the Cathedral.*

The fullest fictional exposition of the Christian heaven in the 20th century has come from C.S. Lewis. While the Edenic paradise is vividly detailed in *Perelandra,* a fantasy set upon an unfallen Venus, the more strictly heavenly paradise is set forth in the dream-allegory *The Great Divorce* (a work which disjoins what Blake had put together in *The Marriage of Heaven and Hell).* Lewis' contemporary, J.R.R. Tolkien, has written his own artful allegory of the heavenly afterlife in the story 'Leaf by Niggle.'

In the poetry of Theodore Roethke heaven is a framing concept.

'All finite things reveal infinitude', Roethke says, in a vein reminiscent of Wordsworth. His verses explore in a variety of ways the imagery of the edge, where finite and infinite meet. Heaven is left without specified content, however, and in this reticence Roethke allies himself with all those moderns who, cautious about the possibility of revelation, remain silent on the question of transcendence.

Leland Ryken
Wheaton College
U. Milo Kaufmann
University of Illinois

Hell

The word *hell* derives from the Anglo-Saxon root *hel* or *hol*, meaning 'to conceal' or 'hide.' In Old Norse mythology, Niflheim was an underground world ruled by Hel or Hela, 'the queen of death.' The most common Hebrew word in the Old Testament for the place of the dead is *Sheol*, which was not, at first, a place of punishment. In the time of the Pharisees, Sheol came to include a place of retribution called *Ge-Hinnom* (Greek *Gehenna*), a name derived from the valley outside Jerusalem where municipal waste was incincerated by continual fires.

In its earliest conception Sheol shared certain general features with Semitic heathenism, especially the view that the departed retained a degree of knowledge of and power over the living. In contrast, Psalm 88:12 depicts Sheol as a place of forgetfulness, in which there is 'no work, or thought, or knowledge, or wisdom' (Ecclesiastes 9:10); all 'love, hatred, and envy has perished' for the dead, who no longer have 'a portion for ever in any thing that is done under the sun' (Ecclesiastes 9:5–6). The overall impression of the Old Testament hell is of a pallid state of monotonous tranquillity (Job 3:17–19) not unlike the classical Hades, a gloomy abode of the dead. In the New Testament the abode of the dead is called 'Hades' and retains the same force as Old Testament 'Sheol.' Tartarus, a dark abyss below Hades, and reserved as a place of punishment, is the Greek equivalent of Gehenna.

Despite minor variations, including disagreement over whether

Sheol is located underground (Numbers 16:30), under water (Jonah 2:7), or under mountains (Job 26:5), Sheol is at first seen as an ethically neutral place inhabited by both the righteous and the evil. Judgment of the dead is a feature of later Old Testament writing, as in the book of Daniel ('Many of those who sleep in the dust of the earth shall awake, some to everlasting life, and some to shame and everlasting contempt', 12:2). Daniel, along with apocalyptic books written between Maccabean and New Testament times, develops the idea of resurrection which came to exercise a profound influence on early Christianity and affected a transition from the neutral Sheol to the retributive Gehenna.

Essential New Testament teaching on hell is contained in Matthew 25:41, 46, where Jesus is depicted at the Last Judgment separating the sheep from the goats and dismissing the damned 'into everlasting fire, prepared for the devil and his angels'. The sins leading to eternal punishment are failures of love, especially in this instance the refusal of charity and hospitality to the disadvantaged. St Paul also specifies that fornicators, idolaters, adulterers, the effeminate, abusers of themselves, drunkards, revilers, and extortioners (1 Corinthians 6:9–10) and those who practise witchcraft, variance, emulations, sedition, and heresy (Galatians 5:20) shall not inherit the kingdom of God.

Each of the synoptic gospels mentions Gehenna, describing it as a place of unquenchable fire (Matthew 5:22; Mark 9:43), of torture (Matthew 5:25–26), of darkness, weeping, and gnashing of teeth (Matthew 8:12; 13:42; Luke 13:28), and of never ending corruption (Mark 9:48). Revelation foresees a general judgment at the end of the millennial period when death and hell deliver up their dead for judgment 'according to their works', whereafter death and hell are to be cast into the lake of fire (Revelation 20:13, 14).

Some of the early Fathers propounded vivid materialistic descriptions of hell (e.g., St Basil of Caesarea, De Spiritu Sancto, 40; St John Chrysostom, Ad Theodorum lapsum, 1.9–10). Most assumed it to be a place of literal fiery torment. In the 3rd century, however, Origen questioned the literal nature of hellfire, identifying hell rather as a spiritual state of separation from God, and in De principiis he advanced the doctrine of apokatastasis or universal salvation. His view was judged heretical at the council of Alexandria in 400, which upheld the opinion of St Augustine in *De civitate Dei* 21.2–10; 22.19 that the damned, while suffering spiritually, are also embodied and burn everlastingly in literal flames. St Thomas Aquinas reiterated this view, arguing that the punishments of hell are twofold: pain of loss of the vision of God and pains of sense – both in proportion to the gravity of wilful, unrepented sin. Among the Reformers, Luther rejected the graphic medieval representations of hell and regarded Jesus' 'descent into hell' as the anguish of his separation from God. Calvin, following Luther, disputed a biblical basis for a literal place called hell, treating the corporeal images of hell in Scripture as figurative for the terrors occasioned by wilful sinfulness.

Anglo-Saxon poetry reflects a popular belief in a connection between hell and morasses, as, for example, in *Beowulf,* where the home of Grendel, a 'feond on helle', is located in the fen districts. Later medieval thought was dominated by Plato's geocentric theory of the sun and planets, according to which each sphere grew more sublime with its distance from the earth up to the final Empyrean or realm of pure essences. Since reality became coarser as it approached the earth's centre, it was logical to think that hell, as the most grotesque of realities, should be located there. Copernican theory challenged the basis on which such ideas were founded and led to attempts to site hell elsewhere. In 1714, for example, Tobias Swinden (*An Enquiry into the Nature and Place of Hell*) suggested the centre of the sun as more plausible because it was both hotter and roomier. Nevertheless the idea of a subterranean hell continued to dominate Christian imagination as it had that of the Old Testament and classical antiquity. Several possible entrances to hell have been proposed. Rabbinic literature often mentions the notorious valley of Hinnom. Lake Avernus was favoured by Virgil, Lucretius, and Livy and echoed by Spenser: 'deepe Avernus hole, /... descends to hell' (*Faerie Queene* 1.5.31). Equally celebrated is Taenarus in the southern Peloponnese, described by Apuleius as one of the 'ventilation holes of the underworld'. In medieval literature and iconography the entrance to hell is often depicted as a mouth, a view deriving from Isaiah 5:14 and recurring in the Psalter of St Swithin's Priory, the famous York Minster Mouth of Hell, and adapted metaphorically in Tennyson's *Charge of the*

Light Brigade: 'Into the mouth of hell / Rode the six hundred' (25-26). The ladder, bridge, and dark wood (cf. Spenser, *Faerie Queene* 1.1.13; Dante, *Inferno,* canto 1) were also considered avenues or pathways to hell.

The signal description of hell and its inhabitants in the Western literary tradition is that of Dante, in his *Inferno,* which provides a stock of graphic images to later writers (and artists). Homiletical literature, particularly that which has a penitential focus, also affords a store of images. Chaucer's Parson, outlining the 'thridde cause that oghte moeve a man to contricioun', provides a harrowing account of the 'Day of Doome' and of 'the horrible peynes of helle.' In so doing he provides a rich compendium of patristic and medieval commentary on the subject (*Canterbury Tales,* 10.157–230). Penitential tracts in subsequent periods almost invariably include similar materials. Among the most celebrated and influential postmedieval accounts of hell in English literature are those of Spenser's *Faerie Queene* and Milton's *Paradise Lost.* Spenser's treatment of hell's torments (1.5.34–35) are largely derived from Ovid's *Metamorphoses* (books 4 and 10), the *Odyssey* (book 11), and the *Aeneid* (book 6). In depicting the physical features of hell in *Paradise Lost,* Milton also borrows from classical sources. Five infernal rivers, Styx, Acheron, Cocytus, Lethe, and Phlegethon, feed into the burning lake; the climate is sulphurous, a 'darkness visible'; hell's portals are ninefold gates guarded by gorgons, hydras, and chimeras where Satan meets Sin and Death. The damned are exposed by turns to 'fierce extremes' of fire and ice, just as Claudio in *Measure for Measure* fears that his soul will 'bathe in fiery floods' or 'reside / in thrilling region of thick-ribbed ice' (3.1.121–22), a torment reflected in Dante (*Inferno,* 32.29–30), categorically confirmed by St Thomas Aquinas (*Summa Theologica,* supp. 3.2.97), and mentioned in a variety of medieval lyrics (e.g., C. Brown, *English Lyrics of the XIIIth Century,* no. 296, line 71).

Milton's imagination, however, was most keenly engaged by the notion of an inner hell, expressed in Satan's cry 'Myself am Hell' (*Paradise Lost,* 4.75). The idea was not original to Milton but had its root in Virgil (*Aeneid,* 6.743) and in patristic commentaries. Among Milton's more immediate literary precedents are Marlowe's *Doctor Faustus,* where Mephistopheles asserts, 'Why, this is hell, nor am I out of it', and Sir Thomas Browne's more prosaic 'I feel sometimes a hell within myself' (*Religio Medici*, 1.51). Nevertheless, Milton's treatment of hell as an inward condition rather than an external location was profoundly influential, especially among the English Romantics. Satan's *non-serviam* speech in book 1 of *Paradise Lost* and his view that 'the mind is its own place' lie behind the statement of Byron's *Manfred*: 'The mind... makes itself /... Is its own origin of ill and end – / And its own place and time' (3.4.129–32). It is also the inspiration for Wordsworth's *Prospectus to the Recluse*, in which he argues that traditional views of heaven and hell can not breed such 'fear and awe' as when 'we look / Into our Minds, into the Mind of Man – / My haunt, and the main region of my song' (38–41), an idea dramatically reworked in Hopkins' sonnet, the 'mind has mountains; cliffs of fall / Frightful, sheer, no-man-fathomed...' (9–10) and echoed in T.S. Eliot's *The Cocktail Party* ('What is hell? Hell is oneself') and in Robert Lowell's *Skunk Hour* ('I myself am hell').

For writers from the 19th century onwards hell has often become a metaphor for the city. Blake's *London* is darkly satanic, for Shelley 'Hell is a city much like London / A populous and smoky city' (*Peter Bell*, 3.1), while Wordsworth places the 'monstrous anthill' London at the centre of the *Prelude*, the point at which in classical epics the hero usually descends into the underworld. A major precedent for the association of the city and hell is *Paradise Lost* (book 9), where Satan issues from hell as one 'in populous city pent' and breaks into the bucolic landscape of Eden. Just as Edenic imagery was assimilated by the tradition of pastoral poetry, the city has in modern writing absorbed the imagery of hell. To the 'modern imagination the city becomes increasingly something hideous and nightmarish', as Northrop Frye observes (*The Modern Century*, 1967, 37), citing the 'fourmillante cité' of Baudelaire, the 'unreal city' of Eliot's Waste Land, and the 'ville tentaculaire' of Verhaeren.

Contemporary literature also reflects the continuing debate concerning the dogma of eternal punishment and the existence of a literal hell. Since the 17th century scepticism concerning hell has been increasingly widespread while at the same time such thinking has been condemned as subversive for undermining the bulwarks of society. Thus William Dodwell concludes that 'since men have learned to ward off the Apprehensions of Eternal Punishment, Progress of Impiety and Immorality among us has been very considerable' (*The Eternity of Future Punishment Asserted and Vindicated*, 1743, 85). Notwithstanding Dr Johnson's firm response to Dr Adams on the meaning of 'damned': 'Sent to Hell, Sir, and punished everlastingly!' (Boswell's *Life of Johnson*, 1960, 1296) the debate has continued. The dismissal of F.D. Maurice from King's College, London, in 1853 for his unorthodox views on eternal punishment, and the rebuttal of such opinions by Joseph Cottle, arguing that they had extinguished 'hell with a Trope' and confuted 'Heaven with a syllogism' (Cottle, *Essays on Socinianism*, 1850, 114, 149) are items in the ongoing controversy.

Stephen Dedalus reflects on the terrors of hell in response to Father Arnall's vivid fire and brimstone sermon in *A Portrait of the Artist as a Young Man* (chapter 3), but his agonies of conviction and spiritual apprehension are short-lived. George Orwell observes, sarcastically, that 'Most Christians profess to believe in Hell. Yet have you ever met a Christian who seemed as afraid of Hell as he was of cancer?... I say that such belief has no reality. It is a sham currency like the money in Samuel Butler's Musical Banks' (*The Collected Essays*, 3.147–48). Yet modern literary pictures of hell are common, from Shaw's depiction of it as culture without pain to Golding's *Pincher Martin*, where hell is viewed as egoism attempting self-creation. In Graham Greene's *Brighton Rock*, the value of positive belief in hell is set against the spiritual emptiness of modern life. Vivid modern reifications of personal damnation occur in works as diverse as Oscar Wilde's *Picture of Dorian Gray* (1890) and Charles Williams' *Descent into Hell* (1937).

Michael Goldberg
University of British Columbia

Holy Spirit

In the Bible, *spirit* originally denoted the mysterious life force of creation, evident in the wind, in breath, and in experiences of ecstatic or charismatic endowment. The overlap of meaning is most clearly seen in Ezekiel 37:9 and John 3:8 and 20:22. Although the early concept was dynamistic in character, Israel's monotheism ensured that this cosmic force was always seen within the Old Testament as God's. The term 'Holy Spirit' itself appears in only two Old Testament passages (Psalm 51:13; Isaiah 63:10–11), and indicates that this mysterious and invisible power partakes of God's awesome purity and splendour. The more common term is 'Spirit of God' (e.g., Genesis 1:2; Job 12:10; Ezekiel 37:7–10); this spirit holds sway in history (Exodus 33:14–17) and is imparted to chosen individuals (e.g., Abraham, Moses, Gideon), especially to the prophets (e.g., Isaiah, Jeremiah, Ezekiel).

In the New Testament Jesus' incarnation is attributed to this Spirit (Luke 1:35; John 1:1–14, 32–33), and his ministry was launched by further endowment following the descent of the dove at his baptism in the Jordan (Mark 1:10; John 1:33–34; Acts 10:38); he was subsequently sent by the Spirit into the desert to be tempted (Matthew 4:1; cf. Milton, *Paradise Regained*, 1.189–95). These events were understood by the early Christians as a fulfilment of Isaiah 61:1–2 (see Luke 4:18), and Jesus himself understood his ministry thus empowered as evidence of the inbreaking of God's final rule (Matthew 12:28). He promised that his disciples would experience the same inspiration in their own ministry (Mark 13:11; cf. Acts 1:8), a promise elaborated in John's gospel in terms of the Spirit as the Paraclete or Comforter (John 14:16–17, 26; 15:26–27; 16:5–15).

Christianity traces its beginning to such an experience of empowering and charismatic endowment by the Spirit at Pentecost (Acts 2:1–4), and the New Testament writers attributed its early expansion to the initiative of the same Spirit acting upon and through various individuals (Acts 6:8–10; 8:9–17; 10:19–20, etc.). The apostles Paul and John in particular present the work of the Spirit in personal renewal as the beginning of the Christian life (John 3:3–8; 7:37–39; Romans 8:9; Galatians 3:2–3), and as the beginning of a transformation which will end in the resurrection of the body (Romans 8:11, 23; 2 Corinthians 1:22; 3:18; 4:16 – 5:5). The Holy Spirit was experienced as coming to expression in a variety of ways (e.g., Romans 5:5; 1 Corinthians 1:4–7; 6:9–11; Galatians 3:5; 5:22–23), and daily life was expected to reflect the Spirit's presence and direction (e.g., Acts 9:31; Romans 8:4–6, 14; 1 John 3:24). This common participation 'in the Spirit' was seen as the basis of the common life of the early believers (1 Corinthians 12:13; Ephesians 4:3–4; Philippians 2:1), and Paul especially expected the worship of the Church to be guided by the Spirit (Romans 12:3–8; 1 Corinthians 12:4–11). Both Paul and John were nevertheless conscious of the need to maintain a critical attitude toward individual claims of inspiration (1 Corinthians 2:12–16; 14:29; 1 Thessalonians 5:19–22; 1 John 4:1-3), one principal criterion being that the Holy Spirit was now also understood as the Spirit of Christ (John 14:26; 16:12–15; Romans 8:9–17; 2 Corinthians 3:17 – 4:6).

The formal doctrine of the Church concerning the Holy Spirit developed much more slowly than did Christology, and in the early period was largely subsumed under it in connection with invocation or discussion of the Trinity, as in the baptismal formulary and catechesis (e.g., St Irenaeus, *Adversus haereses* 2.6.4 and 'Proof of the Apostolic Preaching', 1.1, 6ff.). Sometimes identified by heterodox thinkers with the Word (e.g., Theophilus, *Ad Autolycum*, 2.10; 2.15), or said to have been created by the Son (as in Arianism), the Spirit was recognized as having full divine status with the Father and Son by the Council of Constantinople (AD381). The Nicene Creed asserted that the Holy Spirit 'proceedeth from the Father.' To this statement, in the 6th-century Synod of Braga, was added the *filioque* clause ('and from the Son'), an addition rejected by the Greek Church. Though Pope Leo III declared the *filioque* unnecessary to the Creed, it was included again by Pope Benedict VIII (1014).

Anglo-Saxon poetry reflects this early concern for Trinitarian theology: references are brief and tend to locate or praise the power of the *halig gaest* as an agency of the Godhead. In the tenth Advent Lyric of the *Exeter Book* (10–11), Father and Son are addressed directly, with the comment added: '*Baem inc is gemaene / heahgaest hleofaest*' ('Common to you both is the protecting Holy Spirit').

St Augustine's *De Trinitate* provided another basis for the development of Western doctrine, defining the Holy Spirit as the love which binds the Father and the Son. Peter Lombard's *Sententiae* later identified grace with the action of the Holy Spirit, building on St Ambrose's identification of the water of grace as a 'pouring out of the Holy Spirit' (*De Spiritu Sancto*, 1, introduction 15–18). Ambrose, in turn indebted to Greek writers (ironically including both St Basil the Great and St Athanasius from the other side of the *filioque* controversy), takes issue with heretical interpretations of Amos (especially 4:13) which would make the Spirit 'created' and essentially the 'Spirit of Nature' (2.6.48–55). The identification of the Holy Spirit with grace was contested in the 13th and 14th centuries, with the Scholastics maintaining that the indwelling of the Spirit in individuals spoken of in Scripture is only an 'appropriation.' St Thomas appears to hew a line closer to Augustine than most. Although he identifies the Holy Spirit with the 'gifts of the Holy Spirit' (*1 Sententiae*, 14.2.1), he says that '*Love*... is the proper name of the Holy Spirit, as *Word* is the proper name of the Son' (*Summa Theologica*, 1a.37.1). He adds, however, that it is of the essence of love to be indivisibly a gift: 'A gift is freely given, and expects no return. Its reason is love. What is first given is love; that is the first gift. The Holy Ghost comes forth as the substance of love, and *Gift* is his proper name' (*Summa Theologica*, 1a.38.2).

In Middle English poetry references to the Holy Spirit are often associated with the 'gifts' of the Holy Spirit (e.g., 'Com, shuppere, Holy Gost' by William Herebert, translating the Latin hymn *Veni Creator Spiritus*; cf. R. Greene, *The Early English Carols*, no. 327). Invocations of the Trinity are also common in the Middle English lyric; sometimes these add a prayer for protection to the Holy Spirit. In one such poem occurs an extensive catalogue of symbols of late medieval pneumatology:

> To whome is approched, the holy gost by name,
> The third person, one god in trinite,
> Of parfite loue thow art the gostly flame.
> Emperour of mekeness, pease & tranquyllite,
> My coumford, my counsell, my parfite charite,
> O water of life, O well of consolacion,
> Agaynst all stormes of hard aduersite....
> (C. Brown, *Religious Lyrics of the XVth Century*, no. 51)

The association of the Holy Spirit with the incarnation is persistent in Annunciation lyrics and carols (e.g., Brown, *Religious Lyrics of the XIVth Century*, no. 16, '*Mater Salutaris*'; 18, 'Prayer of the Five Joys'; 60, 'A

Song to the Queen of Heaven'; also R. Greene, *The Early English Carols,* nos. 31, 96, 236), as is, more rarely, the descent of the Holy Spirit in the form of a dove at Christ's baptism as a sign of God's authentication:

> When Jhesus Criste baptyzed was
> The Holy Gost descended with grace;
> The Fader voys was herde in the place:
> *'Hic est Filius meus; ipsum audite.'* (Greene, no. 131)

The Corpus Christi plays include Christ's words from John's gospel about the Comforter (e.g., Chester 15.241–48; 23.194–200) and project a parallel between the life of the Bride of Christ (his Church) and the life of the Virgin Mary his mother. These plays also recall that the Spirit had been given to the prophets in anticipation of the incarnation and New Covenant which they announced (e.g., Chester 8.318–24). In *St Erkenwald,* the miracle of restored life occurs because the Holy Spirit is invoked in prayer. In Chaucer's *Second Nun's Tale,* Cecile assures her brother, in terms from the Apostles' Creed, that those who receive Christ obtain eternal salvation, as 'The Goost, that fro the Fader gan procede, / Hath sowled hem, withouten any drede' (8.328–29).

The Reformation brought few modifications to the doctrine of the Holy Spirit except an increased emphasis on his prompting of the preaching of the gospel. For Luther, 'the Holy Spirit comes and preaches, that is, the Holy Spirit leads you to the Lord, who redeems you' and 'it is the Holy Spirit who sanctifies us' (*Sermon on the Catechism,* 1, *Werke,* 51.164–66). For Calvin it is the 'Communion of the Holy Spirit' which guarantees participation in the covenant; the Spirit not only 'adopts' individuals into the family of God but assures them of their salvation and pours out upon them the water of 'quickening grace' which 'irrigates' their lives for fruitful service (*Institutes,* 3.1.2–3).

Concern for perseverance in the state of grace is, however, a strong theme in Reformation theology. Calvin modifies Augustine's definition of the unpardonable sin – obstinate distrust of forgiveness persisted in until death – saying, 'he sins against the Holy Spirit who, while so constrained by the power of divine truth that he cannot plead ignorance, yet deliberately resists and that merely for the sake of resisting.' He continues: 'Those who are convinced in conscience that what they repudiate and impugn is the word of God, and yet cease not to impugn it, are said to blaspheme against the Spirit [cf. Matthew 12:31], inasmuch as they struggle against the illumination which is the work of the Spirit', and concludes, 'You will perceive that the Apostle speaks not of one particular lapse or two, but of the universal revolt by which the reprobate renounce salvation' (*Institutes*, 3.3.22–23).

When in England Bishop Latimer takes up the question (circa 1562), he has a less defined sense of what the specific 'sin against the Holy Ghost' might be, and reduces the problem to its crux: a refusal to cry out for God's mercy. Latimer is sceptical that anyone can judge whether another has committed this sin (it is not *de facto* in evidence when one is abstinent from worship or resistant to catechism) and counsels against preoccupation with any imagined 'unpardonable' offence: 'Despair not of the mercy of God, for it is immeasurable… for though a man be wicked at this time, yet he may repent, and leave his wickedness tomorrow, and so not commit that sin against the Holy Ghost' (*Sermon* 25). The predicament of Marlowe's *Doctor Faustus* invited from its original audience reflection on such definitions. Offense against the Spirit is considered in quite different terms by George Herbert in his poem on Ephesians 4:30, 'Grieve not the Holy Spirit.' Here, the poet marvels that God's Holy Spirit might 'grieve' when he lapses from the purity of his own commitment ('when I am swore / And crosse thy love'); such knowledge prompts in him tears of contrition.

In Cranmer's *Homilies Appointed to Be Read in Churches* (1562) prayer for help in adversity is to be directed to the Holy Spirit especially ('Concerning Prayer'; cf. Robert Herrick's 'His Letanie, to the Holy Spirit'), as is prayer for 'illumination' or insight (cf. Calvin, *Institutes*, 3.1.4). For many Protestant poets, the Holy Spirit was in fact invoked as 'muse'. Whereas in the Middle Ages the third person of the Trinity had often been pictured as a dove of inspiration coming into the ear of theological writers and biblical translators, writers in a more secular context most often called upon the Virgin Mary to inspire their verse, especially from the time of St Bernard of Clairvaux; she is memorably invoked on a number of occasions by Chaucer. Spenser, however, as a Protestant poet, seeks what he regards as a more appropriate source of inspiration in 'An Hymne of Heavenly Love':

Yet, O most blessed Spirit, pure lampe of light,
Eternall spring of grace and wisedom trew,
Vouchsafe to shed into my barren spright
Some little drop of thy celestial dew,
That may my rhymes with sweet infuse embrew,
And give me words equall unto my thought,
To tell the marveiles by thy mercie wrought. (43–49)

Milton's muse, invoked at the beginning of *Paradise Lost,* recollects Spenser's 'most gentle sprite breathed from above', the spirit of creation. Yet in saying that he intends the Spirit who 'on the secret top / of *Oreb,* or of *Sinai,* didst inspire / That Shepherd, who first taught the chosen Seed' (1.6–8), he suggests a view of the Holy Spirit compatible with both rabbinic and Calvinist formulations. Donne's 'Ascension' concludes: 'And if thy holy Spirit, my Muse did raise, / Deigne at my hands this crown of prayer and praise': only the Holy Spirit can render human words fit homage to Christ. Ben Jonson's 'The Sinner's Sacrifice' makes use of the *filioque* clause for a wider sense of 'inspiration':

Eternal Spirit, God from both proceedings,
Father and Son; the comforter, inbreeding
Pure thoughts in man: with fiery zeal them feeding
For acts of grace. (25–28)

In the later 17th and 18th centuries, an increasing popular emphasis on the Holy Spirit, either in inspiration or as a bestower of charismatic 'gifts of the Spirit', brought about from proponents of 'rational religion' the charges of 'enthusiasm', or ungoverned subjectivity and emotionalism. Dryden's *Religio Laici* (404–16) sees charismatic spirituality as anti-intellectual and in vulgar disrespect of even biblical authority:

The tender Page with horney Fists was gaul'd;
And he was gifted most that loudest baul'd:
The *Spirit* gave the *Doctoral Degree:*
And every member of a *Company*
Was of *his Trade,* and of the *Bible free,*
Plain *Truths* enough for needfull *use* they found;
But men wou'd still be itching to *expound:*

Each was ambitious of th'obscurest place,
No measure ta'n from *Knowledge,* all from GRACE
Study and *Pains* were now no more their Care;
Texts were explain'd by *Fasting,* and by *Prayer:*
This was the Fruit the *private Spirit* brought;
Occasion'd by *great Zeal,* and *little Thought.*

Dean Jonathan Swift, who would have concurred with these sentiments, felt that the Holy Spirit was to be imagined as conferred on prelates episcopally, and not much spoken of otherwise ('On Dr Rundle, Bishop of Derry'). Exacerbating these feelings among conservative Anglicans was the rapid rise in popularity of the evangelicals and especially Methodists after 1730. John and Charles Wesley in particular preached the 'Indwelling of the Holy Spirit in Believers' and their meetings were often attended by 'charismatic manifestations', leading in turn to much literary and even artistic satire (e.g., Kenrick's 'On the Investigation of Truth'; Hogarth's 'Enthusiasm Delineated'). Though the emotional William Cowper might be suspected of 'enthusiasm', his poetry exhibits a typical Calvinist reserve concerning the Holy Spirit, who is invoked only as the 'spirit of instruction' ('Bill of Mortality', 1790).

In literature the tradition of the Holy Spirit as a source of personal inspiration was taken over by the Romantic movement and psychologized in a fashion anticipated to some degree even in Blake. In Blake's *Jerusalem: The Emanation of the Giant Albion,* the prophetic admonition is:

Go, tell them that the worship of God is honouring his gifts
In other men & loving the greatest men best, each according
To his Genius which is the Holy Ghost in man; there is no other
God than that God who is the intellectual foundation of
Humanity. (4.91.8–11)

Blake criticizes the abstraction of Milton's Trinity, and especially the thinness of his treatment of the Holy Spirit: 'in Milton, the Father is Destiny, the Son a Ratio of the five senses, & the Holy Ghost a vacuum!' ('The Marriage of Heaven and Hell'). While he himself prays in orthodox fashion, 'Teach me, O Holy Spirit, the Testimony of Jesus!' (*Jerusalem,* 3.74.14), he fashions his myth of prophetic inspiration for a world in which rationalism has almost displaced spirituality:

> For thus the gospel Sir Isaac [Newton] confutes:
> 'God can only be known by his Attributes;
> And as for the Indwelling of the Holy Ghost
> Or of Christ & his Father, it's all a boast
> And Pride and Vanity of the imagination,
> That disdains to follow this World's Fashion.'
> ('The Everlasting Gospel', 43–48)

In American letters the Romantic sublimation of the Holy Spirit to artistic genius is reflected in the writings of Ralph Waldo Emerson, where it is the brooding Spirit of Nature, the 'Worldsoul' or 'Passive Master' Emerson finds in every religious and artistic high moment:

> In groves of oak...
> Still floats upon the morning wind
> Still whispers to the willing mind,
> One accent of the Holy Ghost
> The heedless world hath never lost. ('Problem', 58–62)

Nineteenth-century texts often reveal a cynicism concerning claims made for the operation of the Holy Spirit in personal affairs. Emily Dickinson, who 'would run away / From Him – and Holy Ghost – and all...' (*Poems*, no. 413), is metaphysically apprehensive about what it might mean to be 'Bride of the Holy Ghost' (no. 817). Charlotte Brontë's Jane Eyre is on the one hand repulsed by her rejected suitor St John Rivers' affected invocations of 'the help of the Holy Spirit to subdue the anger I have roused in him', but says later:

> I mounted to my chamber; locked myself in; fell on my knees; and prayed in my way – a different way to St John's, but effective in its own fashion. I seemed to penetrate very near a Mighty Spirit; and my soul rushed out in gratitude at His feet.

G.M. Hopkins effectively resublimates the Romantic apotheosis of the Spirit of Nature to Creation and the action of the third person of the Trinity in its renewal:

And for all this, nature is never spent;
There lives the dearest freshness deep down things;
And though the last lights off the black West went
Oh, morning, at the brown brink eastward, springs –
Because the Holy Ghost over the bent
World broods with warm breast and with ah! bright wings.
('God's Grandeur')

By contrast, 'Father, Word, and Holy Breath' (*Ulysses*) are alike abstracted from nature for Joyce, whose Stephen Dedalus wonders only briefly if he has 'found the true church all of a sudden in winding up to the end like a reel of cotton some finespun line of reasoning upon insufflation or the imposition of hands or the procession of the Holy Ghost' (*Portrait of the Artist as a Young Man*, chapter 5). Though more self-consciously antagonistic, Joyce bespeaks an affinity with Emerson when he writes of the Irish housewife in his story 'Grace' that 'her faith was bounded by her kitchen, but, if she was put to it, she could believe also in the banshee and in the Holy Ghost.'

Margaret Avison's poem '...Person or a Hymn on and to the Holy Ghost', in the vein of Herbert, sees the Holy Spirit as 'the self-effacing / whose other self was seen / alone by the only one', and prays,

to lead *my* self, effaced
in the known light,
to be in him released
from facelessness,
so that where you
(unseen, unguessed, liable
to grievous hurt) would go
I may show him visible.

An evocation of the Spirit's role in revealing the second person of the Trinity is also found in Larry Woiwode's *Even Tide*, where the Holy Spirit is presented typologically as 'Second Adam's Eve... within the Word walking' (44).

David L. Jeffrey
University of Ottawa
James D.G. Dunn
University of Durham

Incarnation

The term incarnation refers to the unique union of divinity and humanity in Jesus Christ, the study of which is known as Christology. Although variously construed, the doctrine is central to all Christian theological traditions and germane to broader understanding of the relationship between God and creation (cf. Colossians 1:14–20). The New Testament's treatment is declarative rather than explanatory. The prologue to the gospel according to John asserts that 'the Word was made flesh' (1:14) – the Greek sarx denoting not merely the physical body but humanity in its fullness (*Theological Dictionary of the New Testament* 7.139) – as the climax to the creation of the cosmos and the epitome of God's self-revelation. Other passages, notably Philippians 2:5–11, develop implicit themes of descent and ascent and establish the doctrine's paradoxical force.

The New Testament does provide evidence of early disputes with Gnosticism over the question of Jesus' human nature (1 John 4:1–3). Such controversy within Christianity, together with the need to respond to Jewish and pagan refutations, led to doctrinal elaboration during the patristic era. Two distinct and opposing views emerged: one, associated with Alexandria, stressed the divinity of Christ; and the other, associated with Antioch, his humanity – each assailing the inadequacy of the other. Thus St Cyril of Alexandria guarded Christ's divinity by championing the term theotokos – 'God-bearer' – for the Virgin Mary, whereas St Gregory of Nazianzus advocated Jesus' humanity, physical body and human soul: 'For that which he has not assumed, he has not healed; but that which is united to his Godhead, is also saved' (Epistle 101). In 451 the Council of Chalcedon endorsed the 'Tome' (Epistle 28) of Leo I, who argued that by the principle of *communicatio idiomatum* the properties of both the divine and the human natures could be attributed to the single person of Jesus. In its definition, which for a millennium would be accepted almost universally as the basis for further discussion, the council decreed that Jesus be confessed as having 'two natures, without mingling, without change, indivisibly, undividedly [united], the distinction of the natures nowhere removed on account of the union but rather the peculiarity of each nature being kept, and uniting in one person and substance...'

In the centuries following, western European writers turned increasing attention to Jesus' human nature as they grew concerned with matters of soteriology and sacramental theology. St Anselm's argument for the logical necessity of the incarnation (*Cur Deus Homo?*) was followed by scholastic disputes on whether the incarnation would have taken place at all if not for the Fall. Meanwhile, affective devotion to Jesus' humanity was incorporated into the theological schemes of such influential monastic writers as St Bernard of Clairvaux, adopted by mystical writers of the via positiva, and promoted in the vernacular by the Franciscans.

With the Reformation, the controversy between the two major parties of Protestantism... over the real presence of the body and blood of Christ in the Lord's Supper... was responsible for the most detailed Western preoccupation with the intricacies of christology since the ancient church (J. Pelikan, *The Christian Tradition*, 4, 1984, page 158).

The Reformed party stressed the distinction between the two natures of Christ, as in John Calvin's explication of the Apostles' Creed (*Institutes*, 2.2). Lutherans emphasized the unity of his person (Augsburg Confession, article 3), with Luther himself prescribing adherence to the 'Deus incarnatus et humanus Deus' (In *Epistola S. Pauli ad Galatas Commentarius*, 1.3) and declaring that 'to seek God outside of Jesus is the devil' ('extra Iesum quaerere Deum est diabolus', In XV Psalmos Graduum, Psalm 130:1). Reflecting an alternative tradition, more radical Protestants would avoid the intellectual problem altogether, as in the Mennonite Dordrecht Confession (1632): 'But how, or in what manner, this worthy body was prepared, or how the Word became flesh, and He Himself man, we content ourselves with the declaration which the worthy evangelists have given and left in their description thereof...' (article 4).

Modern developments – being heavily influenced by a philosophical aversion to metaphysics and by the rise of the historical method – have tended to focus on existential, psychological, and moral dimensions of the incarnation. In *The Essence of Christianity* (1841), the German positivist Ludwig Feuerbach claimed,

> The incarnation, the mystery of the 'God-man', is... no mysterious composition of contraries, no synthetic fact... it

is an analytic fact – a human word with a human meaning…
And the incarnation has no other significance, no other
effect, than the indubitable certitude of the love of God to
man. (trans. George Eliot, 56–57)

In a similar vein, Emerson declared in his Divinity School Address
(1838) that Jesus' authority lay in his proclamation of the universal
incarnation of God in humanity. The new developments in biblical
criticism were notably represented in Schweitzer's *The Quest for the
Historical Jesus* (1906; translated 1910) and radically epitomized in
Bultmann's 'demythologizing': 'For what God has done in Jesus Christ
is not an historical fact which is capable of historical proof' (*Jesus Christ
and Mythology*, 1958, 80). Reflecting 20th-century developments while
contending with tradition, recent treatments – from the Second Vatican
Council's *Pastoral Constitution on the Church in the Modern World*
(1.1.22) to *The Myth of God Incarnate* (ed. John Hick, 1977) – have
focused on the cultural significance of the doctrine.

Christological concerns appear throughout the history of
English literature. The Dream of the Rood depicts the communicatio
idiomatum graphically and dramatically: 'I saw the journey-ready
beacon / shift in robes and colours; now it was reddened with wet /
drenched with the shedding of blood, now it was sheathed with
treasure' (21b–23, trans. B. Huppél). Reflecting the rise in affective
devotion, medieval lyric poetry on the Passion often employs detailed
description and the language of romantic love. In contrast, the 15th-
century 'A God and yet a man?' cedes both 'witt' and affection,
preferring a simple faith – 'Beleeve and leave to wonder!' (C. Brown,
Religious Lyrics of the XVth Century, no. 120). Julian of Norwich
integrates affective response and theological rigour in her *Showings*,
arguing for the essential unity of her mystical experience on the basis
of the incarnation: 'For I saw full suerly that oure substance is in god,
and also I saw that in oure sensualyte god is…' (Long Text 55, eds.
Colledge and Walsh, 2.566–67.23–25). Whereas medieval mystery
plays featured Jesus' humanity, often in realistic detail (see especially
the York Crucifixion play of the Pinners and Painters), post-
Reformation concern to avoid idolatry and sacrilege led to a ban on
the onstage representation first of God the Father and then of Jesus –
a prohibition which survived in Britain until the 20th century.

The paradox of the incarnation provided apt subject matter for the metaphysical poets, as in Richard Crashaw's 'Hymn on the Holy Nativity' (1652):

> Wellcome all WONDERS in one sight!
> AEternity shutt in a span.
> Sommer in Winter. Day in Night.
> Heaven in earth, and GOD in MAN. (79–82)

While devotion to Jesus' humanity continued, lyrical treatments took a sentimental turn: John Milton's 'Ode on the Morning of Christ's Nativity' – its hymn 'a present to the infant God' – has its direct progeny in Christina Rossetti's 'A Christmas Carol' ('In the bleak mid-winter'), and for Robert Browning the incarnation becomes a symbol of 'archetypal Love'. Paralleling scholarly debate on the historical Jesus, 20th-century literature has often stressed Jesus' humanity: D.H. Lawrence depicts him in sheerly physical, sensual terms in *The Man Who Died*, whereas Dorothy Sayers – offering an orthodox corrective to the other extreme – presents The Man Born to Be King 'realistically and historically', as the one in whom 'the prophecies of the poets had become furnished with a name, a date, and an address.'

In the face of intractable doctrinal dissent, poets of the past two centuries have often turned to broader considerations, particularly those of a literary nature. While Shelley sees 'Imagination' as 'the immortal God which should assume flesh for the redemption of mortal passion' (Preface to *The Cenci*) and Jesus as the supreme poet who 'divulged the sacred and eternal truths [of Platonism]... to mankind' (*A Defence of Poetry*), Auden views the incarnation as 'redeeming' the poetic function: 'Because in Him the Flesh is united to the Word without magical transformation, Imagination is redeemed from promiscuous fornication with her own images' ('The Meditation of Simeon', *For the Time Being*). Addressing matters comprehensively in his own epic meditation, Eliot presents the incarnation as the key to the mysteries of time, eternity, and art: 'The hint half guessed, the gift half understood...' in which 'the impossible union / Of spheres of existence is actual' ('The Dry Salvages').

Robert E. Wright
National Humanities Centre, North Carolina

Predestination

The verb *predestine*, from which the noun is formed, comes from Latin *praedestino,* the Vulgate rendering of *proorizo* (translated 'predestine' in Romans 8:29, 30; Ephesians 1:5, 11, King James Version; also in Acts 4:28, Revised Standard Version).

Biblically speaking, predestination refers to almighty God planning in eternity everything that he would bring about in historical time, particularly the salvation of sinners (Matthew 25:34; Ephesians 1:4; 2 Timothy 1:9; 1 Peter 1:20). The New Testament insists that all saving grace given to human beings in time (knowledge of the gospel, understanding of it and power to respond to it, preservation and final glory) flows from God's eternal predestination. Luke, for example, in Acts bears striking witness to his belief, not merely that Christ was foreordained to die, rise, and reign (Acts 2 and 4), but that salvation comes through prevenient grace (2:47; 11:18, 21–23; 14:25; 15:7–11; 16:14; 18:27) according to divine foreordination (13:48; 18:10).

John records Christ saying that he was sent to save all whom the Father had 'given' him (John 6:37–39; 17:2, 6, 9, 24; 18:9). These are his 'sheep', his 'own' (John 10:14–16, 26–29; 13:1), for whom specifically he prayed (John 17:20). He undertakes to 'draw' them to himself by his Spirit (John 12:32; cf. 6:44; 10:16, 27; 16:8–11); to give them eternal life in and through fellowship with himself and the Father (John 10:28; cf. 5:21; 6:40; 17:2–3; Matthew 11:27); to keep them, losing none (John 6:39; 10:28–29; cf. 17:11, 15; 18:9); to bring them to his glory (14:2–3; cf. 17:24), and raise them immortal (6:39–40; cf. 5:28–29; 11:23–26). Here it is implicit that those who enjoy salvation in Christ do so by virtue of divine grace.

St Paul elaborates: from eternity God had a plan to save a church (Ephesians 3:3–11). The plan was that lost sinners should be set right with God and adopted as his children and heirs through Christ, that they should further be renewed in his image (Ephesians 1:3–6; Romans 8:29), and that the whole company of those undergoing this renewal should grow to the fulness of Christ and eventually be made glorious as he is (Ephesians 4:13; 5:25–27). Believers should rejoice in the certainty that as part of his plan God predestined them personally to share this destiny (Romans 8:28–30; 2 Thessalonians 2:13; 2

Timothy 1:9), graciously choosing them with no regard for their desert and indeed in face of their foreseen ill-desert (Ephesians 2:1–10). From God's sovereign predestinating choice of them flows, first, an effective calling, i.e., a summons to faith and repentance which elicits the response it seeks (cf. 1 Thessalonians 1:5; 2:13); then, through faith, justification, the gift of pardon and acceptance for Jesus' sake; then, the life of sanctification, which from Paul's perspective is glorification begun (2 Corinthians 3:18; 2 Thessalonians 2:13–14); and thereafter glorification in its fulness (Romans 8:30). Paul gives this teaching to Christians, persons who knew themselves 'called', to assure them of present security and final salvation, and to make them realize the extent of their debt to God's mercy, and so lead them into great gratitude for great grace. That salvation is through predestination is thus basic to Paul's view of Christianity.

The biblical theme of predestination has, then, two focal centres. From one standpoint it belongs to the doctrine of God, affirming that whatever happens under God's sovereign providence was foreordained. In this respect it broaches problems such as the existence of evil and the suffering of the innocent. Varying conceptions of God's personhood, rationality, wisdom, goodness, freedom, foreknowledge, and power in relation to his world produce different understandings of foreordination, and issues of theodicy (is God arbitrary? is he the author of sin? are his ways justifiable?) press down on the whole discussion. Such issues are reflected in literature in a variety of ways. In *King Lear,* Gloucester argues that 'As flies to wanton boys, are we to the gods; / They kill us for their sport' (4.1.38–39). In *Paradise Lost* (2.557–61), Milton writes of a group of devils who, sitting apart on a hill,

> reasoned high
> Of Providence, Foreknowledge, Will and Fate –
> Fixed fate, free will, foreknowledge absolute,
> And found no end, in wandering mazes lost.

This is satirical comment on academic discussion in Milton's own age, when, as in the later Middle Ages, much inconclusive speculation on these matters took place. In later years the doctrine of a sovereign, predestining God often yielded to angry renunciation, as, for example, in Hardy's grim commentary at the conclusion to *Tess of the D'Urbervilles:* 'Justice was done, and the President of the Immortals... had ended his sport with Tess.'

From the other standpoint, however, biblical predestination belongs to the doctrine of grace, affirming that God saves some (not all) of a guilty, helpless, corrupt humanity, according to his own free and sovereign choice. In this context what may in one light have appeared disastrous (e.g., the Fall) can prove the necessary ground of future joy. So Milton writes of the *felix culpa:*

> O goodness infinite, goodness immense!
> That all this good of evil shall produce,
> And evil turn to good; more wonderful
> Than that by which creation first brought forth
> Light out of darkness! (*Paradise Lost*, 12.469–73)

This view raises moral and pastoral questions concerning the reality or otherwise of free will and responsibility, the causes of faith and unbelief, the importance or irrelevance of holy living and prayer, and the range and grounds of Christian assurance. Is there, as Hamlet concludes, 'a divinity that shapes our ends, / Rough-hew them how we will' (5.2.10–11), or is it, as Herbert momentarily imagines in 'The Collar', that 'My lines and life are free; free as the road, / Loose as the wind, as large as store'?

Since both sets of questions bear on doxology and devotion together (do I honour or dishonour God by attributing everything to his predestination, including the salvation of those who are saved, myself included, and the damnation of those that are lost?), it is no wonder that they have been hotly discussed in most centuries since St Augustine set the agenda of debate. Periodically the heat has been somewhat mitigated by voices like that of Boethius (*De Consolatione Philosophiae*, 2.m8; 3.m9; 4, pr. 6), who urged restraint of the impulse to rage against divine order, a nuancing of the Augustinian position not unlike that which appealed in the 18th century to Alexander Pope in his rational theodicy *An Essay on Man:*

> All Nature is but Art, unknown to thee;
> All Chance, Direction, which thou canst not see;

All Discord, Harmony not understood;
All partial Evil, universal Good. (1.289–92)

Pope's enlightenment naturalism, however, declared in the next couplet, reflects a very non-Boethian fatalism: 'One truth is clear, "What ever is, is RIGHT".' Such scepticism concerning rational argument on this issue is in its effect not unlike that of Milton (*Paradise Lost* 8.167–84; *Samson Agonistes*, 300–323), but proceeds from a different premise. The lines of the chorus in *Samson Agonistes*, for example, beg to be compared with the earlier lines of Samson himself, who, 'eyeless in Gaza', self-remonstrates:

Yet stay, let me not rashly call in doubt
Divine Prediction; what if all foretold
Had been fulfill'd but through mine own default,
Whom have I to complain of but myself? (43–46)

Until Augustine debated the Pelagians (412–30), Christian teachers had in fact said little about predestination. Combating the fatalism of Gnostics and others, they stressed each person's free will, ability, and responsibility to do right, and the eternal significance of one's present decisions. No one disputed St Clement of Alexandria's view of Romans 8:29 as teaching that God's predestining of those whom he will glorify depends on his foreknowledge of what they will do. Augustine points out (*De fide et operibus*) that even Christians can be lost: the problem of predestination is here linked with the question of final perseverance (*De dono perservantiae, Patrologia Latina*, 45.993–1027). Augustine urged, however, that fallen human beings are morally and spiritually twisted by original sin in the direction of pride and self-assertion against God, so that they cannot choose to love, adore, and serve their Maker (*De praedestinatione sanctorum*). Therefore God must bestow the faith which issues in love, and the gift of perseverance, on anyone whom he is going to save. The foreknowledge spoken of in Romans 8:29 is not passive precognizance but active predetermination: God in sovereign freedom, foreseeing all, chooses out of the corrupt mass of sinful humanity those whose hearts and wills he would change (*Enchiridion*, 107). Christ is central to this predestining purpose, for God first chose him to be Saviour and Head and then chose particular sinners to trust in him and become his spiritual body, the flock of which he is Shepherd. Salvation, first to last, is thus the work of God, who gives to his elect what he requires of them, and knowing this is so will give proper shape to faith, love, and hope. Augustine's predestinarianism became thus a full-scale interpretation of Christian existence.

The reflections of some late medieval philosophers challenged this interpretation fundamentally enough to make it an issue of significant importance for secular literature in the 14th century, bequeathing a legacy of both comic and serious speculation, yet defining the terms of the Reformation and modern debate. William of Occam, for example, elaborated the basis for a distinction between absolute predestination and predestination as foreknowledge – i.e., whether predestination is an act of the will or of the intellect. Adoption of the latter view opens the way to a notion of 'co-operation', by which God decides to elect because of the good works he foresees. In Occam's commentary on Lombard's *Sentences* (*1 Sent.* d.41.q.1G) he thus allows that God may require one to do one's very best to obtain saving grace. Reflecting on the conversion of St Paul and the grace accorded the Virgin Mary (which he finds not to be on the basis of merit, though other cases for him do involve merit), Occam concludes that God predetermines some with cause and some without. Thomas Bradwardine, the 14th-century bishop (and, briefly, Archbishop of Canterbury) takes the strict form of the doctrine of absolute predestination *ante praevisa merita,* but like Albert the Great (*1 Sent.* d.40.a18), he attempts to safeguard the meaningfulness of human freedom by rejecting the *necessitas consequentis* which implies a compulsion of cause and effect and, like Duns Scotus, he feels that 'it is obvious that a predestined person can be damned, because he has free will' (*1 Sent.* d.40.q.1a.1–3). Bradwardine's attack on Pelagian approaches to predestination seeks to counter Occam's emphasis on merit, as well as that of Occam's pupils such as Holcot and Woodham. His *De Causa Dei* elaborates thus a distinction between absolute and 'conditional' necessity (lib. 3), upholding the spontaneity of the will; humans are not at the same level as animals, which have no free 'volitio'. As persons are moved by God, their responsibility is based upon the fact that they are not conscious of this and thus act freely.

It is this distinction which Chaucer has in mind in the beast fable told by his Nun's Priest. The tale is about the almost-successful capture of the rooster Chaunticleer by a devilish fox, a parable about the process and consequences of sin in one of the 'elect' which comically engages the questions of reprobation, election, free will, and necessity. Blaming Chaunticleer for not heeding his prophetic dream of warning ('Thou were ful wel ywarned by thy dremes', 7.3232), the Nun's Priest alludes to the huge body of scholastic discussion of 'certein clerkis' (3234–39), allowing

> But I ne kan nat bulte it to the bren,
> As kan the hooly doctour Augustyn,
> Or Boece, or the bisshop Bradwardyn,
> Wheither that Goddes worthy forwityng
> Streyneth me nedely for to doon a thyng –
> 'Nedely' clepe I symple necessitee –
> Or elles if free choys be graunted me
> To do that same thyng or do it noght
> Though God forwoot it er that it was wroght;
> Or if his wityng streyneth never a deel
> But by necessitee condicioneel. (7.3240–50)

The conclusion of his tale amplifies the question rather than delineating an answer. Similar concerns are taken up again in *Troilus and Criseyde* when the pagan lover, on realizing he has been jilted by Criseyde, 'consoles' himself: 'For al that cometh, cometh by necessitee: / Thus to ben lorn, it is my destinee' (4.958–59). Troilus then goes on to rehearse the arguments concerning whether or not God's foreknowledge destroys 'oure free chois every del' (1059) for more than 120 lines. Here, as in *The Nun's Priest's Tale*, however, the implication is that the 'fre chois... yeven us everychon' (971) is, despite God's foreknowledge and predestination, inescapably bound up with human responsibility: it is that which makes for tragedy, as well as comedy. As Milton's God says in *Paradise Lost* (3.102–19):

> Freely they stood who stood, and fell who fell.
> Not free, what proof could they have giv'n sincere
> Of true allegiance, constant Faith or Love,

Where only what they needs must do, appear'd,
Not what they would? what praise could they receive?
What pleasure I from such obedience paid,
When Will and Reason (Reason also is choice)
Useless and vain, of freedom both despoil'd,
Made passive both, had serv'd necessity,
Not mee. They therefore as to right belong'd,
So were created, nor can justly accuse
Thir maker, or thir making, or thir Fate;
As if Predestination over-rul'd
Thir will, dispos'd by absolute Decree
Or high foreknowledge; they themselves decreed
Thir own revolt, not I: if I foreknew,
Foreknowledge had no influence on their fault,
Which had no less prov'd certain unforeknown.

In the New England Puritanism of Cotton Mather's *Magnalia Christi Americana* (1702), on the other hand, history repeats eternal models precisely because it is predetermined by God from the beginning of time: this is what undergirds his view of the American settlers as the New Covenant elect.

Augustine's account of predestination has been a theological crux in biblical interpretation ever since his day. His thesis has been reaffirmed by some, including St Thomas Aquinas, who, using his Aristotelian paradigm and treating the theme as part of the doctrine of providence, defined predestination as God's 'set way (*ratio*) of directing a rational creature to eternal life as his end' (*Summa Theologica* 1.23.1). Luther, in *De Servo Arbitrio* (*The Bondage of the Will*), used Augustinianism polemically to subvert Erasmus' development of the notion of mankind's meritorious cooperation with enabling grace. Calvin, like Jansenius, defined predestination as a decision (*decretum* or 'decree') which included, alongside the gracious choice of some sinners for salvation, the just reprobation of the rest. Calvin's doctrine, parodied by the drunken Cassio in Shakespeare's *Othello* 'Well, God's above all: and there be souls must be saved, / and there be souls must not be saved' (2.3.105–07) – involved a verbal (not substantial) change from that of Augustine, who had defined predestination as God's choice of sinners to save and had treated reprobation as a separate subject.

The Augustinian formulation favoured by many Puritan thinkers involved a view of both salvation and reprobation operating under the auspices of providence. Daniel Defoe's *Robinson Crusoe* reflects this more resigned view when he looks at his post-shipwreck situation in a positive light: 'I then reflected that God, who was not only righteous but omnipotent, as He had thought fit thus to punish and afflict me, so He was able to deliver me; that if He did not think fit to do it, 'twas my unquestioned duty to resign myself absolutely and entirely to His will; and, on the other hand, it was my duty also to hope in Him, pray to Him, and quietly attend to the dictates and directions of His daily providence.'

Thomas Hobbes presages a secular determinism which has affinities with this doctrine, showing in *Leviathan* that a strict determinist can easily concede human free will so long as he can maintain that individuals must always do what the strict chain of causes obliges them to, a position he concludes to be identical with much Reformation theology.

In the darker Calvinism of Herman Melville, *Moby Dick* is an embittered debate over predestination and free will in which Ahab, the demonic hero, is fated or predestined, as Captain Peleg declares, to be a simulacrum of his biblical forerunner. *Pierre* also struggles with the insoluble conflict of predetermination and free will, reflecting the internal debate of an author who was nurtured on the formulations of the Synod of Dordrecht (1618–19), and whose very rebellion against Calvinism, ironically, is formulated in the vocabulary of Calvinism. (Ahab even considers the Manichean position, asking, 'Be the white whale agent, or be the white whale principal... ?' but without resolution.)

A variety of theologians have chosen rather to modify than simply reaffirm Augustine's thesis. Semi-Pelagians, patristic (e.g., St John Cassian), medieval (e.g., Gabriel Biel), and modern (e.g., Post-Tridentine Roman theologians such as Suarez and Bellarmine and Arminian Protestants such as Watts and Wesley) suspend salvation on a grace-aided human decision, or on a series of decisions which, though divinely foreseen, are not divinely determined. In the 20th century Karl Barth has reconstructed the doctrine in terms of mankind's solidarity in Jesus Christ: he represents Christ as mankind first reprobated on the cross and then elected in the resurrection, and holds that the human race is now actually elect and redeemed in the Mediator. This position, perhaps anticipated to some degree by Aquinas (*Summa Theologica*, 3.q.24.a.4), attempts to parry the accusation of divine arbitrariness and injustice; Barth in fact claims to turn predestination into good news by absorbing it into the gospel, rather than leaving it as a separate dark truth overshadowing the gospel. But the issue is one of theological exegesis: which construction flows naturally from the relevant texts? Does 'predestiny', as the American poet Larry Woiwode puts it, continue to lie like 'a cold spoon on the birthright of speech', or is it the basis for a joyful affirmation of divine providence, such as leads the poet to conclude his volume, 'I love our everlastingly interleaved / Lives predestined and reinstated by / The Word' (*Eventide*, 15.20; epilogue)? The debate continues.

James I. Packer
Regent College
David L. Jeffrey
University of Ottawa

Resurrection

Belief in resurrection is at the core of Christian faith. It has as its foundation the death and rising again of Christ, proclaimed in the gospel as the promise of a future general resurrection when the dead will be raised for judgment and reward. The interdependence of the resurrection of Christ and that at the Last Judgment is succinctly articulated by St Paul when he writes to the church at Corinth that 'if there be no resurrection of the dead, then is Christ not risen: And if Christ be not risen, then is our preaching vain, and your faith is also vain' (1 Corinthians 15:13–14). The New Testament typically does not so much reflect metaphysical speculation as express confidence in the ultimate defeat of death, the end of the curse resulting from the Fall (cf. Romans 6:9–11; 1 Corinthians 15:20–22).

The Christian doctrine of resurrection is distinguished from belief in reincarnation, which usually involves a series of rebirths from which the soul may seek release; nor is it the same as a doctrine of immortality, which concerns only the indestructibility of souls. Resurrection instead has primary reference to bodies. It is literally a 'rising again' (the root meaning of the Greek anastasis and the Latin resurrectio), or a 'rousing up' (egeiro, the Greek verb often used in the New Testament, means 'to awaken' or 'to arouse'). Since this raising up is to judgment and transformation in the life to come, resurrection is also distinguished from mere reanimation, a return to mortal life, which is subject again to death (as in the Lazarus story, John 11).

During Jesus' own ministry he disputed sharply with the Sadducees about the dead (Mark 12:18–17) and demonstrated his power in restoring life on three occasions (Luke 7:11–17; 8:49–56; John 11). Such words and deeds, however, achieved their full significance only in the light of his own resurrection, when, on the 'third day', he triumphed over death. The gospel accounts struggle with the sameness and newness of Jesus' resurrected body: it is the same Jesus who asks to be handled and fed (Luke 24:39, 41), yet he is difficult to recognize (Luke 24:16; John 20:14), disappears or appears at will (Luke 24:36; John 20:19), and finally ascends to heaven (Luke 24:51).

Among the evangelists, John emphasizes that Christ's resurrection life has already begun in believers (e.g., John 6), a process to be completed in resurrection at the end time (6:54; 11:23–26). Paul's message is essentially the same, though he expresses it in the symbolism of baptism; since those who are 'in Christ' have new life here and now, their coming out of the burial waters of baptism is like a resurrection (Romans 6). There is future promise as well: physical death is only a sleep (1 Corinthians 15:51; cf. Matthew 9:24; John 11:11–13), from which believers shall be wakened at the summons of the trumpet (1 Corinthians 15:52; 1 Thessalonians 4:16). The destiny of the believer remains Paul's chief concern, and his themes are sameness and transformation. In the simple image of seed and full-grown grain (1 Corinthians 15; cf. John 12:24) he captures the persistence of the individual but also the radical difference in resurrection, in which one's lowly body will be changed to the likeness of the risen Christ's glorious body (Philippians 3:21).

The Church confessed its belief in the resurrection of the body in the earliest baptismal formulas and later in its creeds ('Christ is risen!' Response 'He is risen indeed! Alleluia!'). At the end of the 1st century, St Clement of Rome used the pagan myth of the phoenix to illustrate God's promise of resurrection (*Epistola 1 ad Corinthios*, *Patrologia Graeca*, 1.261–66). In the next two centuries, writers such as Athenagoras, St Irenaeus, and Tertullian argued for a physical resurrection against gnostic spiritualizing. Origen, however, relied on the Pauline notion of the 'spiritual body' in order to emphasize transformation and discontinuity in resurrection; he also held the controversial belief that all souls, including those of demons, would be redeemed in the life to come.

The Fathers wove together doctrines of immortality (as the postmortem persistence of the individual) and resurrection (as the eschatological reunion of soul with reconstituted body), finding it difficult to hold one without the other: unless the soul persists, there can be no beatific enjoyment of God in the life to come; but without the body the personality has no vehicle of expression, as the incarnation itself attested. Exactly how the raised body could be the same and yet transformed remained a subject of debate. St Augustine, in the closing chapters of *De civitate Dei* defends bodily resurrection against the objections of sceptics. At the same time, he recognizes that if resurrected eyes are to look upon the invisible God, some transformation of present capacities is required (22.11-29).

An Aristotelian understanding of psychophysical unity provided Aquinas a philosophical framework for the belief that the resurrection of the body (and not just the persistence of the soul) was the natural expectation for a future life – though supernatural power would be required to bring it about (*Summa Theologica*, 3a, Supplement 75 – 86; Contra Gentiles, 4.79ff.). The 16th-century Reformers continued to emphasize the raising of Christ and the omnipotence of God, challenging only what they considered unwarranted additions to this belief. Resurrection was affirmed in the Lutheran Augsburg Confession, part 1, article 17, and by Calvin, though he refused to explore the 'corners' of heaven, calling this a 'superfluous investigation of useless matters' (*Institutes*, 3.25).

The earliest extended use of the resurrection theme in English literature is the Old English *Phoenix*, which follows patristic precedent in treating the phoenix myth as an allegory of Christ and his followers: they, covered with the ground until the coming of the consuming and purifying fire, rise from ashes to the life of life. In the Middle English Corpus Christi plays, the resurrection of Christ is portrayed as a triumph over the devil in the harrowing of hell; and the raising of the dead is central in the 'last judgment' plays (see especially the Chester, York, and Towneley cycles). The anonymous author of *St Erkenwald* makes the miraculous reawakening of a righteous pagan long dead the occasion for his spiritual rebirth through Christian baptism; the latter miracle is seen to be of more importance than the revivification of his flesh.

Spenser uses a resurrection allegory in the Redcrosse Knight's battle with the dragon in *The Faerie Queene*. After a day of fighting the knight is knocked into the Well of Life, from which he rises 'new born' (9.34.9), as in Christian baptism; the second night he receives from the Tree of Life a healing balm, the stream which can 'rear again / The senseless corpse appointed for the grave' (9.48.7). Like Christ, he is victorious on the third day.

Shakespeare locates the theme of resurrection in plots which end in reconciliation and harmony. In *All's Well That Ends Well*, Helena is willing to embrace death to set Bertram free; she is indeed believed dead until her sudden reappearance exposes hidden truth and establishes a new beginning. The Christian understanding of resurrection is especially strong in the losses and recoveries of the late plays, though clothed in magic and in pagan classical garb. The threatening seas of *The Tempest* are merciful: lost Ferdinand is restored to Alonso, Milan's misfortune ends in Naples' blessing, and all find themselves 'When no man was his own' (5.1.213). Likewise in *The Winter's Tale*: Paulina's dramatic 're-awakening' of the lifelike 'statue' of Hermione serves to vindicate injured innocence and reward the 'faith' of Leontes. Resurrection is central to John Milton's vision of the loss and regaining of Paradise, for unless death is ultimately defeated God's purposes will not be justified. Christ's victorious resurrection is thus announced before the Fall in *Paradise Lost* (3.245–49) and is later foretold to the fallen but repentant Adam (12.431–35); God promises a second life for mankind in the 'renovation of the just' along with a renewal of heaven and earth (11.61–66). At the end of

Samson Agonistes Milton uses the phoenix as a simile of the resurgence of Samson's power, a pre-Christian harbinger of resurrection.

John Donne's verse provides a variety of resurrection images – from the commonplace pictures of death as 'rest and sleep' from which one wakes to the death of Death ('Death, be not proud') to the alchemical conceit in which the gold of Christ's buried body rises 'all tincture', able not only to change 'leaden and iron wills' but also to transmute sinful bodies into his likeness ('Resurrection, Imperfect'). Elsewhere, the prospect of resurrection and final judgment moves the poet to repentance ('At the round earth's imagined corners'). For George Herbert resurrection becomes the ultimate answer to affliction, from which one will rise with Christ ('Easter Wings').

The poetry of the last two centuries has explored resurrection themes in a variety of ways. In Coleridge's *Rime of the Ancient Mariner* a 'troop of spirits blessed' (349) enlivens the corpses of the mariner's shipmates, fallen through his wanton sin; this 'rising' proves a means to his salvation. Like her American contemporary Emily Dickinson, Christina Rossetti befriends death (in 'Life and Death') for its rest and relief. But while for Dickinson immortality and heaven lie in that rest, Rossetti confesses hope that from the husk will rise the sap of Spring, from fire will come a life remolded ('A Better Resurrection'). For Gerard Manley Hopkins, resurrection hope flashes unexpectedly in the darkness, and its transformation 'at trumpet crash' brings radical discontinuity: without a hint of alchemical magic, this highly combustible 'matchwood', man, is 'immortal diamond' ('That Nature is a Heraclitean Fire and of the Comfort of the Resurrection'). In evident echoing of Paul (1 Corinthians 15:13–14), John Updike challenges romanticized views of resurrection in 'Seven Stanzas at Easter': Make no mistake: if He rose at all it was as His body; if the cells' dissolution did not reverse, the molecules reknit, the amino acids rekindle, the Church will fall... (*Telephone Poles and Other Poems*, 72).

Margaret Avison probes the fear that 'light will burn / and wake the dead' in 'Waking and Sleeping: Christmas' (sunblue), while in the title poem of Christopher Rush's *A Resurrection of a Kind* the dead rise delicately in the evanescence of memory alone.

Examples of resurrection in prose fiction are equally diverse. In Dickens' *A Tale of Two Cities*, Dr Manette is 'recalled to life' by the love of his daughter, and the self-sacrificing Sydney Carton anticipates as he mounts the scaffold resurrection and the redemption of his life in a new future; even Jerry Cruncher's work as 'Resurrection-man' serves the theme as foil. A decidedly non-spiritual interpretation of the raising of the flesh is provided by D.H. Lawrence's *The Man Who Died*, a novel in which the symbolic bird is not the phoenix but the cock (cf. Lawrence's essay 'The Risen Lord', which refashions resurrection into a new kind of life in the body). C.S. Lewis re-creates explicit Christian allegory in Aslan's return to life and his breathing on the stone statues at the castle of the White Witch (*The Lion, the Witch, and the Wardrobe*). In J.R.R. Tolkien's *Lord of the Rings* there are parallels with Christ's resurrection in Gandalf's death and return to life: he falls into an abyss in combat with an evil Balrog, and returns in shining clothes as Gandalf the White, though veiled and not immediately recognized by his followers. A much transmuted development of the theme comes in the early novel of John Gardner, *The Resurrection*, which plays off the philosophically refined thoughts of a professor dying in mid-career against the effects of his dying on himself and on those around him: the issue is not rebirth in an afterlife so much as the struggle of love toward resurrection in the present. In Jack Hodgins' *The Resurrection of Joseph Bourne*, a strange woman of compelling beauty but unknown origin arrives in a port town stinking of death after a deluge, and effects old Bourne's death and his return to life. The miracle leaves no one untouched, and other unexpected personal transformations force decisions about relationships and community – until in the final apocalyptic scene some are destroyed or excluded and the rest join in a dance of reconciled and resurrected life.

Paul W. Gooch
University of Toronto

Second Coming

During his earthly ministry Jesus himself declared that although he was to face death, he would rise from the dead and one day 'come again' (e.g., John 14:2–3), a message reiterated by angelic witnesses at the Ascension (Acts 1:11): 'this same Jesus, which is taken up from you into heaven, shall so come in like manner as ye have seen him go into heaven.' The fundamental relationship between the Ascension and the Second Coming is reflected in all the major creeds of the Church. In the words of the Apostles' Creed, 'He ascended into heaven, And sitteth on the right hand of God the Father Almighty; From thence he shall come to judge the quick and the dead' (*Book of Common Prayer*).

In Matthew 24, in response to a question from his disciples – 'What shall be the sign of thy coming, and of the end of the world?' (v. 3) – Jesus describes at length the circumstances which portend his return. There will be a period of 'great tribulation', and then,

> immediately shall the sun be darkened, and the moon shall not give her light, and the stars shall fall from heaven, and the powers of the heavens shall be shaken: And then shall appear the sign of the Son of man in heaven: and then shall all the tribes of the earth mourn, and they shall see the Son of man coming in the clouds of heaven with power and great glory. And he shall send his angels with a great sound of a trumpet, and they shall gather together his elect from the four winds, from one end of heaven to the other. (vv. 29–31)

Mirroring the expectations of the Old Testament prophets, Jesus talks about a historical judgment to fall upon Jerusalem in the near future (vv. 1–2) and about that destruction as an anticipation of the sacrilege of the last days, the desolation and destruction of Antichrist. His description recalls the imminent 'Day of the Lord' spoken of by Amos (5:18) and Isaiah (2:12ff.), as well as the ultimate 'Day of the Lord' also referred to by the prophets (Joel 3:14–21; Ephesians 1:14–18). The phrase 'day of the Lord' is used widely in the New Testament to indicate the day at which Christ will return to bring history to an end and inaugurate the age to come (e.g., 1 Thessalonians 5:2; 2 Thessalonians 2:2; 2 Peter 3:10); sometimes the expression occurs in other forms (e.g., 'the day of the Lord Jesus', 1 Corinthians 5:5; 2 Corinthians 1:14, 'the day of Jesus Christ', Philippians 1:6; 'the day of God', 2 Peter 3:12; 'the last day', 1 Peter 1:5).

St Paul uses three words to describe the return of Christ:

(1) Greek *parousia* ('presence', 'arrival' – as in 1 Corinthians 16:17; 2 Corinthians 7:7), a word normally used to describe a visit of royalty or one of exalted rank, and here applied to Christ's personal return (Acts 1:11) at the end of the age (Matthew 24:3) in power and glory (24:30) to raise the dead (1 Corinthians 15:23), gather his people to himself (2 Thessalonians 2:1), and destroy evil (1 Thessalonians 2:19; 3:13; 4:15; 5:13); (2) *apokalypsis* ('unveiling' or 'disclosure'), in which his power as God, heretofore partially hidden, is disclosed to the world, which then will of necessity acknowledge his lordship (Philippians 2:10ff.); (3) *epiphaneia* ('appearing'), indicating that it is to be a visible return (2 Thessalonians 2:8); the term is used to designate the incarnation as well, connecting these two events as chief elements in Christ's redemptive work.

John's Patmos vision of the conclusion of human history ends with the promise of 'He which testifieth these things', saying, 'Surely I come quickly', to which the evangelist responds, 'Even so, come, Lord Jesus' (Revelation 22:20). That note of expectancy was prevalent among the early Christians, many of whom expected Christ's return within their own lifetime. When, especially following the destruction of Jerusalem, this did not happen they turned away from preoccupation with the date and manner of Christ's return, observing the words of Jesus that 'of that day and hour knoweth no man, no, not the angels of heaven, but my Father only' (v. 36). Most writers in the period between Augustine and the end of the first millennium were content with the Bishop of Hippo's sentiments as expressed in his *De civitate Dei* (20.30), asserting the fact of the Last Judgment rather than speculating on the time of Christ's return to effect it:

> That the last judgment, then, shall be administered by Jesus Christ in the manner predicted in the sacred writings is denied or doubted by no one, unless by those who, through some incredible animosity or blindness, decline to believe these writings [the Scriptures], though already their truth is demonstrated to all the world. And at or in connection with that judgment the following events shall come to pass, as we have learned: Elias the Tisbite shall come; the Jews shall believe; Antichrist shall persecute; Christ shall judge; the

dead shall rise; the good and the wicked shall be separated; the world shall be burned and renewed. All these things, we believe, shall come to pass; but how, or in what order, human understanding cannot perfectly teach us, but only the experience of the events themselves. My opinion, however, is that they will happen in the order in which I have related them.

As the year 1000 approached, the sabbatarian view of history which made the last age (like the others) to last a thousand years, prompted an expectation of the imminent Second Advent. Commentaries on the book of Revelation began to be written in earnest. The emphasis of vernacular British poems on the subject, like the commentaries themselves and the Latin poem *De Die Judicii* attributed to the Venerable Bede, is still upon the Last Judgment rather than the *parousia* itself: *Christ and Satan* and *Doomsday* III (or *Christ* III) of the Exeter Book, like *Ascension (Christ II)*, emphasize that Christ's coming again will be in severity of judgment, and many will be punished (346b-57). The theme of Christ's Second Coming and prophecies related to it were developed strongly in lections for Advent; after the 12th century, when St Bernard of Clairvaux made the connection between Christ's first and second advent the theme of an important series of sermons, Advent became more widely seen as a season for the examination of Christian conscience preparatory not only for Christmas but for the 'Last Day' or 'Day of the Lord.' Much the same sentiment is expressed in the hymn 'Dies Irae, Dies Illae' of the Franciscan (contemporary and biographer of St Francis) Thomas of Celano. It has often been translated; one of the most powerful versions in English is that by the 17th-century poet Richard Crashaw:

> Oh, that Trump! whose blast shall run
> An even round with th' circling sun,
> And urge the murmuring graves to bring
> Pale mankind forth to meet his King.

When the millennium passed without the Lord's return, 1260 was put forward as another date of the Parousia; it was calculated as concluding a period of forty-two generations (x 30 years), according to an interpretation of the generations of Christ in Matthew's genealogy. Joachim of Fiore's apocalypticism made much of this date, but others were also put forward: 1233, 1300, 1333, and 1400 among them. Some commentators made their calculations on the basis of Daniel 9:24–27. As Morton Bloomfield has shown, *Piers Plowman* participates in the later phase of this apocalyptic expectation. The connection with judgment was emphasized in popular preaching during this period, and this in turn lies behind the Middle English 'Doomsday' lyrics, which are immediately followed in two important manuscripts by poems on the *terminus* of mortal life and repentance (C. Brown, *English Lyrics of the XIIIth Century*, nos. 28a–b, 29a–b). Fourteenth-century lyrics, such as *'Quis Est Iste Qui Uenit de Edom?'* (Brown, *Religious Lyrics of the XIVth Century*, no. 25) and 'How Christ shall Come', followed in the manuscript by a poem on the vision of the Four Horsemen of the Apocalypse (Revelation 6:1–8), suggest a heightened interest in the Parousia itself circa 1325–30. But that Christ's return seemed (in view of many failed predictions) to be somehow far off in a longed-for future is evident in the transference of emphasis once again to *apokalypsis*, a future unveiling of peace and order which finds its poetic counterpart in the idea of a 'once and future king.' The Arthuriad which develops through the alliterative *Morte Arthure* to Malory is 'apocalyptic' romance, but in none of these poems is the 'coming again' parallel sharply focused or clearly realized. The 'Last Judgment' play of York refers to all men seeing Christ descending with his five wounds clearly visible (48.70-71) but offers no further image; N-Town's 'Doomsday' has a stage direction suggesting that Jesus *descendente cum Michaele et Gabriele archangelis* at the outset of the pageant, but then plunges right into the Last Judgment, its principal subject.

With the Reformation new interest in eschatology was awakened, and some older interests downplayed. A late 16th-century hymn of Nikolai Philipp, a Lutheran pastor, 'Wachet auf! ruft uns die Stimme' was composed in 1599 in Westphalia in the midst of a raging epidemic of plague; its great popularity may have led to the tune being adapted by Mendelssohn in his *Elijah*. Philipp's hymn, translated into English by Frances Elizabeth Cox, develops the theme of the sudden arrival of the Bridegroom (Matthew 25:1–13). Calvin,

171

meanwhile, was exceedingly wary of apocalypticism, and studiously avoided making any commentary on the book of Revelation, privately doubting its value to the canon. He both dismissed the late medieval Catholic doctrine that the kingdom of Christ would be realized in an earthly millennium (*Harmony of the Gospels,* on Matthew 24:3) and strove to turn attention away from historical speculation about Christ's return by interpreting Matthew 24:29–31 *in figura,* to refer to the entire history of the Church in the world and awaiting the completion of its redemption:

> Not that the glory and majesty of Christ's kingdom will only appear at his final coming, but that the completion (*complementum*) is delayed till that point – the completion of those things that started at the resurrection... By this way Christ keeps the minds of the faithful in suspense to the last day, in case they should think that there was nothing to the testimony of the prophets on the restoration to come; for it had lain hid for a long time under a dense cloud of troubles... In other words, as long as the Church's pilgrimage in this world lasts, the skies will be dark and cloudy, but as soon as the end of distress arrives, the daylight will break to show his shining majesty. (*Harmony,* on Matthew 24:29)

In English Reformation writers such as John Bale the Second Coming is an urgent subject (*The Image of Bothe Churches,* 1545) but, as in Tyndale, is connected with anti-Catholic polemic. John Knox expresses in his *History of the Reformation in Scotland* the more positive side of British Reformers' expectations of the Second Coming when he sees it as a time of cosmic restitution:

> We believe that the same Lord Jesus shall visibly return for this last Judgment as He was seen to ascend. And then, we firmly believe, the time of refreshing and restitution of all things shall come, so that those who from the beginning have suffered violence, injury, and wrong for righteousness' sake shall inherit that blessed immortality promised them from the beginning. (2.102–03)

Among the most extensive treatments of the Second Coming among English Reformation writers is that by Bishop Hugh Latimer, in his 'Sermon for the Second Sunday in Advent', 1552. Working from his text in Luke 21:25–28, he develops a full biblical exposition on the subject, citing as well Fathers of the Church and dealing with the apocalyptic expectations of Reformers Luther and Bilney (his own mentor). For Latimer the right way to prepare for the 'last day' is not by speculating about the day or the hour but, on the example of Christ, 'by keeping ourselves from superfluous eating and drinking, and in watching and praying.... Therefore Christ addeth, saying, *Vigilate et orate,* 'Watch and pray'...' (*Sermons*, 8).

Yet the instinct to look for a near date for Christ's return is very strong in English Reformation tradition. Even in the 17th century, Henry Vaughan's 'The Dawning' expands upon a hint in George Herbert's poem of the same title to pose a question increasingly upon the minds of English Protestant readers of the Bible: 'Ah! what time wilt thou come? when shall that crie / The *Bridegroome's Comming!* fil the sky?' Vaughan concludes, however, in a prayer which Latimer would have approved:

> when that day, and hour shal come
> In which thy self wil be the Sun,
> Thou'lt find me drest and on my way,
> Watching the Break of thy great day.

In America, the millenarian Sabbath-history of the Puritans developed dramatically, with writers of the stature of Cotton and Increase Mather anticipating the imminent return of Christ, especially to 'His New English Israel' (Cotton Mather, *Wonders of the Invisible World,* 1692; cf. Increase Mather, *The Mystery of Israel's Salvation,* 1699). The eager anticipation expressed in Michael Wigglesworth's poem *The Day of Doom* (1662) is undiminished in the writings of Jonathan Edwards, who expected Christ's Second Coming to inaugurate the millennial kingdom in America, in all probability in New England, 'the most likely of all the American colonies' (*Some Thoughts Concerning the Present Revival of Religion in New England,* 1742).

That the 'day of the Lord' should be not principally thought of as a 'Day of Wrath' but rather as a day of release and redemption is a strong theme in the preaching of the Wesleyan revival of the 18th century. It finds expression in the well-known hymn of Cowper's cousin Martin Madan, a cento, in fact, of hymns by Charles Wesley (nos. 38 and 39 of his *Hymns of Intercession for all Mankind*), and one by John Cennick, the first stanza coming direct from Wesley:

> Lo! he comes, with clouds descending,
>> Once for favoured sinners slain
> Thousand thousand saints attending
>> Swell the triumph of his train:
>>> Hallelujah!
> God appears, on earth to reign!

The last stanza, also Wesley's, concludes with an allusion to Revelation 22:20, 'O come quickly, / Everlasting God, come down!' hearkening back to the theme of the early Church. Another hymn of the Second Coming by an associate of the Wesleys and Whitefield, 'The Alarum' by Richard Kempenfelt, contrasts the 'shriek and despair' of those who have rejected God with the 'glories benign' of the disclosed 'incarnate God' of whom the redeemed sinner need have no further terror:

> O my approving God!
> Washed in thy precious blood,
>> Bold I advance;
> Fearless we range along
> Join the triumphant throng,
> Shout an ecstatic song
>> Through the expanse.

These hymns and poems contrast in their joyous expectation not only the dread anticipation of medieval works on the theme but also a milder and more self-conscious evocation of them in Joseph Addison's 'How Shall I Appear' (*Spectator*, October 18, 1712), to which Addison adds in a note that his concern for the moment when the last trumpet shall sound and the dead arise is with having 'to appear naked and unbodied before Him who made him':

> When rising from the bed of death
>> O'erwhelmed with guilt and fear,

> I see my Maker face to face,
>> Oh, how shall I appear?

Thomas Moore's 'Lord, Who Shall Bear That Day?' relates, in a similar vein, the moment when 'The Saviour shall put forth his radiant head' only to reveal also the countenance of the 'eternal Judge.' Charles Kingsley's strident 'The Day of the Lord at Hand' (1850) strikes a millennial theme, as he almost welcomes the 'last battle' as an opportunity for setting the fallen and sinful world right; in its triumphalist apocalypticism it is reminiscent of Blake's 'Jerusalem.' An American version of some of the same sentiments appears in Julia Ward Howe's 'Battle Hymn of the Republic' (1862), one of the most popular of American patriotic songs, which draws much of its imagery from biblical descriptions of the Second Coming:

> Mine eyes have seen the glory of the coming of the Lord
> He is trampling out the vintage where the grapes of wrath
>> are stored!
> He hath loosed the fateful lightning of his terrible swift sword,
> His truth is marching on.

After the second stanza, for which the variant refrain is 'His day is marching on', the third reads:

> He has sounded forth the trumpet that shall never call retreat;
> He is sifting out the hearts of men before his judgment seat;
> Oh, be swift, my soul, to answer him! be jubilant, my feet!
> Our God is marching on.

The final stanza, with its appeal – 'As he died to make men holy, let us die to make men free' – is an evident recrudescence of the millennialist application of the Parousia. By contrast, John Keble's Advent poems in *The Christian Year* emphasize the age-old liturgical association of the Second Coming with the Advent, especially his poem for the Second Sunday in Advent, 'Not till the freezing blast is still.'

The theme of Christ's coming again occurs in late 19th- and 20th-century writers in a diversity of guises. The best-known modern evocation of 'The Second Coming' is undoubtedly the poem of that title by Yeats. Here, in a realization that 'things fall apart; the centre cannot hold; / Mere anarchy is loosed upon the world', the speaker reflects on the collapse of civilization and its hopes for rational and natural harmony, a reflection which turns to apocalyptic speculation:

> Surely some revelation is at hand;
> Surely the Second Coming is at hand.
> The Second Coming! Hardly are those words out
> When a vast image out of *Spiritus Mundi*
> Troubles my sight....

The image is of the darker side of apocalypse, the 'rough beast, its hour come round at last', which 'slouches toward Bethlehem to be born' – conjuring up associations not with Christ but rather his great antagonist, not with redemption but with tribulation.

In some Catholic writers such as David Jones, the focus is more on 'Sejunction Day', or 'Day of Disjoining' as he calls it, the great 'Uncover' (*apokalypsis*) to Judgment in which a true moral analysis of history will be rendered (*Anathemata*, 5.164; 8.236). Others such as J.R.R. Tolkien and C.S. Lewis have incorporated an eschatological vision of the Second Coming in children's or fantasy fiction (Lewis, *The Last Battle*; Tolkien, *The Return of the King*). *The Second Coming*, by American novelist Walker Percy, uses fundamentalist preaching of an imminent return of Christ to unsettle his protagonist's assurance that his version of the American dream is secure (recalling Yeats, he finds that 'things fall apart'), but then shifts perspective on the title to make the 'second birth' or spiritual regeneration of his anti-hero and anti-heroine the real subject of his story.

David L. Jeffrey
University of Ottawa

THE ACTS OF THE APOSTLES

Abridged from the text of the Revised English Bible

The Ascension   *179*

The Day of Pentecost   *179*

Peter Heals a Crippled Man   *181*

Peter's Defence before the High Priest   *182*

Ananias and Sapphira   *183*

The Apostles Teach in the Temple   *184*

The Counsel of Gamaliel   *185*

The Stoning of Stephen   *186*

Simon the Magician   *187*

Philip and the Ethiopian Eunuch   *188*

The Conversion of Saul   *189*

Saul Escapes from Damascus   *190*

The Conversion of Cornelius   *191*

The Church at Antioch   *193*

Peter Escapes from Herod   *194*

Elymas the Sorcerer   *195*

Paul and Barnabas Turn to the Gentiles   *196*

The Jews Oppose Paul's Mission   *197*

The Council of Jerusalem   *199*

Paul's Journey to Macedonia   *201*

The Conversion of the Philippian Jailer   *202*

Paul Preaches at Thessalonica   *203*

Paul's Speech before the Council of the Areopagus   *204*

Paul Founds the Church at Corinth   *206*

The Church at Ephesus   *206*

The Riot at Ephesus   *208*

Paul Returns to Macedonia   *209*

Paul's Farewell to the Ephesians   *210*

Paul's Final Journey to Jerusalem   *211*

Paul is Arrested in the Temple   *212*

Paul's Defence before the High Priest   *215*

The Jews Plot to Kill Paul   *216*

Paul's Defence before Felix   *217*

Paul Appeals to Caesar   *219*

Paul's Defence before Agrippa   *220*

Shipwreck on the Way to Rome   *221*

Paul's Final Years in Rome   *224*

The Acts of the Apostles

THE ASCENSION
Acts 1:1–3, 6–9, 12–14

In the first part of my work, Theophilus, I gave an account of all that Jesus did and taught from the beginning until the day when he was taken up to heaven, after giving instructions through the Holy Spirit to the apostles whom he had chosen. To these men he showed himself after his death and gave ample proof that he was alive: he was seen by them over a period of forty days and spoke to them about the kingdom of God...

When they were all together, they asked him, 'Lord, is this the time at which you are to restore sovereignty to Israel?' He answered, 'It is not for you to know about dates or times which the Father has set within his own control. But you will receive power when the Holy Spirit comes upon you; and you will bear witness for me in Jerusalem, and throughout all Judaea and Samaria, and even in the farthest corners of the earth.'

After he had said this, he was lifted up before their very eyes, and a cloud took him from their sight...

They then returned to Jerusalem from the hill called Olivet, which is near the city, no farther than a sabbath day's journey. On their arrival they went to the upstairs room where they were lodging: Peter and John and James and Andrew, Philip and Thomas, Bartholomew and Matthew, James son of Alphaeus, Simon the Zealot, and Judas son of James. All these with one accord were constantly at prayer, together with a group of women, and Mary the mother of Jesus, and his brothers...

THE DAY OF PENTECOST
Acts 2:1–8, 13–17, 22–24, 36–38, 41–42

The day of Pentecost had come, and they were all together in one place. Suddenly there came from the sky what sounded like a strong, driving wind, a noise which filled the whole house where they were sitting. And there appeared to them flames like tongues of fire distributed among them and coming to rest on each one. They were all filled with the Holy Spirit and began to talk in other tongues, as the Spirit gave them power of utterance.

Now there were staying in Jerusalem devout Jews drawn from every nation under heaven. At this sound a crowd of them gathered, and were bewildered because each one heard his own language spoken; they were amazed and in astonishment exclaimed, 'Surely these people who are speaking are all Galileans! How is it that each of us can hear them in his own native language?... Others said contemptuously, 'They have been drinking!'

But Peter stood up with the eleven, and in a loud voice addressed the crowd: 'Fellow-Jews, and all who live in Jerusalem, listen and take note of what I say. These people are not drunk, as you suppose; it is only nine in the morning! No, this is what the prophet Joel spoke of: "In the last days, says God, I will pour out my Spirit on all mankind; and your sons and daughters shall prophesy; your young men shall see visions, and your old men shall dream dreams..."

'Men of Israel, hear me: I am speaking of Jesus of Nazareth, singled out by God and made known to you through miracles, portents, and signs, which God worked among you through him, as you well know. By the deliberate will and plan of God he was given into your power, and you killed him, using heathen men to crucify him. But God raised him to life again, setting him free from the pangs of death, because it could not be that death should keep him in its grip...

'Let all Israel then accept as certain that God has made this same Jesus, whom you crucified, both Lord and Messiah.'

When they heard this they were cut to the heart, and said to Peter and the other apostles, 'Friends, what are we to do?' 'Repent', said Peter, 'and be baptized, every one of you, in the name of Jesus the Messiah; then your sins will be forgiven and you will receive the gift of the Holy Spirit...

Those who accepted what he said were baptized, and some three thousand were added to the number of believers that day. They met constantly to hear the apostles teach and to share the common life, to break bread, and to pray...

PETER HEALS A CRIPPLED MAN
Acts 3:1–21, 25 – 4:4

One day at three in the afternoon, the hour of prayer, Peter and John were on their way up to the temple. Now a man who had been a cripple from birth used to be carried there and laid every day by the temple gate called Beautiful to beg from people as they went in. When he saw Peter and John on their way into the temple, he asked for alms. They both fixed their eyes on him, and Peter said, 'Look at us.' Expecting a gift from them, the man was all attention. Peter said, 'I have no silver or gold; but what I have I give you: in the name of Jesus Christ of Nazareth, get up and walk.' Then, grasping him by the right hand he helped him up; and at once his feet and ankles grew strong; he sprang to his feet, and started to walk. He entered the temple with them, leaping and praising God as he went. Everyone saw him walking and praising God, and when they recognized him as the man who used to sit begging at Beautiful Gate they were filled with wonder and amazement at what had happened to him.

While he still clung to Peter and John all the people came running in astonishment towards them in Solomon's Portico, as it is called. Peter saw them coming and met them with these words: 'Men of Israel, why be surprised at this? Why stare at us as if we had made this man walk by some power or godliness of our own? The God of Abraham, Isaac, and Jacob, the God of our fathers, has given the highest honour to his servant Jesus, whom you handed over for trial and disowned in Pilate's court – disowned the holy and righteous one when Pilate had decided to release him. You asked for the reprieve of a murderer, and killed the Prince of life. But God raised him from the dead; of that we are witnesses. The name of Jesus, by awakening faith, has given strength to this man whom you see and know, and this faith has made him completely well as you can all see.

'Now, my friends, I know quite well that you acted in ignorance, as did your rulers; but this is how God fulfilled what he had foretold through all the prophets: that his Messiah would suffer. Repent, therefore, and turn to God, so that your sins may be wiped out. Then the Lord may grant you a time of recovery and send the Messiah appointed for you, that is, Jesus. He must be received into heaven until the time comes for the universal restoration of which God has spoken through his holy prophets from the beginning...

'You are the heirs of the prophets, and of that covenant which God made with your fathers when he said to Abraham, "And in your offspring all the families on earth shall find blessing." When God raised up his servant, he sent him to you first, to bring you blessing by turning every one of you from your wicked ways.'

They were still addressing the people when the chief priests, together with the controller of the temple and the Sadducees, broke in on them, annoyed because they were proclaiming the resurrection from the dead by teaching the people about Jesus. They were arrested and, as it was already evening, put in prison for the night. But many of those who had heard the message became believers, bringing the number of men to about five thousand.

PETER'S DEFENCE BEFORE THE HIGH PRIEST
Acts 4:5–10, 13–21

Next day the Jewish rulers, elders, and scribes met in Jerusalem. There were present Annas the high priest, Caiaphas, John, Alexander, and all who were of the high-priestly family. They brought the apostles before the court and began to interrogate them. 'By what power', they asked, 'or by what name have such men as you done this?' Then Peter, filled with the Holy Spirit, answered, 'Rulers of the people and elders, if it is about help given to a sick man that we are being questioned today, and the means by which he was cured, this is our answer to all of you and to all the people of Israel: it was by the name of Jesus Christ of Nazareth, whom you crucified, and whom God raised from the dead; through him this man stands here before you fit and well...'

Observing that Peter and John were uneducated laymen, they were astonished at their boldness and took note that they had been companions of Jesus; but with the man who had been cured standing in full view beside them, they had nothing to say in reply. So they ordered them to leave the court, and then conferred among themselves. 'What are we to do with these men?' they said. 'It is common knowledge in Jerusalem that a notable miracle has come about through them; and we cannot deny it. But to stop this from spreading farther among the people, we had better caution them never again to speak to anyone in this name.' They then called them in and ordered them to refrain from all public speaking and teaching in the name of Jesus.

But Peter and John replied: 'Is it right in the eyes of God for us to obey you rather than him? Judge for yourselves. We cannot possibly give up speaking about what we have seen and heard.'

With a repeated caution the court discharged them. They could not see how they were to punish them, because the people were all giving glory to God for what had happened...

ANANIAS AND SAPPHIRA
Acts 4:32–35; 5:1–11

The whole company of believers was united in heart and soul. Not one of them claimed any of his possessions as his own; everything was held in common. With great power the apostles bore witness to the resurrection of the Lord Jesus, and all were held in high esteem. There was never a needy person among them, because those who had property in land or houses would sell it, bring the proceeds of the sale, and lay them at the feet of the apostles, to be distributed to any who were in need...

But a man called Ananias sold a property, and with the connivance of his wife Sapphira kept back some of the proceeds, and brought part only to lay at the apostles' feet. Peter said, 'Ananias, how was it that Satan so possessed your mind that you lied to the Holy Spirit by keeping back part of the price of the land? While it remained unsold, did it not remain yours? Even after it was turned into money, was it not still at your own disposal? What made you think of doing this? You have lied not to men but to God.' When Ananias heard these words he dropped dead; and all who heard were awestruck. The younger men rose and covered his body, then carried him out and buried him.

About three hours passed, and his wife came in, unaware of what had happened. Peter asked her, 'Tell me, were you paid such and such a price for the land?' 'Yes,' she replied, 'that was the price.' Peter said, 'Why did the two of you conspire to put the Spirit of the Lord to the test? Those who buried your husband are there at the door, and they will carry you away.' At once she dropped dead at his feet. When the young men came in, they found her dead; and they carried her out and buried her beside her husband.

Great awe fell on the whole church and on all who heard of this.

THE APOSTLES TEACH IN THE TEMPLE
Acts 5:12, 16–32

Many signs and wonders were done among the people by the apostles… and the people from the towns round Jerusalem flocked in, bringing those who were ill or harassed by unclean spirits, and all were cured.

Then the high priest and his colleagues, the Sadducean party, were goaded by jealousy to arrest the apostles and put them in official custody. But during the night, an angel of the Lord opened the prison doors, led them out, and said, 'Go, stand in the temple and tell the people all about this new life.' Accordingly they entered the temple at daybreak and went on with their teaching.

When the high priest arrived with his colleagues they summoned the Sanhedrin, the full Council of the Israelite nation, and sent to the jail for the prisoners. The officers who went to the prison failed to find them there, so they returned and reported, 'We found the jail securely locked at every point, with the warders at their posts by the doors, but on opening them we found no one inside.' When they heard this, the controller of the temple and the chief priests were at a loss to know what could have become of them, until someone came and reported: 'The men you put in prison are standing in the temple teaching the people.' Then the controller went off with the officers and fetched them, but without use of force, for fear of being stoned by the people.

When they had been brought in and made to stand before the

Council, the high priest began his examination. 'We gave you explicit orders', he said, 'to stop teaching in that name; and what has happened? You have filled Jerusalem with your teaching, and you are trying to hold us responsible for that man's death.' Peter replied for the apostles: 'We must obey God rather than men. The God of our fathers raised up Jesus; after you had put him to death by hanging him on a gibbet, God exalted him at his right hand as leader and saviour, to grant Israel repentance and forgiveness of sins. And we are witnesses to all this, as is the Holy Spirit who is given by God to those obedient to him.'

THE COUNSEL OF GAMALIEL
Acts 5:33–42

This touched them on the raw, and they wanted to put them to death. But a member of the Council rose to his feet, a Pharisee called Gamaliel, a teacher of the law held in high regard by all the people. He had the men put outside for a while, and then said, 'Men of Israel, be very careful in deciding what to do with these men. Some time ago Theudas came forward, making claims for himself, and a number of our people, about four hundred, joined him. But he was killed and his whole movement was destroyed and came to nothing. After him came Judas the Galilean at the time of the census; he induced some people to revolt under his leadership, but he too perished and his whole movement was broken up. Now, my advice to you is this: keep clear of these men; let them alone. For if what is being planned and done is human in origin, it will collapse; but if it is from God, you will never be able to stamp it out, and you risk finding yourselves at war with God.'

Convinced by this, they sent for the apostles and had them flogged; then they ordered them to give up speaking in the name of Jesus, and discharged them. The apostles went out from the Council rejoicing that they had been found worthy to suffer humiliation for the sake of the name. And every day they went steadily on with their teaching in the temple and in private houses, telling the good news of Jesus the Messiah.

THE STONING OF STEPHEN
Acts 6:7–12; 7:1–2, 44 – 8:4

The word of God spread more and more widely; the number of disciples in Jerusalem was increasing rapidly, and very many of the priests adhered to the faith.

Stephen, full of grace and power, began to do great wonders and signs among the people. Some members of the synagogue called the Synagogue of Freedmen, comprising Cyrenians and Alexandrians and people from Cilicia and Asia, came forward and argued with Stephen, but could not hold their own against the inspired wisdom with which he spoke. They then put up men to allege that they had heard him make blasphemous statements against Moses and against God. They stirred up the people and the elders and scribes, set upon him and seized him, and brought him before the Council...

Then the high priest asked him, 'Is this true?' He replied, 'My brothers, fathers of this nation, listen to me...

'Our forefathers had the Tent of the Testimony in the desert, as God commanded when he told Moses to make it after the pattern which he had seen. In the next generation, our fathers under Joshua brought it with them when they dispossessed the nations whom God drove out before them, and so it was until the time of David. David found favour with God and begged leave to provide a dwelling-place for the God of Jacob; but it was Solomon who built him a house. However, the Most High does not live in houses made by men; as the prophet says: "Heaven is my throne and earth my footstool. What kind of house will you build for me, says the Lord; where shall my resting-place be? Are not all these things of my own making?"

'How stubborn you are, heathen still at heart and deaf to the truth! You always resist the Holy Spirit. You are just like your fathers! Was there ever a prophet your fathers did not persecute? They killed those who foretold the coming of the righteous one, and now you have betrayed him and murdered him. You received the law given by God's angels and yet you have not kept it.'

This touched them on the raw, and they ground their teeth with fury. But Stephen, filled with the Holy Spirit, and gazing intently up to heaven, saw the glory of God, and Jesus standing at God's right hand. 'Look!' he said. 'I see the heavens opened and the Son of Man standing at the right hand of God.' At this they gave a great shout, and stopped their ears; they made a concerted rush at him, threw him out of the city, and set about stoning him. The witnesses laid their coats at the feet of a young man named Saul. As they stoned him Stephen called out, 'Lord Jesus, receive my spirit.' He fell on his knees and cried aloud, 'Lord, do not hold this sin against them,' and with that he died. Saul was among those who approved of his execution.

That day was the beginning of a time of violent persecution for the church in Jerusalem; and all except the apostles were scattered over the country districts of Judaea and Samaria. Stephen was given burial by devout men, who made a great lamentation for him. Saul, meanwhile, was harrying the church; he entered house after house, seizing men and women and sending them to prison.

As for those who had been scattered, they went through the country preaching the word.

SIMON THE MAGICIAN
Acts 8:5–15, 18–25

Philip came down to a city in Samaria and began proclaiming the Messiah there. As the crowds heard Philip and saw the signs he performed, everyone paid close attention to what he had to say. In many cases of possession the unclean spirits came out with a loud cry, and many paralysed and crippled folk were cured; and there was great rejoicing in that city.

A man named Simon had been in the city for some time and had captivated the Samaritans with his magical arts, making large claims for himself. Everybody, high and low, listened intently to him. 'This man', they said, 'is that power of God which is called "The Great Power".' They listened because they had for so long been captivated by his magic. But when they came to believe Philip, with his good news about the kingdom of God and the name of Jesus Christ, men and women alike were baptized. Even Simon himself believed, and after his baptism was constantly in Philip's company. He was captivated when he saw the powerful signs and miracles that were taking place.

When the apostles in Jerusalem heard that Samaria had accepted the word of God, they sent off Peter and John, who went down there and prayed for the converts, asking that they might receive the Holy Spirit...

When Simon observed that the Spirit was bestowed through the laying on of the apostles' hands, he offered them money and said, 'Give me too the same power, so that anyone I lay my hands on will receive the Holy Spirit.' Peter replied, 'You thought God's gift was for sale? Your money can go with you to damnation! You have neither part nor share in this, for you are corrupt in the eyes of God. Repent of this wickedness of yours and pray the Lord to forgive you for harbouring such a thought. I see that bitter gall and the chains of sin will be your fate.' Simon said to them, 'Pray to the Lord for me, and ask that none of the things you have spoken of may befall me.'

After giving their testimony and speaking the word of the Lord, they took the road back to Jerusalem, bringing the good news to many Samaritan villages on the way.

PHILIP AND THE ETHIOPIAN EUNUCH
Acts 8:26–38

Then the angel of the Lord said to Philip, 'Start out and go south to the road that leads down from Jerusalem to Gaza.' (This is the desert road.) He set out and was on his way when he caught sight of an Ethiopian. This man was a eunuch, a high official of the Kandake, or queen, of Ethiopia, in charge of all her treasure; he had been to Jerusalem on a pilgrimage and was now returning home, sitting in his carriage and reading aloud from the prophet Isaiah. The Spirit said to Philip, 'Go and meet the carriage.' When Philip ran up he heard him reading from the prophet Isaiah and asked, 'Do you understand what you are reading?' He said, 'How can I without someone to guide me?' and invited Philip to get in and sit beside him.

The passage he was reading was this: 'He was led like a sheep to the slaughter; like a lamb that is dumb before the shearer, he does not open his mouth. He has been humiliated and has no redress. Who will be able to speak of his posterity? For he is cut off from the world of the living.'

'Please tell me', said the eunuch to Philip, 'who it is that the prophet is speaking about here: himself or someone else?' Then Philip began and, starting from this passage, he told him the good news of Jesus. As they were going along the road, they came to some water. 'Look,' said the eunuch, 'here is water: what is to prevent my being baptized?' and he ordered the carriage to stop. Then they both went down into the water, Philip and the eunuch, and he baptized him...

THE CONVERSION OF SAUL
Acts 9:1–22

Saul, still breathing murderous threats against the Lord's disciples, went to the high priest and applied for letters to the synagogues at Damascus authorizing him to arrest any followers of the new way whom he found, men or women, and bring them to Jerusalem. While he was still on the road and nearing Damascus, suddenly a light from the sky flashed all around him. He fell to the ground and heard a voice saying, 'Saul, Saul, why are you persecuting me?' 'Tell me, Lord,' he said, 'who you are.' The voice answered, 'I am Jesus, whom you are persecuting. But now get up and go into the city, and you will be told what you have to do.' Meanwhile the men who were travelling with him stood speechless; they heard the voice but could see no one. Saul got up from the ground, but when he opened his eyes he could not see; they led him by the hand and brought him into Damascus. He was blind for three days, and took no food or drink.

There was in Damascus a disciple named Ananias. He had a vision in which he heard the Lord say: 'Ananias!' 'Here I am, Lord,' he answered. The Lord said to him, 'Go to Straight Street, to the house of Judas, and ask for a man from Tarsus named Saul. You will find him at prayer; he has had a vision of a man named Ananias coming in and laying hands on him to restore his sight.' Ananias answered, 'Lord, I have often heard about this man and all the harm he has done your people in Jerusalem. Now he is here with authority

189

from the chief priests to arrest all who invoke your name.' But the Lord replied, 'You must go, for this man is my chosen instrument to bring my name before the nations and their kings, and before the people of Israel. I myself will show him all that he must go through for my name's sake.'

So Ananias went and, on entering the house, laid his hands on him and said, 'Saul, my brother, the Lord Jesus, who appeared to you on your way here, has sent me to you so that you may recover your sight and be filled with the Holy Spirit.' Immediately it was as if scales had fallen from his eyes, and he regained his sight. He got up and was baptized, and when he had eaten his strength returned.

He stayed some time with the disciples in Damascus. Without delay he proclaimed Jesus publicly in the synagogues, declaring him to be the Son of God. All who heard were astounded. 'Is not this the man', they said, 'who was in Jerusalem hunting down those who invoke this name? Did he not come here for the sole purpose of arresting them and taking them before the chief priests?' But Saul went from strength to strength, and confounded the Jews of Damascus with his cogent proofs that Jesus was the Messiah.

SAUL ESCAPES FROM DAMASCUS
Acts 9:23–30

When some time had passed, the Jews hatched a plot against his life; but their plans became known to Saul. They kept watch on the city gates day and night so that they might murder him; but one night some disciples took him and, lowering him in a basket, let him down over the wall.

On reaching Jerusalem he tried to join the disciples, but they were all afraid of him, because they did not believe that he really was a disciple. Barnabas, however, took him and introduced him to the apostles; he described to them how on his journey Saul had seen the Lord and heard his voice, and how at Damascus he had spoken out boldly in the name of Jesus. Saul now stayed with them, moving about freely in Jerusalem. He spoke out boldly and openly in the name of the Lord, talking and debating with the Greek-speaking Jews.

But they planned to murder him, and when the brethren discovered this they escorted him down to Caesarea and sent him away to Tarsus...

THE CONVERSION OF CORNELIUS
Acts 10:1–35, 44 – 11:4, 18

At Caesarea there was a man named Cornelius, a centurion in the Italian Cohort, as it was called. He was a devout man, and he and his whole family joined in the worship of God; he gave generously to help the Jewish people, and was regular in his prayers to God. One day about three in the afternoon he had a vision in which he clearly saw an angel of God come into his room and say, 'Cornelius!' Cornelius stared at him in terror. 'What is it, my lord?' he asked. The angel said, 'Your prayers and acts of charity have gone up to heaven to speak for you before God. Now send to Joppa for a man named Simon, also called Peter: he is lodging with another Simon, a tanner, whose house is by the sea.' When the angel who spoke to him had gone, he summoned two of his servants and a military orderly who was a religious man, told them the whole story, and ordered them to Joppa.

Next day about noon, while they were still on their way and approaching the city, Peter went up on the roof to pray. He grew hungry and wanted something to eat, but while they were getting it ready, he fell into a trance. He saw heaven opened, and something coming down that looked like a great sheet of sailcloth; it was slung by the four corners and was being lowered to the earth, and in it he saw creatures of every kind, four-footed beasts, reptiles, and birds. There came a voice which said to him, 'Get up, Peter, kill and eat.' But Peter answered, 'No, Lord! I have never eaten anything profane or unclean.' The voice came again, a second time: 'It is not for you to call profane what God counts clean.' This happened three times, and then the thing was taken up into heaven.

While Peter was still puzzling over the meaning of the vision he had seen, the messengers from Cornelius had been asking the way to Simon's house, and now arrived at the entrance. They called out and asked if Simon Peter was lodging there. Peter was thinking over the vision, when the Spirit said to him, 'Some men are here looking for you; get up and go downstairs. You may go with them without any misgiving, for it was I who sent them.' Peter came down to the men and said, 'You are looking for me? Here I am. What brings you here?' 'We are from the centurion Cornelius,' they replied, 'a good and religious man, acknowledged as such by the whole Jewish nation. He was directed by a holy angel to send for you to his house and hear what you have to say.' So Peter asked them in and gave them a night's lodging.

Next day he set out with them, accompanied by some members of the congregation at Joppa, and on the following day arrived at Caesarea. Cornelius was expecting them and had called together his relatives and close friends. When Peter arrived, Cornelius came to meet him, and bowed to the ground in deep reverence. But Peter raised him to his feet and said, 'Stand up; I am only a man like you.' Still talking with him he went in and found a large gathering. He said to them, 'I need not tell you that a Jew is forbidden by his religion to visit or associate with anyone of another race. Yet God has shown me clearly that I must not call anyone profane or unclean; that is why I came here without demur when you sent for me. May I ask what was your reason for doing so?'

Cornelius said, 'Three days ago, just about this time, I was in the house here saying the afternoon prayers, when suddenly a man in shining robes stood before me. He said: "Cornelius, your prayer has been heard and your acts of charity have spoken for you before God. Send to Simon Peter at Joppa, and ask him to come; he is lodging in the house of Simon the tanner, by the sea." I sent to you there and then, and you have been good enough to come. So now we are all met here before God, to listen to everything that the Lord has instructed you to say.'

Peter began: 'I now understand how true it is that God has no favourites, but that in every nation those who are god-fearing and do what is right are acceptable to him...'

Peter was still speaking when the Holy Spirit came upon all who were listening to the message. The believers who had come with Peter, men of Jewish birth, were amazed that the gift of the Holy Spirit should have been poured out even on Gentiles, for they could hear

em speaking in tongues of ecstasy and acclaiming the greatness of
od. Then Peter spoke: 'Is anyone prepared to withhold the water of
aptism from these persons, who have received the Holy Spirit just as
e did?' Then he ordered them to be baptized in the name of Jesus
hrist. After that they asked him to stay on with them for a time.

News came to the apostles and the members of the church in
daea that Gentiles too had accepted the word of God; and when
eter came up to Jerusalem those who were of Jewish birth took issue
ith him. 'You have been visiting men who are uncircumcised,' they
id, 'and sitting at table with them!' Peter began by laying before
em the facts as they had happened...

When they heard this their doubts were silenced, and they gave
raise to God. 'This means', they said, 'that God has granted life-
ving repentance to the Gentiles also.'

THE CHURCH AT ANTIOCH
Acts 11:19–26

eanwhile those who had been scattered after the persecution that
ose over Stephen made their way to Phoenicia, Cyprus, and
ntioch, bringing the message to Jews only and to no others. But
ere were some natives of Cyprus and Cyrene among them, and
ese, when they arrived at Antioch, began to speak to Gentiles as
ell, telling them the good news of the Lord Jesus. The power of the
ord was with them, and a great many became believers and turned
the Lord.

The news reached the ears of the church in Jerusalem; and they
nt Barnabas to Antioch. When he arrived and saw the divine grace
work, he rejoiced and encouraged them all to hold fast to the Lord
ith resolute hearts, for he was a good man, full of the Holy Spirit and
faith. And large numbers were won over to the Lord.

He then went off to Tarsus to look for Saul; and when he had
und him, he brought him to Antioch. For a whole year the two of
em lived in fellowship with the church there, and gave instruction
large numbers. It was in Antioch that the disciples first got the
ame of Christians...

PETER ESCAPES FROM HEROD
Acts 12:1–19, 21–23

It was about this time that King Herod launched an attack on certain members of the church. He beheaded James, the brother of John, and, when he saw that the Jews approved, proceeded to arrest Peter also. This happened during the festival of Unleavened Bread. Having secured him, he put him in prison under a military guard, four squads of four men each, meaning to produce him in public after Passover. So, while Peter was held in prison, the church kept praying fervently to God for him.

On the very night before Herod had planned to produce him, Peter was asleep between two soldiers, secured by two chains, while outside the doors sentries kept guard over the prison. All at once an angel of the Lord stood there, and the cell was ablaze with light. He tapped Peter on the shoulder to wake him. 'Quick! Get up!' he said, and the chains fell away from Peter's wrists. The angel said, 'Do up your belt and put on your sandals.' He did so. 'Now wrap your cloak round you and follow me.' Peter followed him out, with no idea that the angel's intervention was real: he thought it was just a vision. They passed the first guard-post, then the second, and reached the iron gate leading out into the city. This opened for them of its own accord; they came out and had walked the length of one street when suddenly the angel left him.

Then Peter came to himself. 'Now I know it is true,' he said: 'the Lord has sent his angel and rescued me from Herod's clutches and from all that the Jewish people were expecting.' Once he had realized this, he made for the house of Mary, the mother of John Mark, where a large company was at prayer. He knocked at the outer door and a maidservant called Rhoda came to answer it. She recognized Peter's voice and was so overjoyed that instead of opening the door she ran in and announced that Peter was standing outside. 'You are crazy,' they told her; but she insisted that it was so. Then they said, 'It must be his angel.'

Peter went on knocking, and when they opened the door and saw him, they were astounded. He motioned to them with his hand to keep quiet, and described to them how the Lord had brought him out of prison. 'Tell James and the members of the church,' he said. Then he left the house and went off elsewhere.

When morning came, there was consternation among the soldiers: what could have become of Peter? Herod made careful search, but failed to find him, so he interrogated the guards and ordered their execution. Afterwards Herod left Judaea to reside for a while at Caesarea...

On an appointed day Herod, attired in his royal robes and seated on the rostrum, addressed the populace; they responded, 'It is a god speaking, not a man!' Instantly an angel of the Lord struck him down, because he had usurped the honour due to God; he was eaten up with worms and so died.

ELYMAS THE SORCERER
Acts 13:1-12

There were in the church at Antioch certain prophets and teachers: Barnabas, Simeon called Niger, Lucius of Cyrene, Manaen, a close friend of Prince Herod, and Saul. While they were offering worship to the Lord and fasting, the Holy Spirit said, 'Set Barnabas and Saul apart for me, to do the work to which I have called them.' Then, after further fasting and prayer, they laid their hands on them and sent them on their way.

These two, sent out on their mission by the Holy Spirit, came down to Seleucia, and from there sailed to Cyprus. Arriving at Salamis, they declared the word of God in the Jewish synagogues; they had John with them as their assistant. They went through the whole island as far as Paphos, and there they came upon a sorcerer, a Jew who posed as a prophet, Barjesus by name. He was in the retinue of the governor, Sergius Paulus, a learned man, who had sent for Barnabas and Saul and wanted to hear the word of God. This Elymas the sorcerer (so his name may be translated) opposed them, trying to turn the governor away from the faith. But Saul, also known as Paul, filled with the Holy Spirit, fixed his eyes on him and said, 'You are a swindler, an out-and-out fraud! You son of the devil and enemy of all goodness, will you never stop perverting the straight ways of the Lord?

Look now, the hand of the Lord strikes: you shall be blind, and for a time you shall not see the light of the sun.' At once mist and darkness came over his eyes, and he groped about for someone to lead him by the hand. When the governor saw what had happened he became a believer, deeply impressed by what he learnt about the Lord.

PAUL AND BARNABAS TURN TO THE GENTILES
Acts 13:13–23, 26–33, 42–46

Sailing from Paphos, Paul and his companions went to Perga in Pamphylia; John, however, left them and returned to Jerusalem. From Perga they continued their journey as far as Pisidian Antioch. On the sabbath they went to synagogue and took their seats; and after the readings from the law and the prophets, the officials of the synagogue sent this message to them: 'Friends, if you have anything to say to the people by way of exhortation, let us hear it.' Paul stood up, raised his hand for silence, and began.

'Listen, men of Israel and you others who worship God! The God of this people, Israel, chose our forefathers. When they were still living as aliens in Egypt, he made them into a great people and, with arm outstretched, brought them out of that country. For some forty years he bore with their conduct in the desert. Then in the Canaanite country, after overthrowing seven nations, whose lands he gave them to be their heritage for some four hundred and fifty years, he appointed judges for them until the time of the prophet Samuel.

'It was then that they asked for a king, and God gave them Saul son of Kish, a man of the tribe of Benjamin. He reigned for forty years before God removed him and appointed David as their king, with this commendation: "I have found David the son of Jesse to be a man after my own heart; he will carry out all my purposes." This is the man from whose descendants God, as he promised, has brought Israel a saviour, Jesus...

'My brothers, who come of Abraham's stock, and others among you who worship God, we are the people to whom this message of salvation has been sent. The people of Jerusalem and their rulers did not recognize Jesus, or understand the words of the prophets which are read sabbath by sabbath; indeed, they fulfilled them by condemning him. Though they failed to find grounds for the sentence of death, they asked Pilate to have him executed. When they had carried out all that the scriptures said about him, they took him down from the gibbet and laid him in a tomb. But God raised him from the dead; and over a period of many days he appeared to those who had come up with him from Galilee to Jerusalem, and they are now his witnesses before our people.

'We are here to give you the good news that God, who made the promise to the fathers, has fulfilled it for the children by raising Jesus from the dead...'

As they were leaving the synagogue they were asked to come again and speak on these subjects next sabbath; and after the congregation had dispersed, many Jews and gentile worshippers went with Paul and Barnabas, who spoke to them and urged them to hold fast to the grace of God.

On the following sabbath almost the whole city gathered to hear the word of God. When the Jews saw the crowds, they were filled with jealous resentment, and contradicted what Paul had said with violent abuse. But Paul and Barnabas were outspoken in their reply. 'It was necessary', they said, 'that the word of God should be declared to you first. But since you reject it and judge yourselves unworthy of eternal life, we now turn to the Gentiles...'

THE JEWS OPPOSE PAUL'S MISSION
Acts 13:49 – 14:28

Thus the word of the Lord spread throughout the region. But the Jews stirred up feeling among those worshippers who were women of standing, and among the leading men of the city; a campaign of persecution was started against Paul and Barnabas, and they were expelled from the district. They shook the dust off their feet in protest against them and went to Iconium. And the disciples were filled with joy and with the Holy Spirit.

At Iconium they went together into the Jewish synagogue and spoke to such purpose that Jews and Greeks in large numbers became believers. But the unconverted Jews stirred up the Gentiles and poisoned their minds against the Christians. So Paul and Barnabas stayed on for some time, and spoke boldly and openly in reliance on the Lord, who confirmed the message of his grace by enabling them to work signs and miracles. The populace was divided, some siding with the Jews, others with the apostles. A move was made by Gentiles and Jews together, with the connivance of the city authorities, to maltreat them and stone them, and when they became aware of this, they made their escape to the Lycaonian cities of Lystra and Derbe and the surrounding country. There they continued to spread the good news.

At Lystra a cripple, lame from birth, who had never walked in his life, sat listening to Paul as he spoke. Paul fixed his eyes on him and, seeing that he had the faith to be cured, said in a loud voice, 'Stand up straight on your feet'; and he sprang up and began to walk. When the crowds saw what Paul had done, they shouted, in their native Lycaonian, 'The gods have come down to us in human form!' They called Barnabas Zeus, and Paul they called Hermes, because he was the spokesman. The priest of Zeus, whose temple was just outside the city, brought oxen and garlands to the gates, and he and the people were about to offer sacrifice.

But when the apostles Barnabas and Paul heard of it, they tore their clothes and rushed into the crowd shouting, 'Men, why are you doing this? We are human beings, just like you. The good news we bring tells you to turn from these follies to the living God, who made heaven and earth and sea and everything in them. In past ages he has allowed all nations to go their own way; and yet he has not left you without some clue to his nature, in the benefits he bestows: he sends you rain from heaven and the crops in their seasons, and gives you food in plenty and keeps you in good heart.' Even with these words they barely managed to prevent the crowd from offering sacrifice to them.

Then Jews from Antioch and Iconium came on the scene and won over the crowds. They stoned Paul, and dragged him out of the city, thinking him dead. The disciples formed a ring round him, and he got to his feet and went into the city. Next day he left with Barnabas for Derbe.

After bringing the good news to that town and gaining many converts, they returned to Lystra, then to Iconium, and then to

Antioch, strengthening the disciples and encouraging them to be true to the faith. They warned them that to enter the kingdom of God we must undergo many hardships. They also appointed for them elders in each congregation, and with prayer and fasting committed them to the Lord in whom they had put their trust.

They passed through Pisidia and came into Pamphylia. When they had delivered the message at Perga, they went down to Attalia, and from there sailed to Antioch, where they had originally been commended to the grace of God for the task which they had now completed. On arrival there, they called the congregation together and reported all that God had accomplished through them, and how he had thrown open the gates of faith to the Gentiles. And they stayed for some time with the disciples there.

THE COUNCIL OF JERUSALEM
Acts 15:1–14, 19–31

Some people who had come down from Judaea began to teach the brotherhood that those who were not circumcised in accordance with Mosaic practice could not be saved. That brought them into fierce dissension and controversy with Paul and Barnabas, and it was arranged that these two and some others from Antioch should go up to Jerusalem to see the apostles and elders about this question.

They were sent on their way by the church, and travelled through Phoenicia and Samaria, telling the full story of the conversion of the Gentiles, and causing great rejoicing among all the Christians.

When they reached Jerusalem they were welcomed by the church and the apostles and elders, and they reported all that God had accomplished through them. But some of the Pharisaic party who had become believers came forward and declared, 'Those Gentiles must be circumcised and told to keep the law of Moses.'

The apostles and elders met to look into this matter, and, after a long debate, Peter rose to address them. 'My friends,' he said, 'in the early days, as you yourselves know, God made his choice among you: from my lips the Gentiles were to hear and believe the message of the gospel. And God, who can read human hearts, showed his approval by giving the Holy Spirit to them as he did to us. He made no difference between them and us; for he purified their hearts by faith. Then why do you now try God's patience by laying on the shoulders of these converts a yoke which neither we nor our forefathers were able to bear? For our belief is that we are saved in the same way as they are: by the grace of the Lord Jesus.'

At that the whole company fell silent and listened to Barnabas and Paul as they described all the signs and portents that God had worked among the Gentiles through them.

When they had finished speaking, James summed up: 'My friends,' he said, 'listen to me. Simon has described how it first happened that God, in his providence, chose from among the Gentiles a people to bear his name...

'In my judgment, therefore, we should impose no irksome restrictions on those of the Gentiles who are turning to God; instead we should instruct them by letter to abstain from things polluted by contact with idols, from fornication, from anything that has been strangled, and from blood. Moses, after all, has never lacked spokesmen in every town for generations past; he is read in the synagogues sabbath by sabbath.'

Then, with the agreement of the whole church, the apostles and elders resolved to choose representatives and send them to Antioch with Paul and Barnabas. They chose two leading men in the community, Judas Barsabbas and Silas, and gave them this letter to deliver:

From the apostles and elders to our brothers of gentile origin in Antioch, Syria, and Cilicia. Greetings!

We have heard that some of our number, without any instructions from us, have disturbed you with their talk and unsettled your minds. In consequence, we have resolved unanimously to send to you our chosen representatives with our well-beloved Barnabas and Paul, who have given up their lives to the cause of our Lord Jesus Christ; so we are sending Judas and Silas, who will, by word of mouth, confirm what is written in this letter. It is the decision of the Holy Spirit, and our decision, to lay no further burden upon you beyond these essentials: you are to abstain from meat that has been offered to idols, from blood, from anything that has been strangled, and from fornication. If you keep yourselves free from these things you will be doing well. Farewell.

So they took their leave and travelled down to Antioch, where they called the congregation together and delivered the letter. When it was read, all rejoiced at the encouragement it brought...

PAUL'S JOURNEY TO MACEDONIA
Acts 15:36 – 16:15

After a while Paul said to Barnabas, 'Let us go back and see how our brothers are getting on in the various towns where we proclaimed the word of the Lord.' Barnabas wanted to take John Mark with them; but Paul insisted that the man who had deserted them in Pamphylia and had not gone on to share in their work was not the man to take with them now. The dispute was so sharp that they parted company. Barnabas took Mark with him and sailed for Cyprus. Paul chose Silas and started on his journey, commended by the brothers to the grace of the Lord. He travelled through Syria and Cilicia bringing new strength to the churches.

He went on to Derbe and then to Lystra, where he found a disciple named Timothy, the son of a Jewish Christian mother and a gentile father, well spoken of by the Christians at Lystra and Iconium. Paul wanted to take him with him when he left, so he had him circumcised out of consideration for the Jews who lived in those parts, for they all knew that his father was a Gentile. As they made their way from town to town they handed on the decisions taken by the apostles and elders in Jerusalem and enjoined their observance. So, day by day, the churches grew stronger in faith and increased in numbers.

They travelled through the Phrygian and Galatian region, prevented by the Holy Spirit from delivering the message in the province of Asia. When they approached the Mysian border they tried to enter Bithynia, but, as the Spirit of Jesus would not allow them, they passed through Mysia and reached the coast at Troas. During the night a vision came to Paul: a Macedonian stood there appealing to him, 'Cross over to Macedonia and help us.' As soon as he had seen this vision, we set about getting a passage to Macedonia, convinced that God had called us to take the good news there.

We sailed from Troas and made a straight run to Samothrace, the next day to Neapolis, and from there to Philippi, a leading city in that district of Macedonia and a Roman colony. Here we stayed for some days, and on the sabbath we went outside the city gate by the riverside, where we thought there would be a place of prayer; we sat down and talked to the women who had gathered there. One of those listening was called Lydia, a dealer in purple fabric, who came from the city of Thyatira; she was a worshipper of God, and the Lord opened her heart to respond to what Paul said. She was baptized, and her household with her, and then she urged us, 'Now that you have accepted me as a believer in the Lord, come and stay at my house.' And she insisted on our going.

THE CONVERSION OF THE PHILIPPIAN JAILER
Acts 16:16–40

Once, on our way to the place of prayer, we met a slave-girl who was possessed by a spirit of divination and brought large profits to her owners by telling fortunes. She followed Paul and the rest of us, shouting, 'These men are servants of the Most High God, and are declaring to you a way of salvation.' She did this day after day, until, in exasperation, Paul rounded on the spirit. 'I command you in the name of Jesus Christ to come out of her,' he said, and it came out instantly.

When the girl's owners saw that their hope of profit had gone, they seized Paul and Silas and dragged them to the city authorities in the main square; bringing them before the magistrates, they alleged, 'These men are causing a disturbance in our city; they are Jews, and they are advocating practices which it is illegal for us Romans to adopt and follow.' The mob joined in the attack; and the magistrates had the prisoners stripped and gave orders for them to be flogged. After a severe beating they were flung into prison and the jailer was ordered to keep them under close guard. In view of these orders, he put them into the inner prison and secured their feet in the stocks.

About midnight Paul and Silas, at their prayers, were singing praises to God, and the other prisoners were listening, when suddenly there was such a violent earthquake that the foundations of the jail were shaken; the doors burst open and all the prisoners found their fetters unfastened. The jailer woke up to see the prison doors wide open and, assuming that the prisoners had escaped, drew his sword intending to kill himself. But Paul shouted, 'Do yourself no harm; we are all here.' The jailer called for lights, rushed in, and threw himself down before Paul and Silas, trembling with fear. He then escorted them out and said, 'Sirs, what must I do to be saved?' They answered, 'Put your trust in the Lord Jesus, and you will be saved, you and your household,' and they imparted the word of the Lord to him and to everyone in his house. At that late hour of the night the jailer took them and washed their wounds, and there and then he and his whole family were baptized. He brought them up into his house, set out a meal, and rejoiced with his whole household in his new-found faith in God.

When daylight came, the magistrates sent their officers with the order, 'Release those men.' The jailer reported these instructions to Paul: 'The magistrates have sent an order for your release. Now you are free to go in peace.' But Paul said to the officers: 'We are Roman citizens! They gave us a public flogging and threw us into prison without trial. Are they now going to smuggle us out by stealth? No indeed! Let them come in person and escort us out.' The officers reported his words to the magistrates. Alarmed to hear that they were Roman citizens, they came and apologized to them, and then escorted them out and requested them to go away from the city. On leaving the prison, they went to Lydia's house, where they met their fellow-Christians and spoke words of encouragement to them, and then they took their departure.

PAUL PREACHES AT THESSALONICA
Acts 17:1–15

They now travelled by way of Amphipolis and Apollonia and came to Thessalonica, where there was a Jewish synagogue. Following his usual practice Paul went to their meetings; and for the next three sabbaths he argued with them, quoting texts of scripture which he expounded and applied to show that the Messiah had to suffer and rise from the dead. 'And this Jesus', he said, 'whom I am proclaiming to you is the Messiah.' Some of them were convinced and joined Paul and Silas, as did a great number of godfearing Gentiles and a good many influential women.

The Jews in their jealousy recruited some ruffians from the dregs of society to gather a mob. They put the city in an uproar, and made for Jason's house with the intention of bringing Paul and Silas before the town assembly. Failing to find them, they dragged Jason himself and some members of the congregation before the magistrates, shouting, 'The men who have made trouble the whole world over have now come here, and Jason has harboured them. All of them flout the emperor's laws, and assert there is a rival king, Jesus.' These words alarmed the mob and the magistrates also, who took security from Jason and the others before letting them go.

As soon as darkness fell, the members of the congregation sent Paul and Silas off to Beroea; and, on arrival, they made their way to the synagogue. The Jews here were more fair-minded than those at Thessalonica: they received the message with great eagerness, studying the scriptures every day to see whether it was true. Many of them therefore became believers, and so did a fair number of Gentiles, women of standing as well as men. But when the Thessalonian Jews learnt that the word of God had now been proclaimed by Paul in Beroea, they followed him there to stir up trouble and rouse the rabble. At once the members of the congregation sent Paul down to the coast, while Silas and Timothy both stayed behind. Paul's escort brought him as far as Athens, and came away with instructions for Silas and Timothy to rejoin him with all speed.

PAUL'S SPEECH BEFORE THE COUNCIL OF THE AREOPAGUS
Acts 17:16–32

While Paul was waiting for them at Athens, he was outraged to see the city so full of idols. He argued in the synagogue with the Jews and gentile worshippers, and also in the city square every day with casual passers-by. Moreover, some of the Epicurean and Stoic philosophers joined issue with him. Some said, 'What can this charlatan be trying to say?' and others, 'He would appear to be a propagandist for foreign deities' – this because he was preaching about Jesus and the resurrection. They brought him to the Council of the Areopagus and asked, 'May we know what this new doctrine is that you propound? You are introducing ideas that sound strange to us, and we should like to know what they mean.' Now, all the Athenians and the resident foreigners had time for nothing except talking or hearing about the latest novelty.

Paul stood up before the Council of the Areopagus and began: 'Men of Athens, I see that in everything that concerns religion you are uncommonly scrupulous. As I was going round looking at the objects of your worship, I noticed among other things an altar bearing the inscription "To an Unknown God". What you worship but do not know – this is what I now proclaim.

'The God who created the world and everything in it, and who is Lord of heaven and earth, does not live in shrines made by human hands. It is not because he lacks anything that he accepts service at our hands, for he is himself the universal giver of life and breath – indeed of everything. He created from one stock every nation of men to inhabit the whole earth's surface. He determined their eras in history and the limits of their territory. They were to seek God in the hope that, groping after him, they might find him; though indeed he is not far from each one of us, for in him we live and move, in him we exist; as some of your own poets have said, "We are also his offspring." Being God's offspring, then, we ought not to suppose that the deity is like an image in gold or silver or stone, shaped by human craftsmanship and design. God has overlooked the age of ignorance; but now he commands men and women everywhere to repent, because he has fixed the day on which he will have the world judged, and justly judged, by a man whom he has designated; of this he has given assurance to all by raising him from the dead.'

When they heard about the raising of the dead, some scoffed; others said, 'We will hear you on this subject some other time.'...

PAUL FOUNDS THE CHURCH AT CORINTH
Acts 18:1–4, 8–18

After this Paul left Athens and went to Corinth. There he met a Jew named Aquila, a native of Pontus, and his wife Priscilla; they had recently arrived from Italy because Claudius had issued an edict that all Jews should leave Rome. Paul approached them and, because he was of the same trade, he made his home with them; they were tentmakers and Paul worked with them. He also held discussions in the synagogue sabbath by sabbath, trying to convince both Jews and Gentiles...

Crispus, the president of the synagogue, became a believer in the Lord, as did all his household; and a number of Corinthians who heard him believed and were baptized. One night in a vision the Lord said to Paul, 'Have no fear: go on with your preaching and do not be silenced. I am with you, and no attack shall harm you, for I have many in this city who are my people.' So he settled there for eighteen months, teaching the word of God among them.

But when Gallio was proconsul of Achaia, the Jews made a concerted attack on Paul and brought him before the court. 'This man', they said, 'is inducing people to worship God in ways that are against the law.' Paul was just about to speak when Gallio declared, 'If it had been a question of crime or grave misdemeanour, I should, of course, have given you Jews a patient hearing, but if it is some bickering about words and names and your Jewish law, you may settle it yourselves. I do not intend to be a judge of these matters.' And he dismissed them from the court. Then they all attacked Sosthenes, the president of the synagogue, and beat him up in full view of the tribunal. But all this left Gallio quite unconcerned.

Paul stayed on at Corinth for some time, and then took leave of the congregation. Accompanied by Priscilla and Aquila, he sailed for Syria, having had his hair cut off at Cenchreae in fulfilment of a vow.

THE CHURCH AT EPHESUS
Acts 18:19 – 19:10, 21–22

They put in at Ephesus, where he parted from his companions; he himself went into the synagogue and held a discussion with the Jews.

He was asked to stay longer, but he declined and set sail from Ephesus, promising, as he took leave of them, 'I shall come back to you if it is God's will.' On landing at Caesarea, he went up and greeted the church; and then went down to Antioch. After some time there he set out again on a journey through the Galatian country and then through Phrygia, bringing new strength to all the disciples.

There arrived at Ephesus a Jew named Apollos, an Alexandrian by birth, an eloquent man, powerful in his use of the scriptures. He had been instructed in the way of the Lord and was full of spiritual fervour; and in his discourses he taught accurately the facts about Jesus, though the only baptism he knew was John's. He now began to speak boldly in the synagogue, where Priscilla and Aquila heard him; they took him in hand and expounded the way to him in greater detail. Finding that he wanted to go across to Achaia, the congregation gave him their support, and wrote to the disciples there to make him welcome. From the time of his arrival, he was very helpful to those who had by God's grace become believers, for he strenuously confuted the Jews, demonstrating publicly from the scriptures that the Messiah is Jesus.

While Apollos was at Corinth, Paul travelled through the inland regions till he came to Ephesus, where he found a number of disciples. When he asked them, 'Did you receive the Holy Spirit when you became believers?' they replied, 'No, we were not even told that there is a Holy Spirit.' He asked, 'Then what baptism were you given?' 'John's baptism,' they answered. Paul said, 'The baptism that John gave was a baptism in token of repentance, and he told the people to put their trust in one who was to come after him, that is, in Jesus.' On hearing this they were baptized into the name of the Lord Jesus; and when Paul had laid his hands on them, the Holy Spirit came upon them and they spoke in tongues of ecstasy and prophesied. There were about a dozen men in all.

During the next three months he attended the synagogue and with persuasive argument spoke boldly about the kingdom of God. When some proved obdurate and would not believe, speaking evil of the new way before the congregation, he withdrew from them, taking the disciples with him, and continued to hold discussions daily in the lecture hall of Tyrannus. This went on for two years, with the result that the whole population of the province of Asia, both Jews and Gentiles, heard the word of the Lord...

When matters had reached this stage, Paul made up his mind to visit Macedonia and Achaia and then go on to Jerusalem. 'After I have been there,' he said, 'I must see Rome also.' He sent two of his assistants, Timothy and Erastus, to Macedonia, while he himself stayed some time longer in the province of Asia.

THE RIOT AT EPHESUS
Acts 19:23–41

It was about this time that the Christian movement gave rise to a serious disturbance. There was a man named Demetrius, a silversmith who made silver shrines of Artemis, and provided considerable employment for the craftsmen. He called a meeting of them and of the workers in allied trades, and addressed them: 'As you men know, our prosperity depends on this industry. But this fellow Paul, as you can see and hear for yourselves, has perverted crowds of people with his propaganda, not only at Ephesus but also in practically the whole of the province of Asia; he tells them that gods made by human hands are not gods at all. There is danger for us here; it is not only that our line of business will be discredited, but also that the sanctuary of the great goddess Artemis will cease to command respect; and then it will not be long before she who is worshipped by all Asia and the civilized world is brought down from her divine pre-eminence.'

On hearing this, they were enraged, and began to shout, 'Great is Artemis of the Ephesians!' The whole city was in an uproar; they made a concerted rush into the theatre, hustling along with them Paul's travelling companions, the Macedonians Gaius and Aristarchus. Paul wanted to appear before the assembly but the other Christians would not let him. Even some of the dignitaries of the province, who were friendly towards him, sent a message urging him not to venture into the theatre. Meanwhile some were shouting one thing, some another, for the assembly was in an uproar and most of them did not know what they had all come for. Some of the crowd explained the trouble to Alexander, whom the Jews had pushed to the front, and he, motioning for silence, attempted to make a defence before the assembly. But when they recognized that he was a Jew, one shout arose from them all: 'Great is Artemis of the Ephesians!' and they kept it up for about two hours.

The town clerk, however, quietened the crowd. 'Citizens of Ephesus,' he said, 'all the world knows that our city of Ephesus is temple warden of the great Artemis and of that image of her which fell from heaven. Since these facts are beyond dispute, your proper course is to keep calm and do nothing rash. These men whom you have brought here as offenders have committed no sacrilege and uttered no blasphemy against our goddess. If, therefore, Demetrius and his craftsmen have a case against anyone, there are assizes and there are proconsuls; let the parties bring their charges and countercharges. But if it is a larger question you are raising, it will be dealt with in the statutory assembly. We certainly run the risk of being charged with riot for this day's work. There is no justification for it, and it would be impossible for us to give any explanation of this turmoil.' With that he dismissed the assembly.

PAUL RETURNS TO MACEDONIA
Acts 20:1–12

When the disturbance was over, Paul sent for the disciples and, after encouraging them, said goodbye and set out on his journey to Macedonia. He travelled through that region, constantly giving encouragement to the Christians, and finally reached Greece. When he had spent three months there and was on the point of embarking for Syria, a plot was laid against him by the Jews, so he decided to return by way of Macedonia. He was accompanied by Sopater son of Pyrrhus from Beroea, Aristarchus and Secundus from Thessalonica, Gaius of Derbe, and Timothy, and from Asia Tychicus and Trophimus. These went ahead and waited for us at Troas; we ourselves sailed from Philippi after the Passover season, and five days later rejoined them at Troas, where we spent a week.

On the Saturday night, when we gathered for the breaking of bread, Paul, who was to leave next day, addressed the congregation and went on speaking until midnight. Now there were many lamps in the upstairs room where we were assembled, and a young man named Eutychus, who was sitting on the window-ledge, grew more and more drowsy as Paul went on talking, until, completely overcome by sleep, he fell from the third storey to the ground, and was picked up dead. Paul went down, threw himself upon him, and clasped him in his arms. 'Do not distress yourselves,' he said to them; 'he is alive.' He then went upstairs, broke bread and ate, and after much conversation, which lasted until dawn, he departed. And they took the boy home, greatly relieved that he was alive.

PAUL'S FAREWELL TO THE EPHESIANS
Acts 20:13–19, 22–32, 36–38

We went on ahead to the ship and embarked for Assos, where we were to take Paul aboard; this was the arrangement he had made, since he was going to travel by road. When he met us at Assos, we took him aboard and proceeded to Mitylene. We sailed from there and next day arrived off Chios. On the second day we made Samos, and the following day we reached Miletus. Paul had decided to bypass Ephesus and so avoid having to spend time in the province of Asia; he was eager to be in Jerusalem on the day of Pentecost, if that were possible. He did, however, send from Miletus to Ephesus and summon the elders of the church. When they joined him, he spoke to them as follows.

'You know how, from the day that I first set foot in the province of Asia, I spent my whole time with you, serving the Lord in all humility amid the sorrows and trials that came upon me through the intrigues of the Jews... Now, as you see, I am constrained by the Spirit to go to Jerusalem. I do not know what will befall me there, except that in city after city the Holy Spirit assures me that imprisonment and hardships await me. For myself, I set no store by life; all I want is to finish the race, and complete the task which the Lord Jesus assigned to me, that of bearing my testimony to the gospel of God's grace.

'One thing more: I have gone about among you proclaiming the kingdom, but now I know that none of you will ever see my face

210

again. That being so, I here and now declare that no one's fate can be laid at my door; I have kept back nothing; I have disclosed to you the whole purpose of God. Keep guard over yourselves and over all the flock of which the Holy Spirit has given you charge, as shepherds of the church of the Lord, which he won for himself by his own blood. I know that when I am gone, savage wolves will come in among you and will not spare the flock. Even from your own number men will arise who will distort the truth in order to get the disciples to break away and follow them. So be on the alert; remember how with tears I never ceased to warn each one of you night and day for three years.

'And now I commend you to God and to the word of his grace, which has power to build you up and give you your heritage among all those whom God has made his own...'

As he finished speaking, he knelt down with them all and prayed. There were loud cries of sorrow from them all, as they folded Paul in their arms and kissed him; what distressed them most was his saying that they would never see his face again. Then they escorted him to the ship.

PAUL'S FINAL JOURNEY TO JERUSALEM
Acts 21:1–4, 7–8, 10–17

We tore ourselves away from them and, putting to sea, made a straight run and came to Cos; next day to Rhodes, and thence to Patara. There we found a ship bound for Phoenicia, so we went aboard and sailed in her. We came in sight of Cyprus and, leaving it to port, we continued our voyage to Syria and put in at Tyre, where the ship was to unload her cargo. We sought out the disciples and stayed there a week...

We made the passage from Tyre and reached Ptolemais, where we greeted the brotherhood and spent a day with them. Next day we left and came to Caesarea, where we went to the home of Philip the evangelist... When we had been there several days, a prophet named Agabus arrived from Judaea. He came to us, took Paul's belt, bound his own feet and hands with it, and said, 'These are the words of the Holy Spirit: Thus will the Jews in Jerusalem bind the man to whom this belt belongs, and hand him over to the Gentiles.' When we heard this, we and the local people begged and implored Paul to abandon his visit to Jerusalem. Then Paul gave his answer: 'Why all these tears? Why are you trying to weaken my resolution? I am ready, not merely to be bound, but even to die at Jerusalem for the name of the Lord Jesus.' So, as he would not be dissuaded, we gave up and said, 'The Lord's will be done.'

At the end of our stay we packed our baggage and took the road up to Jerusalem. Some of the disciples from Caesarea came along with us, to direct us to a Cypriot named Mnason, a Christian from the early days, with whom we were to spend the night. On our arrival at Jerusalem, the congregation welcomed us gladly.

PAUL IS ARRESTED IN THE TEMPLE
Acts 21:18 – 22:29

Next day Paul paid a visit to James; we accompanied him, and all the elders were present. After greeting them, he described in detail all that God had done among the Gentiles by means of his ministry. When they heard this, they gave praise to God. Then they said to Paul: 'You observe, brother, how many thousands of converts we have among the Jews, all of them staunch upholders of the law. Now they have been given certain information about you: it is said that you teach all the Jews in the gentile world to turn their backs on Moses, and tell them not to circumcise their children or follow our way of life. What is to be done, then? They are sure to hear that you have arrived. Our proposal is this: we have four men here who are under a vow; take them with you and go through the ritual of purification together, and pay their expenses, so that they may have their heads shaved; then everyone will know that there is nothing in the reports they have heard about you, but that you are yourself a practising Jew and observe the law. As for the gentile converts, we sent them our decision that they should abstain from meat that has been offered to idols, from blood, from anything that has been strangled, and from fornication.' So Paul took the men, and next day, after going through the ritual of purification with them, he went into the temple to give notice of the date when the period of purification would end and the offering be made for each of them.

But just before the seven days were up, the Jews from the province of Asia saw him in the temple. They stirred up all the crowd and seized him, shouting, 'Help us, men of Israel! This is the fellow who attacks our people, our law, and this sanctuary, and spreads his teaching the whole world over. What is more, he has brought Gentiles into the temple and profaned this holy place.' They had previously seen Trophimus the Ephesian with him in the city, and assumed that Paul had brought him into the temple.

The whole city was in a turmoil, and people came running from all directions. They seized Paul and dragged him out of the temple, and at once the doors were shut. They were bent on killing him, but word came to the officer commanding the cohort that all Jerusalem was in an uproar. He immediately took a force of soldiers with their centurions and came down at the double to deal with the riot. When the crowd saw the commandant and his troops, they stopped beating Paul. As soon as the commandant could reach Paul, he arrested him and ordered him to be shackled with two chains; he enquired who he was and what he had been doing. Some in the crowd shouted one thing, some another, and as the commandant could not get at the truth because of the hubbub, he ordered him to be taken to the barracks. When Paul reached the steps, he found himself carried up by the soldiers because of the violence of the mob; for the whole crowd was at their heels yelling, 'Kill him!'

Just before he was taken into the barracks Paul said to the commandant, 'May I have a word with you?' The commandant said, 'So you speak Greek? Then you are not the Egyptian who started a revolt some time ago and led a force of four thousand terrorists out into the desert?' Paul replied, 'I am a Jew from Tarsus in Cilicia, a citizen of no mean city. May I have your permission to speak to the people?' When this was given, Paul stood on the steps and raised his hand to call for the attention of the people. As soon as quiet was restored, he addressed them in the Jewish language:

'Brothers and fathers, give me a hearing while I put my case to you.' When they heard him speaking to them in their own language, they listened more quietly. 'I am a true-born Jew,' he began, 'a native of Tarsus in Cilicia. I was brought up in this city, and as a pupil of Gamaliel I was thoroughly trained in every point of our ancestral law. I have always been ardent in God's service, as you all are today. And so I persecuted this movement to the death, arresting its followers, men and women alike, and committing them to prison, as the high priest and the whole Council of Elders can testify. It was they who gave me letters to our fellow-Jews at Damascus, and I was on my way to make arrests there also and bring the prisoners to Jerusalem for punishment. What happened to me on my journey was this: when I was nearing Damascus, about midday, a great light suddenly flashed from the sky all around me. I fell to the ground, and heard a voice saying: "Saul, Saul, why do you persecute me?" I answered, "Tell me, Lord, who you are." "I am Jesus of Nazareth, whom you are persecuting," he said. My companions saw the light, but did not hear the voice that spoke to me. "What shall I do, Lord?" I asked, and he replied, "Get up, and go on to Damascus; there you will be told all that you are appointed to do." As I had been blinded by the brilliance of that light, my companions led me by the hand, and so I came to Damascus.

'There a man called Ananias, a devout observer of the law and well spoken of by all the Jews who lived there, came and stood beside me, and said, "Saul, my brother, receive your sight again!" Instantly I recovered my sight and saw him. He went on: "The God of our fathers appointed you to know his will and to see the Righteous One and to hear him speak, because you are to be his witness to tell the world what you have seen and heard. Do not delay. Be baptized at once and wash away your sins, calling on his name."

'After my return to Jerusalem, as I was praying in the temple I fell into a trance and saw him there, speaking to me. "Make haste", he said, "and leave Jerusalem quickly, for they will not accept your testimony about me." "But surely, Lord," I answered, "they know that I imprisoned those who believe in you and flogged them in every synagogue; when the blood of Stephen your witness was shed I stood by, approving, and I looked after the clothes of those who killed him." He said to me, "Go, for I mean to send you far away to the Gentiles."'

Up to this point the crowd had given him a hearing; but now they began to shout, 'Down with the scoundrel! He is not fit to be alive!' And as they were yelling and waving their cloaks and flinging dust in the air, the commandant ordered him to be brought into the barracks, and gave instructions that he should be examined under the lash, to find out what reason there was for such an outcry against him. But when they tied him up for the flogging, Paul said to the centurion who was standing there, 'Does the law allow you to flog a Roman citizen, and an unconvicted one at that?' When the centurion heard this, he went and reported to the commandant: 'What are you about? This man is a Roman citizen.' The commandant came to Paul and asked, 'Tell me, are you a Roman citizen?' 'Yes,' said he. The commandant rejoined, 'Citizenship cost me a large sum of money.' Paul said, 'It was mine by birth.' Then those who were about to examine him promptly withdrew; and the commandant himself was alarmed when he realized that Paul was a Roman citizen and that he had put him in irons.

PAUL'S DEFENCE BEFORE THE HIGH PRIEST
Acts 22:30 – 23:11

The following day, wishing to be quite sure what charge the Jews were bringing against Paul, he released him and ordered the chief priests and the entire Council to assemble. He then brought Paul down to stand before them.

With his eyes steadily fixed on the Council, Paul said, 'My brothers, all my life to this day I have lived with a perfectly clear conscience before God.' At this the high priest Ananias ordered his attendants to strike him on the mouth. Paul retorted, 'God will strike you, you whitewashed wall! You sit there to judge me in accordance with the law; then, in defiance of the law, you order me to be struck!' The attendants said, 'Would you insult God's high priest?' 'Brothers,' said Paul, 'I had no idea he was high priest; scripture, I know, says: "You shall not abuse the ruler of your people."'

Well aware that one section of them were Sadducees and the other Pharisees, Paul called out in the Council, 'My brothers, I am a Pharisee, a Pharisee born and bred; and the issue in this trial is our hope of the resurrection of the dead.' At these words the Pharisees and Sadducees fell out among themselves, and the assembly was divided. (The Sadducees deny that there is any resurrection or angel or spirit, but the Pharisees believe in all three.) A great uproar ensued; and some of the scribes belonging to the Pharisaic party openly took sides and declared, 'We find no fault with this man; perhaps an angel or spirit has spoken to him.' In the mounting dissension, the commandant was afraid that Paul would be torn to pieces, so he ordered the troops to go down, pull him out of the crowd, and bring him into the barracks.

The following night the Lord appeared to him and said, 'Keep up your courage! You have affirmed the truth about me in Jerusalem, and you must do the same in Rome.'

THE JEWS PLOT TO KILL PAUL
Acts 23:12–35

When day broke, the Jews banded together and took an oath not to eat or drink until they had killed Paul. There were more than forty in the conspiracy; they went to the chief priests and elders and said, 'We have bound ourselves by a solemn oath not to taste food until we have killed Paul. It is now up to you and the rest of the Council to apply to the commandant to have him brought down to you on the pretext of a closer investigation of his case; we have arranged to make away with him before he reaches you.'

The son of Paul's sister, however, learnt of the plot and, going to the barracks, obtained entry, and reported it to Paul, who called one of the centurions and said, 'Take this young man to the commandant; he has something to report.' The centurion brought him to the commandant and explained, 'The prisoner Paul sent for me and asked me to bring this young man to you; he has something to tell you.' The commandant took him by the arm, drew him aside, and asked him, 'What is it you have to report?' He replied, 'The Jews have agreed on a plan: they will request you to bring Paul down to the Council tomorrow on the pretext of obtaining more precise information about him. Do not listen to them; for a party more than forty strong are lying in wait for him, and they have sworn not to eat or drink until they have done away with him. They are now ready, waiting only for your consent.' The commandant dismissed the young man, with orders not to let anyone know that he had given him this information.

He then summoned two of his centurions and gave them these orders: 'Have two hundred infantry ready to proceed to Caesarea, together with seventy cavalrymen and two hundred light-armed troops; parade them three hours after sunset, and provide mounts for Paul so that he may be conducted under safe escort to Felix the governor.' And he wrote a letter to this effect:

> From Claudius Lysias to His Excellency the Governor Felix. Greeting.
>
> This man was seized by the Jews and was on the point of being murdered when I intervened with the troops, and, on discovering that he was a Roman citizen, I removed him to safety. As I wished to ascertain the ground of their charge against him, I brought him down to their Council. I found that their case had to do with controversial matters of their law, but there was no charge against him which merited death or imprisonment. Information, however, has now been brought to my notice of an attempt to be made on the man's life, so I am sending him to you without delay, and have instructed his accusers to state their case against him before you.

Acting on their orders, the infantry took custody of Paul and brought him by night to Antipatris. Next day they returned to their barracks, leaving the cavalry to escort him the rest of the way. When the cavalry reached Caesarea, they delivered the letter to the governor, and handed Paul over to him. He read the letter, and asked him what province he was from; and learning that he was from Cilicia he said, 'I will hear your case when your accusers arrive.' He ordered him to be held in custody at his headquarters in Herod's palace.

PAUL'S DEFENCE BEFORE FELIX
Acts 24:1–26

Five days later the high priest Ananias came down, accompanied by some of the elders and an advocate named Tertullus, to lay before the governor their charge against Paul. When the prisoner was called, Tertullus opened the case.

'Your excellency,' he said to Felix, 'we owe it to you that we enjoy unbroken peace, and it is due to your provident care that, in all kinds of ways and in all sorts of places, improvements are being made for the good of this nation. We appreciate this, and are most grateful to you. And now, not to take up too much of your time, I crave your indulgence for a brief statement of our case. We have found this man to be a pest, a fomenter of discord among the Jews all over the world, a ringleader of the sect of the Nazarenes. He made an attempt to profane the temple and we arrested him. If you examine him yourself you can ascertain the truth of all the charges we bring against him.' The Jews supported the charge, alleging that the facts were as he stated.

The governor then motioned to Paul to speak, and he replied as follows: 'Knowing as I do that for many years you have administered justice to this nation, I make my defence with confidence. As you can ascertain for yourself, it is not more than twelve days since I went up to Jerusalem on a pilgrimage. They did not find me in the temple arguing with anyone or collecting a crowd, or in the synagogues or anywhere else in the city; and they cannot make good the charges they now bring against me. But this much I will admit: I am a follower of the new way (the "sect" they speak of), and it is in that manner that I worship the God of our fathers; for I believe all that is written in the law and the prophets, and in reliance on God I hold the hope, which my accusers too accept, that there is to be a resurrection of good and wicked alike. Accordingly I, no less than they, train myself to keep at all times a clear conscience before God and man.

'After an absence of several years I came to bring charitable gifts to my nation and to offer sacrifices. I was ritually purified and engaged in this service when they found me in the temple; I had no crowd with me, and there was no disturbance. But some Jews from the province of Asia were there, and if they had any charge against me, it is they who ought to have been in court to state it. Failing that, it is for these persons here present to say what crime they discovered when I was brought before the Council, apart from this one declaration which I made as I stood there: "The issue in my trial before you today is the resurrection of the dead."'

Then Felix, who was well informed about the new way, adjourned the hearing. 'I will decide your case when Lysias the commanding officer comes down,' he said. He gave orders to the centurion to keep Paul under open arrest and not to prevent any of his friends from making themselves useful to him.

Some days later Felix came with his wife Drusilla, who was a Jewess, and sent for Paul. He let him talk to him about faith in Christ Jesus, but when the discourse turned to questions of morals, self-control, and the coming judgment, Felix became alarmed and exclaimed, 'Enough for now! When I find it convenient I will send for you again.' He also had hopes of a bribe from Paul, so he sent for him frequently and talked with him.

PAUL APPEALS TO CAESAR
Acts 24:27 – 25:2, 6–12

When two years had passed, Felix was succeeded by Porcius Festus. Wishing to curry favour with the Jews, Felix left Paul in custody.

Three days after taking up his appointment, Festus went up from Caesarea to Jerusalem, where the chief priests and the Jewish leaders laid before him their charge against Paul...

After spending eight or ten days at most in Jerusalem, he went down to Caesarea, and next day he took his seat in court and ordered Paul to be brought before him. When he appeared, the Jews who had come down from Jerusalem stood round bringing many grave charges, which they were unable to prove. Paul protested: 'I have committed no offence against the Jewish law, or against the temple, or against the emperor.' Festus, anxious to ingratiate himself with the Jews, turned to Paul and asked, 'Are you willing to go up to Jerusalem and stand trial on these charges before me there?' But Paul said, 'I am now standing before the emperor's tribunal; that is where I ought to be tried. I have committed no offence against the Jews, as you very well know. If I am guilty of any capital crime, I do not ask to escape the death penalty; if, however, there is no substance in the charges which these men bring against me, it is not open to anyone to hand me over to them. I appeal to Caesar!' Then Festus, after conferring with his advisers, replied, 'You have appealed to Caesar: to Caesar you shall go!'

PAUL'S DEFENCE BEFORE AGRIPPA
Acts 25:13–23; 26:1–8, 22–32

Some days later King Agrippa and Bernice arrived at Caesarea on a courtesy visit to Festus. They spent some time there, and during their stay Festus raised Paul's case with the king. 'There is a man here', he said, 'left in custody by Felix; and when I was in Jerusalem the chief priests and elders of the Jews brought a charge against him, demanding his condemnation. I replied that it was not Roman practice to hand a man over before he had been confronted with his accusers and given an opportunity of answering the charge. So when they had come here with me I lost no time, but took my seat in court the very next day and ordered the man to be brought before me. When his accusers rose to speak, they brought none of the charges I was expecting; they merely had certain points of disagreement with him about their religion, and about someone called Jesus, a dead man whom Paul alleged to be alive. Finding myself out of my depth in such discussions, I asked if he was willing to go to Jerusalem and stand trial there on these issues. But Paul appealed to be remanded in custody for his imperial majesty's decision, and I ordered him to be detained until I could send him to the emperor.' Agrippa said to Festus, 'I should rather like to hear the man myself.' 'You shall hear him tomorrow,' he answered.

Next day Agrippa and Bernice came in full state and entered the audience-chamber accompanied by high-ranking officers and prominent citizens; and on the orders of Festus, Paul was brought in...

Agrippa said to Paul: 'You have our permission to give an account of yourself.' Then Paul stretched out his hand and began his defence.

'I consider myself fortunate, King Agrippa, that it is before you I am to make my defence today on all the charges brought against me by the Jews, particularly as you are expert in all our Jewish customs and controversies. I beg you therefore to give me a patient hearing.

'My life from my youth up, a life spent from the first among my nation and in Jerusalem, is familiar to all Jews. Indeed they have known me long enough to testify, if they would, that I belonged to the strictest group in our religion: I was a Pharisee. It is the hope based on the promise God made to our forefathers that has led to my being on trial today. Our twelve tribes worship with intense devotion night and day in the hope of seeing the fulfilment of that promise; and for this very hope I am accused, your majesty, and accused by Jews. Why should Jews find it incredible that God should raise the dead?...

I assert nothing beyond what was foretold by the prophets and by Moses: that the Messiah would suffer and that, as the first to rise from the dead, he would announce the dawn both to the Jewish people and to the Gentiles.'

While Paul was thus making his defence, Festus shouted at the top of his voice, 'Paul, you are raving; too much study is driving you mad.' 'I am not mad, your excellency,' said Paul; 'what I am asserting is sober truth. The king is well versed in these matters, and I can speak freely to him. I do not believe that he can be unaware of any of these facts, for this has been no hole-and-corner business. King Agrippa, do you believe the prophets? I know you do.' Agrippa said to Paul, 'With a little more of your persuasion you will make a Christian of me.' 'Little or much,' said Paul, 'I wish to God that not only you, but all those who are listening to me today, might become what I am – apart from these chains!'

With that the king rose, and with him the governor, Bernice, and the rest of the company, and after they had withdrawn they talked it over. 'This man', they agreed, 'is doing nothing that deserves death or imprisonment.' Agrippa said to Festus, 'The fellow could have been discharged, if he had not appealed to the emperor.'

SHIPWRECK ON THE WAY TO ROME
Acts 27:1 – 28:6

When it was decided that we should sail for Italy, Paul and some other prisoners were handed over to a centurion named Julius, of the Augustan Cohort. We embarked in a ship of Adramyttium, bound for ports in the province of Asia, and put out to sea. Aristarchus, a Macedonian from Thessalonica, came with us. Next day we landed at Sidon, and Julius very considerately allowed Paul to go to his friends to be cared for. Leaving Sidon we sailed under the lee of Cyprus because of the head winds, then across the open sea off the coast of Cilicia and Pamphylia, and so reached Myra in Lycia.

There the centurion found an Alexandrian vessel bound for Italy and put us on board. For a good many days we made little headway, and we were hard put to it to reach Cnidus. Then, as the wind continued against us, off Salmone we began to sail under the lee of Crete, and, hugging the coast, struggled on to a place called Fair Havens, not far from the town of Lasea.

By now much time had been lost, and with the Fast already over, it was dangerous to go on with the voyage. So Paul gave them this warning: 'I can see, gentlemen, that this voyage will be disastrous; it will mean heavy loss, not only of ship and cargo but also of life.' But the centurion paid more attention to the captain and to the owner of the ship than to what Paul said; and as the harbour was unsuitable for wintering, the majority were in favour of putting to sea, hoping, if they could get so far, to winter at Phoenix, a Cretan harbour facing south-west and north-west. When a southerly breeze sprang up, they thought that their purpose was as good as achieved, and, weighing anchor, they sailed along the coast of Crete hugging the land. But before very long a violent wind, the Northeaster as they call it, swept down from the landward side. It caught the ship and, as it was impossible to keep head to wind, we had to give way and run before it. As we passed under the lee of a small island called Cauda, we managed with a struggle to get the ship's boat under control. When they had hoisted it on board, they made use of tackle to brace the ship. Then, afraid of running on to the sandbanks of Syrtis, they put out a sea-anchor and let her drift. Next day, as we were making very heavy weather, they began to lighten the ship; and on the third day they jettisoned the ship's gear with their own hands. For days on end there was no sign of either sun or stars, the storm was raging unabated, and our last hopes of coming through alive began to fade.

When they had gone for a long time without food, Paul stood up among them and said, 'You should have taken my advice, gentlemen, not to put out from Crete: then you would have avoided this damage and loss. But now I urge you not to lose heart; not a single life will be lost, only the ship. Last night there stood by me an angel of the God whose I am and whom I worship. "Do not be afraid, Paul," he said; "it is ordained that you shall appear before Caesar; and, be assured, God has granted you the lives of all who are sailing with you." So take heart, men! I trust God: it will turn out as I have been told; we are to be cast ashore on an island.'

The fourteenth night came and we were still drifting in the Adriatic Sea. At midnight the sailors felt that land was getting nearer, so they took a sounding and found twenty fathoms. Sounding again after a short interval they found fifteen fathoms; then, fearing that we might be cast ashore on a rugged coast, they let go four anchors from the stern and prayed for daylight to come. The sailors tried to abandon ship; they had already lowered the ship's boat, pretending they were going to lay out anchors from the bows, when Paul said to the centurion and the soldiers, 'Unless these men stay on board you cannot reach safety.' At that the soldiers cut the ropes of the boat and let it drop away.

Shortly before daybreak Paul urged them all to take some food. 'For the last fourteen days', he said, 'you have lived in suspense and gone hungry; you have eaten nothing. So have something to eat, I beg you; your lives depend on it. Remember, not a hair of your heads will be lost.' With these words, he took bread, gave thanks to God in front of them all, broke it, and began eating. Then they plucked up courage, and began to take food themselves. All told there were on board two hundred and seventy-six of us. After they had eaten as much as they wanted, they lightened the ship by dumping the grain into the sea.

When day broke, they did not recognize the land, but they sighted a bay with a sandy beach, on which they decided, if possible, to run ashore. So they slipped the anchors and let them go; at the same time they loosened the lashings of the steering-paddles, set the foresail to the wind, and let her drive to the beach. But they found themselves caught between cross-currents and ran the ship aground, so that the bow stuck fast and remained immovable, while the stern was being pounded to pieces by the breakers. The soldiers thought they had better kill the prisoners for fear that any should swim away and escape; but the centurion was determined to bring Paul safely through, and prevented them from carrying out their plan. He gave orders that those who could swim should jump overboard first and get to land; the rest were to follow, some on planks, some on parts of the ship. And thus it was that all came safely to land.

Once we had made our way to safety, we identified the island as Malta. The natives treated us with uncommon kindness: because it had started to rain and was cold they lit a bonfire and made us all welcome. Paul had got together an armful of sticks and put them on the fire, when a viper, driven out by the heat, fastened on his hand. The natives, seeing the snake hanging on to his hand, said to one another, 'The man must be a murderer; he may have escaped from the sea, but divine justice would not let him live.' Paul, however, shook off the snake into the fire and was none the worse. They still expected him to swell up or suddenly drop down dead, but after waiting a long time without seeing anything out of the way happen to him, they changed their minds and said, 'He is a god.' ...

PAUL'S FINAL YEARS IN ROME
Acts 28:11–23, 30–31

Three months had passed when we put to sea in a ship which had wintered in the island; she was the *Castor and Pollux* of Alexandria. We landed at Syracuse and spent three days there; then we sailed up the coast and arrived at Rhegium. Next day a south wind sprang up and we reached Puteoli in two days. There we found fellow-Christians and were invited to stay a week with them. And so to Rome. The Christians there had had news of us and came out to meet us as far as Appii Forum and the Three Taverns, and when Paul saw them, he gave thanks to God and took courage.

When we entered Rome Paul was allowed to lodge privately, with a soldier in charge of him. Three days later he called together the local Jewish leaders, and when they were assembled, he said to them: 'My brothers, I never did anything against our people or against the customs of our forefathers; yet I was arrested in Jerusalem and handed over to the Romans. They examined me and would have liked to release me because there was no capital charge against me; but the Jews objected, and I had no option but to appeal to Caesar; not that I had any accusation to bring against my own people. This is why I have asked to see and talk to you; it is for loyalty to the hope of Israel that I am in these chains.' They replied, 'We have had no communication about you from Judaea, nor has any countryman of ours arrived with any report or gossip to your discredit. We should like to hear from you what your views are; all we know about this sect is that no one has a good word to say for it.'

So they fixed a day, and came in large numbers to his lodging. From dawn to dusk he put his case to them; he spoke urgently of the kingdom of God and sought to convince them about Jesus by appealing to the law of Moses and the prophets...

He stayed there two full years at his own expense, with a welcome for all who came to him; he proclaimed the kingdom of God and taught the facts about the Lord Jesus Christ quite openly and without hindrance.

THE GENERAL EPISTLES

The Epistle of James   228

The Epistle to the Hebrews   235
Abridged from the text of the New Revised Standard Version

The First Epistle of Peter   248

The Epistle of Jude   256

The Second Epistle of Peter   258

The Epistle of James

FAITHFUL LIVING
James 1:1–25

James, a servant[1] of God and of the Lord Jesus Christ, to the twelve tribes in the Dispersion: Greetings.

My brothers and sisters,[2] whenever you face trials of any kind, consider it nothing but joy, because you know that the testing of your faith produces endurance; and let endurance have its full effect, so that you may be mature and complete, lacking in nothing.

If any of you is lacking in wisdom, ask God, who gives to all generously and ungrudgingly, and it will be given you. But ask in faith, never doubting, for the one who doubts is like a wave of the sea, driven and tossed by the wind; for the doubter, being double-minded and unstable in every way, must not expect to receive anything from the Lord.

Let the believer[3] who is lowly boast in being raised up, and the rich in being brought low, because the rich will disappear like a flower in the field. For the sun rises with its scorching heat and withers the field; its flower falls, and its beauty perishes. It is the same with the rich; in the midst of a busy life, they will wither away.

Blessed is anyone who endures temptation. Such a one has stood the test and will receive the crown of life that the Lord[4] has promised to those who love him. No one, when tempted, should say, 'I am being tempted by God'; for God cannot be tempted by evil and he himself tempts no one. But one is tempted by one's own desire, being lured and enticed by it; then, when that desire has conceived, it gives birth to sin, and that sin, when it is fully grown, gives birth to death. Do not be deceived, my beloved.[5]

Every generous act of giving, with every perfect gift, is from above, coming down from the Father of lights, with whom there is no variation or shadow due to change.[6] In fulfilment of his own purpose he gave us birth by the word of truth, so that we would become a kind of first fruits of his creatures.

You must understand this, my beloved:[5] let everyone be quick to listen, slow to speak, slow to anger; for your anger does not produce God's righteousness. Therefore rid yourselves of all sordidness and rank growth of wickedness, and welcome with meekness the implanted word that has the power to save your souls.

But be doers of the word, and not merely hearers who deceive themselves. For if any are hearers of the word and not doers,[7] they are like those who look at themselves in a mirror; for they look at themselves and, on going away, immediately forget what they were like. But those who look into the perfect law, the law of liberty, and persevere, being not hearers who forget but doers who act – they will be blessed in their doing.

THE LAW OF LOVE
James 1:26 – 2:13

If any think they are religious, and do not bridle their tongues but deceive their hearts, their religion is worthless. Religion that is pure and undefiled before God, the Father, is this: to care for orphans and widows in their distress, and to keep oneself unstained by the world.

My brothers and sisters,[8] do you with your acts of favouritism really believe in our glorious Lord Jesus Christ?[9] For if a person with gold rings and in fine clothes comes into your assembly, and if a poor person in dirty clothes also comes in, and if you take notice of the one wearing the fine clothes and say, 'Have a seat here, please', while to the one who is poor you say, 'Stand there', or, 'Sit at my feet',[10] have you not made distinctions among yourselves, and become judges with evil thoughts? Listen, my beloved brothers and sisters.[2] Has not God chosen the poor in the world to be rich in faith and to be heirs of the kingdom that he has promised to those who love him? But you have dishonoured the poor. Is it not the rich who oppress you? Is it not they who drag you into court? Is it not they who blaspheme the excellent name that was invoked over you?

You do well if you really fulfil the royal law according to the scripture, 'You shall love your neighbour as yourself.' But if you show partiality, you commit sin and are convicted by the law as transgressors. For whoever keeps the whole law but fails in one point has become accountable for all of it. For the one who said, 'You shall not commit adultery', also said, 'You shall not murder.' Now if you do not commit adultery but if you murder, you have become a transgressor of the law. So speak and so act as those who are to be judged by the law of liberty. For judgment will be without mercy to anyone who has shown no mercy; mercy triumphs over judgment.

FAITH AND WORKS
James 2:14–26

What good is it, my brothers and sisters,[2] if you say you have faith but do not have works? Can faith save you? If a brother or sister is naked and lacks daily food, and one of you says to them, 'Go in peace; keep warm and eat your fill', and yet you do not supply their bodily needs, what is the good of that? So faith by itself, if it has no works, is dead.

But someone will say, 'You have faith and I have works.' Show me your faith without works, and I by my works will show you my faith. You believe that God is one; you do well. Even the demons believe – and shudder. Do you want to be shown, you senseless person, that faith without works is barren? Was not our ancestor Abraham justified by works when he offered his son Isaac on the altar? You see that faith was active along with his works, and faith was brought to completion by the works. Thus the scripture was fulfilled that says, 'Abraham believed God, and it was reckoned to him as righteousness', and he was called the friend of God. You see that a person is justified by works and not by faith alone. Likewise, was not Rahab the prostitute also justified by works when she welcomed the messengers and sent them out by another road? For just as the body without the spirit is dead, so faith without works is also dead.

SELF-CONTROL
James 3:1 – 4:10

Not many of you should become teachers, my brothers and sisters, for you know that we who teach will be judged with greater strictness. For all of us make many mistakes. Anyone who makes no mistakes in speaking is perfect, able to keep the whole body in check with a bridle. If we put bits into the mouths of horses to make them obey us, we guide their whole bodies. Or look at ships: though they are so large that it takes strong winds to drive them, yet they are guided by a very small rudder wherever the will of the pilot directs. So also the tongue is a small member, yet it boasts of great exploits.

How great a forest is set ablaze by a small fire! And the tongue is a fire. The tongue is placed among our members as a world of iniquity; it stains the whole body, sets on fire the cycle of nature,[11] and is itself set on fire by hell.[12] For every species of beast and bird, of reptile and sea creature, can be tamed and has been tamed by the human species, but no one can tame the tongue – a restless evil, full of deadly poison. With it we bless the Lord and Father, and with it we curse those who are made in the likeness of God. From the same mouth come blessing and cursing. My brothers and sisters,[8] this ought not to be so. Does a spring pour forth from the same opening both fresh and brackish water? Can a fig tree, my brothers and sisters,[8] yield olives, or a grapevine figs? No more can salt water yield fresh.

Who is wise and understanding among you? Show by your good life that your works are done with gentleness born of wisdom. But if you have bitter envy and selfish ambition in your hearts, do not be boastful and false to the truth. Such wisdom does not come down from above, but is earthly, unspiritual, devilish. For where there is envy and selfish ambition, there will also be disorder and wickedness of every kind. But the wisdom from above is first pure, then peaceable, gentle, willing to yield, full of mercy and good fruits, without a trace of partiality or hypocrisy. And a harvest of righteousness is sown in peace for[13] those who make peace.

Those conflicts and disputes among you, where do they come from? Do they not come from your cravings that are at war within you? You want something and do not have it; so you commit murder. And you covet[14] something and cannot obtain it; so you engage in disputes and conflicts. You do not have, because you do not ask. You ask and do not receive, because you ask wrongly, in order to spend what you get on your pleasures. Adulterers! Do you not know that friendship with the world is enmity with God? Therefore whoever wishes to be a friend of the world becomes an enemy of God. Or do you suppose that it is for nothing that the scripture says, 'God[15] yearns jealously for the spirit that he has made to dwell in us'? But he gives all the more grace; therefore it says,

> 'God opposes the proud,
> but gives grace to the humble.'

Submit yourselves therefore to God. Resist the devil, and he will flee from you. Draw near to God, and he will draw near to you. Cleanse your hands, you sinners, and purify your hearts, you double-minded. Lament and mourn and weep. Let your laughter be turned into mourning and your joy into dejection. Humble yourselves before the Lord, and he will exalt you.

HUMILITY AND JUSTICE
James 4:11 – 5:6

Do not speak evil against one another, brothers and sisters.[2] Whoever speaks evil against another or judges another, speaks evil against the law and judges the law; but if you judge the law, you are not a doer of the law but a judge. There is one lawgiver and judge who is able to save and to destroy. So who, then, are you to judge your neighbour?

Come now, you who say, 'Today or tomorrow we will go to such and such a town and spend a year there, doing business and making money.' Yet you do not even know what tomorrow will bring. What is your life? For you are a mist that appears for a little while and then vanishes. Instead you ought to say, 'If the Lord wishes, we will live and do this or that.' As it is, you boast in your arrogance; all such boasting is evil. Anyone, then, who knows the right thing to do and fails to do it, commits sin.

Come now, you rich people, weep and wail for the miseries that are coming to you. Your riches have rotted, and your clothes are moth-eaten. Your gold and silver have rusted, and their rust will be evidence against you, and it will eat your flesh like fire. You have laid up treasure[16] for the last days. Listen! The wages of the labourers who mowed your fields, which you kept back by fraud, cry out, and the cries of the harvesters have reached the ears of the Lord of hosts. You have lived on the earth in luxury and in pleasure; you have fattened your hearts on a day of slaughter. You have condemned and murdered the righteous one, who does not resist you.

PATIENCE AND PRAYER
James 5:7–20

Be patient, therefore, beloved,[2] until the coming of the Lord. The farmer waits for the precious crop from the earth, being patient with it until it receives the early and the late rains. You also must be patient. Strengthen your hearts, for the coming of the Lord is near.[17] Beloved,[18] do not grumble against one another, so that you may not be judged. See, the Judge is standing at the doors! As an example of suffering and patience, beloved,[2] take the prophets who spoke in the name of the Lord. Indeed we call blessed those who showed endurance. You have heard of the endurance of Job, and you have seen the purpose of the Lord, how the Lord is compassionate and merciful.

Above all, my beloved,[2] do not swear, either by heaven or by earth or by any other oath, but let your 'Yes' be yes and your 'No' be no, so that you may not fall under condemnation.

Are any among you suffering? They should pray. Are any cheerful? They should sing songs of praise. Are any among you sick? They should call for the elders of the church and have them pray over them, anointing them with oil in the name of the Lord. The prayer of faith will save the sick, and the Lord will raise them up; and anyone who has committed sins will be forgiven. Therefore confess your sins to one another, and pray for one another, so that you may be healed. The prayer of the righteous is powerful and effective. Elijah was a human being like us, and he prayed fervently that it might not rain, and for three years and six months it did not rain on the earth. Then he prayed again, and the heaven gave rain and the earth yielded its harvest.

My brothers and sisters,[8] if anyone among you wanders from the truth and is brought back by another, you should know that whoever brings back a sinner from wandering will save the sinner's[19] soul from death and will cover a multitude of sins.

Alternative readings

1. Gk *slave*
2. Gk *brothers*
3. Gk *brother*
4. Gk *he*; other ancient authorities read *God*
5. Gk *my beloved brothers*
6. Other ancient authorities read *variation due to a shadow of turning*
7. Gk *at the face of his birth*
8. Gk *My brothers*
9. Or *hold the faith of our glorious Lord Jesus Christ without acts of favouritism*
10. Gk *sit under my footstool*
11. Or *wheel of birth*
12. Gk *Gehenna*
13. Or *by*
14. Or *you murder and you covet*
15. Gk *He*
16. Or *will eat your flesh, since you have stored up fire*
17. Or *is at hand*
18. Gk *Brothers*
19. Gk *his*

The Epistle to the Hebrews

JESUS IS GREATER THAN THE ANGELS
Hebrews 1:1–5, 14; 2:1–3, 5–11, 14–18

Long ago God spoke to our ancestors in many and various ways by the prophets, but in these last days he has spoken to us by a Son, whom he appointed heir of all things, through whom he also created the worlds. He is the reflection of God's glory and the exact imprint of God's very being, and he sustains all things by his powerful word. When he had made purification for sins, he sat down at the right hand of the Majesty on high, having become as much superior to angels as the name he has inherited is more excellent than theirs.

For to which of the angels did God ever say,

'You are my Son;
today I have begotten you'?

Or again,

'I will be his Father,
and he will be my Son'?...

Are not all angels spirits in the divine service, sent to serve for the sake of those who are to inherit salvation?

Therefore we must pay greater attention to what we have heard, so that we do not drift away from it. For if the message declared through angels was valid, and every transgression or disobedience received a just penalty, how can we escape if we neglect so great a salvation?...

Now God did not subject the coming world, about which we are speaking, to angels. But someone has testified somewhere,

'What are human beings that you are mindful of them,
or mortals, that you care for them?
You have made them for a little while lower than the angels;

you have crowned them with glory and honour,
subjecting all things under their feet.'

Now in subjecting all things to them, God left nothing outside their control. As it is, we do not yet see everything in subjection to them, but we do see Jesus, who for a little while was made lower than the angels, now crowned with glory and honour because of the suffering of death, so that by the grace of God he might taste death for everyone.

It was fitting that God, for whom and through whom all things exist, in bringing many children to glory, should make the pioneer of their salvation perfect through sufferings. For the one who sanctifies and those who are sanctified all have one Father. For this reason Jesus is not ashamed to call them brothers and sisters...

Since, therefore, the children share flesh and blood, he himself likewise shared the same things, so that through death he might destroy the one who has the power of death, that is, the devil, and free those who all their lives were held in slavery by the fear of death. For it is clear that he did not come to help angels, but the descendants of Abraham. Therefore he had to become like his brothers and sisters in every respect, so that he might be a merciful and faithful high priest in the service of God, to make a sacrifice of atonement for the sins of the people. Because he himself was tested by what he suffered, he is able to help those who are being tested.

JESUS IS GREATER THAN MOSES
Hebrews 3:1–3, 12–19; 4:11–13

Therefore, brothers and sisters, holy partners in a heavenly calling, consider that Jesus, the apostle and high priest of our confession, was faithful to the one who appointed him, just as Moses also 'was faithful in all God's house.' Yet Jesus is worthy of more glory than Moses, just as the builder of a house has more honour than the house itself...

Take care, brothers and sisters, that none of you may have an evil, unbelieving heart that turns away from the living God. But exhort one another every day, as long as it is called 'today', so that none of you may be hardened by the deceitfulness of sin. For we have become partners of Christ, if only we hold our first confidence firm to the end. As it is said,

> 'Today, if you hear his voice,
> do not harden your hearts as in the rebellion.'

Now who were they who heard and yet were rebellious? Was it not all those who left Egypt under the leadership of Moses? But with whom was he angry for forty years? Was it not those who sinned, whose bodies fell in the wilderness? And to whom did he swear that they would not enter his rest, if not to those who were disobedient? So we see that they were unable to enter because of unbelief...

Let us therefore make every effort to enter that rest, so that no one may fall through such disobedience as theirs.

Indeed, the word of God is living and active, sharper than any two-edged sword, piercing until it divides soul from spirit, joints from marrow; it is able to judge the thoughts and intentions of the heart. And before him no creature is hidden, but all are naked and laid bare to the eyes of the one to whom we must render an account.

JESUS IS GREATER THAN AARON
Hebrews 4:14–16; 5:7–10; 7:1–12, 23–27; 8:5–6

Since, then, we have a great high priest who has passed through the heavens, Jesus, the Son of God, let us hold fast to our confession. For we do not have a high priest who is unable to sympathize with our weaknesses, but we have one who in every respect has been tested as we are, yet without sin. Let us therefore approach the throne of grace with boldness, so that we may receive mercy and find grace to help in time of need...

In the days of his flesh, Jesus offered up prayers and supplications, with loud cries and tears, to the one who was able to save him from death, and he was heard because of his reverent submission. Although he was a Son, he learned obedience through what he suffered; and having been made perfect, he became the source of eternal salvation for all who obey him, having been designated by

God a high priest according to the order of Melchizedek... This 'King Melchizedek of Salem, priest of the Most High God, met Abraham as he was returning from defeating the kings and blessed him'; and to him Abraham apportioned 'one-tenth of everything'. His name, in the first place, means 'king of righteousness'; next he is also king of Salem, that is, 'king of peace'. Without father, without mother, without genealogy, having neither beginning of days nor end of life, but resembling the Son of God, he remains a priest for ever.

See how great he is! Even Abraham the patriarch gave him a tenth of the spoils. And those descendants of Levi who receive the priestly office have a commandment in the law to collect tithes from the people, that is, from their kindred, though these also are descended from Abraham. But this man, who does not belong to their ancestry, collected tithes from Abraham and blessed him who had received the promises. It is beyond dispute that the inferior is blessed by the superior. In the one case, tithes are received by those who are mortal; in the other, by one of whom it is testified that he lives. One might even say that Levi himself, who receives tithes, paid tithes through Abraham, for he was still in the loins of his ancestor when Melchizedek met him.

Now if perfection had been attainable through the levitical priesthood – for the people received the law under this priesthood – what further need would there have been to speak of another priest arising according to the order of Melchizedek, rather than one according to the order of Aaron? For when there is a change in the priesthood, there is necessarily a change in the law as well...

Furthermore, the former priests were many in number, because they were prevented by death from continuing in office; but he holds his priesthood permanently, because he continues for ever. Consequently he is able for all time to save those who approach God through him, since he always lives to make intercession for them.

For it was fitting that we should have such a high priest, holy, blameless, undefiled, separated from sinners, and exalted above the heavens. Unlike the other high priests, he has no need to offer sacrifices day after day, first for his own sins, and then for those of the people; this he did once for all when he offered himself....

They offer worship in a sanctuary that is a sketch and shadow of the heavenly one; for Moses, when he was about to erect the tent, was warned, 'See that you make everything according to the pattern that was shown you on the mountain.' But Jesus has now obtained a more excellent ministry, and to that degree he is the mediator of a better covenant, which has been enacted through better promises.

THE NEW COVENANT
Hebrews 8:7 – 9:7, 11–12, 24–28

For if that first covenant had been faultless, there would have been no need to look for a second one.

God finds fault with them when he says:

'The days are surely coming, says the Lord,
when I will establish a new covenant with the house of
Israel
and with the house of Judah;
not like the covenant that I made with their ancestors,
on the day when I took them by the hand to lead them out
of the land of Egypt;
for they did not continue in my covenant,
and so I had no concern for them, says the Lord.
This is the covenant that I will make with the house of
Israel
after those days, says the Lord:
I will put my laws in their minds,
and write them on their hearts,
and I will be their God,
and they shall be my people.
And they shall not teach one another
or say to each other, "Know the Lord",
for they shall all know me,
from the least of them to the greatest.
For I will be merciful towards their iniquities,
and I will remember their sins no more.'

In speaking of 'a new covenant', he has made the first one obsolete. And what is obsolete and growing old will soon disappear.

Now even the first covenant had regulations for worship and an earthly sanctuary. For a tent was constructed, the first one, in which were the lampstand, the table, and the bread of the Presence; this is called the Holy Place. Behind the second curtain was a tent called the Holy of Holies. In it stood the golden altar of incense and the ark of the covenant overlaid on all sides with gold, in which there were a golden urn holding the manna, and Aaron's rod that budded, and the tablets of the covenant; above it were the cherubim of glory overshadowing the mercy-seat. Of these things we cannot speak now in detail.

Such preparations having been made, the priests go continually into the first tent to carry out their ritual duties; but only the high priest goes into the second, and he but once a year, and not without taking the blood that he offers for himself and for the sins committed unintentionally by the people...

But when Christ came as a high priest of the good things that have come, then through the greater and perfect tent (not made with hands, that is, not of this creation), he entered once for all into the Holy Place, not with the blood of goats and calves, but with his own blood, thus obtaining eternal redemption...

For Christ did not enter a sanctuary made by human hands, a mere copy of the true one, but he entered into heaven itself, now to appear in the presence of God on our behalf. Nor was it to offer himself again and again, as the high priest enters the Holy Place year after year with blood that is not his own; for then he would have had to suffer again and again since the foundation of the world. But as it is, he has appeared once for all at the end of the age to remove sin by the sacrifice of himself. And just as it is appointed for mortals to die once, and after that the judgment, so Christ, having been offered once to bear the sins of many, will appear a second time, not to deal with sin, but to save those who are eagerly waiting for him...

CONFIDENCE IN GOD
Hebrews 10:19–39

Therefore, my friends, since we have confidence to enter the sanctuary by the blood of Jesus, by the new and living way that he opened for us through the curtain (that is, through his flesh), and since we have a great priest over the house of God, let us approach with a true heart in full assurance of faith, with our hearts sprinkled clean from an evil conscience and our bodies washed with pure water. Let us hold fast to the confession of our hope without wavering, for he who has promised is faithful. And let us consider how to provoke one another to love and good deeds, not neglecting to meet together, as is the habit of some, but encouraging one another, and all the more as you see the Day approaching.

For if we wilfully persist in sin after having received the knowledge of the truth, there no longer remains a sacrifice for sins, but a fearful prospect of judgment, and a fury of fire that will consume the adversaries. Anyone who has violated the law of Moses dies without mercy 'on the testimony of two or three witnesses.' How much worse punishment do you think will be deserved by those who have spurned the Son of God, profaned the blood of the covenant by which they were sanctified, and outraged the Spirit of grace? For we know the one who said, 'Vengeance is mine, I will repay.' And again, 'The Lord will judge his people.' It is a fearful thing to fall into the hands of the living God.

But recall those earlier days when, after you had been enlightened, you endured a hard struggle with sufferings, sometimes being publicly exposed to abuse and persecution, and sometimes being partners with those so treated. For you had compassion for those who were in prison, and you cheerfully accepted the plundering of your possessions, knowing that you yourselves possessed something better and more lasting. Do not, therefore, abandon that confidence of yours; it brings a great reward. For you need endurance, so that when you have done the will of God, you may receive what was promised. For yet

> 'in a very little while,
> the one who is coming will come and will not delay;
> but my righteous one will live by faith.
> My soul takes no pleasure in anyone who shrinks back.'

But we are not among those who shrink back and so are lost, but among those who have faith and so are saved.

HEROES OF FAITH
Hebrews 11:1–40

Now faith is the assurance of things hoped for, the conviction of things not seen. Indeed, by faith our ancestors received approval. By faith we understand that the worlds were prepared by the word of God, so that what is seen was made from things that are not visible.

By faith Abel offered to God a more acceptable sacrifice than Cain's. Through this he received approval as righteous, God himself giving approval to his gifts; he died, but through his faith he still speaks. By faith Enoch was taken so that he did not experience death; and 'he was not found, because God had taken him.' For it was attested before he was taken away that 'he had pleased God.' And without faith it is impossible to please God, for whoever would approach him must believe that he exists and that he rewards those who seek him. By faith Noah, warned by God about events as yet unseen, respected the warning and built an ark to save his household; by this he condemned the world and became an heir to the righteousness that is in accordance with faith.

By faith Abraham obeyed when he was called to set out for a place that he was to receive as an inheritance; and he set out, not knowing where he was going. By faith he stayed for a time in the land he had been promised, as in a foreign land, living in tents, as did Isaac and Jacob, who were heirs with him of the same promise. For he looked forward to the city that has foundations, whose architect and builder is God. By faith he received power of procreation, even though he was too old – and Sarah herself was barren – because he considered him faithful who had promised. Therefore from one person, and this one as good as dead, descendants were born, 'as many as the stars of heaven and as the innumerable grains of sand by the seashore.'

All of these died in faith without having received the promises, but from a distance they saw and greeted them. They confessed that they were strangers and foreigners on the earth, for people who speak in this way make it clear that they are seeking a homeland. If they had been thinking of the land that they had left behind, they would have had opportunity to return. But as it is, they desire a better country, that is, a heavenly one. Therefore God is not ashamed to be called their God; indeed, he has prepared a city for them.

By faith Abraham, when put to the test, offered up Isaac. He who had received the promises was ready to offer up his only son, of whom he had been told, 'It is through Isaac that descendants shall be named after you.' He considered the fact that God is able even to raise someone from the dead – and figuratively speaking, he did receive him back. By faith Isaac invoked blessings for the future on Jacob and Esau. By faith Jacob, when dying, blessed each of the sons of Joseph, 'bowing in worship over the top of his staff.' By faith Joseph, at the end of his life, made mention of the exodus of the Israelites and gave instructions about his burial.

By faith Moses was hidden by his parents for three months after his birth, because they saw that the child was beautiful; and they were not afraid of the king's edict. By faith Moses, when he was grown up, refused to be called a son of Pharaoh's daughter, choosing rather to share ill-treatment with the people of God than to enjoy the fleeting pleasures of sin. He considered abuse suffered for the Christ to be greater wealth than the treasures of Egypt, for he was looking ahead to the reward. By faith he left Egypt, unafraid of the king's anger; for he persevered as though he saw him who is invisible. By faith he kept the Passover and the sprinkling of blood, so that the destroyer of the firstborn would not touch the firstborn of Israel.

By faith the people passed through the Red Sea as if it were dry land, but when the Egyptians attempted to do so they were drowned. By faith the walls of Jericho fell after they had been encircled for seven days. By faith Rahab the prostitute did not perish with those who were disobedient, because she had received the spies in peace.

And what more should I say? For time would fail me to tell of Gideon, Barak, Samson, Jephthah, of David and Samuel and the prophets – who through faith conquered kingdoms, administered justice, obtained promises, shut the mouths of lions, quenched raging fire, escaped the edge of the sword, won strength out of weakness, became mighty in war, put foreign armies to flight. Women received their dead by resurrection. Others were tortured, refusing to accept release, in order to obtain a better resurrection. Others suffered mocking and flogging, and even chains and imprisonment. They were stoned to death, they were sawn in two, they were killed by the sword; they went about in skins of sheep and goats, destitute, persecuted, tormented – of whom the world was not worthy. They wandered in deserts and mountains, and in caves and holes in the ground.

Yet all these, though they were commended for their faith, did not receive what was promised, since God had provided something better so that they would not, without us, be made perfect.

A CALL FOR PERSEVERENCE
Hebrews 12:1–19, 22–25, 28–29

Therefore, since we are surrounded by so great a cloud of witnesses, let us also lay aside every weight and the sin that clings so closely, and let us run with perseverance the race that is set before us, looking to Jesus the pioneer and perfecter of our faith, who for the sake of the joy that was set before him endured the cross, disregarding its shame, and has taken his seat at the right hand of the throne of God.

Consider him who endured such hostility against himself from sinners, so that you may not grow weary or lose heart. In your struggle against sin you have not yet resisted to the point of shedding your blood. And you have forgotten the exhortation that addresses you as children –

'My child, do not regard lightly the discipline of the Lord,
or lose heart when you are punished by him;
for the Lord disciplines those whom he loves,
and chastises every child whom he accepts.'

Endure trials for the sake of discipline. God is treating you as children; for what child is there whom a parent does not discipline? If you do not have that discipline in which all children share, then you are illegitimate and not his children. Moreover, we had human parents to discipline us, and we respected them. Should we not be even more willing to be subject to the Father of spirits and live? For they disciplined us for a short time as seemed best to them, but he disciplines us for our good, in order that we may share his holiness.

Now, discipline always seems painful rather than pleasant at the time, but later it yields the peaceful fruit of righteousness to those who have been trained by it.

Therefore lift your drooping hands and strengthen your weak knees, and make straight paths for your feet, so that what is lame may not be put out of joint, but rather be healed.

Pursue peace with everyone, and the holiness without which no one will see the Lord. See to it that no one fails to obtain the grace of God; that no root of bitterness springs up and causes trouble, and through it many become defiled. See to it that no one becomes like Esau, an immoral and godless person, who sold his birthright for a single meal. You know that later, when he wanted to inherit the blessing, he was rejected, for he found no chance to repent, even though he sought the blessing with tears.

You have not come to something that can be touched, a blazing fire, and darkness, and gloom, and a tempest, and the sound of a trumpet, and a voice whose words made the hearers beg that not another word be spoken to them... But you have come to Mount Zion and to the city of the living God, the heavenly Jerusalem, and to innumerable angels in festal gathering, and to the assembly of the firstborn who are enrolled in heaven, and to God the judge of all, and to the spirits of the righteous made perfect, and to Jesus, the mediator of a new covenant, and to the sprinkled blood that speaks a better word than the blood of Abel.

See that you do not refuse the one who is speaking; for if they did not escape when they refused the one who warned them on earth, how much less will we escape if we reject the one who warns from heaven!... Therefore, since we are receiving a kingdom that cannot be shaken, let us give thanks, by which we offer to God an acceptable worship with reverence and awe; for indeed our God is a consuming fire.

FINAL EXHORTATIONS
Hebrews 13:1–25

Let mutual love continue. Do not neglect to show hospitality to strangers, for by doing that some have entertained angels without knowing it. Remember those who are in prison, as though you were in prison with them; those who are being tortured, as though you yourselves were being tortured. Let marriage be held in honour by all, and let the marriage bed be kept undefiled; for God will judge fornicators and adulterers. Keep your lives free from the love of money, and be content with what you have; for he has said, 'I will never leave you or forsake you.' So we can say with confidence,

'The Lord is my helper;
I will not be afraid.
What can anyone do to me?'

Remember your leaders, those who spoke the word of God to you; consider the outcome of their way of life, and imitate their faith. Jesus Christ is the same yesterday and today and for ever. Do not be carried away by all kinds of strange teachings; for it is well for the heart to be strengthened by grace, not by regulations about food, which have not benefited those who observe them. We have an altar from which those who officiate in the tent have no right to eat. For the bodies of those animals whose blood is brought into the sanctuary by the high priest as a sacrifice for sin are burned outside the camp. Therefore Jesus also suffered outside the city gate in order to sanctify the people by his own blood. Let us then go to him outside the camp and bear the abuse he endured. For here we have no lasting city, but we are looking for the city that is to come. Through him, then, let us continually offer a sacrifice of praise to God, that is, the fruit of lips that confess his name. Do not neglect to do good and to share what you have, for such sacrifices are pleasing to God.

Obey your leaders and submit to them, for they are keeping watch over your souls and will give an account. Let them do this with joy and not with sighing – for that would be harmful to you.

Pray for us; we are sure that we have a clear conscience, desiring to act honourably in all things. I urge you all the more to do this, so that I may be restored to you very soon.

Now may the God of peace, who brought back from the dead our Lord Jesus, the great shepherd of the sheep, by the blood of the eternal covenant, make you complete in everything good so that you may do his will, working among us that which is pleasing in his sight, through Jesus Christ, to whom be the glory for ever and ever. Amen.

I appeal to you, brothers and sisters, bear with my word of exhortation, for I have written to you briefly. I want you to know that our brother Timothy has been set free; and if he comes in time, he will be with me when I see you. Greet all your leaders and all the saints. Those from Italy send you greetings. Grace be with all of you.

The First Epistle of Peter

THE CHILDREN OF GOD
1 Peter 1:1 – 2:3

Peter, an apostle of Jesus Christ, to the exiles of the Dispersion in Pontus, Galatia, Cappadocia, Asia, and Bithynia, who have been chosen and destined by God the Father and sanctified by the Spirit to be obedient to Jesus Christ and to be sprinkled with his blood:

May grace and peace be yours in abundance.

Blessed be the God and Father of our Lord Jesus Christ! By his great mercy he has given us a new birth into a living hope through the resurrection of Jesus Christ from the dead, and into an inheritance that is imperishable, undefiled, and unfading, kept in heaven for you, who are being protected by the power of God through faith for a salvation ready to be revealed in the last time. In this you rejoice,[1] even if now for a little while you have had to suffer various trials, so that the genuineness of your faith – being more precious than gold that, though perishable, is tested by fire – may be found to result in praise and glory and honour when Jesus Christ is revealed. Although you have not seen him,[2] you love him; and even though you do not see him now, you believe in him and rejoice with an indescribable and glorious joy, for you are receiving the outcome of your faith, the salvation of your souls.

Concerning this salvation, the prophets who prophesied of the grace that was to be yours made careful search and inquiry, inquiring about the person or time that the Spirit of Christ within them indicated, when it testified in advance to the sufferings destined for Christ and the subsequent glory. It was revealed to them that they were serving not themselves but you, in regard to the things that have now been announced to you through those who brought you good news by the Holy Spirit sent from heaven – things into which angels long to look!

Therefore prepare your minds for action;[3] discipline yourselves;

set all your hope on the grace that Jesus Christ will bring you when he is revealed. Like obedient children, do not be conformed to the desires that you formerly had in ignorance. Instead, as he who called you is holy, be holy yourselves in all your conduct; for it is written, 'You shall be holy, for I am holy.'

If you invoke as Father the one who judges all people impartially according to their deeds, live in reverent fear during the time of your exile. You know that you were ransomed from the futile ways inherited from your ancestors, not with perishable things like silver or gold, but with the precious blood of Christ, like that of a lamb without defect or blemish. He was destined before the foundation of the world, but was revealed at the end of the ages for your sake. Through him you have come to trust in God, who raised him from the dead and gave him glory, so that your faith and hope are set on God.

Now that you have purified your souls by your obedience to the truth[4] so that you have genuine mutual love, love one another deeply[5] from the heart.[6] You have been born anew, not of perishable but of imperishable seed, through the living and enduring word of God.[7] For

> 'All flesh is like grass
> and all its glory like the flower of grass.
> The grass withers,
> and the flower falls,
> but the word of the Lord endures for ever.'

That word is the good news that was announced to you.

Rid yourselves, therefore, of all malice, and all guile, insincerity, envy, and all slander. Like newborn infants, long for the pure, spiritual milk, so that by it you may grow into salvation – if indeed you have tasted that the Lord is good.

THE PEOPLE OF GOD
1 Peter 2:4–10

Come to him, a living stone, though rejected by mortals yet chosen and precious in God's sight, and like living stones, let yourselves be built[8] into a spiritual house, to be a holy priesthood, to offer spiritual sacrifices acceptable to God through Jesus Christ. For it stands in scripture:

> 'See, I am laying in Zion a stone,
> a cornerstone chosen and precious;
> and whoever believes in him[9] will not be put to shame.'

To you then who believe, he is precious; but for those who do not believe,

> 'The stone that the builders rejected
> has become the very head of the corner',

and

> 'A stone that makes them stumble,
> and a rock that makes them fall.'

They stumble because they disobey the word, as they were destined to do.

But you are a chosen race, a royal priesthood, a holy nation, God's own people,[10] in order that you may proclaim the mighty acts of him who called you out of darkness into his marvellous light.

> Once you were not a people,
> but now you are God's people;
> once you had not received mercy,
> but now you have received mercy.

RESPECT FOR AUTHORITY
1 Peter 2:11 – 3:12

Beloved, I urge you as aliens and exiles to abstain from the desires of the flesh that wage war against the soul. Conduct yourselves honourably among the Gentiles, so that, though they malign you as evildoers, they may see your honourable deeds and glorify God when he comes to judge. [11]

For the Lord's sake accept the authority of every human institution,[12] whether of the emperor as supreme, or of governors, as sent by him to punish those who do wrong and to praise those who do right. For it is God's will that by doing right you should silence the ignorance of the foolish. As servants[13] of God, live as free people, yet do not use your freedom as a pretext for evil. Honour everyone. Love the family of believers.[14] Fear God. Honour the emperor.

Slaves, accept the authority of your masters with all deference, not only those who are kind and gentle but also those who are harsh. For it is to your credit if, being aware of God, you endure pain while suffering unjustly. If you endure when you are beaten for doing wrong, where is the credit in that? But if you endure when you do right and suffer for it, you have God's approval. For to this you have been called, because Christ also suffered for you, leaving you an example, so that you should follow in his steps.

> 'He committed no sin,
> and no deceit was found in his mouth.'

When he was abused, he did not return abuse; when he suffered, he did not threaten; but he entrusted himself to the one who judges justly. He himself bore our sins in his body on the cross,[15] so that, free from sins, we might live for righteousness; by his wounds[16] you have been healed. For you were going astray like sheep, but now you have returned to the shepherd and guardian of your souls.

Wives, in the same way, accept the authority of your husbands, so that, even if some of them do not obey the word, they may be won over without a word by their wives' conduct, when they see the purity and reverence of your lives. Do not adorn yourselves outwardly by braiding your hair, and by wearing gold ornaments or fine clothing; rather, let your adornment be the inner self with the lasting beauty of a gentle and quiet spirit, which is very precious in God's sight. It was in this way long ago that the holy women who hoped in God used to adorn themselves by accepting the authority of their husbands. Thus Sarah obeyed Abraham and called him lord. You have become her daughters as long as you do what is good and never let fears alarm you.

Husbands, in the same way, show consideration for your wives in your life together, paying honour to the woman as the weaker sex,[17] since they too are also heirs of the gracious gift of life – so that nothing may hinder your prayers.

Finally, all of you, have unity of spirit, sympathy, love for one another, a tender heart, and a humble mind. Do not repay evil for evil or abuse for abuse; but, on the contrary, repay with a blessing. It is for this that you were called – that you might inherit a blessing. For

> 'Those who desire life
> and desire to see good days,
> let them keep their tongues from evil
> and their lips from speaking deceit;
> let them turn away from evil and do good;
> let them seek peace and pursue it.
> For the eyes of the Lord are on the righteous,
> and his ears are open to their prayer.
> But the face of the Lord is against those who do evil.'

SUFFERING AND GLORY
1 Peter 3:13 – 5:14

Now who will harm you if you are eager to do what is good? But even if you do suffer for doing what is right, you are blessed. Do not fear what they fear,[18] and do not be intimidated, but in your hearts sanctify Christ as Lord. Always be ready to make your defence to anyone who demands from you an account of the hope that is in you; yet do it with gentleness and reverence.[19] Keep your conscience clear, so that, when you are maligned, those who abuse you for your good conduct in Christ may be put to shame. For it is better to suffer for doing good, if suffering should be God's will, than to suffer for doing evil. For Christ also suffered[20] for sins once for all, the righteous for the unrighteous, in order to bring you[21] to God. He was put to death in the flesh, but made alive in the spirit, in which also he went and made a proclamation to the spirits in prison, who in former times did not obey, when God waited patiently in the days of Noah, during the building of the ark, in which a few, that is, eight people, were saved through water. And baptism, which this prefigured, now saves you – not as a removal of dirt from the body, but as an appeal to God for[22] a good conscience, through the resurrection of Jesus Christ, who has gone into heaven and is at the right hand of God, with angels, authorities, and powers made subject to him.

Since therefore Christ suffered in the flesh,[23] arm yourselves also with the same intention (for whoever has suffered in the flesh has finished with sin), so as to live for the rest of your earthly life[24] no longer by human desires but by the will of God. You have already spent enough time in doing what the Gentiles like to do, living in licentiousness, passions, drunkenness, revels, carousing, and lawless idolatry. They are surprised that you no longer join them in the same excesses of dissipation, and so they blaspheme.[25] But they will have to give an account to him who stands ready to judge the living and the dead. For this is the reason the gospel was proclaimed even to the dead, so that, though they had been judged in the flesh as everyone is judged, they might live in the spirit as God does.

The end of all things is near;[26] therefore be serious and discipline yourselves for the sake of your prayers. Above all, maintain constant love for one another, for love covers a multitude of sins. Be hospitable to one another without complaining. Like good stewards of the manifold grace of God, serve one another with whatever gift each of you has received. Whoever speaks must do so as one speaking the very words of God; whoever serves must do so with the strength that God supplies, so that God may be glorified in all things through Jesus Christ. To him belong the glory and the power for ever and ever. Amen.

Beloved, do not be surprised at the fiery ordeal that is taking place among you to test you, as though something strange were happening to you. But rejoice in so far as you are sharing Christ's sufferings, so that you may also be glad and shout for joy when his glory is revealed. If you are reviled for the name of Christ, you are blessed, because the spirit of glory,[27] which is the Spirit of God, is resting on you.[28] But let none of you suffer as a murderer, a thief, a criminal, or even as a mischief-maker. Yet if any of you suffers as a Christian, do not consider it a disgrace, but glorify God because you bear this name. For the time has come for judgment to begin with the household of God; if it begins with us, what will be the end for those who do not obey the gospel of God? And

'If it is hard for the righteous to be saved,
what will become of the ungodly and the sinners?'

Therefore, let those suffering in accordance with God's will entrust themselves to a faithful Creator, while continuing to do good.

Now as an elder myself and a witness of the sufferings of Christ, as well as one who shares in the glory to be revealed, I exhort the elders among you to tend the flock of God that is in your charge, exercising the oversight,[29] not under compulsion but willingly, as God would have you do it[30] – not for sordid gain but eagerly. Do not lord it over those in your charge, but be examples to the flock. And when the chief shepherd appears, you will win the crown of glory that never fades away. In the same way, you who are younger must accept the authority of the elders.[31] And all of you must clothe yourselves with humility in your dealings with one another, for

> 'God opposes the proud,
> but gives grace to the humble.'

Humble yourselves therefore under the mighty hand of God, so that he may exalt you in due time. Cast all your anxiety on him, because he cares for you. Discipline yourselves; keep alert.[32] Like a roaring lion your adversary the devil prowls around, looking for someone to devour. Resist him, steadfast in your faith, for you know that your brothers and sisters[33] throughout the world are undergoing the same kinds of suffering. And after you have suffered for a little while, the God of all grace, who has called you to his eternal glory in Christ, will himself restore, support, strengthen, and establish you. To him be the power for ever and ever. Amen.

Through Silvanus, whom I consider a faithful brother, I have written this short letter to encourage you, and to testify that this is the true grace of God. Stand fast in it. Your sister church in Babylon,[34] chosen together with you, sends you greetings; and so does my son Mark. Greet one another with a kiss of love. Peace to all of you who are in Christ.[35]

Alternative renderings

1. Or *Rejoice in this*
2. Other ancient authorities read *known*
3. Gk *gird up the loins of your mind*
4. Other ancient authorities add *through the Spirit*
5. Or *constantly*
6. Other ancient authorities read *a pure heart*
7. Or *through the word of the living and enduring God*
8. Or *you yourselves are being built*
9. Or *it*
10. Gk *a people for his possession*
11. Gk *God on the day of visitation*
12. Or *every institution ordained for human beings*
13. Gk *slaves*
14. Gk *Love the brotherhood*
15. Or *carried up our sins in his body to the tree*
16. Gk *bruise*
17. Gk *vessel*
18. Gk *their fear*
19. Or *respect*
20. Other ancient authorities read *died*
21. Other ancient authorities read *us*
22. Or *a pledge to God from*
23. Other ancient authorities add *for us*; others, *for you*
24. Gk *rest of the time in the flesh*
25. Or *they malign you*
26. Or *is at hand*
27. Other ancient authorities add *and of power*
28. Other ancient authorities add *On their part he is blasphemed, but on your part he is glorified*
29. Other ancient authorities lack *exercising the oversight*
30. Other ancient authorities lack *as God would have you do it*
31. Or *of those who are older*
32. Or *be vigilant*
33. Gk *your brotherhood*
34. Gk *She who is*
35. Other ancient authorities add *Amen*

The Epistle of Jude

Jude,[1] a servant[2] of Jesus Christ and brother of James, to those who are called, who are beloved[3] in[4] God the Father and kept safe for[4]Jesus Christ:

May mercy, peace, and love be yours in abundance.

Beloved, while eagerly preparing to write to you about the salvation we share, I find it necessary to write and appeal to you to contend for the faith that was once for all entrusted to the saints. For certain intruders have stolen in among you, people who long ago were designated for this condemnation as ungodly, who pervert the grace of our God into licentiousness and deny our only Master and Lord, Jesus Christ.[5]

Now I desire to remind you, though you are fully informed, that the Lord, who once for all saved[6] a people out of the land of Egypt, afterwards destroyed those who did not believe. And the angels who did not keep their own position, but left their proper dwelling, he has kept in eternal chains in deepest darkness for the judgment of the great day. Likewise, Sodom and Gomorrah and the surrounding cities, which, in the same manner as they, indulged in sexual immorality and pursued unnatural lust,[7] serve as an example by undergoing a punishment of eternal fire.

Yet in the same way these dreamers also defile the flesh, reject authority, and slander the glorious ones.[8] But when the archangel Michael contended with the devil and disputed about the body of Moses, he did not dare to bring a condemnation of slander[9] against him, but said, 'The Lord rebuke you!' But these people slander whatever they do not understand, and they are destroyed by those things that, like irrational animals, they know by instinct. Woe to them! For they go the way of Cain, and abandon themselves to Balaam's error for the sake of gain, and perish in Korah's rebellion. These are blemishes[10] on your love-feasts, while they feast with you without fear, feeding themselves.[11] They are waterless clouds carried along by the winds; autumn trees without fruit, twice dead, uprooted; wild waves of the sea, casting up the foam of their own shame; wandering stars, for whom the deepest darkness has been reserved for ever.

It was also about these that Enoch, in the seventh generation from Adam, prophesied, saying, 'See, the Lord is coming[12] with tens of thousands of his holy ones, to execute judgment on all, and to convict everyone of all the deeds of ungodliness that they have committed in such an ungodly way, and of all the harsh things that ungodly sinners have spoken against him.' These are grumblers and malcontents; they indulge their own lusts; they are bombastic in speech, flattering people to their own advantage.

But you, beloved, must remember the predictions of the apostles of our Lord Jesus Christ; for they said to you, 'In the last time there will be scoffers, indulging their own ungodly lusts.' It is these worldly people, devoid of the Spirit, who are causing divisions. But you, beloved, build yourselves up on your most holy faith; pray in the Holy Spirit; keep yourselves in the love of God; look forward to the mercy of our Lord Jesus Christ that leads to[13] eternal life. And have mercy on some who are wavering; save others by snatching them out of the fire; and have mercy on still others with fear, hating even the tunic defiled by their bodies. [14]

Now to him who is able to keep you from falling, and to make you stand without blemish in the presence of his glory with rejoicing, to the only God our Saviour, through Jesus Christ our Lord, be glory, majesty, power, and authority, before all time and now and for ever. Amen.

Alternative renderings

1. Gk *Judas*
2. Gk *slave*
3. Other ancient authorities read *sanctified*
4. Or *by*
5. Or *the only Master and our Lord Jesus Christ*
6. Other ancient authorities read *though you were once for all fully informed, that Jesus* (or *Joshua*) *who saved*
7. Gk *went after other flesh*
8. Or *angels*; Gk *glories*
9. Or *condemnation for blasphemy*
10. Or *reefs*
11. Or *without fear. They are shepherds who care only for themselves*
12. Gk *came*
13. Gk *Christ to*
14. Gk *by the flesh*. The Greek text of verses 22–23 is uncertain at several points

The Second Epistle of Peter

THE CHRISTIAN CALLING
2 Peter 1:1–18

Simeon[1] Peter, a servant[2] and apostle of Jesus Christ, to those who have received a faith as precious as ours through the righteousness of our God and Saviour Jesus Christ:[3]

May grace and peace be yours in abundance in the knowledge of God and of Jesus our Lord.

His divine power has given us everything needed for life and godliness, through the knowledge of him who called us by[4] his own glory and goodness. Thus he has given us, through these things, his precious and very great promises, so that through them you may escape from the corruption that is in the world because of lust, and may become participants in the divine nature. For this very reason, you must make every effort to support your faith with goodness, and goodness with knowledge, and knowledge with self-control, and self-control with endurance, and endurance with godliness, and godliness with mutual[5] affection, and mutual[5] affection with love. For if these things are yours and are increasing among you, they keep you from being ineffective and unfruitful in the knowledge of our Lord Jesus Christ. For anyone who lacks these things is nearsighted and blind, and is forgetful of the cleansing of past sins. Therefore, brothers and sisters,[6] be all the more eager to confirm your call and election, for if you do this, you will never stumble. For in this way, entry into the eternal kingdom of our Lord and Saviour Jesus Christ will be richly provided for you.

Therefore I intend to keep on reminding you of these things, though you know them already and are established in the truth that has come to you. I think it right, as long as I am in this body,[7] to refresh your memory, since I know that my death[8] will come soon, as indeed our Lord Jesus Christ has made clear to me. And I will make every effort so that after my departure you may be able at any time to recall these things.

For we did not follow cleverly devised myths when we made known to you the power and coming of our Lord Jesus Christ, but we had been eyewitnesses of his majesty. For he received honour and glory from God the Father when that voice was conveyed to him by the Majestic Glory, saying, 'This is my Son, my Beloved,[9] with whom I am well pleased.' We ourselves heard this voice come from heaven, while we were with him on the holy mountain.

TRUE AND FALSE PROPHETS
2 Peter 1:19 – 2:22

So we have the prophetic message more fully confirmed. You will do well to be attentive to this as to a lamp shining in a dark place, until the day dawns and the morning star rises in your hearts. First of all you must understand this, that no prophecy of scripture is a matter of one's own interpretation, because no prophecy ever came by human will, but men and women moved by the Holy Spirit spoke from God.[10]

But false prophets also arose among the people, just as there will be false teachers among you, who will secretly bring in destructive opinions. They will even deny the Master who bought them – bringing swift destruction on themselves. Even so, many will follow their licentious ways, and because of these teachers[11] the way of truth will be maligned. And in their greed they will exploit you with deceptive words. Their condemnation, pronounced against them long ago, has not been idle, and their destruction is not asleep.

For if God did not spare the angels when they sinned, but cast them into hell[12] and committed them to chains[13] of deepest darkness to be kept until the judgment; and if he did not spare the ancient world, even though he saved Noah, a herald of righteousness, with seven others, when he brought a flood on a world of the ungodly; and if by turning the cities of Sodom and Gomorrah to ashes he condemned them to extinction[14] and made them an example of what is coming to the ungodly;[15] and if he rescued Lot, a righteous man greatly distressed by the licentiousness of the lawless (for that righteous man, living among them day after day, was tormented in his righteous soul by their lawless deeds that he saw and heard), then the

Lord knows how to rescue the godly from trial, and to keep the unrighteous under punishment until the day of judgment – especially those who indulge their flesh in depraved lust, and who despise authority.

Bold and wilful, they are not afraid to slander the glorious ones,[16] whereas angels, though greater in might and power, do not bring against them a slanderous judgment from the Lord.[17] These people, however, are like irrational animals, mere creatures of instinct, born to be caught and killed. They slander what they do not understand, and when those creatures are destroyed,[18] they also will be destroyed, suffering[19] the penalty for doing wrong. They count it a pleasure to revel in the daytime. They are blots and blemishes, revelling in their dissipation[20] while they feast with you. They have eyes full of adultery, insatiable for sin. They entice unsteady souls. They have hearts trained in greed. Accursed children! They have left the straight road and have gone astray, following the road of Balaam son of Bosor,[21] who loved the wages of doing wrong, but was rebuked for his own transgression; a speechless donkey spoke with a human voice and restrained the prophet's madness.

These are waterless springs and mists driven by a storm; for them the deepest darkness has been reserved. For they speak bombastic nonsense, and with licentious desires of the flesh they entice people who have just[22] escaped from those who live in error. They promise them freedom, but they themselves are slaves of corruption; for people are slaves to whatever masters them. For if, after they have escaped the defilements of the world through the knowledge of our Lord and Saviour Jesus Christ, they are again entangled in them and overpowered, the last state has become worse for them than the first. For it would have been better for them never to have known the way of righteousness than, after knowing it, to turn back from the holy commandment that was passed on to them. It has happened to them according to the true proverb,

'The dog turns back to its own vomit',

and,

'The sow is washed only to wallow in the mud.'

LIVING IN THE LAST DAYS
2 Peter 3:1–18

This is now, beloved, the second letter I am writing to you; in them I am trying to arouse your sincere intention by reminding you that you should remember the words spoken in the past by the holy prophets, and the commandment of the Lord and Saviour spoken through your apostles. First of all you must understand this, that in the last days scoffers will come, scoffing and indulging their own lusts and saying, 'Where is the promise of his coming? For ever since our ancestors died,[23] all things continue as they were from the beginning of creation!' They deliberately ignore this fact, that by the word of God heavens existed long ago and an earth was formed out of water and by means of water, through which the world of that time was deluged with water and perished. But by the same word the present heavens and earth have been reserved for fire, being kept until the day of judgment and destruction of the godless.

But do not ignore this one fact, beloved, that with the Lord one day is like a thousand years, and a thousand years are like one day. The Lord is not slow about his promise, as some think of slowness, but is patient with you,[24] not wanting any to perish, but all to come to repentance. But the day of the Lord will come like a thief, and then the heavens will pass away with a loud noise, and the elements will be dissolved with fire, and the earth and everything that is done on it will be disclosed.[25]

Since all these things are to be dissolved in this way, what sort of people ought you to be in leading lives of holiness and godliness, waiting for and hastening[26] the coming of the day of God, because of which the heavens will be set ablaze and dissolved, and the elements will melt with fire? But, in accordance with his promise, we wait for new heavens and a new earth, where righteousness is at home.

Therefore, beloved, while you are waiting for these things, strive to be found by him at peace, without spot or blemish; and regard the patience of our Lord as salvation. So also our beloved brother Paul wrote to you according to the wisdom given to him, speaking of this as he does in all his letters. There are some things in them hard to understand, which the ignorant and unstable twist to their own destruction, as they do the other scriptures. You therefore, beloved, since you are forewarned, beware that you are not carried away with the error of the lawless and lose your own stability. But grow in the grace and knowledge of our Lord and Saviour Jesus Christ. To him be the glory both now and to the day of eternity. Amen.[27]

Alternative renderings

1. Other ancient authorities read *Simon*
2. Gk *slave*
3. Or *of our God and the Saviour Jesus Christ*
4. Other ancient authorities read *through*
5. Gk *brotherly*
6. Gk *brothers*
7. Gk *tent*
8. Gk *the putting off of my tent*
9. Other ancient authorities read *my beloved Son*
10. Other ancient authorities read *but moved by the Holy Spirit saints of God spoke*
11. Gk *because of them*
12. Gk *Tartaros*
13. Other ancient authorities read *pits*
14. Other ancient authorities lack *to extinction*
15. Other ancient authorites read *an example to those who were to be ungodly*
16. Or *angels*; Gk *glories*
17. Other ancient authorities read *before the Lord*; others lack the phrase
18. Gk *in their destruction*
19. Other ancient authorities read *receiving*
20. Other ancient authorities read *love-feasts*
21. Other ancient authorities read *Beor*
22. Other ancient authorities read *actually*
23. Gk *our fathers fell asleep*
24. Other ancient authorities read *on your account*
25. Other ancient authorities read *will be burned up*
26. Or *earnestly desiring*
27. Other ancient authorities lack *Amen*

THE EPISTLES OF PAUL

The Epistle to the Galatians   265

The First Epistle to the Thessalonians   274

The Second Epistle to the Thessalonians   279

The First Epistle to the Corinthians   282
Abridged from the text of the Revised English Bible

The Second Epistle to the Corinthians   300
Abridged from the text of the Revised English Bible

The Epistle to the Romans   312
Abridged from the text of the Revised English Bible

The Epistle to the Colossians   331

The Epistle to Philemon   337

The Epistle to the Ephesians   339

The Epistle to the Philippians   347

The First Epistle to Timothy   353

The Epistle to Titus   360

The Second Epistle to Timothy   363

The Epistle to the Galatians

THE APOSTLE TO THE GENTILES
Galatians 1:1 – 3:5

From Paul, an apostle commissioned not by any human authority or human act, but by Jesus Christ and God the Father who raised him from the dead. I and all the friends now with me send greetings to the churches of Galatia.

Grace to you and peace from God the Father and our Lord Jesus Christ, who gave himself for our sins, to rescue us out of the present wicked age as our God and Father willed; to him be glory for ever and ever! Amen.

I am astonished to find you turning away so quickly from him who called you by grace, and following a different gospel. Not that it is in fact another gospel; only there are some who unsettle your minds by trying to distort the gospel of Christ. But should anyone, even I myself or an angel from heaven, preach a gospel other than the gospel I preached to you, let him be banned! I warned you in the past and now I warn you again: if anyone preaches a gospel other than the gospel you received, let him be banned!

Now do I sound as if I were asking for human approval and not for God's alone? Am I currying favour with men? If I were still seeking human favour, I should be no servant of Christ. I must make it clear to you, my friends, that the gospel you heard me preach is not of human origin. I did not take it over from anyone; no one taught it me; I received it through a revelation of Jesus Christ.

You have heard what my manner of life was when I was still a practising Jew: how savagely I persecuted the church of God and tried to destroy it; and how in the practice of our national religion I outstripped most of my Jewish contemporaries by my boundless devotion to the traditions of my ancestors. But then in his good pleasure God, who from my birth had set me apart, and who had called me through his grace, chose to reveal his Son in and through me, in order that I might proclaim him among the Gentiles. Immediately, without consulting a single person, without going up to Jerusalem to see those who were apostles before me, I went off to Arabia, and afterwards returned to Damascus.

Three years later I did go up to Jerusalem to get to know Cephas, and I stayed two weeks with him. I saw none of the other apostles, except James, the Lord's brother. What I write is plain truth; God knows I am not lying!

Then I left for the regions of Syria and Cilicia. I was still unknown by sight to the Christian congregations in Judaea; they had simply heard it said, 'Our former persecutor is preaching the good news of the faith which once he tried to destroy', and they praised God for what had happened to me. Fourteen years later, I went up again to Jerusalem with Barnabas, and we took Titus with us. I went in response to a revelation from God; I explained, at a private interview with those of repute, the gospel which I preach to the Gentiles, to make sure that the race I had run and was running should not be in vain. Not even my companion Titus, Greek though he is, was compelled to be circumcised. That course was urged only as a concession to certain sham Christians, intruders who had sneaked in to spy on the liberty we enjoy in the fellowship of Christ Jesus. These men wanted to bring us into bondage, but not for one moment did I yield to their dictation; I was determined that the full truth of the gospel should be maintained for you.

As for those reputed to be something (not that their importance matters to me: God does not recognize these personal distinctions) – these men of repute, I say, imparted nothing further to me. On the contrary, they saw that I had been entrusted to take the gospel to the Gentiles as surely as Peter had been entrusted to take it to the Jews; for the same God who was at work in Peter's mission to the Jews was also at work in mine to the Gentiles.

Recognizing, then, the privilege bestowed on me, those who are reputed to be pillars of the community, James, Cephas, and John, accepted Barnabas and myself as partners and shook hands on it: the agreement was that we should go to the Gentiles, while they went to the Jews. All they asked was that we should keep in mind the poor, the very thing I have always made it my business to do.

But when Cephas came to Antioch, I opposed him to his face, because he was clearly in the wrong. For until some messengers came from James, he was taking his meals with gentile Christians; but after they came he drew back and began to hold aloof, because he was afraid of the Jews. The other Jewish Christians showed the same lack of principle; even Barnabas was carried away and played false like the rest. But when I saw that their conduct did not square with the truth of the gospel, I said to Cephas in front of the whole congregation, 'If you, a Jew born and bred, live like a Gentile, and not like a Jew, how can you insist that Gentiles must live like Jews?'

We ourselves are Jews by birth, not gentile sinners; yet we know that no one is ever justified by doing what the law requires, but only through faith in Christ Jesus. So we too have put our faith in Jesus Christ, in order that we might be justified through this faith, and not through actions dictated by law; for no human being can be justified by keeping the law.

If then, in seeking to be justified in Christ, we ourselves no less than the Gentiles turn out to be sinners, does that mean that Christ is a promoter of sin? Of course not! On the contrary, it is only if I start building up again all I have pulled down that I prove to be one who breaks the law. For through the law I died to law – to live for God. I have been crucified with Christ: the life I now live is not my life, but the life which Christ lives in me; and my present mortal life is lived by faith in the Son of God, who loved me and gave himself up for me. I will not nullify the grace of God; if righteousness comes by law, then Christ died for nothing.

You stupid Galatians! You must have been bewitched – you before whose eyes Jesus Christ was openly displayed on the cross! Answer me one question: did you receive the Spirit by keeping the law or by believing the gospel message? Can you really be so stupid? You started with the spiritual; do you now look to the material to make you perfect? Is all you have experienced to come to nothing – surely not! When God gives you the Spirit and works miracles among you, is it because you keep the law, or is it because you have faith in the gospel message?

THE HEIRS OF ABRAHAM
Galatians 3:6–29

Look at Abraham: he put his faith in God, and that faith was counted to him as righteousness. You may take it, then, that it is those who have faith who are Abraham's sons. And scripture, foreseeing that God would justify the Gentiles through faith, declared the gospel to Abraham beforehand: 'In you all nations shall find blessing.' Thus it is those with faith who share the blessing with faithful Abraham.

On the other hand, those who rely on obedience to the law are under a curse; for scripture says, 'Cursed is everyone who does not persevere in doing everything that is written in the book of the law.' It is evident that no one is ever justified before God by means of the law, because we read, 'He shall gain life who is justified through faith.' Now the law does not operate on the basis of faith, for we read, 'He who does this shall gain life by what he does.' Christ bought us freedom from the curse of the law by coming under the curse for our sake; for scripture says, 'Cursed is everyone who is hanged on a gibbet.' The purpose of this was that the blessing of Abraham should in Jesus Christ be extended to the Gentiles, so that we might receive the promised Spirit through faith.

My friends, let me give you an illustration. When a man's will and testament has been duly executed, no one else can set it aside or add a codicil. Now, the promises were pronounced to Abraham and to his 'issue'. It does not say 'issues' in the plural, but 'your issue' in the singular; and by 'issue' is meant Christ. My point is this: a testament, or covenant, had already been validated by God; a law made four hundred and thirty years later cannot invalidate it and so render its promises ineffective. If the inheritance is by legal right, then it is not by promise; but it was by promise that God bestowed it as a free gift on Abraham.

Then what of the law? It was added to make wrongdoing a legal offence; it was an interim measure pending the arrival of the 'issue' to whom the promise was made. It was promulgated through angels, and there was an intermediary; but an intermediary is not needed for one party acting alone, and God is one.

Does the law, then, contradict the promises? Of course not! If a law had been given which had power to bestow life, then righteousness would indeed have come from keeping the law. But scripture has declared the whole world to be prisoners in subjection to sin, so that faith in Jesus Christ should be the ground on which the promised blessing is given to those who believe.

Before this faith came, we were close prisoners in the custody of law, pending the revelation of faith. The law was thus put in charge of us until Christ should come, when we should be justified through faith; and now that faith has come, its charge is at an end.

It is through faith that you are all sons of God in union with Christ Jesus. Baptized into union with him, you have all put on Christ like a garment. There is no such thing as Jew and Greek, slave and freeman, male and female; for you are all one person in Christ Jesus. So if you belong to Christ, you are the 'issue' of Abraham and heirs by virtue of the promise.

THE FREEDOM OF FAITH
Galatians 4:1 – 5:15

This is what I mean: so long as the heir is a minor, he is no better off than a slave, even though the whole estate is his; he is subject to guardians and trustees until the date set by his father. So it was with us: during our minority we were slaves, subject to the elemental spirits of the universe, but when the appointed time came, God sent his Son, born of a woman, born under the law, to buy freedom for those who were under the law, in order that we might attain the status of sons.

To prove that you are sons, God has sent into our hearts the Spirit of his Son, crying 'Abba, Father!' You are therefore no longer a slave but a son, and if a son, an heir by God's own act.

Formerly, when you did not know God, you were slaves to gods who are not gods at all. But now that you do acknowledge God – or rather, now that he has acknowledged you – how can you turn back to those feeble and bankrupt elemental spirits? Why do you propose to enter their service all over again? You keep special days and months and seasons and years. I am afraid that all my hard work on you may have been wasted.

Put yourselves in my place, my friends, I beg you, as I put myself in yours. You never did me any wrong: it was bodily illness, as you will remember, that originally led to my bringing you the gospel, and you resisted any temptation to show scorn or disgust at my physical condition; on the contrary you welcomed me as if I were an angel of God, as you might have welcomed Christ Jesus himself. What has become of the happiness you felt then? I believe you would have torn out your eyes and given them to me, had that been possible! Have I now made myself your enemy by being frank with you?

Others are lavishing attention on you, but without sincerity: what they really want is to isolate you so that you may lavish attention on them. To be the object of sincere attentions is always good, and not just when I am with you. You are my own children, and I am in labour with you all over again until you come to have the form of Christ. How I wish I could be with you now, for then I could modify my tone; as it is, I am at my wits' end about you.

Tell me now, you that are so anxious to be under law, will you not listen to what the law says? It is written there that Abraham had two sons, the one by a slave, the other by a free-born woman. The slave's son was born in the ordinary course of nature, but the free woman's through God's promise. This is an allegory: the two women stand for two covenants. The one covenant comes from Mount Sinai; that is Hagar, and her children are born into slavery. Sinai is a mountain in Arabia and represents the Jerusalem of today, for she and her children are in slavery. But the heavenly Jerusalem is the free woman; she is our mother. For scripture says, 'Rejoice, O barren woman who never bore a child; break into a shout of joy, you who have never been in labour; for the deserted wife will have more children than she who lives with her husband.'

Now you, my friends, like Isaac, are children of God's promise, but just as in those days the natural-born son persecuted the spiritual son, so it is today. Yet what does scripture say? 'Drive out the slave and her son, for the son of the slave shall not share the inheritance with the son of the free woman.' You see, then, my friends, we are no slave's children; our mother is the free woman. It is for freedom that Christ set us free. Stand firm, therefore, and refuse to submit again to the yoke of slavery.

Mark my words: I, Paul, say to you that if you get yourself circumcised Christ will benefit you no more. I impress on you once again that every man who accepts circumcision is under obligation to keep the entire law. When you seek to be justified by way of law, you are cut off from Christ: you have put yourselves outside God's grace. For it is by the Spirit and through faith that we hope to attain that righteousness which we eagerly await. If we are in union with Christ Jesus, circumcision makes no difference at all, nor does the lack of it; the only thing that counts is faith expressing itself through love.

You were running well; who was it hindered you from following the truth? Whatever persuasion was used, it did not come from God who called you. 'A little leaven', remember, 'leavens all the dough'. The Lord gives me confidence that you will not adopt the wrong view; but whoever it is who is unsettling your minds must bear God's judgment. As for me, my friends, if I am still advocating circumcision, then why am I still being persecuted? To do that would be to strip the cross of all offence. Those agitators had better go the whole way and make eunuchs of themselves!

THE GUIDANCE OF THE SPIRIT
Galatians 5:16 – 6:10

You, my friends, were called to be free; only beware of turning your freedom into licence for your unspiritual nature. Instead, serve one another in love; for the whole law is summed up in a single commandment: 'Love your neighbour as yourself.' But if you go on fighting one another, tooth and nail, all you can expect is mutual destruction.

What I mean is this: be guided by the Spirit and you will not gratify the desires of your unspiritual nature. That nature sets its desires against the Spirit, while the Spirit fights against it. They are in conflict with one another so that you cannot do what you want. But if you are led by the Spirit, you are not subject to law.

Anyone can see the behaviour that belongs to the unspiritual nature: fornication, indecency, and debauchery; idolatry and sorcery; quarrels, a contentious temper, envy, fits of rage, selfish ambitions, dissensions, party intrigues, and jealousies; drinking bouts, orgies, and the like. I warn you, as I warned you before, that no one who behaves like that will ever inherit the kingdom of God.

But the harvest of the Spirit is love, joy, peace, patience, kindness, goodness, fidelity, gentleness, and self-control. Against such things there is no law. Those who belong to Christ Jesus have crucified the old nature with its passions and desires. If the Spirit is the source of our life, let the Spirit also direct its course.

We must not be conceited, inciting one another to rivalry, jealous of one another. If anyone is caught doing something wrong, you, my friends, who live by the Spirit must gently set him right. Look to yourself, each one of you: you also may be tempted. Carry one another's burdens, and in this way you will fulfil the law of Christ.

If anyone imagines himself to be somebody when he is nothing, he is deluding himself. Each of you should examine his own conduct, and then he can measure his achievement by comparing himself with himself and not with anyone else; for everyone has his own burden to bear.

When anyone is under instruction in the faith, he should give his teacher a share of whatever good things he has.

Make no mistake about this: God is not to be fooled; everyone reaps what he sows. If he sows in the field of his unspiritual nature, he will reap from it a harvest of corruption; but if he sows in the field of the Spirit, he will reap from it a harvest of eternal life. Let us never tire of doing good, for if we do not slacken our efforts we shall in due time reap our harvest. Therefore, as opportunity offers, let us work for the good of all, especially members of the household of the faith.

FINAL ADVICE
Galatians 6:11–18

Look how big the letters are, now that I am writing to you in my own hand. It is those who want to be outwardly in good standing who are trying to force circumcision on you; their sole object is to escape persecution for the cross of Christ. Even those who do accept circumcision are not thoroughgoing observers of the law; they want you to be circumcised just in order to boast of your submission to that outward rite. God forbid that I should boast of anything but the cross of our Lord Jesus Christ, through which the world is crucified to me and I to the world! Circumcision is nothing; uncircumcision is nothing; the only thing that counts is new creation! All who take this principle for their guide, peace and mercy be upon them, the Israel of God!

In future let no one make trouble for me, for I bear the marks of Jesus branded on my body.

The grace of our Lord Jesus Christ be with you, my friends. Amen.

The First Epistle to the Thessalonians

PAUL'S LOVE FOR THE THESSALONIANS
1 Thessalonians 1:1 – 3:13

From Paul, Silvanus, and Timothy to the church of the Thessalonians who belong to God the Father and the Lord Jesus Christ.

Grace to you and peace.

We always thank God for you all, and mention you in our prayers. We continually call to mind, before our God and Father, how your faith has shown itself in action, your love in labour, and your hope of our Lord Jesus Christ in perseverance. My dear friends, beloved by God, we are certain that he has chosen you, because when we brought you the gospel we did not bring it in mere words but in the power of the Holy Spirit and with strong conviction. You know what we were like for your sake when we were with you.

You, in turn, followed the example set by us and by the Lord; the welcome you gave the message meant grave suffering for you, yet you rejoiced in the Holy Spirit; and so you have become a model for all believers in Macedonia and in Achaia. From you the word of the Lord rang out; and not in Macedonia and Achaia alone, but everywhere your faith in God has become common knowledge. No words of ours are needed; everyone is spreading the story of our visit to you: how you turned from idols to be servants of the true and living God, and to wait expectantly for his Son from heaven, whom he raised from the dead, Jesus our deliverer from the retribution to come.

You know for yourselves, my friends, that our visit to you was not fruitless. Far from it! After all the injury and outrage which as you know we had suffered at Philippi, by the help of our God we declared the gospel of God to you frankly and fearlessly in face of great opposition. The appeal we make does not spring from delusion or sordid motive or from any attempt to deceive; but God has approved us as fit to be entrusted with the gospel. So when we preach, we do not curry favour with men; we seek only the favour of God, who is continually testing our hearts. We have never resorted to flattery, as you have cause to know; nor, as God is our witness, have our words ever been a cloak for greed. We have never sought honour from men, not from you or from anyone else, although as Christ's own envoys we might have made our weight felt; but we were as gentle with you as a nurse caring for her children. Our affection was so deep that we were determined to share with you not only the gospel of God but our very selves; that is how dear you had become to us! You remember, my friends, our toil and drudgery; night and day we worked for a living, rather than be a burden to any of you while we proclaimed to you the good news of God.

We call you to witness, yes and God himself, how devout and just and blameless was our conduct towards you who are believers. As you well know, we dealt with each one of you as a father deals with his children; we appealed to you, we encouraged you, we urged you, to live lives worthy of the God who calls you into his kingdom and glory.

We have reason to thank God continually because, when we handed on God's message, you accepted it, not as the word of men, but as what it truly is, the very word of God at work in you who are believers. You, my friends, have followed the example of the Christians in the churches of God in Judaea: you have been treated by your own countrymen as they were treated by the Jews, who killed the Lord Jesus and the prophets and drove us out, and are so heedless of God's will and such enemies of their fellow-men that they hinder us from telling the Gentiles how they may be saved. All this time they have been making up the full measure of their guilt. But now retribution has overtaken them for good and all!

My friends, when for a short spell you were lost to us – out of sight but not out of mind – we were exceedingly anxious to see you again. So we made up our minds to visit you – I, Paul, more than once – but Satan thwarted us. For what hope or joy or triumphal crown is there for us when we stand before our Lord Jesus at his coming? What indeed but you? You are our glory and our joy.

So when we could bear it no longer, we decided to stay on alone at Athens, and sent Timothy, our colleague and a fellow-worker with God in the service of the gospel of Christ, to encourage you to stand firm for the faith and under all these hardships remain unshaken. You know that this is our appointed lot, for when we were with you we warned you that we were bound to suffer hardship; and so it has turned out, as you have found. This was why I could bear it no longer and sent to find out about your faith; I was afraid that the tempter might have tempted you and our labour might be wasted.

But now Timothy has just returned from his visit to you, bringing good news of your faith and love. He tells us that you always think kindly of us, and are as anxious to see us as we are to see you. So amid all our difficulties and hardships we are reassured, my friends, by the news of your faith. It is the breath of life to us to know that you stand firm in the Lord. What thanks can we give to God in return for you? What thanks for all the joy you have brought us, making us rejoice before our God while we pray most earnestly night and day to be allowed to see you again and to make good whatever is lacking in your faith?

May our God and Father himself, and our Lord Jesus, open the way for us to come to you; and may the Lord make your love increase and overflow to one another and to everyone, as our love does to you. May he make your hearts firm, so that you may stand before our God and Father holy and faultless when our Lord Jesus comes with all those who are his own.

THE CHRISTIAN WAY OF LIFE
1 Thessalonians 4:1–12

And now, friends, we have one thing to ask of you, as fellow-Christians. We passed on to you the tradition of the way we must live if we are to please God; you are indeed already following it, but we beg you to do so yet more thoroughly. You know the rules we gave you in the name of the Lord Jesus. This is the will of God, that you should be holy: you must abstain from fornication; each one of you must learn to gain mastery over his body, to hallow and honour it, not giving way to lust like the pagans who know nothing of God; no one must do his fellow-Christian wrong in this matter, or infringe his rights. As we impressed on you before, the Lord punishes all such offences. For God called us to holiness, not to impurity. Anyone therefore who flouts these rules is flouting not man but the God who bestows on you his Holy Spirit.

About love of the brotherhood you need no words of mine, for you are yourselves taught by God to love one another, and you are in fact practising this rule of love towards all your fellow-Christians throughout Macedonia. Yet we appeal to you, friends, to do better still. Let it be your ambition to live quietly and attend to your own business; and to work with your hands, as we told you, so that you may command the respect of those outside your own number, and at the same time never be in want.

THE CHRISTIAN HOPE
1 Thessalonians 4:13 – 5:11

We wish you not to remain in ignorance, friends, about those who sleep in death; you should not grieve like the rest of mankind, who have no hope. We believe that Jesus died and rose again; so too will God bring those who died as Christians to be with Jesus.

This we tell you as a word from the Lord: those of us who are still alive when the Lord comes will have no advantage over those who have died; when the command is given, when the archangel's voice is heard, when God's trumpet sounds, then the Lord himself will descend from heaven; first the Christian dead will rise, then we who are still alive shall join them, caught up in clouds to meet the Lord in the air. Thus we shall always be with the Lord. Console one another, then, with these words.

About dates and times, my friends, there is no need to write to you, for you yourselves know perfectly well that the day of the Lord comes like a thief in the night. While they are saying, 'All is peaceful, all secure', destruction is upon them, sudden as the pangs that come on a woman in childbirth; and there will be no escape. But you, friends, are not in the dark; the day will not come upon you like a thief. You are all children of light, children of day. We do not belong to night and darkness, and we must not sleep like the rest, but keep awake and sober. Sleepers sleep at night, and drunkards get drunk at night, but we, who belong to the daylight, must keep sober, armed with the breastplate of faith and love, and the hope of salvation for a helmet. God has not destined us for retribution, but for the full attainment of salvation through our Lord Jesus Christ. He died for us so that awake or asleep we might live in company with him. Therefore encourage one another, build one another up – as indeed you do.

FINAL EXHORTATIONS
1 Thessalonians 5:12–28

We beg you, friends, to acknowledge those who are working so hard among you, and are your leaders and counsellors in the Lord's fellowship. Hold them in the highest esteem and affection for the work they do.

Live at peace among yourselves. We urge you, friends, to rebuke the idle, encourage the faint-hearted, support the weak, and be patient with everyone.

See to it that no one pays back wrong for wrong, but always aim at what is best for each other and for all.

Always be joyful; pray continually; give thanks whatever happens; for this is what God wills for you in Christ Jesus.

Do not stifle inspiration or despise prophetic utterances, but test them all; keep hold of what is good and avoid all forms of evil.

May God himself, the God of peace, make you holy through and through, and keep you sound in spirit, soul, and body, free of any fault when our Lord Jesus Christ comes. He who calls you keeps faith; he will do it.

Friends, pray for us also.

Greet all our fellow-Christians with the kiss of peace.

I adjure you by the Lord to have this letter read to them all.

The grace of our Lord Jesus Christ be with you!

The Second Epistle to the Thessalonians

THE SECOND COMING OF CHRIST
2 Thessalonians 1:1 – 2:12

From Paul, Silvanus, and Timothy to the church of the Thessalonians who belong to God our Father and the Lord Jesus Christ.

Grace to you and peace from God the Father and the Lord Jesus Christ.

Friends, we are always bound to thank God for you, and it is right that we should, because your faith keeps on increasing and the love you all have for each other grows ever greater. Indeed we boast about you among the churches of God, because your faith remains so steadfast under all the persecutions and troubles you endure. This points to the justice of God's judgment; you will be proved worthy of the kingdom of God, for which indeed you are suffering. It is just that God should balance the account by sending affliction to those who afflict you, and relief to you who are afflicted, and to us as well, when the Lord Jesus is revealed from heaven with his mighty angels in blazing fire. Then he will mete out punishment to those who refuse to acknowledge God and who will not obey the gospel of our Lord Jesus. They will suffer the penalty of eternal destruction, cut off from the presence of the Lord and the splendour of his might, when on the great day he comes to reveal his glory among his own and his majesty among all believers; and therefore among you, since you believed the testimony we brought you.

With this in mind we pray for you always, that our God may count you worthy of your calling, and that his power may bring to fulfilment every good purpose and every act inspired by faith, so that the name of our Lord Jesus may be glorified in you, and you in him, according to the grace of our God and the Lord Jesus Christ.

Now about the coming of our Lord Jesus Christ, when he is to gather us to himself: I beg you, my friends, do not suddenly lose your heads, do not be alarmed by any prophetic utterance, any pronouncement, or any letter purporting to come from us, alleging that the day of the Lord is already here. Let no one deceive you in any way. That day cannot come before the final rebellion against God, when wickedness will be revealed in human form, the man doomed to destruction. He is the adversary who raises himself up against every so-called god or object of worship, and even enthrones himself in God's temple claiming to be God. Do you not remember that I told you this while I was still with you? You know, too, about the restraining power which ensures that he will be revealed only at his appointed time; for already the secret forces of wickedness are at work, secret only for the present until the restraining hand is removed from the scene. Then he will be revealed, the wicked one whom the Lord Jesus will destroy with the breath of his mouth and annihilate by the radiance of his presence. The coming of the wicked one is the work of Satan; it will be attended by all the powerful signs and miracles that falsehood can devise, all the deception that sinfulness can impose on those doomed to destruction, because they did not open their minds to love of the truth and so find salvation. That is why God puts them under a compelling delusion, which makes them believe what is false, so that all who have not believed the truth but made sinfulness their choice may be brought to judgment.

FURTHER INSTRUCTIONS AND ENCOURAGEMENT
2 Thessalonians 2:13 – 3:18

We are always bound to thank God for you, my friends beloved by the Lord. From the beginning of time God chose you to find salvation in the Spirit who consecrates you and in the truth you believe. It was for this that he called you through the gospel we brought, so that you might come to possess the splendour of our Lord Jesus Christ.

Stand firm then, my friends, and hold fast to the traditions which you have learned from us by word or by letter. And may our Lord Jesus Christ himself and God our Father, who has shown us such love, and in his grace has given us such unfailing encouragement and so sure a hope, still encourage and strengthen you in every good deed and word.

And now, friends, pray for us, that the word of the Lord may have everywhere the swift and glorious success it has had among you, and that we may be rescued from wrong-headed and wicked people; for not all have faith. But the Lord keeps faith, and he will strengthen you and guard you from the evil one; and in the Lord we have confidence about you, that you are doing and will continue to do what we tell you. May the Lord direct your hearts towards God's love and the steadfastness of Christ.

These are our instructions to you, friends, in the name of our Lord Jesus Christ: hold aloof from every Christian who falls into idle habits, and disregards the tradition you received from us. You yourselves know how you ought to follow our example: you never saw us idling; we did not accept free hospitality from anyone; night and day in toil and drudgery we worked for a living, rather than be a burden to any of you – not because we do not have the right to maintenance, but to set an example for you to follow. Already during our stay with you we laid down this rule: anyone who will not work shall not eat. We mention this because we hear that some of you are idling their time away, minding everybody's business but their own. We instruct and urge such people in the name of the Lord Jesus Christ to settle down to work and earn a living.

My friends, you must never tire of doing right. If anyone disobeys the instructions given in my letter, single him out, and have nothing to do with him until he is ashamed of himself. I do not mean treat him as an enemy, but admonish him as one of the family.

May the Lord of peace himself give you peace at all times and in all ways. The Lord be with you all.

This greeting is in my own handwriting; all genuine letters of mine bear the same signature – Paul.

The grace of our Lord Jesus Christ be with you all.

The First Epistle to the Corinthians

THE WISDOM OF GOD
1 Corinthians 1:1–3, 10–13, 17 – 2:16

From Paul, apostle of Christ Jesus by God's call and by his will, together with our colleague Sosthenes, to God's church at Corinth, dedicated to him in Christ Jesus, called to be his people, along with all who invoke the name of our Lord Jesus Christ wherever they may be – their Lord as well as ours.

Grace and peace to you from God our Father and the Lord Jesus Christ.

I appeal to you, my friends, in the name of our Lord Jesus Christ: agree among yourselves, and avoid divisions; let there be complete unity of mind and thought. My friends, it has been brought to my notice by Chloe's people that there are quarrels among you. What I mean is this: each of you is saying, 'I am for Paul,' or 'I am for Apollos'; 'I am for Cephas,' or 'I am for Christ.' Surely Christ has not been divided! Was it Paul who was crucified for you? Was it in Paul's name that you were baptized?... Christ did not send me to baptize, but to proclaim the gospel; and to do it without recourse to the skills of rhetoric, lest the cross of Christ be robbed of its effect.

The message of the cross is sheer folly to those on the way to destruction, but to us, who are on the way to salvation, it is the power of God. Scripture says, 'I will destroy the wisdom of the wise, and bring to nothing the cleverness of the clever.' Where is your wise man now, your man of learning, your subtle debater of this present age? God has made the wisdom of this world look foolish! As God in his wisdom ordained, the world failed to find him by its wisdom, and he chose by the folly of the gospel to save those who have faith. Jews demand signs, Greeks look for wisdom, but we proclaim Christ nailed to the cross; and though this is an offence to Jews and folly to

Gentiles, yet to those who are called, Jews and Greeks alike, he is the power of God and the wisdom of God.

The folly of God is wiser than human wisdom, and the weakness of God stronger than human strength. My friends, think what sort of people you are, whom God has called. Few of you are wise by any human standard, few powerful or of noble birth. Yet, to shame the wise, God has chosen what the world counts folly, and to shame what is strong, God has chosen what the world counts weakness. He has chosen things without rank or standing in the world, mere nothings, to overthrow the existing order. So no place is left for any human pride in the presence of God. By God's act you are in Christ Jesus; God has made him our wisdom, and in him we have our righteousness, our holiness, our liberation. Therefore, in the words of scripture, 'If anyone must boast, let him boast of the Lord.'

So it was, my friends, that I came to you, without any pretensions to eloquence or wisdom in declaring the truth about God. I resolved that while I was with you I would not claim to know anything but Jesus Christ – Christ nailed to the cross. I came before you in weakness, in fear, in great trepidation. The word I spoke, the gospel I proclaimed, did not sway you with clever arguments; it carried conviction by spiritual power, so that your faith might be built not on human wisdom but on the power of God.

Among the mature I do speak words of wisdom, though not a wisdom belonging to this present age or to its governing powers, already in decline; I speak God's hidden wisdom, his secret purpose framed from the very beginning to bring us to our destined glory. None of the powers that rule the world has known that wisdom; if they had, they would not have crucified the Lord of glory. Scripture speaks of 'things beyond our seeing, things beyond our hearing, things beyond our imagining, all prepared by God for those who love him'; and these are what God has revealed to us through the Spirit. For the Spirit explores everything, even the depths of God's own nature. Who knows what a human being is but the human spirit within him? In the same way, only the Spirit of God knows what God is. And we have received this Spirit from God, not the spirit of the world, so that we may know all that God has lavished on us; and, because we are interpreting spiritual truths to those who have the

Spirit, we speak of these gifts of God in words taught us not by our human wisdom but by the Spirit. An unspiritual person refuses what belongs to the Spirit of God; it is folly to him; he cannot grasp it, because it needs to be judged in the light of the Spirit. But a spiritual person can judge the worth of everything, yet is not himself subject to judgment by others. Scripture indeed asks, 'Who can know the mind of the Lord or be his counsellor?' Yet we possess the mind of Christ.

THE TEMPLE OF GOD
1 Corinthians 3:1–17

But I could not talk to you, my friends, as people who have the Spirit; I had to deal with you on the natural plane, as infants in Christ. I fed you on milk, instead of solid food, for which you were not yet ready. Indeed, you are still not ready for it; you are still on the merely natural plane. Can you not see that as long as there is jealousy and strife among you, you are unspiritual, living on the purely human level? When one declares, 'I am for Paul,' and another, 'I am for Apollos,' are you not all too human?

After all, what is Apollos? What is Paul? Simply God's agents in bringing you to faith. Each of us performed the task which the Lord assigned to him: I planted the seed, and Apollos watered it; but God made it grow. It is not the gardeners with their planting and watering who count, but God who makes it grow. Whether they plant or water, they work as a team, though each will get his own pay for his own labour. We are fellow-workers in God's service; and you are God's garden.

Or again, you are God's building. God gave me the privilege of laying the foundation like a skilled master builder; others put up the building. Let each take care how he builds. There can be no other foundation than the one already laid: I mean Jesus Christ himself. If anyone builds on that foundation with gold, silver, and precious stones, or with wood, hay, and straw, the work that each does will at last be brought to light; the day of judgment will expose it. For that day dawns in fire, and the fire will test the worth of each person's work. If anyone's building survives, he will be rewarded; if it burns down, he will have to bear the loss; yet he will escape with his life, though only by passing through the fire. Surely you know that you are God's temple, where the Spirit of God dwells. Anyone who destroys God's temple will himself be destroyed by God, because the temple of God is holy; and you are that temple.

AN APPEAL FOR HUMILITY
1 Corinthians 4:6-21

My friends, I have applied all this to Apollos and myself for your benefit, so that you may take our case as an example, and learn the true meaning of 'nothing beyond what stands written', and may not be inflated with pride as you take sides in support of one against another. My friend, who makes you so important? What do you possess that was not given you? And if you received it as a gift, why take the credit to yourself?

No doubt you already have all you could desire; you have come into your fortune already! Without us you have come into your kingdom. How I wish you had indeed come into your kingdom; then you might share it with us! For it seems to me God has made us apostles the last act in the show, like men condemned to death in the arena, a spectacle to the whole universe – to angels as well as men. We are fools for Christ's sake, while you are sensible Christians! We are weak; you are powerful! You are honoured; we are in disgrace! To this day we go hungry and thirsty and in rags; we are beaten up; we wander from place to place; we wear ourselves out earning a living with our own hands. People curse us, and we bless; they persecute us, and we submit; they slander us, and we try to be conciliatory. To this day we are treated as the scum of the earth, as the dregs of humanity.

I am not writing this to shame you, but to bring you to reason; for you are my dear children. You may have thousands of tutors in Christ, but you have only one father; for in Christ Jesus you are my offspring, and mine alone, through the preaching of the gospel. I appeal to you therefore to follow my example. That is why I have sent Timothy, who is a dear son to me and a trustworthy Christian, to remind you of my way of life in Christ, something I teach everywhere in all the churches. There are certain persons who are filled with self-importance because they think I am not coming to Corinth. I shall come very soon, if it is the Lord's will; and then I shall take the measure of these self-important people, not by what they say, but by what they can do, for the kingdom of God is not a matter of words, but of power. Choose, then: am I to come to you with a rod in my hand, or with love and a gentle spirit?

MATTERS OF SEX AND MARRIAGE
1 Corinthians 5:1–13; 6:12 – 7:17, 25–35

I actually hear reports of sexual immorality among you, immorality such as even pagans do not tolerate: the union of a man with his stepmother. And you are proud of yourselves! You ought to have gone into mourning; anyone who behaves like that should be turned out of your community. For my part, though I am absent in body, I am present in spirit, and have already reached my judgment on the man who did this thing, as if I were indeed present: when you are all assembled in the name of our Lord Jesus, and I am with you in spirit, through the power of our Lord Jesus you are to consign this man to Satan for the destruction of his body, so that his spirit may be saved on the day of the Lord.

Your self-satisfaction ill becomes you. Have you never heard the saying, 'A little leaven leavens all the dough'? Get rid of the old leaven and then you will be a new batch of unleavened dough. Indeed you already are, because Christ our Passover lamb has been sacrificed. So we who observe the festival must not use the old leaven, the leaven of depravity and wickedness, but only the unleavened bread which is sincerity and truth.

In my letter I wrote that you must have nothing to do with those who are sexually immoral. I was not, of course, referring to people in general who are immoral or extortioners or swindlers or idolaters; to avoid them you would have to withdraw from society altogether. I meant that you must have nothing to do with any so-called Christian who leads an immoral life, or is extortionate, idolatrous, a slanderer, a drunkard, or a swindler; with anyone like that you should not even eat. What business of mine is it to judge outsiders? God is their judge. But within the fellowship, you are the judges: 'Root out the wrongdoer from your community.'…

'I am free to do anything,' you say. Yes, but not everything does good. No doubt I am free to do anything, but I for one will not let anything make free with me. 'Food is for the belly and the belly for food,' you say. True; and one day God will put an end to both. But the body is not for fornication; it is for the Lord – and the Lord for the body. God not only raised our Lord from the dead; he will also raise us by his power. Do you not know that your bodies are limbs and organs of Christ? Shall I then take parts of Christ's body and make them over to a prostitute? Never! You surely know that anyone who joins himself to a prostitute becomes physically one with her, for scripture says, 'The two shall become one flesh'; but anyone who joins himself to the Lord is one with him spiritually. Have nothing to do with fornication. Every other sin that one may commit is outside the body; but the fornicator sins against his own body. Do you not know that your body is a temple of the indwelling Holy Spirit, and the Spirit is God's gift to you? You do not belong to yourselves; you were bought at a price. Then honour God in your body.

Now for the matters you wrote about. You say, 'It is a good thing for a man not to have intercourse with a woman.' Rather, in the face of so much immorality, let each man have his own wife and each woman her own husband. The husband must give the wife what is due to her, and equally the wife must give the husband his due. The wife cannot claim her body as her own; it is her husband's. Equally, the husband cannot claim his body as his own; it is his wife's. Do not deny yourselves to one another, except when you agree to devote yourselves to prayer for a time, and to come together again afterwards; otherwise, through lack of self-control, you may be tempted by Satan. I say this by way of concession, not command. I should like everyone to be as I myself am; but each person has the gift God has granted him, one this gift and another that.

To the unmarried and to widows I say this: it is a good thing if like me they stay as they are; but if they do not have self-control, they should marry. It is better to be married than burn with desire.

To the married I give this ruling, which is not mine but the Lord's: a wife must not separate herself from her husband – if she does, she must either remain unmarried or be reconciled to her husband – and the husband must not divorce his wife.

To the rest I say this, as my own word, not as the Lord's: if a Christian has a wife who is not a believer, and she is willing to live with him, he must not divorce her; and if a woman has a husband who is not a believer, and he is willing to live with her, she must not divorce him. For the husband now belongs to God through his Christian wife, and the wife through her Christian husband. Otherwise your children would not belong to God, whereas in fact they do. If however the unbelieving partner wishes for a separation, it should be granted; in such cases the Christian husband or wife is not bound by the marriage. God's call is a call to live in peace. But remember: a wife may save her husband; and a husband may save his wife.

However that may be, each one should accept the lot which the Lord has assigned him and continue as he was when God called him. That is the rule I give in all the churches...

About the unmarried, I have no instructions from the Lord, but I give my opinion as one who by the Lord's mercy is fit to be trusted. I think the best way for a man to live in a time of stress like the present is this – to remain as he is. Are you bound in marriage? Do not seek a dissolution. Has your marriage been dissolved? Do not seek a wife. But if you do marry, you are not doing anything wrong, nor does a girl if she marries; it is only that those who marry will have hardships to endure, and my aim is to spare you.

What I mean, my friends, is this: the time we live in will not last long. While it lasts, married men should be as if they had no wives; mourners should be as if they had nothing to grieve them, the joyful as if they did not rejoice; those who buy should be as if they possessed nothing, and those who use the world's wealth as if they did not have full use of it. For the world as we know it is passing away.

I want you to be free from anxious care. An unmarried man is concerned with the Lord's business; his aim is to please the Lord. But a married man is concerned with worldly affairs; his aim is to please his wife, and he is pulled in two directions. The unmarried woman or girl is concerned with the Lord's business; her aim is to be dedicated to him in body as in spirit. But the married woman is concerned with worldly affairs; her aim is to please her husband.

In saying this I am thinking simply of your own good. I have no wish to keep you on a tight rein; I only want you to be beyond criticism and be free from distraction in your devotion to the Lord.

MEAT OFFERED TO IDOLS
1 Corinthians 8:1–13; 9:19–23; 10:1 – 11:1

Now about meat consecrated to heathen deities.

Of course 'We all have knowledge,' as you say. 'Knowledge' inflates a man, whereas love builds him up. If anyone fancies that he has some kind of knowledge, he does not yet know in the true sense of knowing. But if anyone loves God, he is known by God.

Well then, about eating this consecrated meat: of course, as you say, 'A false god has no real existence, and there is no god but one.' Even though there be so-called gods, whether in heaven or on earth – and indeed there are many such gods and many such lords – yet for us there is one God, the Father, from whom are all things, and we exist for him; there is one Lord, Jesus Christ, through whom are all things, and we exist through him.

But not everyone possesses this knowledge. There are some who have been so accustomed to idolatry that they still think of this meat as consecrated to the idol, and their conscience, being weak, is defiled by eating it. Certainly food will not bring us into God's presence: if we do not eat, we are none the worse, and if we do eat, we are none the better. But be careful that this liberty of yours does not become a pitfall for the weak. If one of them sees you sitting down to a meal in a heathen temple – you with your 'knowledge' – will not his conscience be emboldened to eat meat consecrated to the heathen deity? This 'knowledge' of yours destroys the weak, the fellow-Christian for whom Christ died. In sinning against your brothers and sisters in this way and wounding their conscience, weak as it is, you sin against Christ. Therefore, if food be the downfall of a fellow-Christian, I will never eat meat again, for I will not be the cause of a fellow-Christian's downfall...

I am free and own no master; but I have made myself everyone's servant, to win over as many as possible. To Jews I behaved like a Jew, to win Jews; that is, to win those under the law I behaved as if under the law, though not myself subject to the law. To win those outside that law, I behaved as if outside the law, though not myself outside God's law, but subject to the law of Christ. To the weak I became weak, to win the weak. To them all I have become everything in turn, so that in one way or another I may save some. All this I do for the sake of the gospel, to have a share in its blessings...

Let me remind you, my friends, that our ancestors were all under the cloud, and all of them passed through the Red Sea; so they all received baptism into the fellowship of Moses in cloud and sea. They all ate the same supernatural food, and all drank the same supernatural drink; for they drank from the supernatural rock that accompanied their travels – and that rock was Christ. Yet most of them were not accepted by God, for the wilderness was strewn with their corpses.

These events happened as warnings to us not to set our desires on evil things as they did. Do not be idolaters, like some of them; as scripture says, 'The people sat down to feast and rose up to revel.' Let us not commit fornication; some of them did, and twenty-three thousand died in one day. Let us not put the Lord to the test as some of them did; they were destroyed by the snakes. Do not grumble as some of them did; they were destroyed by the Destroyer.

All these things that happened to them were symbolic, and were recorded as a warning for us, upon whom the end of the ages has come. If you think you are standing firm, take care, or you may fall. So far you have faced no trial beyond human endurance; God keeps faith and will not let you be tested beyond your powers, but when the test comes he will at the same time provide a way out and so enable you to endure. So then, my dear friends, have nothing to do with idolatry. I appeal to you as sensible people; form your own judgment on what I say. When we bless the cup of blessing, is it not a means of sharing in the blood of Christ? When we break the bread, is it not a means of sharing in the body of Christ? Because there is one loaf, we, though many, are one body; for it is one loaf of which we all partake.

Consider Jewish practice: are not those who eat the sacrificial meal partners in the altar? What do I imply by this? That meat consecrated to an idol is anything more than meat, or that an idol is anything more than an idol? No, I mean that pagan sacrifices are offered (in the words of scripture) 'to demons and to that which is not God'; and I will not have you become partners with demons. You cannot drink the cup of the Lord and the cup of demons. You cannot partake of the Lord's table and the table of demons. Are we to provoke the Lord? Are we stronger than he is?

'We are free to do anything,' you say. Yes, but not everything is good for us. We are free to do anything, but not everything builds up the community. You should each look after the interests of others, not your own. You may eat anything sold in the meat market without raising questions of conscience; 'for the earth is the Lord's and all that is in it'.

If an unbeliever invites you to a meal and you accept, eat whatever is put before you, without raising questions of conscience. But if somebody says to you, 'This food has been offered in sacrifice,' then, out of consideration for him and for conscience' sake, do not eat it – not your conscience, I mean, but his.

'What?' you say. 'Is my freedom to be called in question by another's conscience? If I partake with thankfulness, why am I blamed for eating food over which I have said grace?' You may eat or drink, or do anything else, provided it is all done to the glory of God; give no offence to Jews, or Greeks, or to the church of God. For my part I always try to be considerate to everyone, not seeking my own good but the good of the many, so that they may be saved. Follow my example as I follow Christ's.

THE LORD'S SUPPER
1 Corinthians 11:17–34

In giving you these instructions I come to something I cannot commend: your meetings tend to do more harm than good. To begin with, I am told that when you meet as a congregation you fall into sharply divided groups. I believe there is some truth in it, for divisions are bound to arise among you if only to show which of your members are genuine. The result is that when you meet as a congregation, it is not the Lord's Supper you eat; when it comes to eating, each of you takes his own supper, one goes hungry and another has too much to drink. Have you no homes of your own to eat and drink in? Or are you so contemptuous of the church of God that you shame its poorer members? What am I to say? Can I commend you? On this point, certainly not!

For the tradition which I handed on to you came to me from the Lord himself: that on the night of his arrest the Lord Jesus took bread, and after giving thanks to God broke it and said: 'This is my body, which is for you; do this in memory of me.' In the same way, he took the cup after supper, and said: 'This cup is the new covenant sealed by my blood. Whenever you drink it, do this in memory of me.' For every time you eat this bread and drink the cup, you proclaim the death of the Lord, until he comes.

It follows that anyone who eats the bread or drinks the cup of the Lord unworthily will be guilty of offending against the body and blood of the Lord. Everyone must test himself before eating from the bread and drinking from the cup. For he who eats and drinks eats and drinks judgment on himself if he does not discern the body. That is why many of you are feeble and sick, and a number have died. But if we examined ourselves, we should not fall under judgment. When, however, we do fall under the Lord's judgment, he is disciplining us to save us from being condemned with the rest of the world.

Therefore, my friends, when you meet for this meal, wait for one another. If you are hungry, eat at home, so that in meeting together you may not fall under judgment. The other matters I will settle when I come.

GIFTS OF THE SPIRIT
1 Corinthians 12:1–14, 26–31

About gifts of the Spirit, my friends, I want there to be no misunderstanding.

You know how, in the days when you were still pagan, you used to be carried away by some impulse or other to those dumb heathen gods. For this reason I must impress upon you that no one who says 'A curse on Jesus!' can be speaking under the influence of the Spirit of God; and no one can say 'Jesus is Lord!' except under the influence of the Holy Spirit.

There are varieties of gifts, but the same Spirit. There are varieties of service, but the same Lord. There are varieties of activity, but in all of them and in everyone the same God is active. In each of us the Spirit is seen to be at work for some useful purpose. One, through the Spirit, has the gift of wise speech, while another, by the power of the same Spirit, can put the deepest knowledge into words. Another, by the same Spirit, is granted faith; another, by the one Spirit, gifts of healing, and another miraculous powers; another has the gift of prophecy, and another the ability to distinguish true spirits from false; yet another has the gift of tongues of various kinds, and another the ability to interpret them. But all these gifts are the activity of one and the same Spirit, distributing them to each individual at will.

Christ is like a single body with its many limbs and organs, which, many as they are, together make up one body; for in the one Spirit we were all brought into one body by baptism, whether Jews or Greeks, slaves or free; we were all given that one Spirit to drink.

A body is not a single organ, but many... If one part suffers, all suffer together; if one flourishes, all rejoice together.

Now you are Christ's body, and each of you a limb or organ of it. Within our community God has appointed in the first place apostles, in the second place prophets, thirdly teachers; then miracle-workers, then those who have gifts of healing, or ability to help others or power to guide them, or the gift of tongues of various kinds. Are all apostles? All prophets? All teachers? Do all work miracles? Do all have gifts of healing? Do all speak in tongues of ecstasy? Can all interpret them? The higher gifts are those you should prize. But I can show you an even better way.

THE GIFT OF LOVE
1 Corinthians 13:1–13

I may speak in tongues of men or of angels, but if I have no love, I am a sounding gong or a clanging cymbal. I may have the gift of prophecy and the knowledge of every hidden truth; I may have faith enough to move mountains; but if I have no love, I am nothing. I may give all I possess to the needy, I may give my body to be burnt, but if I have no love, I gain nothing by it.

Love is patient and kind. Love envies no one, is never boastful, never conceited, never rude; love is never selfish, never quick to take offence. Love keeps no score of wrongs, takes no pleasure in the sins of others, but delights in the truth. There is nothing love cannot face; there is no limit to its faith, its hope, its endurance.

Love will never come to an end. Prophecies will cease; tongues of ecstasy will fall silent; knowledge will vanish. For our knowledge and our prophecy alike are partial, and the partial vanishes when wholeness comes. When I was a child I spoke like a child, thought like a child, reasoned like a child; but when I grew up I finished with childish things. At present we see only puzzling reflections in a mirror, but one day we shall see face to face. My knowledge now is partial; then it will be whole, like God's knowledge of me. There are three things that last for ever: faith, hope, and love; and the greatest of the three is love.

THE GIFTS OF TONGUES AND PROPHECY
1 Corinthians 14:1–19, 26–31, 39–40

Make love your aim; then be eager for the gifts of the Spirit, above all for prophecy. If anyone speaks in tongues he is talking with God, not with men and women; no one understands him, for he speaks divine mysteries in the Spirit. On the other hand, if anyone prophesies, he is talking to men and women, and his words have power to build; they stimulate and they encourage. Speaking in tongues may build up the speaker himself, but it is prophecy that builds up a Christian community. I am happy for you all to speak in tongues, but happier still for you to prophesy. The prophet is worth more than one who speaks in tongues – unless indeed he can explain its meaning, and so help to build up the community. Suppose, my friends, that when I come to you I speak in tongues: what good shall I do you unless what I say contains something by way of revelation, or enlightenment, or prophecy, or instruction?

Even with inanimate things that produce sounds – a flute, say, or a lyre – unless their notes are distinct, how can you tell what tune is being played? Or again, if the trumpet-call is not clear, who will prepare for battle? In the same way, if what you say in tongues yields no precise meaning, how can anyone tell what is being said? You will be talking to empty air. There are any number of different languages in the world; nowhere is without language. If I do not know the speaker's language, his words will be gibberish to me, and mine to him. You are, I know, eager for gifts of the Spirit; then aspire above all to excel in those which build up the church.

Anyone who speaks in tongues should pray for the ability to interpret. If I use such language in prayer, my spirit prays, but my mind is barren. What then? I will pray with my spirit, but also with my mind; I will sing hymns with my spirit, but with my mind as well. Suppose you are praising God with the spirit alone: how will an ordinary person who is present be able to say 'Amen' to your thanksgiving, when he does not know what you are saying? Your prayer of thanksgiving may be splendid, but it is no help to the other person. Thank God, I am more gifted in tongues than any of you, but in the congregation I would rather speak five intelligible words, for the benefit of others as well as myself, than thousands of words in the language of ecstasy...

To sum up, my friends: when you meet for worship, each of you contributing a hymn, some instruction, a revelation, an ecstatic utterance, or its interpretation, see that all of these aim to build up the church. If anyone speaks in tongues, only two should speak, or at most three, one at a time, and someone must interpret. If there is no interpreter, they should keep silent and speak to themselves and to God. Of the prophets, two or three may speak, while the rest exercise their judgment upon what is said. If someone else present receives a revelation, let the first speaker stop. You can all prophesy, one at a time, so that all may receive instruction and encouragement...

In short, my friends, be eager to prophesy; do not forbid speaking in tongues; but let all be done decently and in order.

THE RESURRECTION OF THE DEAD
1 Corinthians 15:1–58

And now, my friends, I must remind you of the gospel that I preached to you; the gospel which you received, on which you have taken your stand, and which is now bringing you salvation. Remember the terms in which I preached the gospel to you – for I assume that you hold it fast and that your conversion was not in vain.

First and foremost, I handed on to you the tradition I had received: that Christ died for our sins, in accordance with the scriptures; that he was buried; that he was raised to life on the third day, in accordance with the scriptures; and that he appeared to Cephas, and afterwards to the Twelve. Then he appeared to over five hundred of our brothers at once, most of whom are still alive, though some have died. Then he appeared to James, and afterwards to all the apostles.

Last of all he appeared to me too; it was like a sudden, abnormal birth. For I am the least of the apostles, indeed not fit to be called an apostle, because I had persecuted the church of God. However, by God's grace I am what I am, and his grace to me has not proved vain; in my labours I have outdone them all – not I, indeed, but the grace of God working with me. But no matter whether it was I or they! This is what we all proclaim, and this is what you believed.

Now if this is what we proclaim, that Christ was raised from the dead, how can some of you say there is no resurrection of the dead? If there is no resurrection, then Christ was not raised; and if Christ was not raised, then our gospel is null and void, and so too is your faith; and we turn out to have given false evidence about God, because we bore witness that he raised Christ to life, whereas, if the dead are not raised, he did not raise him. For if the dead are not raised, it follows that Christ was not raised; and if Christ was not raised, your faith has nothing to it and you are still in your old state of sin. It follows also that those who have died within Christ's fellowship are utterly lost. If it is for this life only that Christ has given us hope, we of all people are most to be pitied.

But the truth is, Christ was raised to life – the firstfruits of the harvest of the dead. For since it was a man who brought death into the world, a man also brought resurrection of the dead. As in Adam all die, so in Christ all will be brought to life; but each in proper order: Christ the firstfruits, and afterwards, at his coming, those who belong to Christ. Then comes the end, when he delivers up the kingdom to God the Father, after deposing every sovereignty, authority, and power. For he is destined to reign until God has put all enemies under his feet; and the last enemy to be deposed is death. Scripture says, 'He has put all things in subjection under his feet.' But in saying 'all things', it clearly means to exclude God who made all things subject to him; and when all things are subject to him, then the Son himself will also be made subject to God who made all things subject to him, and thus God will be all in all.

Again, there are those who receive baptism on behalf of the dead. What do you suppose they are doing? If the dead are not raised to life at all, what do they mean by being baptized on their behalf?

And why do we ourselves face danger hour by hour? Every day I die: I swear it by my pride in you, my friends – for in Christ Jesus our Lord I am proud of you. With no more than human hopes, what would have been the point of my fighting those wild beasts at Ephesus? If the dead are never raised to life, 'Let us eat and drink, for tomorrow we die.'

Make no mistake: 'Bad company ruins good character.' Wake up, be sober, and stop sinning: some of you have no knowledge of God – to your shame I say it.

But, you may ask, how are the dead raised? In what kind of body? What stupid questions! The seed you sow does not come to life unless it has first died; and what you sow is not the body that shall be, but a bare grain, of wheat perhaps, or something else; and God gives it the body of his choice, each seed its own particular body. All flesh is not the same: there is human flesh, flesh of beasts, of birds, and of fishes – all different. There are heavenly bodies and earthly bodies; and the splendour of the heavenly bodies is one thing, the splendour of the earthly another. The sun has a splendour of its own, the moon another splendour, and the stars yet another; and one star differs from another in brightness. So it is with the resurrection of the dead: what is sown as a perishable thing is raised imperishable. Sown in humiliation, it is raised in glory; sown in weakness, it is raised in power; sown a physical body, it is raised a spiritual body.

If there is such a thing as a physical body, there is also a spiritual body. It is in this sense that scripture says, 'The first man, Adam, became a living creature,' whereas the last Adam has become a life-giving spirit. Observe, the spiritual does not come first; the physical body comes first, and then the spiritual. The first man is from earth, made of dust: the second man is from heaven. The man made of dust is the pattern of all who are made of dust, and the heavenly man is the pattern of all the heavenly. As we have worn the likeness of the man made of dust, so we shall wear the likeness of the heavenly man.

What I mean, my friends, is this: flesh and blood can never possess the kingdom of God, the perishable cannot possess the imperishable. Listen! I will unfold a mystery: we shall not all die, but we shall all be changed in a flash, in the twinkling of an eye, at the last trumpet-call. For the trumpet will sound, and the dead will rise imperishable, and we shall be changed. This perishable body must be clothed with the imperishable, and what is mortal with immortality. And when this perishable body has been clothed with the imperishable and our mortality has been clothed with immortality, then the saying of scripture will come true: 'Death is swallowed up; victory is won!' 'O Death, where is your victory? O Death, where is your sting?' The sting of death is sin, and sin gains its power from the law. But thanks be to God! He gives us victory through our Lord Jesus Christ.

Therefore, my dear friends, stand firm and immovable, and work for the Lord always, work without limit, since you know that in the Lord your labour cannot be lost.

FINAL INSTRUCTIONS
1 Corinthians 16:1–6, 19–24

Now about the collection in aid of God's people: you should follow the instructions I gave to our churches in Galatia. Every Sunday each of you is to put aside and keep by him whatever he can afford, so that there need be no collecting when I come. When I arrive, I will give letters of introduction to persons approved by you, and send them to carry your gift to Jerusalem. If it seems right for me to go as well, they can travel with me.

I shall come to Corinth after passing through Macedonia – for I am travelling by way of Macedonia – and I may stay some time with you, perhaps even for the whole winter; and then you can help me on my way wherever I go next…

Greetings from the churches of Asia. Many greetings in the Lord from Aquila and Prisca and the church that meets in their house.

Greetings from the whole brotherhood. Greet one another with the kiss of peace.

This greeting is in my own hand – Paul.

If anyone does not love the Lord, let him be outcast. Marana tha – Come, Lord!

The grace of the Lord Jesus be with you.

My love to you all in Christ Jesus.

The Second Epistle to the Corinthians

A TIME TO CONSOLE AND FORGIVE
2 Corinthians 1:1–11, 15–17, 23 – 2:11

From Paul, apostle of Christ Jesus by God's will, and our colleague Timothy, to God's church at Corinth, together with all God's people throughout the whole of Achaia. Grace and peace to you from God our Father and the Lord Jesus Christ.

Praise be to the God and Father of our Lord Jesus Christ, the all-merciful Father, the God whose consolation never fails us! He consoles us in all our troubles, so that we in turn may be able to console others in any trouble of theirs and to share with them the consolation we ourselves receive from God. As Christ's suffering exceeds all measure and extends to us, so too it is through Christ that our consolation has no limit. If distress is our lot, it is the price we pay for your consolation and your salvation; if our lot is consolation, it is to help us to bring you consolation, and strength to face with fortitude the same sufferings we now endure. And our hope for you is firmly grounded; for we know that if you share in the suffering, you share also in the consolation.

In saying this, my friends, we should like you to know how serious was the trouble that came upon us in the province of Asia. The burden of it was far too heavy for us to bear, so heavy that we even despaired of life. Indeed, we felt in our hearts that we had received a death sentence. This was meant to teach us to place reliance not on ourselves, but on God who raises the dead. From such mortal peril God delivered us; and he will deliver us again, he on whom our hope is fixed. Yes, he will continue to deliver us, while you co-operate by praying for us. Then, with so many people praying for our deliverance, there will be many to give thanks on our behalf for God's gracious favour towards us...

It was because I felt so confident about all this that I had intended to come first of all to you and give you the benefit of a double visit: I meant to visit you on my way to Macedonia and, after leaving Macedonia, to return to you, and you could then have sent me on my way to Judaea. That was my intention; did I lightly change my mind?...

I appeal to God as my witness and stake my life upon it: it was out of consideration for you that I did not after all come to Corinth. It is not that we have control of your faith; rather we are working with you for your happiness. For it is by that faith that you stand. So I made up my mind that my next visit to you must not be another painful one. If I cause pain to you, who is left to cheer me up, except you whom I have offended? This is precisely the point I made in my letter: I did not want, I said, to come and be made miserable by the very people who ought to have made me happy; and I had sufficient confidence in you all to know that for me to be happy is for all of you to be happy. That letter I sent you came out of great distress and anxiety; how many tears I shed as I wrote it! Not because I wanted to cause you pain; rather I wanted you to know the love, the more than ordinary love, that I have for you.

Any injury that has been done has not been done to me; to some extent (I do not want to make too much of it) it has been done to you all. The penalty on which the general meeting has agreed has met the offence well enough. Something very different is called for now: you must forgive the offender and put heart into him; the man's distress must not be made so severe as to overwhelm him. I urge you therefore to reassure him of your love for him. I wrote, I may say, to see how you stood the test, whether you fully accepted my authority. But anyone who has your forgiveness has mine too; and when I speak of forgiving (so far as there is anything for me to forgive), I mean that as the representative of Christ I have forgiven him for your sake. For Satan must not be allowed to get the better of us; we know his wiles all too well.

THE GLORY OF CHRIST
2 Corinthians 3:1 – 5:10, 14–21

Are we beginning all over again to produce our credentials? Do we, like some people, need letters of introduction to you, or from you?

No, you are all the letter we need, a letter written on our heart; anyone can see it for what it is and read it for himself. And as for you, it is plain that you are a letter that has come from Christ, given to us to deliver; a letter written not with ink but with the Spirit of the living God, written not on stone tablets but on the pages of the human heart.

It is in full reliance upon God, through Christ, that we make such claims. There is no question of our having sufficient power in ourselves: we cannot claim anything as our own. The power we have comes from God; it is he who has empowered us as ministers of a new covenant, not written but spiritual; for the written law condemns to death, but the Spirit gives life.

The ministry that brought death, and that was engraved in written form on stone, was inaugurated with such glory that the Israelites could not keep their eyes on Moses, even though the glory on his face was soon to fade. How much greater, then, must be the glory of the ministry of the Spirit! If glory accompanied the ministry that brought condemnation, how much richer in glory must be the ministry that brings acquittal! Indeed, the glory that once was is now no glory at all; it is outshone by a still greater glory. For if what was to fade away had its glory, how much greater is the glory of what endures!

With such a hope as this we speak out boldly; it is not for us to do as Moses did: he put a veil over his face to keep the Israelites from gazing at the end of what was fading away. In any case their minds had become closed, for that same veil is there to this very day when the lesson is read from the old covenant; and it is never lifted, because only in Christ is it taken away. Indeed to this very day, every time the law of Moses is read, a veil lies over the mind of the hearer. But (as scripture says) 'Whenever he turns to the Lord the veil is removed.' Now the Lord of whom this passage speaks is the Spirit; and where the Spirit of the Lord is, there is liberty. And because for us there is no veil over the face, we all see as in a mirror the glory of the Lord, and we are being transformed into his likeness with ever-increasing glory, through the power of the Lord who is the Spirit.

Since God in his mercy has given us this ministry, we never lose heart. We have renounced the deeds that people hide for very shame; we do not practise cunning or distort the word of God. It is by declaring the truth openly that we recommend ourselves to the conscience of our fellow-men in the sight of God. If our gospel is veiled at all, it is veiled only for those on the way to destruction; their unbelieving minds are so blinded by the god of this passing age that the gospel of the glory of Christ, who is the image of God, cannot dawn upon them and bring them light. It is not ourselves that we proclaim; we proclaim Christ Jesus as Lord, and ourselves as your servants for Jesus' sake. For the God who said, 'Out of darkness light shall shine,' has caused his light to shine in our hearts, the light which is knowledge of the glory of God in the face of Jesus Christ.

But we have only earthenware jars to hold this treasure, and this proves that such transcendent power does not come from us; it is God's alone. We are hard pressed, but never cornered; bewildered, but never at our wits' end; hunted, but never abandoned to our fate; struck down, but never killed. Wherever we go we carry with us in our body the death that Jesus died, so that in this body also the life that Jesus lives may be revealed. For Jesus' sake we are all our life being handed over to death, so that the life of Jesus may be revealed in this mortal body of ours. Thus death is at work in us, but life in you.

But scripture says, 'I believed, and therefore I spoke out,' and we too, in the same spirit of faith, believe and therefore speak out; for we know that he who raised the Lord Jesus to life will with Jesus raise us too, and bring us to his presence, and you with us. Indeed, all this is for your sake, so that, as the abounding grace of God is shared by more and more, the greater may be the chorus of thanksgiving that rises to the glory of God.

No wonder we do not lose heart! Though our outward humanity is in decay, yet day by day we are inwardly renewed. Our troubles are slight and short-lived, and their outcome is an eternal glory which far outweighs them, provided our eyes are fixed, not on the things that are seen, but on the things that are unseen; for what is seen is transient, what is unseen is eternal. We know that if the earthly frame that houses us today is demolished, we possess a building which God has provided – a house not made by human hands, eternal and in heaven. In this present body we groan, yearning to be covered by our heavenly habitation put on over this one, in the hope that, being thus clothed, we shall not find ourselves naked. We groan indeed, we who are enclosed within this earthly frame; we are oppressed because we do not want to have the old body stripped off. What we want is to be covered by the new body put on over it, so that our mortality may be absorbed into life immortal. It is for this destiny that God himself has been shaping us; and as a pledge of it he has given us the Spirit.

Therefore we never cease to be confident. We know that so long as we are at home in the body we are exiles from the Lord; faith is our guide, not sight. We are confident, I say, and would rather be exiled from the body and make our home with the Lord. That is why it is our ambition, wherever we are, at home or in exile, to be acceptable to him. For we must all have our lives laid open before the tribunal of Christ, where each must receive what is due to him for his conduct in the body, good or bad...

For the love of Christ controls us once we have reached the conclusion that one man died for all and therefore all mankind has died. He died for all so that those who live should cease to live for themselves, and should live for him who for their sake died and was raised to life. With us therefore worldly standards have ceased to count in our estimate of anyone; even if once they counted in our understanding of Christ, they do so now no longer. For anyone united to Christ, there is a new creation: the old order has gone; a new order has already begun.

All this has been the work of God. He has reconciled us to himself through Christ, and has enlisted us in this ministry of reconciliation: God was in Christ reconciling the world to himself, no longer holding people's misdeeds against them, and has entrusted us with the message of reconciliation. We are therefore Christ's ambassadors. It is as if God were appealing to you through us: we implore you in Christ's name, be reconciled to God! Christ was innocent of sin, and yet for our sake God made him one with human sinfulness, so that in him we might be made one with the righteousness of God.

AN APPEAL FROM THE HEART
2 Corinthians 6:1–13; 7:3–13; 8:1–7, 13–17; 9:6–8

Sharing in God's work, we make this appeal: you have received the grace of God; do not let it come to nothing. He has said:

In the hour of my favour I answered you;
on the day of deliverance I came to your aid.

This is the hour of favour, this the day of deliverance.

Lest our ministry be brought into discredit, we avoid giving any offence in anything. As God's ministers, we try to recommend ourselves in all circumstances by our steadfast endurance: in affliction, hardship, and distress; when flogged, imprisoned, mobbed; overworked, sleepless, starving. We recommend ourselves by innocent behaviour and grasp of truth, by patience and kindliness, by gifts of the Holy Spirit, by unaffected love, by declaring the truth, by the power of God. We wield the weapons of righteousness in right hand and left. Honour and dishonour, praise and blame, are alike our lot: we are the impostors who speak the truth, the unknown men whom all men know; dying we still live on; disciplined by suffering, we are not done to death; in our sorrows we have always cause for joy; poor ourselves, we bring wealth to many; penniless, we own the world.

We have spoken very frankly to you, friends in Corinth; we have opened our heart to you. There is no constraint on our part; any constraint there may be is in you. In fair exchange then (if I may speak to you like a father) open your hearts to us...

My words are no reflection on you. I have told you before that, come death, come life, your place in our hearts is secure. I am speaking to you with great frankness, but my pride in you is just as great. In all our many troubles my cup is full of consolation and overflows with joy.

Even when we reached Macedonia we still found no relief; instead trouble met us at every turn, fights without and fears within. But God, who brings comfort to the downcast, has comforted us by the arrival of Titus, and not merely by his arrival, but by his being so greatly encouraged about you. He has told us how you long for me, how sorry you are, and how eager to take my side; and that has made me happier still.

Even if I did hurt you by the letter I sent, I do not now regret it. I did regret it; but now that I see the letter gave you pain, though only for a time, I am happy – not because of the pain but because the pain led to a change of heart. You bore the pain as God would have you bear it, and so you came to no harm from what we did. Pain borne in God's way brings no regrets but a change of heart leading to salvation; pain borne in the world's way brings death. You bore your pain in God's way, and just look at the results: it made you take the matter seriously and vindicate yourselves; it made you indignant and apprehensive; it aroused your longing for me, your devotion, and your eagerness to see justice done! At every point you have cleared yourselves of blame. And so, although I did send you that letter, it was not the offender or his victim that most concerned me. My aim in writing was to help to make plain to you, in the sight of God, how truly you are devoted to us. That is why we have been so encouraged.

But besides being encouraged ourselves, we have also been delighted beyond everything by seeing how happy Titus is: you have all helped to set his mind completely at rest…

We must tell you, friends, about the grace that God has given to the churches in Macedonia. The troubles they have been through have tried them hard, yet in all this they have been so exuberantly happy that from the depths of their poverty they have shown themselves lavishly open-handed. Going to the limit of their resources, as I can testify, and even beyond that limit, they begged us most insistently, and on their own initiative, to be allowed to share in this generous service to their fellow-Christians. And their giving surpassed our expectations; for first of all they gave themselves to the Lord and, under God, to us. The upshot is that we have asked Titus, since he has already made a beginning, to bring your share in this further work of generosity also to completion. You are so rich in everything – in faith, speech, knowledge, and diligence of every kind, as well as in the love you have for us – that you should surely show yourselves equally lavish in this generous service!…

There is no question of relieving others at the cost of hardship to yourselves; it is a question of equality. At the moment your surplus meets their need, but one day your need may be met from their surplus. The aim is equality; as scripture has it, 'Those who gathered more did not have too much, and those who gathered less did not have too little.'

I thank God that he has made Titus as keen on your behalf as we are! So keen is he that he not only welcomed our request; it is by his own choice he is now leaving to come to you…

Remember: sow sparingly, and you will reap sparingly; sow bountifully, and you will reap bountifully. Each person should give as he has decided for himself; there should be no reluctance, no sense of compulsion; God loves a cheerful giver. And it is in God's power to provide you with all good gifts in abundance, so that, with every need always met to the full, you may have something to spare for every good cause...

PAUL DEFENDS HIS MINISTRY
2 Corinthians 10:1–5, 9 – 12:13

I, Paul, appeal to you by the gentleness and magnanimity of Christ – I who am so timid (you say) when face to face with you, so courageous when I am away from you. Spare me when I come, I beg you, the need for that courage and self-assurance, which I reckon I could confidently display against those who assume my behaviour to be dictated by human weakness. Weak and human we may be, but that does not dictate the way we fight our battles. The weapons we wield are not merely human; they are strong enough with God's help to demolish strongholds. We demolish sophistries and all that rears its proud head against the knowledge of God; we compel every human thought to surrender in obedience to Christ...

So you must not think of me as one who tries to scare you by the letters he writes. 'His letters', so it is said, 'are weighty and powerful; but when he is present he is unimpressive, and as a speaker he is beneath contempt.' People who talk in that way should reckon with this: my actions when I come will show the same man as my letters showed while I was absent.

We should not dare to class ourselves or compare ourselves with any of those who commend themselves. What fools they are to measure themselves on their own, to find in themselves their standard of comparison! As for us, our boasting will not go beyond the proper limits; and our sphere is determined by the limit God laid down for us, which permitted us to come as far as Corinth. We are not overstretching our commission, as we would be if we had never come to you; but we were the first to reach as far as Corinth in the work of the gospel of

Christ. And we do not boast of work done where others have laboured, work beyond our proper sphere. Our hope is rather that, as your faith grows, we may attain a position among you greater than ever before, but still within the limits of our sphere. Then we can carry the gospel to lands that lie beyond you, never priding ourselves on work already done in anyone else's sphere. If anyone would boast, let him boast of the Lord. For it is not the one who recommends himself, but the one whom the Lord recommends, who is to be accepted.

I should like you to bear with me in a little foolishness; please bear with me. I am jealous for you, with the jealousy of God; for I betrothed you to Christ, thinking to present you as a chaste virgin to her true and only husband. Now I am afraid that, as the serpent in his cunning seduced Eve, your thoughts may be corrupted and you may lose your single-hearted devotion to Christ. For if some newcomer proclaims another Jesus, not the Jesus whom we proclaimed, or if you receive a spirit different from the Spirit already given to you, or a gospel different from the gospel you have already accepted, you put up with that well enough. I am not aware of being in any way inferior to those super-apostles. I may be no speaker, but knowledge I do have; at all times we have made known to you the full truth.

Or was this my offence, that I made no charge for preaching the gospel of God, humbling myself in order to exalt you? I robbed other churches – by accepting support from them to serve you. If I ran short while I was with you, I did not become a charge on anyone; my needs were fully met by friends from Macedonia; I made it a rule, as I always shall, never to be a burden to you. As surely as the truth of Christ is in me, nothing shall bar me from boasting about this throughout Achaia. Why? Because I do not love you? God knows I do.

And I shall go on doing as I am doing now, to cut the ground from under those who would seize any chance to put their vaunted apostleship on the same level as ours. Such people are sham apostles, confidence tricksters masquerading as apostles of Christ. And no wonder! Satan himself masquerades as an angel of light, so it is easy enough for his agents to masquerade as agents of good. But their fate will match their deeds.

I repeat: let no one take me for a fool; but if you must, then give me the privilege of a fool, and let me have my little boast like others.

In boasting so confidently I am not speaking like a Christian, but like a fool. So many people brag of their earthly distinctions that I shall do so too. How gladly you put up with fools, being yourselves so wise! If someone tyrannizes over you, exploits you, gets you in his clutches, puts on airs, and hits you in the face, you put up with it. And you call me a weakling! I admit the reproach.

But if there is to be bravado (and I am still speaking as a fool), I can indulge in it too. Are they Hebrews? So am I. Israelites? So am I. Abraham's descendants? So am I. Are they servants of Christ? I am mad to speak like this, but I can outdo them: more often overworked, more often imprisoned, scourged more severely, many a time face to face with death. Five times the Jews have given me the thirty-nine strokes; three times I have been beaten with rods; once I was stoned; three times I have been shipwrecked, and for twenty-four hours I was adrift on the open sea. I have been constantly on the road; I have met dangers from rivers, dangers from robbers, dangers from my fellow-countrymen, dangers from foreigners, dangers in the town, dangers in the wilderness, dangers at sea, dangers from false Christians. I have toiled and drudged and often gone without sleep; I have been hungry and thirsty and have often gone without food; I have suffered from cold and exposure.

Apart from these external things, there is the responsibility that weighs on me every day, my anxious concern for all the churches. Is anyone weak? I share his weakness. If anyone brings about the downfall of another, does my heart not burn with anger? If boasting there must be, I will boast of the things that show up my weakness. He who is blessed for ever, the God and Father of the Lord Jesus, knows that what I say is true. When I was in Damascus, the commissioner of King Aretas kept the city under observation to have me arrested; and I was let down in a basket, through a window in the wall, and so escaped his clutches.

It may do no good, but I must go on with my boasting; I come now to visions and revelations granted by the Lord. I know a Christian man who fourteen years ago (whether in the body or out of the body, I do not know – God knows) was caught up as far as the third heaven. And I know that this same man (whether in the body or apart from the body, I do not know – God knows) was caught up into paradise, and heard words so secret that human lips may not repeat them.

About such a man I am ready to boast; but I will not boast on my own account, except of my weaknesses. If I chose to boast, it would not be the boast of a fool, for I should be speaking the truth. But I refrain, because I do not want anyone to form an estimate of me which goes beyond the evidence of his own eyes and ears. To keep me from being unduly elated by the magnificence of such revelations, I was given a thorn in my flesh, a messenger of Satan sent to buffet me; this was to save me from being unduly elated. Three times I begged the Lord to rid me of it, but his answer was: 'My grace is all you need; power is most fully seen in weakness.' I am therefore happy to boast of my weaknesses, because then the power of Christ will rest upon me. So I am content with a life of weakness, insult, hardship, persecution, and distress, all for Christ's sake; for when I am weak, then I am strong.

I am being very foolish, but it was you who drove me to it; my credentials should have come from you. In nothing did I prove inferior to those super-apostles, even if I am a nobody. The signs of an apostle were there in the work I did among you, marked by unfailing endurance, by signs, portents, and miracles. Is there any way in which you were treated worse than the other churches – except this, that I was never a charge on you? Forgive me for being so unfair!

FINAL WARNINGS
2 Corinthians 12:14, 20 – 13:14

I am now getting ready to pay you a third visit; and... I fear that when I come I may find you different from what I wish, and you may find me to be what you do not wish. I fear I may find quarrelling and jealousy, angry tempers and personal rivalries, backbiting and gossip, arrogance and general disorder. I am afraid that when I come my God may humiliate me again in your presence, that I may have cause to grieve over many who were sinning before and have not repented of their unclean lives, their fornication and sensuality.

This will be my third visit to you. As scripture says, 'Every charge must be established on the evidence of two or three witnesses': to those who sinned before, and to everyone else, I repeat the warning I gave last time; on my second visit I gave it in person, and now I give it while absent. It is that when I come this time, I will show no leniency. Then you will have the proof you seek of the Christ who speaks through me, the Christ who, far from being weak with you, makes his power felt among you. True, he died on the cross in weakness, but he lives by the power of God; so you will find that we who share his weakness shall live with him by the power of God.

Examine yourselves: are you living the life of faith? Put yourselves to the test. Surely you recognize that Jesus Christ is among you? If not, you have failed the test. I hope you will come to see that we have not failed. Our prayer to God is that you may do no wrong, not that we should win approval; we want you to do what is right, even if we should seem failures. We have no power to act against the truth, but only for it. We are happy to be weak at any time if only you are strong. Our prayer, then, is for your amendment. In writing this letter before I come, my aim is to spare myself, when I do come, any sharp exercise of authority – authority which the Lord gave me for building up and not for pulling down.

And now, my friends, farewell. Mend your ways; take our appeal to heart; agree with one another; live in peace; and the God of love and peace will be with you. Greet one another with the kiss of peace. All God's people send you greetings.

The grace of the Lord Jesus Christ, and the love of God, and the fellowship of the Holy Spirit, be with you all.

The Epistle to the Romans

PAUL'S LOVE FOR THE ROMANS
Romans 1:1, 5–12

From Paul, servant of Christ Jesus, called by God to be an apostle and set apart for the service of his gospel… to bring people of all nations to faith and obedience in his name, including you who have heard the call and belong to Jesus Christ.

I send greetings to all of you in Rome, who are loved by God and called to be his people. Grace and peace to you from God our Father and the Lord Jesus Christ.

Let me begin by thanking my God, through Jesus Christ, for you all, because the story of your faith is being told all over the world. God is my witness, to whom I offer the service of my spirit by preaching the gospel of his Son: God knows that I make mention of you in my prayers continually, and am always asking that by his will I may, somehow or other, at long last succeed in coming to visit you. For I long to see you; I want to bring you some spiritual gift to make you strong; or rather, I want us to be encouraged by one another's faith when I am with you, I by yours and you by mine.

GOD'S JUDGMENT ON HUMAN SIN
Romans 1:16–26, 29 – 2:16

For I am not ashamed of the gospel. It is the saving power of God for everyone who has faith – the Jew first, but the Greek also – because in it the righteousness of God is seen at work, beginning in faith and ending in faith; as scripture says, 'Whoever is justified through faith shall gain life.'

Divine retribution is to be seen at work, falling from heaven on all the impiety and wickedness of men and women who in their wickedness suppress the truth. For all that can be known of God lies plain before their eyes; indeed God himself has disclosed it to them. Ever since the world began his invisible attributes, that is to say his everlasting power and deity, have been visible to the eye of reason, in the things he has made. Their conduct, therefore, is indefensible; knowing God, they have refused to honour him as God, or to render him thanks. Hence all their thinking has ended in futility, and their misguided minds are plunged in darkness. They boast of their wisdom, but they have made fools of themselves, exchanging the glory of the immortal God for an image shaped like mortal man, even for images like birds, beasts, and reptiles.

For this reason God has given them up to their own vile desires, and the consequent degradation of their bodies. They have exchanged the truth of God for a lie, and have offered reverence and worship to created things instead of to the Creator. Blessed is he for ever, Amen. As a result God has given them up to shameful passions...

They are filled with every kind of wickedness, villainy, greed, and malice; they are one mass of envy, murder, rivalry, treachery, and malevolence; gossips and scandalmongers; and blasphemers, insolent, arrogant, and boastful; they invent new kinds of vice, they show no respect to parents, they are without sense or fidelity, without natural affection or pity. They know well enough the just decree of God, that those who behave like this deserve to die; yet they not only do these things themselves but approve such conduct in others.

You have no defence, then, whoever you may be, when you sit in judgment – for in judging others you condemn yourself, since you, the judge, are equally guilty. We all know that God's judgment on those who commit such crimes is just; and do you imagine – you that pass judgment on the guilty while committing the same crimes yourself – do you imagine that you, any more than they, will escape the judgment of God? Or do you despise his wealth of kindness and tolerance and patience, failing to see that God's kindness is meant to lead you to repentance? In the obstinate impenitence of your heart you are laying up for yourself a store of retribution against the day of retribution, when God's just judgment will be revealed, and he will pay everyone for what he has done. To those who pursue glory, honour, and immortality by steady persistence in well-doing, he will give eternal life; but the retribution of his wrath awaits those who are governed by selfish ambition, who refuse obedience to truth and take evil for their guide. There will be affliction and distress for every human being who is a wrongdoer, for the Jew first and for the Greek also; but for everyone who does right there will be glory, honour, and peace, for the Jew first and also for the Greek. God has no favourites.

Those who have sinned outside the pale of the law of Moses will perish outside the law, and all who have sinned under that law will be judged by it. None will be justified before God by hearing the law, but by doing it. When Gentiles who do not possess the law carry out its precepts by the light of nature, then, although they have no law, they are their own law; they show that what the law requires is inscribed on their hearts, and to this their conscience gives supporting witness, since their own thoughts argue the case, sometimes against them, sometimes even for them. So it will be on the day when, according to my gospel, God will judge the secrets of human hearts through Christ Jesus.

GOD WILL JUSTIFY BOTH JEW AND GENTILE
Romans 2:17–22, 25 – 3:1, 9–12, 19–31

But as for you who bear the name of Jew and rely on the law: you take pride in your God; you know his will; taught by the law, you know what really matters; you are confident that you are a guide to the blind, a light to those in darkness, an instructor of the foolish, and a teacher of the immature, because you possess in the law the embodiment of knowledge and truth. You teach others, then; do you not teach yourself? You proclaim, 'Do not steal'; but are you yourself a thief? You say, 'Do not commit adultery'; but are you an adulterer?...

Circumcision has value, provided you keep the law; but if you break the law, then your circumcision is as if it had never been. Equally, if an uncircumcised man keeps the precepts of the law, will he not count as circumcised? He may be physically uncircumcised, but by fulfilling the law he will pass judgment on you who break it, for all your written code and your circumcision. It is not externals that make a Jew, nor an external mark in the flesh that makes circumcision.

The real Jew is one who is inwardly a Jew, and his circumcision is of the heart, spiritual not literal; he receives his commendation not from men but from God.

Then what advantage has the Jew? …are we Jews any better off? No, not at all! For we have already drawn up the indictment that all, Jews and Greeks alike, are under the power of sin. Scripture says:

> There is no one righteous; no, not one;
> no one who understands, no one who seeks God.
> All have swerved aside, all alike have become debased;
> there is no one to show kindness: no, not one…

Now all the words of the law are addressed, as we know, to those who are under the law, so that no one may have anything to say in self-defence, and the whole world may be exposed to God's judgment. For no human being can be justified in the sight of God by keeping the law: law brings only the consciousness of sin.

But now, quite independently of law, though with the law and the prophets bearing witness to it, the righteousness of God has been made known; it is effective through faith in Christ for all who have such faith – all, without distinction. For all alike have sinned, and are deprived of the divine glory; and all are justified by God's free grace alone, through his act of liberation in the person of Christ Jesus. For God designed him to be the means of expiating sin by his death, effective through faith. God meant by this to demonstrate his justice, because in his forbearance he had overlooked the sins of the past – to demonstrate his justice now in the present, showing that he is himself just and also justifies anyone who puts his faith in Jesus.

What room then is left for human pride? It is excluded. And on what principle? The keeping of the law would not exclude it, but faith does. For our argument is that people are justified by faith quite apart from any question of keeping the law.

Do you suppose God is the God of the Jews alone? Is he not the God of Gentiles also? Certainly, of Gentiles also. For if the Lord is indeed one, he will justify the circumcised by their faith and the uncircumcised through their faith. Does this mean that we are using faith to undermine the law? By no means: we are upholding the law.

ABRAHAM: FATHER OF THE FAITHFUL
Romans 4:1–12, 23–25

What, then, are we to say about Abraham, our ancestor by natural descent? If Abraham was justified by anything he did, then he has grounds for pride. But not in the eyes of God! For what does scripture say? 'Abraham put his faith in God, and that faith was counted to him as righteousness.'

Now if someone does a piece of work, his wages are not 'counted' to be a gift; they are paid as his due. But if someone without any work to his credit simply puts his faith in him who acquits the wrongdoer, then his faith is indeed 'counted as righteousness'. In the same sense David speaks of the happiness of the man whom God 'counts' as righteous, apart from any good works: 'Happy are they', he says, 'whose lawless deeds are forgiven, whose sins are blotted out; happy is the man whose sin the Lord does not count against him.'

Is this happiness confined to the circumcised, or is it for the uncircumcised also? We have just been saying: 'Abraham's faith was counted as righteousness.' In what circumstances was it so counted? Was he circumcised at the time, or not? He was not yet circumcised, but uncircumcised; he received circumcision later as the sign and hallmark of that righteousness which faith had given him while he was still uncircumcised. It follows that he is the father of all who have faith when uncircumcised, and so have righteousness 'counted' to them; and at the same time he is the father of the circumcised, provided they are not merely circumcised, but also follow that path of faith which our father Abraham trod while he was still uncircumcised...

The words 'counted to him' were meant to apply not only to Abraham but to us; our faith too is to be 'counted', the faith in the God who raised Jesus our Lord from the dead; for he was given up to death for our misdeeds, and raised to life for our justification.

THE GRACE OF GOD FOR ALL HUMANITY
Romans 5:1–21

Therefore, now that we have been justified through faith, we are at peace with God through our Lord Jesus Christ, who has given us access to that grace in which we now live; and we exult in the hope of the divine glory that is to be ours. More than this: we even exult in our present sufferings, because we know that suffering is a source of endurance, endurance of approval, and approval of hope. Such hope is no fantasy; through the Holy Spirit he has given us, God's love has flooded our hearts.

It was while we were still helpless that, at the appointed time, Christ died for the wicked. Even for a just man one of us would hardly die, though perhaps for a good man one might actually brave death; but Christ died for us while we were yet sinners, and that is God's proof of his love towards us. And so, since we have now been justified by Christ's sacrificial death, we shall all the more certainly be saved through him from final retribution. For if, when we were God's enemies, we were reconciled to him through the death of his Son, how much more, now that we have been reconciled, shall we be saved by his life! But that is not all: we also exult in God through our Lord Jesus, through whom we have now been granted reconciliation.

What does this imply? It was through one man that sin entered the world, and through sin death, and thus death pervaded the whole human race, inasmuch as all have sinned. For sin was already in the world before there was law; and although in the absence of law no reckoning is kept of sin, death held sway from Adam to Moses, even over those who had not sinned as Adam did, by disobeying a direct command – and Adam foreshadows the man who was to come. But God's act of grace is out of all proportion to Adam's wrongdoing. For if the wrongdoing of that one man brought death upon so many, its effect is vastly exceeded by the grace of God and the gift that came to so many by the grace of the one man, Jesus Christ. And again, the gift of God is not to be compared in its effect with that one man's sin; for the judicial action, following on the one offence, resulted in a verdict of condemnation, but the act of grace, following on so many misdeeds, resulted in a verdict of acquittal. If, by the wrongdoing of one man, death established its reign through that one man, much more shall those who in far greater measure receive grace and the gift of righteousness live and reign through the one man, Jesus Christ.

It follows, then, that as the result of one misdeed was condemnation for all people, so the result of one righteous act is acquittal and life for all. For as through the disobedience of one man many were made sinners, so through the obedience of one man many will be made righteous. Law intruded into this process to multiply law-breaking. But where sin was multiplied, grace immeasurably exceeded it, in order that, as sin established its reign by way of death, so God's grace might establish its reign in righteousness, and result in eternal life through Jesus Christ our Lord.

NO LONGER SLAVES TO SIN
Romans 6:1–23; 7:5–25

What are we to say, then? Shall we persist in sin, so that there may be all the more grace? Certainly not! We died to sin: how can we live in it any longer? Have you forgotten that when we were baptized into union with Christ Jesus we were baptized into his death? By that baptism into his death we were buried with him, in order that, as Christ was raised from the dead by the glorious power of the Father, so also we might set out on a new life.

For if we have become identified with him in his death, we shall also be identified with him in his resurrection. We know that our old humanity has been crucified with Christ, for the destruction of the sinful self, so that we may no longer be slaves to sin, because death cancels the claims of sin. But if we thus died with Christ, we believe that we shall also live with him, knowing as we do that Christ, once raised from the dead, is never to die again: he is no longer under the dominion of death. When he died, he died to sin, once for all, and now that he lives, he lives to God. In the same way you must regard yourselves as dead to sin and alive to God, in union with Christ Jesus.

Therefore sin must no longer reign in your mortal body, exacting obedience to the body's desires. You must no longer put any part of it at sin's disposal, as an implement for doing wrong. Put yourselves instead at the disposal of God; think of yourselves as raised from death to life, and yield your bodies to God as implements for doing right. Sin shall no longer be your master, for you are no longer under law, but under grace.

What then? Are we to sin, because we are not under law but

under grace? Of course not! You know well enough that if you bind yourselves to obey a master, you are slaves of the master you obey; and this is true whether the master is sin and the outcome death, or obedience and the outcome righteousness. Once you were slaves of sin, but now, thank God, you have yielded wholehearted obedience to that pattern of teaching to which you were made subject; emancipated from sin, you have become slaves of righteousness (to use language that suits your human weakness). As you once yielded your bodies to the service of impurity and lawlessness, making for moral anarchy, so now you must yield them to the service of righteousness, making for a holy life.

When you were slaves of sin, you were free from the control of righteousness. And what gain did that bring you? Things that now make you ashamed, for their end is death. But now, freed from the commands of sin and bound to the service of God, you have gains that lead to holiness, and the end is eternal life. For sin pays a wage, and the wage is death, but God gives freely, and his gift is eternal life in union with Christ Jesus our Lord...

While we lived on the level of mere human nature, the sinful passions evoked by the law were active in our bodies, and bore fruit for death. But now, having died to that which held us bound, we are released from the law, to serve God in a new way, the way of the spirit in contrast to the old way of a written code.

What follows? Is the law identical with sin? Of course not! Yet had it not been for the law I should never have become acquainted with sin. For example, I should never have known what it was to covet, if the law had not said, 'You shall not covet.' Through that commandment sin found its opportunity, and produced in me all kinds of wrong desires. In the absence of law, sin is devoid of life. There was a time when, in the absence of law, I was fully alive; but when the commandment came, sin sprang to life and I died. The commandment which should have led to life proved in my experience to lead to death, because in the commandment sin found its opportunity to seduce me, and through the commandment killed me. So then, the law in itself is holy and the commandment is holy and just and good.

Are we therefore to say that this good thing caused my death?

Of course not! It was sin that killed me, and thereby sin exposed its true character: it used a good thing to bring about my death, and so, through the commandment, sin became more sinful than ever. We know that the law is spiritual; but I am not: I am unspiritual, sold as a slave to sin. I do not even acknowledge my own actions as mine, for what I do is not what I want to do, but what I detest. But if what I do is against my will, then clearly I agree with the law and hold it to be admirable. This means that it is no longer I who perform the action, but sin that dwells in me. For I know that nothing good dwells in me – my unspiritual self, I mean – for though the will to do good is there, the ability to effect it is not. The good which I want to do, I fail to do; but what I do is the wrong which is against my will; and if what I do is against my will, clearly it is no longer I who am the agent, but sin that has its dwelling in me.

I discover this principle, then: that when I want to do right, only wrong is within my reach. In my inmost self I delight in the law of God, but I perceive in my outward actions a different law, fighting against the law that my mind approves, and making me a prisoner under the law of sin which controls my conduct. Wretched creature that I am, who is there to rescue me from this state of death? Who but God? Thanks be to him through Jesus Christ our Lord!

LIFE IN THE SPIRIT
Romans 7:25 – 8:39

To sum up then: left to myself I serve God's law with my mind, but with my unspiritual nature I serve the law of sin.

It follows that there is now no condemnation for those who are united with Christ Jesus. In Christ Jesus the life-giving law of the Spirit has set you free from the law of sin and death. What the law could not do, because human weakness robbed it of all potency, God has done: by sending his own Son in the likeness of our sinful nature and to deal with sin, he has passed judgment against sin within that very nature, so that the commandment of the law may find fulfilment in us, whose conduct is no longer controlled by the old nature, but by the Spirit.

Those who live on the level of the old nature have their outlook formed by it, and that spells death; but those who live on the level of the spirit have the spiritual outlook, and that is life and peace. For the outlook of the unspiritual nature is enmity with God; it is not subject to the law of God and indeed it cannot be; those who live under its control cannot please God.

But you do not live like that. You live by the spirit, since God's Spirit dwells in you; and anyone who does not possess the Spirit of Christ does not belong to Christ. But if Christ is in you, then although the body is dead because of sin, yet the Spirit is your life because you have been justified. Moreover, if the Spirit of him who raised Jesus from the dead dwells in you, then the God who raised Christ Jesus from the dead will also give new life to your mortal bodies through his indwelling Spirit.

It follows, my friends, that our old nature has no claim on us; we are not obliged to live in that way. If you do so, you must die. But if by the Spirit you put to death the base pursuits of the body, then you will live.

For all who are led by the Spirit of God are sons of God. The Spirit you have received is not a spirit of slavery, leading you back into a life of fear, but a Spirit of adoption, enabling us to cry 'Abba! Father!' The Spirit of God affirms to our spirit that we are God's children; and if children, then heirs, heirs of God and fellow-heirs with Christ; but we must share his sufferings if we are also to share his glory.

For I reckon that the sufferings we now endure bear no comparison with the glory, as yet unrevealed, which is in store for us. The created universe is waiting with eager expectation for God's sons to be revealed. It was made subject to frustration, not of its own choice but by the will of him who subjected it, yet with the hope that the universe itself is to be freed from the shackles of mortality and is to enter upon the glorious liberty of the children of God. Up to the present, as we know, the whole created universe in all its parts groans as if in the pangs of childbirth. What is more, we also, to whom the Spirit is given as the firstfruits of the harvest to come, are groaning inwardly while we look forward eagerly to our adoption, our liberation from mortality. It was with this hope that we were saved. Now to see something is no longer to hope: why hope for what is already seen? But if we hope for something we do not yet see, then we look forward to it eagerly and with patience.

In the same way the Spirit comes to the aid of our weakness. We do not even know how we ought to pray, but through our inarticulate groans the Spirit himself is pleading for us, and God who searches our inmost being knows what the Spirit means, because he pleads for God's people as God himself wills; and in everything, as we know, he co-operates for good with those who love God and are called according to his purpose. For those whom God knew before ever they were, he also ordained to share the likeness of his Son, so that he might be the eldest among a large family of brothers; and those whom he foreordained, he also called, and those whom he called he also justified, and those whom he justified he also glorified.

With all this in mind, what are we to say? If God is on our side, who is against us? He did not spare his own Son, but gave him up for us all; how can he fail to lavish every other gift upon us? Who will bring a charge against those whom God has chosen? Not God, who acquits! Who will pronounce judgment? Not Christ, who died, or rather rose again; not Christ, who is at God's right hand and pleads our cause! Then what can separate us from the love of Christ? Can affliction or hardship? Can persecution, hunger, nakedness, danger, or sword? 'We are being done to death for your sake all day long,' as scripture says; 'we have been treated like sheep for slaughter' – and yet, throughout it all, overwhelming victory is ours through him who loved us. For I am convinced that there is nothing in death or life, in the realm of spirits or superhuman powers, in the world as it is or the world as it shall be, in the forces of the universe, in heights or depths – nothing in all creation that can separate us from the love of God in Christ Jesus our Lord.

THE TRUE ISRAEL OF GOD
Romans 9:1–7, 25 – 10:4, 9–13; 11:1–6, 13–36

I am speaking the truth as a Christian; my conscience, enlightened by the Holy Spirit, assures me that I do not lie when I tell you that there is great grief and unceasing sorrow in my heart. I would even pray to be an outcast myself, cut off from Christ, if it would help my brothers, my kinsfolk by natural descent. They are descendants of Israel, chosen to be God's sons; theirs is the glory of the divine presence, theirs the covenants, the law, the temple worship, and the promises. The patriarchs are theirs, and from them by natural descent came the Messiah. May God, supreme above all, be blessed for ever! Amen.

It cannot be that God's word has proved false. Not all the offspring of Israel are truly Israel, nor does being Abraham's descendants make them all his true children; …as he says in Hosea: 'Those who were not my people I will call my people, and the unloved I will call beloved. In the very place where they were told, "You are no people of mine," they shall be called sons of the living God.' But about Israel Isaiah makes this proclamation: 'Though the Israelites be countless as the sands of the sea, only a remnant shall be saved, for the Lord's sentence on the land will be summary and final'; as also he said previously, 'If the Lord of Hosts had not left us descendants, we should have become like Sodom, and no better than Gomorrah.'

Then what are we to say? That Gentiles, who made no effort after righteousness, nevertheless achieved it, a righteousness based on faith; whereas Israel made great efforts after a law of righteousness, but never attained to it. Why was this? Because their efforts were not based on faith but, mistakenly, on deeds. They tripped over the 'stone' mentioned in scripture: 'Here I lay in Zion a stone to trip over, a rock to stumble against; but he who has faith in it will not be put to shame.'

Friends, my heart's desire and my prayer to God is for their salvation. To their zeal for God I can testify; but it is an ill-informed zeal. For they ignore God's way of righteousness, and try to set up their own, and therefore they have not submitted themselves to God's righteousness; for Christ is the end of the law and brings righteousness for everyone who has faith…

If the confession 'Jesus is Lord' is on your lips, and the faith that God raised him from the dead is in your heart, you will find salvation. For faith in the heart leads to righteousness, and confession on the lips leads to salvation. Scripture says, 'No one who has faith in him will be put to shame': there is no distinction between Jew and Greek, because the same Lord is Lord of all, and has riches enough for all who call on him. For 'Everyone who calls on the name of the Lord will be saved.'…

I ask, then: Has God rejected his people? Of course not! I am an Israelite myself, of the stock of Abraham, of the tribe of Benjamin. God has not rejected the people he acknowledged of old as his own. Surely you know what scripture says in the story of Elijah -how he pleads with God against Israel: 'Lord, they have killed your prophets, they have torn down your altars, and I alone am left, and they are seeking my life.' But what was the divine word to him? 'I have left myself seven thousand men who have not knelt to Baal.' In just the same way at the present time a 'remnant' has come into being, chosen by the grace of God. But if it is by grace, then it does not rest on deeds, or grace would cease to be grace...

It is to you Gentiles that I am speaking. As an apostle to the Gentiles, I make much of that ministry, yet always in the hope of stirring those of my own race to envy, and so saving some of them. For if their rejection has meant the reconciliation of the world, what will their acceptance mean? Nothing less than life from the dead! If the first loaf is holy, so is the whole batch. If the root is holy, so are the branches. But if some of the branches have been lopped off, and you, a wild olive, have been grafted in among them, and have come to share the same root and sap as the olive, do not make yourself superior to the branches. If you do, remember that you do not sustain the root: the root sustains you.

You will say, 'Branches were lopped off so that I might be grafted in.' Very well: they were lopped off for lack of faith, and by faith you hold your place. Put away your pride, and be on your guard; for if God did not spare the natural branches, no more will he spare you. Observe the kindness and the severity of God – severity to those who fell away, divine kindness to you provided that you remain within its scope; otherwise you too will be cut off, whereas they, if they do not continue faithless, will be grafted in, since it is in God's power to graft them in again. For if you were cut from your native wild olive and against nature grafted into the cultivated olive, how much more readily will they, the natural olive branches, be grafted into their native stock!

There is a divine secret here, my friends, which I want to share with you, to keep you from thinking yourselves wise: this partial hardening has come on Israel only until the Gentiles have been admitted in full strength; once that has happened, the whole of Israel will be saved, in accordance with scripture:

> From Zion shall come the Deliverer;
> he shall remove wickedness from Jacob.
> And this is the covenant I will grant them,
> when I take away their sins.

Judged by their response to the gospel, they are God's enemies for your sake; but judged by his choice, they are dear to him for the sake of the patriarchs; for the gracious gifts of God and his calling are irrevocable. Just as formerly you were disobedient to God, but now have received mercy because of their disobedience, so now, because of the mercy shown to you, they have proved disobedient, but only in order that they too may receive mercy. For in shutting all mankind in the prison of their disobedience, God's purpose was to show mercy to all mankind.

> How deep are the wealth
> and the wisdom and the knowledge of God!
> How inscrutable his judgments,
> how unsearchable his ways!
> 'Who knows the mind of the Lord?
> Who has been his counsellor?'
> 'Who has made a gift to him first,
> and earned a gift in return?'
> From him and through him and for him all things exist –
> to him be glory for ever! Amen.

CHRISTIAN LIFE AND DUTY
Romans 12:1 – 13:14

Therefore, my friends, I implore you by God's mercy to offer your very selves to him: a living sacrifice, dedicated and fit for his acceptance, the worship offered by mind and heart. Conform no longer to the pattern of this present world, but be transformed by the renewal of your minds. Then you will be able to discern the will of God, and to know what is good, acceptable, and perfect.

By authority of the grace God has given me I say to everyone among you: do not think too highly of yourself, but form a sober estimate based on the measure of faith that God has dealt to each of you. For just as in a single human body there are many limbs and organs, all with different functions, so we who are united with Christ, though many, form one body, and belong to one another as its limbs and organs.

Let us use the different gifts allotted to each of us by God's grace: the gift of inspired utterance, for example, let us use in proportion to our faith; the gift of administration to administer, the gift of teaching to teach, the gift of counselling to counsel. If you give to charity, give without grudging; if you are a leader, lead with enthusiasm; if you help others in distress, do it cheerfully.

Love in all sincerity, loathing evil and holding fast to the good. Let love of the Christian community show itself in mutual affection. Esteem others more highly than yourself.

With unflagging zeal, aglow with the Spirit, serve the Lord. Let hope keep you joyful; in trouble stand firm; persist in prayer; contribute to the needs of God's people, and practise hospitality. Call down blessings on your persecutors – blessings, not curses. Rejoice with those who rejoice, weep with those who weep. Live in agreement with one another. Do not be proud, but be ready to mix with humble people. Do not keep thinking how wise you are.

Never pay back evil for evil. Let your aims be such as all count honourable. If possible, so far as it lies with you, live at peace with all. My dear friends, do not seek revenge, but leave a place for divine retribution; for there is a text which reads, 'Vengeance is mine, says the Lord, I will repay.' But there is another text: 'If your enemy is hungry, feed him; if he is thirsty, give him a drink; by doing this you will heap live coals on his head.' Do not let evil conquer you, but use good to conquer evil.

Every person must submit to the authorities in power, for all authority comes from God, and the existing authorities are instituted by him. It follows that anyone who rebels against authority is resisting a divine institution, and those who resist have themselves to thank for the punishment they will receive. Governments hold no terrors for the law-abiding but only for the criminal. You wish to have no fear of the authorities? Then continue to do right and you will have their approval, for they are God's agents working for your good. But if you are doing wrong, then you will have cause to fear them; it is not for nothing that they hold the power of the sword, for they are God's agents of punishment bringing retribution on the offender. That is why you are obliged to submit. It is an obligation imposed not merely by fear of retribution but by conscience. That is also why you pay taxes. The authorities are in God's service and it is to this they devote their energies.

Discharge your obligations to everyone; pay tax and levy, reverence and respect, to those to whom they are due. Leave no debt outstanding, but remember the debt of love you owe one another. He who loves his neighbour has met every requirement of the law. The commandments, 'You shall not commit adultery, you shall not commit murder, you shall not steal, you shall not covet,' and any other commandment there may be, are all summed up in the one rule, 'Love your neighbour as yourself.' Love cannot wrong a neighbour; therefore love is the fulfilment of the law.

Always remember that this is the hour of crisis: it is high time for you to wake out of sleep, for deliverance is nearer to us now than it was when first we believed. It is far on in the night; day is near. Let us therefore throw off the deeds of darkness and put on the armour of light. Let us behave with decency as befits the day: no drunken orgies, no debauchery or vice, no quarrels or jealousies! Let Christ Jesus himself be the armour that you wear; give your unspiritual nature no opportunity to satisfy its desires.

CHRISTIAN TOLERANCE
Romans 14:1 – 15:7

Accept anyone who is weak in faith without debate about his misgivings. For instance, one person may have faith strong enough to eat all kinds of food, while another who is weaker eats only vegetables. Those who eat meat must not look down on those who do not, and those who do not eat meat must not pass judgment on those who do; for God has accepted them. Who are you to pass judgment on someone else's servant? Whether he stands or falls is his own Master's business; and stand he will, because his Master has power to enable him to stand.

Again, some make a distinction between this day and that; others regard all days alike. Everyone must act on his own convictions. Those who honour the day honour the Lord, and those who eat meat also honour the Lord, since when they eat they give thanks to God; and those who abstain have the Lord in mind when abstaining, since they too give thanks to God.

For none of us lives, and equally none of us dies, for himself alone. If we live, we live for the Lord; and if we die, we die for the Lord. So whether we live or die, we belong to the Lord. This is why Christ died and lived again, to establish his lordship over both dead and living. You, then, why do you pass judgment on your fellow-Christian? And you, why do you look down on your fellow-Christian? We shall all stand before God's tribunal; for we read in scripture, 'As I live, says the Lord, to me every knee shall bow and every tongue acknowledge God.' So, you see, each of us will be answerable to God.

Let us therefore cease judging one another, but rather make up our minds to place no obstacle or stumbling block in a fellow-Christian's way. All that I know of the Lord Jesus convinces me that nothing is impure in itself; only, if anyone considers something impure, then for him it is impure. If your fellow-Christian is outraged by what you eat, then you are no longer guided by love. Do not by your eating be the ruin of one for whom Christ died! You must not let what you think good be brought into disrepute; for the kingdom of God is not eating and drinking, but justice, peace, and joy, inspired by the Holy Spirit. Everyone who shows himself a servant of Christ in this way is acceptable to God and approved by men.

Let us, then, pursue the things that make for peace and build up the common life. Do not destroy the work of God for the sake of food. Everything is pure in itself, but it is wrong to eat if by eating you cause another to stumble. It is right to abstain from eating meat or drinking wine or from anything else which causes a fellow-Christian to stumble. If you have some firm conviction, keep it between yourself and God. Anyone who can make his decision without misgivings is fortunate. But anyone who has misgivings and yet eats is guilty, because his action does not arise from conviction, and anything which does not arise from conviction is sin. Those of us who are strong must accept as our own burden the tender scruples of the weak, and not just please ourselves. Each of us must consider his neighbour and think what is for his good and will build up the common life. Christ too did not please himself; to him apply the words of scripture, 'The reproaches of those who reproached you fell on me.' The scriptures written long ago were all written for our instruction, in order that through the encouragement they give us we may maintain our hope with perseverance. And may God, the source of all perseverance and all encouragement, grant that you may agree with one another after the manner of Christ Jesus, and so with one mind and one voice may praise the God and Father of our Lord Jesus Christ.

In a word, accept one another as Christ accepted us, to the glory of God.

FINAL ADVICE AND DOXOLOGY
Romans 15:14–16, 23–24; 16:1–5, 17–18, 25–27

My friends, I have no doubt in my own mind that you yourselves are full of goodness and equipped with knowledge of every kind, well able to give advice to one another; nevertheless I have written to refresh your memory, and written somewhat boldly at times, in virtue of the gift I have from God. His grace has made me a minister of Christ Jesus to the Gentiles; and in the service of the gospel of God it is my priestly task to offer the Gentiles to him as an acceptable sacrifice, consecrated by the Holy Spirit...

But now I have no further scope in these parts, and I have been longing for many years to visit you on my way to Spain; for I hope to see you in passing, and to be sent on my way there with your support after having enjoyed your company for a while...

I commend to you Phoebe, a fellow-Christian who is a minister in the church at Cenchreae. Give her, in the fellowship of the Lord, a welcome worthy of God's people, and support her in any business in which she may need your help, for she has herself been a good friend to many, including myself.

Give my greetings to Prisca and Aquila, my fellow-workers in Christ Jesus. They risked their necks to save my life, and not I alone but all the gentile churches are grateful to them. Greet also the church that meets at their house...

I implore you, my friends, keep an eye on those who stir up quarrels and lead others astray, contrary to the teaching you received. Avoid them; such people are servants not of Christ our Lord but of their own appetites, and they seduce the minds of simple people with smooth and specious words...

To him who has power to make you stand firm, according to my gospel and the proclamation of Jesus Christ, according to the revelation of that divine secret kept in silence for long ages but now disclosed, and by the eternal God's command made known to all nations through prophetic scriptures, to bring them to faith and obedience – to the only wise God through Jesus Christ be glory for endless ages! Amen.

The Epistle to the Colossians

PAUL'S LOVE FOR THE COLOSSIANS
Colossians 1:1–12

From Paul, by the will of God apostle of Christ Jesus, and our colleague Timothy, to God's people at Colossae, our fellow-believers in Christ.

Grace to you and peace from God our Father.

In all our prayers to God, the Father of our Lord Jesus Christ, we thank him for you, because we have heard of your faith in Christ Jesus and the love you bear towards all God's people; both spring from that hope stored up for you in heaven of which you learned when the message of the true gospel first came to you. That same gospel is bearing fruit and making new growth the whole world over, as it does among you and has done since the day when you heard of God's grace and learned what it truly is. It was Epaphras, our dear fellow-servant and a trusted worker for Christ on our behalf, who taught you this, and it is he who has brought us news of the love the Spirit has awakened in you.

This is why, ever since we first heard about you, we have not ceased to pray for you. We ask God that you may receive from him full insight into his will, all wisdom and spiritual understanding, so that your manner of life may be worthy of the Lord and entirely pleasing to him. We pray that you may bear fruit in active goodness of every kind, and grow in knowledge of God. In his glorious might may he give you ample strength to meet with fortitude and patience whatever comes; and to give joyful thanks to the Father who has made you fit to share the heritage of God's people in the realm of light.

THE SUPREMACY OF CHRIST
Colossians 1:13 – 2:15

He rescued us from the domain of darkness and brought us into the kingdom of his dear Son, through whom our release is secured and our sins are forgiven. He is the image of the invisible God; his is the primacy over all creation. In him everything in heaven and on earth was created, not only things visible but also the invisible orders of thrones, sovereignties, authorities, and powers: the whole universe has been created through him and for him. He exists before all things, and all things are held together in him. He is the head of the body, the church. He is its origin, the first to return from the dead, to become in all things supreme. For in him God in all his fullness chose to dwell, and through him to reconcile all things to himself, making peace through the shedding of his blood on the cross – all things, whether on earth or in heaven.

Formerly you yourselves were alienated from God, his enemies in heart and mind, as your evil deeds showed. But now by Christ's death in his body of flesh and blood God has reconciled you to himself, so that he may bring you into his own presence, holy and without blame or blemish. Yet you must persevere in faith, firm on your foundations and never to be dislodged from the hope offered in the gospel you accepted. This is the gospel which has been proclaimed in the whole creation under heaven, the gospel of which I, Paul, became a minister.

It is now my joy to suffer for you; for the sake of Christ's body, the church, I am completing what still remains for Christ to suffer in my own person. I became a servant of the church by virtue of the task assigned to me by God for your benefit: to put God's word into full effect, that secret purpose hidden for long ages and through many generations, but now disclosed to God's people. To them he chose to make known what a wealth of glory is offered to the Gentiles in this secret purpose: Christ in you, the hope of glory.

He it is whom we proclaim. We teach everyone and instruct everyone in all the ways of wisdom, so as to present each one of you as a mature member of Christ's body. To this end I am toiling strenuously with all the energy and power of Christ at work in me. I want you to know how strenuous are my exertions for you and the Laodiceans, and for all who have never set eyes on me. My aim is to keep them in good heart and united in love, so that they may come to the full wealth of conviction which understanding brings, and grasp God's secret, which is Christ himself, in whom lie hidden all the treasures of wisdom and knowledge. I tell you this to make sure no one talks you into error by specious arguments. I may be absent in body, but in spirit I am with you, and rejoice to see your unbroken ranks and the solid front which your faith in Christ presents.

Therefore, since you have accepted Christ Jesus as Lord, live in union with him. Be rooted in him, be built in him, grow strong in the faith as you were taught; let your hearts overflow with thankfulness. Be on your guard; let no one capture your minds with hollow and delusive speculations, based on traditions of human teaching and centred on the elemental spirits of the universe and not on Christ.

For it is in Christ that the Godhead in all its fullness dwells embodied, it is in him you have been brought to fulfilment. Every power and authority in the universe is subject to him as head. In him also you were circumcised, not in a physical sense, but by the stripping away of the old nature, which is Christ's way of circumcision. For you were buried with him in baptism, and in that baptism you were also raised to life with him through your faith in the active power of God, who raised him from the dead. And although you were dead because of your sins and your uncircumcision, he has brought you to life with Christ. For he has forgiven us all our sins; he has cancelled the bond which was outstanding against us with its legal demands; he has set it aside, nailing it to the cross. There he disarmed the cosmic powers and authorities and made a public spectacle of them, leading them as captives in his triumphal procession.

LIVING AS THE BODY OF CHRIST
Colossians 2:16 – 4:6

Allow no one, therefore, to take you to task about what you eat or drink, or over the observance of festival, new moon, or sabbath. These are no more than a shadow of what was to come; the reality is Christ's. You are not to be disqualified by the decision of people who go in for self-mortification and angel-worship and access to some visionary world. Such people, bursting with the futile conceit of worldly minds, lose their hold upon the head; yet it is from the head that the whole body, with all its joints and ligaments, has its needs supplied, and thus knit together grows according to God's design.

Did you not die with Christ and pass beyond reach of the elemental spirits of the universe? Then why behave as though you were still living the life of the world? Why let people dictate to you: 'Do not handle this, do not taste that, do not touch the other' – referring to things that must all perish as they are used? That is to follow human rules and regulations. Such conduct may have an air of wisdom, with its forced piety, its self-mortification, and its severity to the body; but it is of no use at all in combating sensuality.

Were you not raised to life with Christ? Then aspire to the realm above, where Christ is, seated at God's right hand, and fix your thoughts on that higher realm, not on this earthly life. You died; and now your life lies hidden with Christ in God. When Christ, who is our life, is revealed, then you too will be revealed with him in glory.

So put to death those parts of you which belong to the earth – fornication, indecency, lust, evil desires, and the ruthless greed which is nothing less than idolatry; on these divine retribution falls. This is the way you yourselves once lived; but now have done with rage, bad temper, malice, slander, filthy talk – banish them all from your lips! Do not lie to one another, now that you have discarded the old human nature and the conduct that goes with it, and have put on the new nature which is constantly being renewed in the image of its Creator and brought to know God. There is no question here of Greek and Jew, circumcised and uncircumcised, barbarian, Scythian, slave and freeman; but Christ is all, and is in all.

Put on, then, garments that suit God's chosen and beloved people: compassion, kindness, humility, gentleness, patience. Be tolerant with one another and forgiving, if any of you has cause for complaint: you must forgive as the Lord forgave you. Finally, to bind everything together and complete the whole, there must be love. Let Christ's peace be arbiter in your decisions, the peace to which you were called as members of a single body. Always be thankful. Let the gospel of Christ dwell among you in all its richness; teach and instruct one another with all the wisdom it gives you. With psalms and hymns and spiritual songs, sing from the heart in gratitude to God. Let every word and action, everything you do, be in the name of the Lord Jesus, and give thanks through him to God the Father.

Wives, be subject to your husbands; that is your Christian duty.

Husbands, love your wives and do not be harsh with them. Children, obey your parents in everything, for that is pleasing to God and is the Christian way. Fathers, do not exasperate your children, in case they lose heart. Slaves, give entire obedience to your earthly masters, not merely to catch their eye or curry favour with them, but with single-mindedness, out of reverence for the Lord. Whatever you are doing, put your whole heart into it, as if you were doing it for the Lord and not for men, knowing that there is a master who will give you an inheritance as a reward for your service. Christ is the master you must serve. Wrongdoers will pay for the wrong they do; there will be no favouritism. Masters, be just and fair to your slaves, knowing that you too have a master in heaven.

Persevere in prayer, with minds alert and with thankful hearts; and include us in your prayers, asking God to provide an opening for the gospel, that we may proclaim the secret of Christ, for which indeed I am in prison. Pray that I may make the secret plain, as it is my duty to do.

Be wise in your dealings with outsiders, but use your opportunities to the full. Let your words always be gracious, never insipid; learn how best to respond to each person you meet.

GREETINGS FROM PAUL'S CO-WORKERS
Colossians 4:7–18

You will hear all my news from Tychicus, our dear brother and trustworthy helper and fellow-servant in the Lord's work. I am sending him to you for this purpose, to let you know how we are and to put fresh heart into you. With him comes Onesimus, our trustworthy and dear brother, who is one of yourselves. They will tell you all that has happened here.

Aristarchus, Christ's captive like myself, sends his greetings; so does Mark, the cousin of Barnabas (you have had instructions about him; if he comes, make him welcome), and Jesus Justus. Of the Jewish Christians, these are the only ones working with me for the kingdom of God, and they have been a great comfort to me. Greetings from Epaphras, servant of Christ, who is one of yourselves. He prays hard for you all the time, that you may stand fast, as mature Christians, fully determined to do the will of God. I can vouch for him, that he works tirelessly for you and the people at Laodicea and Hierapolis. Greetings to you from our dear friend Luke, the doctor, and from Demas. Give our greetings to the Christians at Laodicea, and to Nympha and the congregation that meets at her house. Once this letter has been read among you, see that it is read also to the church at Laodicea, and that you in turn read my letter to Laodicea. Give Archippus this message: 'See that you carry out fully the duty entrusted to you in the Lord's service.'

I add this greeting in my own hand – Paul. Remember I am in prison. Grace be with you.

The Epistle to Philemon

Philemon 1:1–25

From Paul, a prisoner of Christ Jesus, and our colleague Timothy, to Philemon our dear friend and fellow-worker, together with Apphia our sister, and Archippus our comrade-in-arms, and the church that meets at your house.

Grace to you and peace from God our Father and the Lord Jesus Christ.

I thank my God always when I mention you in my prayers, for I hear of your love and faith towards the Lord Jesus and for all God's people. My prayer is that the faith you hold in common with us may deepen your understanding of all the blessings which belong to us as we are brought closer to Christ. Your love has brought me much joy and encouragement; through you God's people have been much refreshed.

Accordingly, although in Christ I might feel free to dictate where your duty lies, yet, because of that same love, I would rather appeal to you. Ambassador as I am of Christ Jesus, and now his prisoner, I, Paul, appeal to you about my child, whose father I have become in this prison. I mean Onesimus, once so useless to you, but now useful indeed, both to you and to me. In sending him back to you I am sending my heart. I should have liked to keep him with me, to look after me on your behalf, here in prison for the gospel, but I did not want to do anything without your consent, so that your kindness might be a matter not of compulsion, but of your own free will. Perhaps this is why you lost him for a time to receive him back for good – no longer as a slave, but as more than a slave: as a dear brother, very dear to me, and still dearer to you, both as a man and as a Christian.

If, then, you think of me as your partner in the faith, welcome him as you would welcome me. If he did you any wrong and owes you anything, put it down to my account. Here is my signature: Paul. I will repay you – not to mention that you owe me your very self. Yes, brother, I am asking this favour of you as a fellow-Christian; set my mind at rest.

I write to you confident that you will meet my wishes; I know that you will in fact do more than I ask. And one last thing: have a room ready for me, for I hope through the prayers of you all to be restored to you.

Epaphras, a captive of Christ Jesus like myself, sends you greetings. So do my fellow-workers Mark, Aristarchus, Demas, and Luke.

The grace of the Lord Jesus Christ be with your spirit!

The Epistle to the Ephesians

THE SECRET PURPOSE OF GOD
Ephesians 1:1 – 2:10

From Paul, by the will of God apostle of Christ Jesus, to God's people at Ephesus, to the faithful, incorporate in Christ Jesus.

Grace to you and peace from God our Father and the Lord Jesus Christ.

Blessed be the God and Father of our Lord Jesus Christ, who has conferred on us in Christ every spiritual blessing in the heavenly realms. Before the foundation of the world he chose us in Christ to be his people, to be without blemish in his sight, to be full of love; and he predestined us to be adopted as his children through Jesus Christ. This was his will and pleasure in order that the glory of his gracious gift, so graciously conferred on us in his Beloved, might redound to his praise. In Christ our release is secured and our sins forgiven through the shedding of his blood. In the richness of his grace God has lavished on us all wisdom and insight. He has made known to us his secret purpose, in accordance with the plan which he determined beforehand in Christ, to be put into effect when the time was ripe: namely, that the universe, everything in heaven and on earth, might be brought into a unity in Christ.

In Christ indeed we have been given our share in the heritage, as was decreed in his design whose purpose is everywhere at work; for it was his will that we, who were the first to set our hope on Christ, should cause his glory to be praised. And in Christ you also – once you had heard the message of the truth, the good news of your salvation, and had believed it – in him you were stamped with the seal of the promised Holy Spirit; and that Spirit is a pledge of the inheritance which will be ours when God has redeemed what is his own, to his glory and praise.

Because of all this, now that I have heard of your faith in the Lord Jesus and the love you bear towards all God's people, I never cease to give thanks for you when I mention you in my prayers. I pray that the God of our Lord Jesus Christ, the all-glorious Father, may confer on you the spiritual gifts of wisdom and vision, with the knowledge of him that they bring. I pray that your inward eyes may be enlightened, so that you may know what is the hope to which he calls you, how rich and glorious is the share he offers you among his people in their inheritance, and how vast are the resources of his power open to us who have faith. His mighty strength was seen at work when he raised Christ from the dead, and enthroned him at his right hand in the heavenly realms, far above all government and authority, all power and dominion, and any title of sovereignty that commands allegiance, not only in this age but also in the age to come. He put all things in subjection beneath his feet, and gave him as head over all things to the church which is his body, the fullness of him who is filling the universe in all its parts.

You once were dead because of your sins and wickedness; you followed the ways of this present world order, obeying the commander of the spiritual powers of the air, the spirit now at work among God's rebel subjects. We too were once of their number: we were ruled by our physical desires, and did what instinct and evil imagination suggested. In our natural condition we lay under the condemnation of God like the rest of mankind. But God is rich in mercy, and because of his great love for us, he brought us to life with Christ when we were dead because of our sins; it is by grace you are saved. And he raised us up in union with Christ Jesus and enthroned us with him in the heavenly realms, so that he might display in the ages to come how immense are the resources of his grace, and how great his kindness to us in Christ Jesus. For it is by grace you are saved through faith; it is not your own doing. It is God's gift, not a reward for work done. There is nothing for anyone to boast of; we are God's handiwork, created in Christ Jesus for the life of good deeds which God designed for us.

THE NEW HUMANITY
Ephesians 2:11 – 3:21

Remember then your former condition, Gentiles as you are by birth, 'the uncircumcised' as you are called by those who call themselves 'the circumcised' because of a physical rite. You were at that time separate from Christ, excluded from the community of Israel, strangers to God's covenants and the promise that goes with them. Yours was a world without hope and without God. Once you were far off, but now in union with Christ Jesus you have been brought near through the shedding of Christ's blood. For he is himself our peace. Gentiles and Jews, he has made the two one, and in his own body of flesh and blood has broken down the barrier of enmity which separated them; for he annulled the law with its rules and regulations, so as to create out of the two a single new humanity in himself, thereby making peace. This was his purpose, to reconcile the two in a single body to God through the cross, by which he killed the enmity. So he came and proclaimed the good news: peace to you who were far off, and peace to those who were near; for through him we both alike have access to the Father in the one Spirit.

Thus you are no longer aliens in a foreign land, but fellow-citizens with God's people, members of God's household. You are built on the foundation of the apostles and prophets, with Christ Jesus himself as the corner-stone. In him the whole building is bonded together and grows into a holy temple in the Lord. In him you also are being built with all the others into a spiritual dwelling for God.

With this in mind I pray for you, I, Paul, who for the sake of you Gentiles am now the prisoner of Christ Jesus – for surely you have heard how God's gift of grace to me was designed for your benefit. It was by a revelation that his secret purpose was made known to me. I have already written you a brief account of this, and by reading it you can see that I understand the secret purpose of Christ. In former generations that secret was not disclosed to mankind; but now by inspiration it has been revealed to his holy apostles and prophets, that through the gospel the Gentiles are joint heirs with the Jews, part of the same body, sharers together in the promise made in Christ Jesus. Such is the gospel of which I was made a minister by God's unmerited gift, so powerfully at work in me. To me, who am less than the least of all God's people, he has granted the privilege of proclaiming to the Gentiles the good news of the unfathomable riches of Christ, and of bringing to light how this hidden purpose was to be put into effect. It lay concealed for long ages with God the Creator of the universe, in order that now, through the church, the wisdom of God in its infinite variety might be made known to the rulers and authorities in the heavenly realms. This accords with his age-long purpose, which he accomplished in Christ Jesus our Lord, in whom we have freedom of access to God, with the confidence born of trust in him. I beg you, then, not to lose heart over my sufferings for you; indeed, they are your glory.

With this in mind, then, I kneel in prayer to the Father, from whom every family in heaven and on earth takes its name, that out of the treasures of his glory he may grant you inward strength and power through his Spirit, that through faith Christ may dwell in your hearts in love. With deep roots and firm foundations may you, in company with all God's people, be strong to grasp what is the breadth and length and height and depth of Christ's love, and to know it, though it is beyond knowledge. So may you be filled with the very fullness of God.

Now to him who is able through the power which is at work among us to do immeasurably more than all we can ask or conceive, to him be glory in the church and in Christ Jesus from generation to generation for evermore! Amen.

SPIRITUAL GROWTH
Ephesians 4:1-16

I implore you then – I, a prisoner for the Lord's sake: as God has called you, live up to your calling. Be humble always and gentle, and patient too, putting up with one another's failings in the spirit of love. Spare no effort to make fast with bonds of peace the unity which the Spirit gives. There is one body and one Spirit, just as there is one hope held out in God's call to you; one Lord, one faith, one baptism; one God and Father of all, who is over all and through all and in all.

But each of us has been given a special gift, a particular share in the bounty of Christ. That is why scripture says:

He ascended into the heights;
he took captives into captivity;
he gave gifts to men.

Now, the word 'ascended' implies that he also descended to the lowest level, down to the very earth. He who descended is none other than he who ascended far above all heavens, so that he might fill the universe. And it is he who has given some to be apostles, some prophets, some evangelists, some pastors and teachers, to equip God's people for work in his service, for the building up of the body of Christ, until we all attain to the unity inherent in our faith and in our knowledge of the Son of God – to mature manhood, measured by nothing less than the full stature of Christ. We are no longer to be children, tossed about by the waves and whirled around by every fresh gust of teaching, dupes of cunning rogues and their deceitful schemes. Rather we are to maintain the truth in a spirit of love; so shall we fully grow up into Christ. He is the head, and on him the whole body depends. Bonded and held together by every constituent joint, the whole frame grows through the proper functioning of each part, and builds itself up in love.

LIVING THE CHRISTIAN LIFE
Ephesians 4:17 – 6:9

Here then is my word to you, and I urge it on you in the Lord's name: give up living as pagans do with their futile notions. Their minds are closed, they are alienated from the life that is in God, because ignorance prevails among them and their hearts have grown hard as stone. Dead to all feeling, they have abandoned themselves to vice, and there is no indecency that they do not practise. But that is not how you learned Christ. For were you not told about him, were you not as Christians taught the truth as it is in Jesus? Renouncing your former way of life, you must lay aside the old human nature which, deluded by its desires, is in process of decay: you must be renewed in mind and spirit, and put on the new nature created in God's likeness, which shows itself in the upright and devout life called for by the truth.

Then have done with falsehood and speak the truth to each other, for we belong to one another as parts of one body.

If you are angry, do not be led into sin; do not let sunset find you nursing your anger; and give no foothold to the devil.

343

The thief must give up stealing, and work hard with his hands to earn an honest living, so that he may have something to share with the needy.

Let no offensive talk pass your lips, only what is good and helpful to the occasion, so that it brings a blessing to those who hear it. Do not grieve the Holy Spirit of God, for that Spirit is the seal with which you were marked for the day of final liberation. Have done with all spite and bad temper, with rage, insults, and slander, with evil of any kind. Be generous to one another, tender-hearted, forgiving one another as God in Christ forgave you.

In a word, as God's dear children, you must be like him. Live in love as Christ loved you and gave himself up on your behalf, an offering and sacrifice whose fragrance is pleasing to God.

Fornication and indecency of any kind, or ruthless greed, must not be so much as mentioned among you, as befits the people of God. No coarse, stupid, or flippant talk: these things are out of place; you should rather be thanking God. For be very sure of this: no one given to fornication or vice, or the greed which makes an idol of gain, has any share in the kingdom of Christ and of God. Let no one deceive you with shallow arguments; it is for these things that divine retribution falls on God's rebel subjects. Have nothing to do with them. Though you once were darkness, now as Christians you are light. Prove yourselves at home in the light, for where light is, there is a harvest of goodness, righteousness, and truth. Learn to judge for yourselves what is pleasing to the Lord; take no part in the barren deeds of darkness, but show them up for what they are. It would be shameful even to mention what is done in secret. But everything is shown up by being exposed to the light, and whatever is exposed to the light itself becomes light. That is why it is said:

Awake, sleeper,
rise from the dead,
and Christ will shine upon you.

Take great care, then, how you behave: act sensibly, not like simpletons. Use the present opportunity to the full, for these are evil days. Do not be foolish, but understand what the will of the Lord is. Do not give way to drunkenness and the ruin that goes with it, but let the Holy Spirit fill you: speak to one another in psalms, hymns, and songs; sing and make music from your heart to the Lord; and in the name of our Lord Jesus Christ give thanks every day for everything to our God and Father.

Be subject to one another out of reverence for Christ.

Wives, be subject to your husbands as though to the Lord; for the man is the head of the woman, just as Christ is the head of the church. Christ is, indeed, the saviour of that body; but just as the church is subject to Christ, so must women be subject to their husbands in everything.

Husbands, love your wives, as Christ loved the church and gave himself up for it, to consecrate and cleanse it by water and word, so that he might present the church to himself all glorious, with no stain or wrinkle or anything of the sort, but holy and without blemish. In the same way men ought to love their wives, as they love their own bodies. In loving his wife a man loves himself. For no one ever hated his own body; on the contrary, he keeps it nourished and warm, and that is how Christ treats the church, because it is his body, of which we are living parts. 'This is why' (in the words of scripture) 'a man shall leave his father and mother and be united to his wife, and the two shall become one flesh.' There is hidden here a great truth, which I take to refer to Christ and to the church. But it applies also to each one of you: the husband must love his wife as his very self, and the wife must show reverence for her husband.

Children, obey your parents; for it is only right that you should. 'Honour your father and your mother' is the first commandment to carry a promise with it: 'that it may be well with you and that you may live long on the earth.'

Fathers, do not goad your children to resentment, but bring them up in the discipline and instruction of the Lord.

Slaves, give single-minded obedience to your earthly masters with fear and trembling, as if to Christ. Do it not merely to catch their eye or curry favour with them, but as slaves of Christ do the will of God wholeheartedly. Give cheerful service, as slaves of the Lord rather than of men. You know that whatever good anyone may do, slave or free, will be repaid by the Lord.

Masters, treat your slaves in the same spirit: give up using threats, and remember that you both have the same Master in heaven; there is no favouritism with him.

THE ARMOUR OF GOD
Ephesians 6:10–20

Finally, find your strength in the Lord, in his mighty power. Put on the full armour provided by God, so that you may be able to stand firm against the stratagems of the devil. For our struggle is not against human foes, but against cosmic powers, against the authorities and potentates of this dark age, against the superhuman forces of evil in the heavenly realms. Therefore, take up the armour of God; then you will be able to withstand them on the evil day and, after doing your utmost, to stand your ground. Stand fast, I say. Fasten on the belt of truth; for a breastplate put on integrity; let the shoes on your feet be the gospel of peace, to give you firm footing; and, with all these, take up the great shield of faith, with which you will be able to quench all the burning arrows of the evil one. Accept salvation as your helmet, and the sword which the Spirit gives you, the word of God. Constantly ask God's help in prayer, and pray always in the power of the Spirit. To this end keep watch and persevere, always interceding for all God's people. Pray also for me, that I may be granted the right words when I speak, and may boldly and freely make known the hidden purpose of the gospel, for which I am an ambassador – in chains. Pray that I may speak of it boldly, as is my duty.

You will want to know how I am and what I am doing; Tychicus will give you all the news. He is our dear brother and trustworthy helper in the Lord's work. I am sending him to you on purpose to let you have news of us and to put fresh heart into you.

Peace to the community and love with faith, from God the Father and the Lord Jesus Christ. God's grace be with all who love our Lord Jesus Christ with undying love.

The Epistle to the Philippians

PAUL'S LOVE FOR THE PHILIPPIANS
Philippians 1:1–26

From Paul and Timothy, servants of Christ Jesus, to all God's people at Philippi, who are incorporate in Christ Jesus, with the bishops and deacons.

Grace to you and peace from God our Father and the Lord Jesus Christ.

I thank my God every time I think of you; whenever I pray for you all, my prayers are always joyful, because of the part you have taken in the work of the gospel from the first day until now. Of this I am confident, that he who started the good work in you will bring it to completion by the day of Christ Jesus. It is only natural that I should feel like this about you all, because I have great affection for you, knowing that, both while I am kept in prison and when I am called on to defend the truth of the gospel, you all share in this privilege of mine. God knows how I long for you all with the deep yearning of Christ Jesus himself. And this is my prayer, that your love may grow ever richer in knowledge and insight of every kind, enabling you to learn by experience what things really matter. Then on the day of Christ you will be flawless and without blame, yielding the full harvest of righteousness that comes through Jesus Christ, to the glory and praise of God.

My friends, I want you to understand that the progress of the gospel has actually been helped by what has happened to me. It has become common knowledge throughout the imperial guard, and indeed among the public at large, that my imprisonment is in Christ's cause; and my being in prison has given most of our fellow-Christians confidence to speak the word of God fearlessly and with extraordinary courage.

Some, it is true, proclaim Christ in a jealous and quarrelsome spirit, but some do it in goodwill. These are moved by love, knowing that it is to defend the gospel that I am where I am; the others are moved by selfish ambition and present Christ from mixed motives, meaning to cause me distress as I lie in prison. What does it matter? One way or another, whether sincerely or not, Christ is proclaimed; and for that I rejoice.

Yes, and I shall go on rejoicing; for I know well that the issue will be my deliverance, because you are praying for me and the Spirit of Jesus Christ is given me for support. It is my confident hope that nothing will daunt me or prevent me from speaking boldly; and that now as always Christ will display his greatness in me, whether the verdict be life or death. For to me life is Christ, and death is gain. If I am to go on living in the body there is fruitful work for me to do. Which then am I to choose? I cannot tell. I am pulled two ways: my own desire is to depart and be with Christ – that is better by far; but for your sake the greater need is for me to remain in the body. This convinces me: I am sure I shall remain, and stand by you all to ensure your progress and joy in the faith, so that on my account you may have even more cause for pride in Christ Jesus – through seeing me restored to you.

SPIRITUAL UNITY IN CHRIST
Philippians 1:27 – 2:18

Whatever happens, let your conduct be worthy of the gospel of Christ, so that whether or not I come and see you for myself I may hear that you are standing firm, united in spirit and in mind, side by side in the struggle to advance the gospel faith, meeting your opponents without so much as a tremor. This is a sure sign to them that destruction is in store for them and salvation for you, a sign from God himself; for you have been granted the privilege not only of believing in Christ but also of suffering for him. Your conflict is the same as mine; once you saw me in it, and now you hear I am in it still.

If then our common life in Christ yields anything to stir the heart, any consolation of love, any participation in the Spirit, any warmth of affection or compassion, fill up my cup of happiness by thinking and feeling alike, with the same love for one another and a

348

common attitude of mind. Leave no room for selfish ambition and vanity, but humbly reckon others better than yourselves. Look to each other's interests and not merely to your own.

Take to heart among yourselves what you find in Christ Jesus: 'He was in the form of God; yet he laid no claim to equality with God, but made himself nothing, assuming the form of a slave. Bearing the human likeness, sharing the human lot, he humbled himself, and was obedient, even to the point of death, death on a cross! Therefore God raised him to the heights and bestowed on him the name above all names, that at the name of Jesus every knee should bow – in heaven, on earth, and in the depths – and every tongue acclaim, "Jesus Christ is Lord", to the glory of God the Father.'

So you too, my friends, must be obedient, as always; even more, now that I am absent, than when I was with you. You must work out your own salvation in fear and trembling; for it is God who works in you, inspiring both the will and the deed, for his own chosen purpose.

Do everything without grumbling or argument. Show yourselves innocent and above reproach, faultless children of God in a crooked and depraved generation, in which you shine like stars in a dark world and proffer the word of life. Then you will be my pride on the day of Christ, proof that I did not run my race in vain or labour in vain. But if my life-blood is to be poured out to complete the sacrifice and offering up of your faith, I rejoice and share my joy with you all. You too must rejoice and share your joy with me.

PLANS AND COMMENDATIONS
Philippians 2:19 – 3:1a

I hope, in the Lord Jesus, to send Timothy to you soon; it will cheer me up to have news of you. I have no one else here like him, who has a genuine concern for your affairs; they are all bent on their own interests, not on those of Christ Jesus. But Timothy's record is known to you: you know that he has been at my side in the service of the gospel like a son working under his father. So he is the one I mean to send as soon as I see how things go with me; and I am confident, in the Lord, that I shall be coming myself before long.

I have decided I must also send our brother Epaphroditus, my fellow-worker and comrade, whom you commissioned to attend to my needs. He has been missing you all, and was upset because you heard he was ill. Indeed he was dangerously ill, but God was merciful to him; and not only to him but to me, to spare me one sorrow on top of another. For this reason I am all the more eager to send him and give you the happiness of seeing him again; that will relieve my anxiety as well. Welcome him then in the fellowship of the Lord with wholehearted delight. You should honour people like him; in Christ's cause he came near to death, risking his life to render me the service you could not give. And now, my friends, I wish you joy in the Lord.

PAUL'S FAITH AND EXAMPLE
Philippians 3:1b – 4:3

To repeat what I have written to you before is no trouble to me, and it is a safeguard for you. Be on your guard against those dogs, those who do nothing but harm and who insist on mutilation – 'circumcision' I will not call it; we are the circumcision, we who worship by the Spirit of God, whose pride is in Christ Jesus, and who put no confidence in the physical. It is not that I am myself without grounds for such confidence. If anyone makes claims of that kind, I can make a stronger case for myself: circumcised on my eighth day, Israelite by race, of the tribe of Benjamin, a Hebrew born and bred; in my practice of the law a Pharisee, in zeal for religion a persecutor of the church, by the law's standard of righteousness without fault. But all such assets I have written off because of Christ. More than that, I count everything sheer loss, far outweighed by the gain of knowing Christ Jesus my Lord, for whose sake I did in fact forfeit everything. I count it so much rubbish, for the sake of gaining Christ and finding myself in union with him, with no righteousness of my own based on the law, nothing but the righteousness which comes from faith in Christ, given by God in response to faith. My one desire is to know Christ and the power of his resurrection, and to share his sufferings in growing conformity with his death, in hope of somehow attaining the resurrection from the dead.

It is not that I have already achieved this. I have not yet reached perfection, but I press on, hoping to take hold of that for which Christ once took hold of me. My friends, I do not claim to have hold of it yet. What I do say is this: forgetting what is behind and straining towards what lies ahead, I press towards the finishing line, to win the heavenly prize to which God has called me in Christ Jesus.

We who are mature should keep to this way of thinking. If on any point you think differently, this also God will make plain to you. Only let our conduct be consistent with what we have already attained.

Join together, my friends, in following my example. You have us for a model; imitate those whose way of life conforms to it. As I have often told you, and now tell you with tears, there are many whose way of life makes them enemies of the cross of Christ. They are heading for destruction, they make appetite their god, they take pride in what should bring shame; their minds are set on earthly things. We, by contrast, are citizens of heaven, and from heaven we expect our deliverer to come, the Lord Jesus Christ. He will transfigure our humble bodies, and give them a form like that of his own glorious body, by that power which enables him to make all things subject to himself. This, my dear friends, whom I love and long for, my joy and crown, this is what it means to stand firm in the Lord.

Euodia and Syntyche, I appeal to you both: agree together in the Lord. Yes, and you too, my loyal comrade, I ask you to help these women, who shared my struggles in the cause of the gospel, with Clement and my other fellow-workers, who are enrolled in the book of life.

JOY AND PEACE IN CHRIST
Philippians 4:4–23

I wish you joy in the Lord always. Again I say: all joy be yours.

Be known to everyone for your consideration of others.

The Lord is near; do not be anxious, but in everything make your requests known to God in prayer and petition with thanksgiving. Then the peace of God, which is beyond all understanding, will guard your hearts and your thoughts in Christ Jesus.

And now, my friends, all that is true, all that is noble, all that is just and pure, all that is lovable and attractive, whatever is excellent and admirable – fill your thoughts with these things.

Put into practice the lessons I taught you, the tradition I have passed on, all that you heard me say or saw me do; and the God of peace will be with you.

It is a great joy to me in the Lord that after so long your care for me has now revived. I know you always cared; it was opportunity you lacked. Not that I am speaking of want, for I have learned to be self-sufficient whatever my circumstances. I know what it is to have nothing, and I know what it is to have plenty. I have been thoroughly initiated into fullness and hunger, plenty and poverty. I am able to face anything through him who gives me strength. All the same, it was kind of you to share the burden of my troubles.

You Philippians are aware that, when I set out from Macedonia in the early days of my mission, yours was the only church to share with me in the giving and receiving; more than once you contributed to my needs, even at Thessalonica. Do not think I set my heart on the gift; all I care for is the interest mounting up in your account. I have been paid in full; I have all I need and more, now that I have received from Epaphroditus what you sent. It is a fragrant offering, an acceptable sacrifice, pleasing to God. And my God will supply all your needs out of the magnificence of his riches in Christ Jesus. To our God and Father be glory for ever and ever! Amen.

Give my greetings, in the fellowship of Christ Jesus, to each one of God's people. My colleagues send their greetings to you, and so do all God's people here, particularly those in the emperor's service.

The grace of our Lord Jesus Christ be with your spirit.

The First Epistle to Timothy

KEEPING THE FAITH
1 Timothy 1:1-14

From Paul, apostle of Christ Jesus by command of God our Saviour and Christ Jesus our hope, to Timothy his true-born son in the faith.

Grace, mercy, and peace to you from God the Father and Christ Jesus our Lord.

When I was starting for Macedonia, I urged you to stay on at Ephesus. You were to instruct certain people to give up teaching erroneous doctrines and devoting themselves to interminable myths and genealogies, which give rise to mere speculation, and do not further God's plan for us, which works through faith.

This instruction has love as its goal, the love which springs from a pure heart, a good conscience, and a genuine faith. Through lack of these some people have gone astray into a wilderness of words. They set out to be teachers of the law, although they do not understand either the words they use or the subjects about which they are so dogmatic.

We all know that the law is an admirable thing, provided we treat it as law, recognizing that it is designed not for good citizens, but for the lawless and unruly, the impious and sinful, the irreligious and worldly, for parricides and matricides, murderers and fornicators, perverts, kidnappers, liars, perjurers – in fact all whose behaviour flouts the sound teaching which conforms with the gospel entrusted to me, the gospel which tells of the glory of the ever-blessed God.

I give thanks to Christ Jesus our Lord, who has made me equal to the task; I thank him for judging me worthy of trust and appointing me to his service – although in the past I had met him with abuse and persecution and outrage. But because I acted in the ignorance of unbelief I was dealt with mercifully; the grace of our Lord was lavished upon me, along with the faith and love which are ours in Christ Jesus.

Here is a saying you may trust, one that merits full acceptance:

'Christ Jesus came into the world to save sinners'; and among them I stand first. But I was mercifully dealt with for this very purpose, that Jesus Christ might find in me the first occasion for displaying his inexhaustible patience, and that I might be typical of all who were in future to have faith in him and gain eternal life. To the King eternal, immortal, invisible, the only God, be honour and glory for ever and ever! Amen.

In laying this charge upon you, Timothy my son, I am guided by those prophetic utterances which first directed me to you. Encouraged by them, fight the good fight with faith and a clear conscience. It was through spurning conscience that certain persons made shipwreck of their faith, among them Hymenaeus and Alexander, whom I consigned to Satan, in the hope that through this discipline they might learn not to be blasphemous.

First of all, then, I urge that petitions, prayers, intercessions, and thanksgivings be offered for everyone, for sovereigns and for all in high office so that we may lead a tranquil and quiet life, free to practise our religion with dignity. Such prayer is right, and approved by God our Saviour, whose will it is that all should find salvation and come to know the truth. For there is one God, and there is one mediator between God and man, Christ Jesus, himself man, who sacrificed himself to win freedom for all mankind, revealing God's purpose at God's good time; of this I was appointed herald and apostle (this is no lie, it is the truth), to instruct the Gentiles in the true faith.

It is my desire, therefore, that everywhere prayers be said by the men of the congregation, who shall lift up their hands with a pure intention, without anger or argument. Women must dress in becoming manner, modestly and soberly, not with elaborate hair-styles, not adorned with gold or pearls or expensive clothes, but with good deeds, as befits women who claim to be religious. Their role is to learn, listening quietly and with due submission. I do not permit women to teach or dictate to the men; they should keep quiet. For Adam was created first, and Eve afterwards; moreover it was not Adam who was deceived; it was the woman who, yielding to deception, fell into sin. But salvation for the woman will be in the bearing of children, provided she continues in faith, love, and holiness, with modesty.

QUALIFICATIONS FOR CHURCH LEADERS
1 Timothy 1:15 – 3:16

Here is a saying you may trust: 'To aspire to leadership is an honourable ambition.' A bishop, therefore, must be above reproach, husband of one wife, sober, temperate, courteous, hospitable, and a good teacher; he must not be given to drink or brawling, but be of a forbearing disposition, avoiding quarrels, and not avaricious. He must be one who manages his own household well and controls his children without losing his dignity, for if a man does not know how to manage his own family, how can he take charge of a congregation of God's people? He should not be a recent convert; conceit might bring on him the devil's punishment. He must moreover have a good reputation with the outside world, so that he may not be exposed to scandal and be caught in the devil's snare.

Deacons, likewise, must be dignified, not indulging in double talk, given neither to excessive drinking nor to money-grubbing. They must be men who combine a clear conscience with a firm hold on the mystery of the faith. And they too must first undergo scrutiny, and only if they are of unimpeachable character may they serve as deacons. Women in this office must likewise be dignified, not scandalmongers, but sober, and trustworthy in every way. A deacon must be the husband of one wife, and good at managing his children and his own household. For deacons with a good record of service are entitled to high standing and the right to be heard on matters of the Christian faith.

I am hoping to come to you before long, but I write this in case I am delayed, to let you know what is proper conduct in God's household, that is, the church of the living God, the pillar and bulwark of the truth. And great beyond all question is the mystery of our religion:

> He was manifested in flesh,
> vindicated in spirit,
> seen by angels;
> he was proclaimed among the nations,
> believed in throughout the world,
> raised to heavenly glory.

SPIRITUAL TRUTH AND DISCIPLINE
1 Timothy 4:1 – 5:2

The Spirit explicitly warns us that in time to come some will forsake the faith and surrender their minds to subversive spirits and demon-inspired doctrines, through the plausible falsehoods of those whose consciences have been permanently branded. They will forbid marriage, and insist on abstinence from foods which God created to be enjoyed with thanksgiving by believers who have come to knowledge of the truth. Everything that God has created is good, and nothing is to be rejected provided it is accepted with thanksgiving, for it is then made holy by God's word and by prayer.

By offering such advice as this to the brotherhood you will prove to be a good servant of Christ Jesus, nurtured in the precepts of our faith and of the sound instruction which you have followed. Have nothing to do with superstitious myths, mere old wives' tales. Keep yourself in training for the practice of religion; for while the training of the body brings limited benefit, the benefits of religion are without limit, since it holds out promise not only for this life but also for the life to come. Here is a saying you may trust, one that merits full acceptance. 'This is why we labour and struggle, because we have set our hope on the living God, who is the Saviour of all' – the Saviour, above all, of believers.

Insist on these things in your teaching. Let no one underrate you because you are young, but be to believers an example in speech and behaviour, in love, fidelity, and purity. Until I arrive devote yourself to the public reading of the scriptures, to exhortation, and to teaching. Do not neglect the spiritual endowment given you when, under the guidance of prophecy, the elders laid their hands on you.

Make these matters your business, make them your absorbing interest, so that your progress may be plain to all. Persevere in them, keeping close watch on yourself and on your teaching; by doing so you will save both yourself and your hearers.

Never be harsh with an older man; appeal to him as if he were your father. Treat the younger men as brothers, the older women as mothers, and the younger as your sisters, in all purity.

CONCERNING WIDOWS AND ELDERS
1 Timothy 5:3–22

Enrol as widows only those who are widows in the fullest sense. If a widow has children or grandchildren, they should learn as their first duty to show loyalty to the family and so repay what they owe to their parents and grandparents; for that has God's approval. But a widow in the full sense, one who is alone in the world, puts all her trust in God, and regularly, night and day, attends the meetings for prayer and worship. A widow given to self-indulgence, however, is as good as dead. Add these instructions to the rest, so that the widows may be above reproach. And if anyone does not make provision for his relations, and especially for members of his own household, he has denied the faith and is worse than an unbeliever.

A widow under sixty years of age should not be put on the roll. An enrolled widow must have been the wife of one husband, and must have gained a reputation for good deeds, by taking care of children, by showing hospitality, by washing the feet of God's people, by supporting those in distress – in short, by doing good at every opportunity.

Do not admit younger widows to the roll; for if they let their passions distract them from Christ's service they will want to marry again, and so be guilty of breaking their earlier vow to him. Besides, in going round from house to house they would learn to be idle, indeed worse than idle, gossips and busybodies, speaking of things better left unspoken. For that reason it is my wish that young widows should marry again, have children, and manage a household; then they will give the enemy no occasion for scandal. For there have in fact been some who have taken the wrong turning and gone over to Satan.

If a Christian woman has widows in her family, she must support them; the congregation must be relieved of the burden, so that it may be free to support those who are widows in the full sense.

Elders who give good service as leaders should be reckoned worthy of a double stipend, in particular those who work hard at preaching and teaching. For scripture says, 'You shall not muzzle an ox while it is treading out the grain'; besides, 'The worker earns his pay.'

Do not entertain a charge against an elder unless it is supported by two or three witnesses. Those who do commit sins you must rebuke in public, to put fear into the others. Before God and Christ Jesus and the angels who are his chosen, I solemnly charge you: maintain these rules, never prejudging the issue, but acting with strict impartiality. Do not be over-hasty in the laying on of hands, or you may find yourself implicated in other people's misdeeds; keep yourself above reproach.

FURTHER ADVICE ON THE SPIRITUAL LIFE
1 Timothy 5:22 – 6:21

Stop drinking only water; in view of your frequent ailments take a little wine to help your digestion.

There are people whose offences are so obvious that they precede them into court, and others whose offences have not yet caught up with them. So too with good deeds; they may be obvious, but, even if they are not, they cannot be concealed for ever.

All who wear the yoke of slavery must consider their masters worthy of all respect, so that the name of God and the Christian teaching are not brought into disrepute. Slaves of Christian masters must not take liberties with them just because they are their brothers. Quite the contrary: they must do their work all the better because those who receive the benefit of their service are one with them in faith and love.

This is what you are to teach and preach. Anyone who teaches otherwise, and does not devote himself to sound precepts – that is, those of our Lord Jesus Christ – and to good religious teaching, is a pompous ignoramus with a morbid enthusiasm for mere speculations and quibbles. These give rise to jealousy, quarrelling, slander, base suspicions, and endless wrangles – all typical of those whose minds are corrupted and who have lost their grip of the truth. They think religion should yield dividends; and of course religion does yield high dividends, but only to those who are content with what they have. We brought nothing into this world, and we can take nothing out; if we have food and clothing let us rest content. Those who want to be rich fall into temptations and snares and into many foolish and harmful desires which plunge people into ruin and destruction. The love of money is the root of all evil, and in pursuit of it some have wandered from the faith and spiked themselves on many a painful thorn.

But you, man of God, must shun all that, and pursue justice, piety, integrity, love, fortitude, and gentleness. Run the great race of faith and take hold of eternal life, for to this you were called, when you confessed your faith nobly before many witnesses. Now in the presence of God, who gives life to all things, and of Jesus Christ, who himself made that noble confession in his testimony before Pontius Pilate, I charge you to obey your orders without fault or failure until the appearance of our Lord Jesus Christ which God will bring about in his own good time. He is the blessed and only Sovereign, King of kings and Lord of lords; he alone possesses immortality, dwelling in unapproachable light; him no one has ever seen or can ever see; to him be honour and dominion for ever! Amen.

Instruct those who are rich in this world's goods not to be proud, and to fix their hopes not on so uncertain a thing as money, but on God, who richly provides all things for us to enjoy. They are to do good and to be rich in well-doing, to be ready to give generously and to share with others, and so acquire a treasure which will form a good foundation for the future. Then they will grasp the life that is life indeed.

Timothy, keep safe what has been entrusted to you. Turn a deaf ear to empty and irreligious chatter, and the contradictions of 'knowledge' so-called, for by laying claim to it some have strayed far from the faith.

Grace be with you all!

The Epistle to Titus

From Paul, servant of God and apostle of Jesus Christ, marked as such by the faith of God's chosen people and the knowledge of the truth enshrined in our religion with its hope of eternal life, which God, who does not lie, promised long ages ago, and now in his own good time has openly declared in the proclamation entrusted to me by command of God our Saviour.

To Titus, my true-born son in the faith which we share. Grace and peace to you from God the Father and Jesus Christ our Saviour.

My intention in leaving you behind in Crete was that you should deal with any outstanding matters, and in particular should appoint elders in each town in accordance with the principles I have laid down: Are they men of unimpeachable character? Is each the husband of one wife? Are their children believers, not open to any charge of dissipation or indiscipline? For as God's steward a bishop must be a man of unimpeachable character. He must not be overbearing or short-tempered or given to drink; no brawler, no money-grubber, but hospitable, right-minded, temperate, just, devout, and self-controlled. He must keep firm hold of the true doctrine, so that he may be well able both to appeal to his hearers with sound teaching and to refute those who raise objections.

There are many, especially among Jewish converts, who are undisciplined, who talk wildly and lead others astray. Such men must be muzzled, because they are ruining whole families by teaching what they should not, and all for sordid gain. It was a Cretan prophet, one of their own countrymen, who said, 'Cretans were ever liars, vicious brutes, lazy gluttons' – and how truly he spoke! All the more reason why you should rebuke them sharply, so that they may be restored to a sound faith, instead of paying heed to Jewish myths and to human commandments, the work of those who turn their backs on the truth.

To the pure all things are pure; but nothing is pure to tainted disbelievers, tainted both in reason and in conscience. They profess to know God but by their actions deny him; they are detestable and disobedient, disqualified for any good work.

For your part, what you say must be in keeping with sound doctrine. The older men should be sober, dignified, and temperate, sound in faith, love, and fortitude. The older women, similarly, should be reverent in their demeanour, not scandalmongers or slaves to excessive drinking; they must set a high standard, and so teach the younger women to be loving wives and mothers, to be temperate, chaste, busy at home, and kind, respecting the authority of their husbands. Then the gospel will not be brought into disrepute.

Urge the younger men, similarly, to be temperate in all things, and set them an example of good conduct yourself. In your teaching you must show integrity and seriousness, and offer sound instruction to which none can take exception. Any opponent will be at a loss when he finds nothing to say to our discredit.

Slaves are to respect their masters' authority in everything and to give them satisfaction; they are not to answer back, nor to pilfer, but are to show themselves absolutely trustworthy. In all this they will add lustre to the doctrine of God our Saviour.

For the grace of God has dawned upon the world with healing for all mankind; and by it we are disciplined to renounce godless ways and worldly desires, and to live a life of temperance, honesty, and godliness in the present age, looking forward to the happy fulfilment of our hope when the splendour of our great God and Saviour Christ Jesus will appear. He it is who sacrificed himself for us, to set us free from all wickedness and to make us his own people, pure and eager to do good.

These are your themes; urge them and argue them with an authority which no one can disregard.

Remind everyone to be submissive to the government and the authorities, and to obey them; to be ready for any honourable work; to slander no one, to avoid quarrels, and always to show forbearance and a gentle disposition to all.

There was a time when we too were lost in folly and disobedience and were slaves to passions and pleasures of every kind. Our days were passed in malice and envy; hateful ourselves, we loathed one another. 'But when the kindness and generosity of God our Saviour dawned upon the world, then, not for any good deeds of our own, but because he was merciful, he saved us through the water of rebirth and the renewing power of the Holy Spirit, which he lavished upon us through Jesus Christ our Saviour, so that, justified by his grace, we might in hope become heirs to eternal life.' That is a saying you may trust.

Such are the points I want you to insist on, so that those who have come to believe in God may be sure to devote themselves to good works. These precepts are good in themselves and also useful to society. But avoid foolish speculations, genealogies, quarrels, and controversies over the law; they are unprofitable and futile.

If someone is contentious, he should be allowed a second warning; after that, have nothing more to do with him, recognizing that anyone like that has a distorted mind and stands self-condemned in his sin.

Once I have sent Artemas or Tychicus to you, join me at Nicopolis as soon as you can, for that is where I have decided to spend the winter. Do your utmost to help Zenas the lawyer and Apollos on their travels, and see that they are not short of anything. And our own people must be taught to devote themselves to good works to meet urgent needs; they must not be unproductive.

All who are with me send you greetings. My greetings to our friends in the faith. Grace be with you all!

The Second Epistle to Timothy

THE DEMANDS OF THE GOSPEL
2 Timothy 1:1 – 2:10

From Paul, apostle of Christ Jesus by the will of God, whose promise of life is fulfilled in Christ Jesus, to Timothy his dear son.

Grace, mercy, and peace to you from God the Father and Christ Jesus our Lord.

I give thanks to the God of my forefathers, whom I worship with a clear conscience, when I mention you in my prayers as I do constantly night and day; when I remember the tears you shed, I long to see you again and so make my happiness complete. I am reminded of the sincerity of your faith, a faith which was alive in Lois your grandmother and Eunice your mother before you, and which, I am confident, now lives in you.

That is why I remind you to stir into flame the gift from God which is yours through the laying on of my hands. For the spirit that God gave us is no cowardly spirit, but one to inspire power, love, and self-discipline. So never be ashamed of your testimony to our Lord, nor of me imprisoned for his sake, but through the power that comes from God accept your share of suffering for the sake of the gospel. It is he who has brought us salvation and called us to a dedicated life, not for any merit of ours but for his own purpose and of his own grace, granted to us in Christ Jesus from all eternity, and now at length disclosed by the appearance on earth of our Saviour Jesus Christ. He has broken the power of death and brought life and immortality to light through the gospel.

Of this gospel I have been appointed herald, apostle, and teacher. That is the reason for my present plight; but I am not ashamed of it, because I know whom I have trusted, and am confident of his power to keep safe what he has put into my charge until the great day. Hold to the outline of sound teaching which you heard from me, living by the faith and love which are ours in Christ Jesus.

Keep safe the treasure put into our charge, with the help of the Holy Spirit dwelling within us.

As you are aware, everyone in the province of Asia deserted me, including Phygelus and Hermogenes. But may the Lord's mercy rest on the house of Onesiphorus! He has often relieved me in my troubles; he was not ashamed to visit a prisoner, but when he came to Rome took pains to search me out until he found me. The Lord grant that he find mercy from the Lord on the great day! You know as well as anyone the many services he rendered at Ephesus.

Take strength, my son, from the grace of God which is ours in Christ Jesus. You heard my teaching in the presence of many witnesses; hand on that teaching to reliable men who in turn will be qualified to teach others.

Take your share of hardship, like a good soldier of Christ Jesus. A soldier on active service must not let himself be involved in the affairs of everyday life if he is to give satisfaction to his commanding officer. Again, no athlete wins a prize unless he abides by the rules. The farmer who does the work has first claim on the crop. Reflect on what I am saying, and the Lord will help you to full understanding.

Remember the theme of my gospel: Jesus Christ, risen from the dead, born of David's line. For preaching this I am exposed to hardship, even to the point of being fettered like a criminal; but the word of God is not fettered. All this I endure for the sake of God's chosen ones, in the hope that they too may attain the glorious and eternal salvation which is in Christ Jesus.

TRUE CHRISTIANITY
2 Timothy 2:11 – 4:8

Here is a saying you may trust:

> If we died with him, we shall live with him;
> if we endure, we shall reign with him;
> if we disown him, he will disown us;
> if we are faithless, he remains faithful,
> for he cannot disown himself.

Keep on reminding people of this, and charge them solemnly before God to stop disputing about mere words; it does no good, and only ruins those who listen. Try hard to show yourself worthy of God's approval, as a worker with no cause for shame; keep strictly to the true gospel, avoiding empty and irreligious chatter; those who indulge in it will stray farther and farther into godless ways, and the infection of their teaching will spread like gangrene. Such are Hymenaeus and Philetus; in saying that our resurrection has already taken place they are wide of the truth and undermine people's faith. But God has laid a foundation-stone, and it stands firm, bearing this inscription: 'The Lord knows his own' and 'Everyone who takes the Lord's name upon his lips must forsake wickedness.' Now in any great house there are not only utensils of gold and silver, but also others of wood or earthenware; the former are valued, the latter held cheap. Anyone who cleanses himself from all this wickedness will be a vessel valued and dedicated, a thing useful to the master of the house, and fit for any honourable purpose.

Turn from the wayward passions of youth, and pursue justice, integrity, love, and peace together with all who worship the Lord in singleness of mind; have nothing to do with foolish and wild speculations. You know they breed quarrels, and a servant of the Lord must not be quarrelsome; he must be kindly towards all. He should be a good teacher, tolerant, and gentle when he must discipline those who oppose him. God may then grant them a change of heart and lead them to recognize the truth; thus they may come to their senses and escape from the devil's snare in which they have been trapped and held at his will.

Remember, the final age of this world is to be a time of turmoil! People will love nothing but self and money; they will be boastful, arrogant, and abusive; disobedient to parents, devoid of gratitude, piety, and natural affection; they will be implacable in their hatreds, scandalmongers, uncontrolled and violent, hostile to all goodness, perfidious, foolhardy, swollen with self-importance. They will love their pleasures more than their God. While preserving the outward form of religion, they are a standing denial of its power. Keep clear of them. They are the sort that insinuate themselves into private houses and there get silly women into their clutches, women burdened with

THE EPISTLES OF PAUL

sins and carried away by all kinds of desires, always wanting to be taught but incapable of attaining to a knowledge of the truth. As Jannes and Jambres opposed Moses, so these men oppose the truth; their warped minds disqualify them from grasping the faith. Their successes will be short-lived; like those opponents of Moses, they will come to be recognized by everyone for the fools they are.

But you, my son, have observed closely my teaching and manner of life, my resolution, my faithfulness, patience, and spirit of love, and my fortitude under persecution and suffering – all I went through at Antioch, at Iconium, at Lystra, and the persecutions I endured; and from all of them the Lord rescued me. Persecution will indeed come to everyone who wants to live a godly life as a follower of Christ Jesus, whereas evildoers and charlatans will progress from bad to worse, deceiving and deceived. But for your part, stand by the truths you have learned and are assured of. Remember from whom you learned them; remember that from early childhood you have been familiar with the sacred writings which have power to make you wise and lead you to salvation through faith in Christ Jesus. All inspired scripture has its use for teaching the truth and refuting error, or for reformation of manners and discipline in right living, so that the man of God may be capable and equipped for good work of every kind.

Before God, and before Christ Jesus who is to judge the living and the dead, I charge you solemnly by his coming appearance and his reign, proclaim the message, press it home in season and out of season, use argument, reproof, and appeal, with all the patience that teaching requires. For the time will come when people will not stand sound teaching, but each will follow his own whim and gather a crowd of teachers to tickle his fancy. They will stop their ears to the truth and turn to fables. But you must keep your head whatever happens; put up with hardship, work to spread the gospel, discharge all the duties of your calling.

As for me, my life is already being poured out on the altar, and the hour for my departure is upon me. I have run the great race, I have finished the course, I have kept the faith. And now there awaits me the garland of righteousness which the Lord, the righteous Judge, will award to me on the great day, and not to me alone, but to all who have set their hearts on his coming appearance.

FINAL INSTRUCTIONS
2 Timothy 4:9–22

Do your best to join me soon. Demas, his heart set on this present world, has deserted me and gone to Thessalonica; Crescens is away in Galatia, Titus in Dalmatia; apart from Luke I have no one with me. Get hold of Mark and bring him with you; he is a great help to me. Tychicus I have sent to Ephesus. When you come, bring the cloak I left with Carpus at Troas, and the books, particularly my notebooks.

Alexander the coppersmith did me a great deal of harm. The Lord will deal with him as he deserves, but you had better be on your guard against him, for he is bitterly opposed to everything we teach. At the first hearing of my case no one came into court to support me; they all left me in the lurch; I pray that it may not be counted against them. But the Lord stood by me and lent me strength, so that I might be his instrument in making the full proclamation of the gospel for the whole pagan world to hear; and thus I was rescued from the lion's jaws. The Lord will rescue me from every attempt to do me harm, and bring me safely into his heavenly kingdom. Glory to him for ever and ever! Amen.

Greetings to Prisca and Aquila, and the household of Onesiphorus.

Erastus stayed behind at Corinth, and Trophimus I left ill at Miletus. Do try to get here before winter.

Greetings from Eubulus, Pudens, Linus, and Claudia, and from all the brotherhood here.

The Lord be with your spirit. Grace be with you all!

THE EPISTLES OF JOHN

The First Epistle of John   370

The Second Epistle of John   376

The Third Epistle of John   377

The First Epistle of John

GOD IS LIGHT
1 John 1:1 – 2:17

Something which has existed since the beginning, which we have heard, which we have seen with our own eyes, which we have watched and touched with our own hands, the Word of life – this is our theme. That life was made visible; we saw it and are giving our testimony, declaring to you the eternal life, which was present to the Father and has been revealed to us. We are declaring to you what we have seen and heard, so that you too may share our life. Our life is shared with the Father and with his Son Jesus Christ. We are writing this to you so that our joy may be complete.

This is what we have heard from him and are declaring to you: God is light, and there is no darkness in him at all. If we say that we share in God's life while we are living in darkness, we are lying, because we are not living the truth. But if we live in light, as he is in light, we have a share in another's life, and the blood of Jesus, his Son, cleanses us from all sin. If we say, 'We have no sin', we are deceiving ourselves, and truth has no place in us; if we acknowledge our sins, he is trustworthy and upright, so that he will forgive our sins and will cleanse us from all evil. If we say, 'We have never sinned', we make him a liar, and his word has no place in us.

My children, I am writing this to prevent you from sinning; but if anyone does sin, we have an advocate with the Father, Jesus Christ, the upright. He is the sacrifice to expiate our sins, and not only ours, but also those of the whole world.

In this way we know that we have come to know him, if we keep his commandments. Whoever says, 'I know him' without keeping his commandments, is a liar, and truth has no place in him. But anyone who does keep his word, in such a one God's love truly reaches its perfection. This is the proof that we are in God. Whoever claims to remain in him must act as he acted.

My dear friends, this is not a new commandment I am writing for you, but an old commandment that you have had from the beginning; the old commandment is the message you have heard. Yet in another way, I am writing a new commandment for you – and this is true for you, just as much as for him – for darkness is passing away and the true light is already shining. Whoever claims to be in light but hates his brother is still in darkness. Anyone who loves his brother remains in light and there is in him nothing to make him fall away. But whoever hates his brother is in darkness and is walking about in darkness not knowing where he is going, because darkness has blinded him.

I am writing to you, children, because your sins have been forgiven through his name. I am writing to you, fathers, because you have come to know the One who has existed since the beginning. I am writing to you, young people, because you have overcome the Evil One. I have written to you, children, because you have come to know the Father. I have written to you, parents, because you have come to know the One who has existed since the beginning. I have written to you, young people, because you are strong, and God's word remains in you, and you have overcome the Evil One.

Do not love the world or what is in the world. If anyone does love the world, the love of the Father finds no place in him, because everything there is in the world – disordered bodily desires, disordered desires of the eyes, pride in possession – is not from the Father but is from the world. And the world, with all its disordered desires, is passing away. But whoever does the will of God remains for ever.

THE COMING OF THE ANTICHRIST
1 John 2:18–27

Children, this is the final hour; you have heard that the Antichrist is coming, and now many Antichrists have already come; from this we know that it is the final hour. They have gone from among us, but they never really belonged to us; if they had belonged to us, they would have stayed with us. But this was to prove that not one of them belonged to us. But you have been anointed by the Holy One, and have all received knowledge. I have written to you not because you are ignorant of the truth, but because you are well aware of it, and because no lie can come from the truth. Who is the liar, if not one who claims that Jesus is not the Christ? This is the Antichrist, who denies both the Father and the Son. Whoever denies the Son cannot have the Father either; whoever acknowledges the Son has the Father too. Let what you heard in the beginning remain in you; as long as what you heard in the beginning remains in you, you will remain in the Son and in the Father. And the promise he made you himself is eternal life.

So much have I written to you about those who are trying to lead you astray. But as for you, the anointing you received from him remains in you, and you do not need anyone to teach you; since the anointing he gave you teaches you everything, and since it is true, not false, remain in him just as he has taught you.

GOD'S CHILDREN
1 John 2:28 – 3:10

Therefore remain in him now, children, so that when he appears we may be fearless, and not shrink from him in shame at his coming.

If you know that he is upright you must recognize that everyone whose life is upright is a child of his. You must see what great love the Father has lavished on us by letting us be called God's children – which is what we are! The reason why the world does not acknowledge us is that it did not acknowledge him. My dear friends, we are already God's children, but what we shall be in the future has not yet been revealed. We are well aware that when he appears we shall be like him, because we shall see him as he really is. Whoever treasures this hope of him purifies himself, to be as pure as he is.

Whoever sins, acts wickedly, because all sin is wickedness. Now you are well aware that he has appeared in order to take sins away, and that in him there is no sin. No one who remains in him sins, and whoever sins has neither seen him nor recognized him. Children, do not let anyone lead you astray. Whoever acts uprightly is upright, just as he is upright. Whoever lives sinfully belongs to the devil, since the devil has been a sinner from the beginning. This was the purpose of the appearing of the Son of God, to undo the work of the devil. No one who is a child of God sins because God's seed remains in him. Nor can he sin, because he is a child of God. This is what distinguishes the children of God from the children of the devil: whoever does not live uprightly and does not love his brother is not from God.

LOVE ONE ANOTHER
1 John 3:11 – 4:6

This is the message which you heard from the beginning, that we must love one another, not to be like Cain, who was from the Evil One and murdered his brother. And why did he murder his brother? Because his own actions were evil and his brother's upright. Do not be surprised, brothers, if the world hates you. We are well aware that we have passed over from death to life because we love our brothers. Whoever does not love, remains in death. Anyone who hates his brother is a murderer, and you are well aware that no murderer has eternal life remaining in him. This is the proof of love, that he laid down his life for us, and we too ought to lay down our lives for our brothers. If anyone is well-off in worldly possessions and sees his brother in need but closes his heart to him, how can the love of God be remaining in him?

Children, our love must be not just words or mere talk, but something active and genuine. This will be the proof that we belong to the truth, and it will convince us in his presence, even if our own feelings condemn us, that God is greater than our feelings and knows all things. My dear friends, if our own feelings do not condemn us, we can be fearless before God, and whatever we ask we shall receive from him, because we keep his commandments and do what is acceptable to him.

His commandment is this, that we should believe in the name of his Son Jesus Christ and that we should love one another as he commanded us. Whoever keeps his commandments remains in God, and God in him. And this is the proof that he remains in us: the Spirit that he has given us.

GOD IS LOVE
1 John 4:7 – 5:5

My dear friends, not every spirit is to be trusted, but test the spirits to see whether they are from God, for many false prophets are at large in the world. This is the proof of the spirit of God: any spirit which acknowledges Jesus Christ, come in human nature, is from God, and no spirit which fails to acknowledge Jesus is from God; it is the spirit of Antichrist, whose coming you have heard of; he is already at large in the world. Children, you are from God and have overcome them, because he who is in you is greater than he who is in the world. They are from the world, and therefore the world inspires what they say, and listens to them. We are from God; whoever recognizes God listens to us; anyone who is not from God refuses to listen to us. This is how we can distinguish the spirit of truth from the spirit of falsehood.

My dear friends, let us love one another, since love is from God and everyone who loves is a child of God and knows God. Whoever fails to love does not know God, because God is love. This is the revelation of God's love for us, that God sent his only Son into the world that we might have life through him. Love consists in this: it is not we who loved God, but God loved us and sent his Son to expiate our sins. My dear friends, if God loved us so much, we too should love one another. No one has ever seen God, but as long as we love one another God remains in us and his love comes to its perfection in us.

This is the proof that we remain in him and he in us, that he has given us a share in his Spirit. We ourselves have seen and testify that the Father sent his Son as Saviour of the world. Anyone who acknowledges that Jesus is the Son of God, God remains in him and he in God. We have recognized for ourselves, and put our faith in, the love God has for us.

God is love, and whoever remains in love remains in God and God in him. Love comes to its perfection in us when we can face the Day of Judgment fearlessly, because even in this world we have become as he is. In love there is no room for fear, but perfect love drives out fear, because fear implies punishment and no one who is afraid has come to perfection in love. Let us love, then, because he first loved us. Anyone who says 'I love God' and hates his brother, is a liar, since whoever does not love the brother whom he can see cannot love God whom he has not seen. Indeed this is the commandment we have received from him, that whoever loves God, must also love his brother.

Whoever believes that Jesus is the Christ is a child of God, and whoever loves the father loves the son. In this way we know that we love God's children, when we love God and keep his commandments. This is what the love of God is: keeping his commandments. Nor are his commandments burdensome, because every child of God overcomes the world. And this is the victory that has overcome the world – our faith. Who can overcome the world but the one who believes that Jesus is the Son of God?

THE WAY TO ETERNAL LIFE
1 John 5:6–21

He it is who came by water and blood, Jesus Christ, not with water alone but with water and blood, and it is the Spirit that bears witness, for the Spirit is Truth. So there are three witnesses, the Spirit, water and blood; and the three of them coincide. If we accept the testimony of human witnesses, God's testimony is greater, for this is God's testimony which he gave about his Son. Whoever believes in the Son of God has this testimony within him, and whoever does not believe is making God a liar, because he has not believed the testimony God has given about his Son. This is the testimony: God has given us eternal life, and this life is in his Son. Whoever has the Son has life, and whoever has not the Son of God has not life.

I have written this to you who believe in the name of the Son of God so that you may know that you have eternal life.

Our fearlessness towards him consists in this, that if we ask anything in accordance with his will he hears us. And if we know that he listens to whatever we ask him, we know that we already possess whatever we have asked of him. If anyone sees his brother commit a sin that is not a deadly sin, he has only to pray, and God will give life to this brother – provided that it is not a deadly sin. There is sin that leads to death and I am not saying you must pray about that. Every kind of wickedness is sin, but not all sin leads to death.

We are well aware that no one who is a child of God sins, because he who was born from God protects him, and the Evil One has no hold over him. We are well aware that we are from God, and the whole world is in the power of the Evil One. We are well aware also that the Son of God has come, and has given us understanding so that we may know the One who is true. We are in the One who is true as we are in his Son, Jesus Christ. He is the true God and this is eternal life.

Children, be on your guard against false gods.

The Second Epistle of John

From the Elder: my greetings to the Lady, the chosen one, and to her children, whom I love in truth – and I am not the only one, for so do all who have come to know the Truth – because of the truth that remains in us and will be with us for ever. In our life of truth and love, we shall have grace, faithful love and peace from God the Father and from Jesus Christ, the Son of the Father.

It has given me great joy to find that children of yours have been living the life of truth as we were commanded by the Father. And now I am asking you – dear lady, not as though I were writing you a new commandment, but only the one which we have had from the beginning – that we should love one another.

To love is to live according to his commandments: this is the commandment which you have heard since the beginning, to live a life of love.

There are many deceivers at large in the world, refusing to acknowledge Jesus Christ as coming in human nature. They are the Deceiver; they are the Antichrist. Watch yourselves, or all our work will be lost and you will forfeit your full reward. If anybody does not remain in the teaching of Christ but goes beyond it, he does not have God with him: only those who remain in what he taught can have the Father and the Son with them. If anyone comes to you bringing a different doctrine, you must not receive him into your house or even give him a greeting. Whoever greets him has a share in his wicked activities.

There are several things I have to tell you, but I have thought it best not to trust them to paper and ink. I hope instead to visit you and talk to you in person, so that our joy may be complete.

Greetings to you from the children of your sister, the chosen one.

The Third Epistle of John

3 John 1:1–15

From the Elder: greetings to my dear friend Gaius, whom I love in truth.

My dear friend, I hope everything is going happily with you and that you are as well physically as you are spiritually. It was a great joy to me when some brothers came and told of your faithfulness to the truth, and of your life in the truth. It is always my greatest joy to hear that my children are living according to the truth.

My dear friend, you have done loyal work in helping these brothers, even though they were strangers to you. They are a proof to the whole Church of your love and it would be a kindness if you could help them on their journey as God would approve. It was entirely for the sake of the name that they set out, without depending on the non-believers for anything: it is our duty to welcome people of this sort and contribute our share to their work for the truth.

I have written a note for the members of the church, but Diotrephes, who enjoys being in charge of it, refuses to accept us. So if I come, I shall tell everyone how he has behaved, and about the wicked accusations he has been circulating against us. As if that were not enough, he not only refuses to welcome our brothers, but prevents from doing so other people who would have liked to, and expels them from the church. My dear friend, never follow a bad example, but keep following the good one; whoever does what is right is from God, but no one who does what is wrong has ever seen God.

Demetrius has been approved by everyone, and indeed by Truth itself. We too will vouch for him and you know that our testimony is true.

There were several things I had to tell you but I would rather not trust them to pen and ink. However, I hope to see you soon and talk to you in person. Peace be with you; greetings from your friends; greet each of our friends by name.

Index of Primary Sources

Abrams, M.H.   77

Addison, Joseph   174

Aelred of Riveaulx   64, 69

Ambrose, St   142

Andrewes, Lancelot   98

Anselm, St   151

Apuleius   137

Aquinas, St Thomas   64, 65, 69, 75, 82, 84, 87, 103, 104, 109, 127, 128, 137, 138, 160, 161, 162, 164

Arnold, Matthew   78, 88, 113

Athenagoras   164

Auden, W.H.   153

Augustine, St   63, 64, 77, 87, 90, 91, 92, 95, 96, 97, 102, 103, 104, 105, 118, 137, 143, 144, 156, 157, 158, 160, 164, 169

Avison, Margaret   96, 149, 166

Bale, John   172

Barrow, Isaac   72, 73

Barth, John   101

Barth, Karl   162

Basil of Caesarea, St   136

Baudelaire, Charles Pierre   139

Baxter, Richard   109

Bayly   93

Bede   91, 170

Bellarmine   161

Belloc, Hilaire   130

Bentham, Jeremy   76, 78

Bernard of Clairvaux, St   64, 79, 145, 151, 170

Biel, Gabriel   161

Blake, William   122, 134, 139, 147, 175

Blish, James   88

Boehme, Jacob   76

Boethius, A.M.S.   118, 156

Bolt, Robert   87

Boswell, James   140

Bradwardine, Thomas   126, 158

Brontë, Charlotte   148

Browne, Sir Thomas   68, 109, 110, 139

Browne, William   99

Browning, Robert   87, 113, 134, 153

Bryant, William Cullen   114

Bultmann, Rudolf   152

Bunyan, John   70, 83, 93, 94, 100, 120, 128, 133

Burnet   110

Burton, Robert   99

Butler, Samuel   87, 88

Byron, George, Lord   77, 100, 113, 139

Calvin, John   67, 92, 93, 94, 105, 133, 137, 144, 151, 160, 164, 171

Canes, John   109

Carlyle, Thomas   77, 96

Cassian, St John   161

Cennick, John   174

Chaucer, Geoffrey   66, 85, 91, 97, 104, 118, 123, 127, 138, 144, 145, 159

Chesterton, G.K.   79, 115

Chillingworth, William   109

Chrysostom, St John   91, 97, 128, 136

Clark, Samuel   72

Clement of Rome, St   21, 164

Coleridge, Samuel Taylor   77, 86, 113, 123, 166

Copley, Anthony   99

Cottle, Joseph   140

Cowper, William   73, 74, 75, 95, 100, 109, 112, 121, 122, 130, 147, 174

Cranmer, Thomas   106, 145

Crashaw, Richard   70, 133, 153, 170

Cyril of Alexandria, St   150

Dante Alighieri   66, 95, 132, 134, 138

Defoe, Daniel   87, 93, 161

della Mirandola, Pico   108, 119

Dent   93

Descartes, René   83

Dickens, Charles   78, 94, 96, 166

Dickinson, Emily   101, 134, 148, 166

Dodwell, William   139

Donne, John   93, 96, 99, 106, 107, 110, 120, 127, 133, 145, 146, 166

Dostoevski, Feodor M.   96

Dryden, John   88, 93, 110, 111, 133, 146

Dunbar, William   66

Edwards, Jonathan   173

Eliot, T.S.   80, 96, 114, 131, 134, 139, 153

Emerson, Ralph Waldo   122, 123, 148, 152

Empiricus, Sextus   108

Erasmus   105, 160

Feuerbach, Ludwig   151

Fichte, Johann Gottlieb   123

Fielding, Henry   73, 95

Fletcher, Giles   98, 133

Fletcher, John   109

Fletcher, Phineas   99

Freud, Sigmund   88

Frye, Northrop   139

Gardner, John   167

Goethe, Johann Wolfgang von   86

Golding, William   140

Gower, John   66

Greene, Graham   115, 140

Gregory of Nazianzus, St   150

Gregory the Great, St   91

Gregory, Lady   100

Hardy, Thomas   113, 156

Herbert, George   68, 85, 99, 106, 107, 120, 121, 128, 133, 145, 149, 156, 166, 173

Herebert, William   143

Herrick, Robert   85, 133, 145

Hoadley, Bishop Benjamin   72

Hobbes, Thomas   72, 161

Hodgins, Jack   167

Hogarth   147

Homer   138

Hooker, Richard   109

Hopkins, G.M.   113, 130, 131, 134, 139, 148, 166

Howe, Julia Ward   122, 175

Irenaeus, St   21, 56, 142, 164

Jerome, St   62, 63

Joachim of Fiore   171

Johnson, Samuel   140

Jones, David   115, 176

Jonson, Ben   146

Josephus, Flavius   89
Joyce, James   88, 114, 140, 149
Julian of Norwich   152
Keble, John   80, 95, 175
Kempenfelt, Richard   174
Kenrick   147
Kierkegaard, Søren   91, 110
Kingsley, Charles   113, 175
Knox, John   172
Langland, William   66, 83, 104
Latimer, Bishop Hugh   145, 173
Law, William   72
Lawrence, D.H.   79, 153, 167
Lewis, C.S.   83, 115, 134, 167, 176
Livy   137
Locke, John   68, 83, 111
Lombard, Peter   142, 158
Lowell, James Russell   114
Lowell, Robert   139
Loyola, St Ignatius   91
Lucretius   137
Luther, Martin   91, 93, 104, 105, 112, 137, 151, 160
MacLeish, Archibald   101
Madan, Martin   174
Malory, Sir Thomas   171
Marlowe, Christopher   86, 100, 103, 127, 133, 138, 145
Marvell, Andrew   87, 99
Mather, Cotton   160, 173
Mather, Increase   173
Maurice, F.D.   140
Melville, Herman   114, 161
Miller, Arthur   101
Milton, John   70, 83, 87, 100, 109, 120, 123, 133, 138, 139,
141, 145, 147, 153, 155, 156, 157, 159, 160, 165, 166
Mirk, John   67
Montaigne, Michel de   83, 108, 109, 114, 122
Moore, Thomas   175
More, Hannah   73, 74, 112
More, Henry   70
More, St Thomas   87, 106
Morris, William   113
Newman, John Henry   95
Newton, John   95, 100, 130
Nietzsche, Friedrich Wilhelm   86
Norris, John   68
O'Connor, Flannery   116
Origen   24, 118, 136, 164
Orwell, George   140
Ovid   138
Owen, John   109
Paine, Thomas   122
Pascal, Blaise   91, 108, 109, 110
Patmore, Coventry   79
Percy, Walker   176
Philipp, Nikolai   171
Plato   62
Pope, Alexander   111, 129, 156, 157
Prior, Matthew   71
Pseudo-Dionysius   65
Rahner, K.   90
Richard of St Victor   65
Roethke, Theodore   101, 134, 135
Rolle, Richard   66, 91
Rossetti, Christina   79, 113, 153, 166

Rousseau, Jean-Jacques   122
Rowe, Elizabeth   109, 112
Rush, Christopher   166
Ruskin, John   78
Ryman, Friar James   92
Sackville, Thomas   97
Sayers, Dorothy L.   153
Schelling, F.W.J. von   76
Schweitzer, Albert   152
Shakespeare, William   69, 84, 85, 87, 92, 100, 127, 133, 155, 159
Shaw, George Bernard   79, 96, 113
Shelley, Percy Bysshe   76, 77, 85, 113, 139, 153
Sibbes, Richard   134
Sidney, Sir Philip   106
Simon, Father   109, 110, 114
Skelton, John   97
Smart, Christopher   75, 120, 129, 130
Spenser, Edmund   69, 85, 98, 100, 106, 120, 132, 137, 138, 145, 146, 165
Spurgeon, C.H.   96
Steele, R.   73
Stillingfleet, Edward   109
Suarez   161
Swift, Jonathan   71, 93, 94, 100, 111, 147
Swinburne, A.C.   113
Swinden, Tobias   137
Taylor, Bishop Jeremy   84, 107, 108, 111, 128
Tennyson, Alfred, Lord   134, 137

Tertullian   103, 164
Theophilus   142
Thomas of Celano   91, 170
Thomas, R.S.   115
Thompson, Francis   95, 113, 130, 134
Tillotson, Archbishop John   68, 72, 88, 109
Tolkien, J.R.R.   134, 167, 176
Toplady, Augustus   94
Traherne, Thomas   133
Updike, John   115, 166
Vaughan, Henry   107, 108, 133, 173
Virgil   111, 137, 138
Voltaire, F.   122
Wapull, George   98
Watts, Isaac   112, 161
Wesley, Charles   120, 147, 174
Wesley, John   71, 93, 94, 107, 109, 112, 147, 161
Whitefield, George   72, 75, 94
Whitman, Walt   122
Wigglesworth, Michael   173
Wilberforce, William   95
Wilbur, Richard   131
Wilde, Oscar   85, 87, 88, 113, 140
William of Occam   158
Williams, Charles   140
Winthrop, John   68
Woiwode, Larry   149, 162
Wood, Nathaniel   86
Wordsworth, William 76, 88, 95, 112, 113, 123, 134, 135, 139
Yeats, W.B.   176